E X P L O R I N G
SCOTLAND

FODOR'S TRAVEL PUBLICATIONS, INC.

NEW YORK • TORONTO • LONDON • SYDNEY • AUCKLAND

HTTP://WWW.FODORS.COM/

Copyright © The Automobile Association 1997
Maps copyright © The Automobile Association 1997
Mountain High Maps Image (S) copyright © 1993 Digital Wisdom, Inc.

Published in the United States by Fodor's Travel Publications, Inc.
Published in the United Kingdom by AA Publishing.

Fodor's and Fodor's Exploring Guides are registered trademarks of Fodor's Travel Publications, Inc.

ISBN 0–679–03214–2
Second Edition

Fodor's Exploring Scotland

Author: **Gilbert Summers**
Revision verifier: **Gilbert Summers**
Front Cover Silhouette: **Catherine Karnow/Woodfin Camp**

Special Sales
Fodor's Travel Publications are available at special discounts for bulk purchases (100 copies or more) for sales promotions or premiums. Special editions, including personalized covers, excerpts of existing guides, and corporate imprints, can be created in large quantities for special needs. For more information, contact your local bookseller or write to Special Markets, Fodor's Travel Publications, 201 East 50th Street, New York, NY 10022.

PRINTED IN ITALY BY PRINTERS TRENTO S.R.L.
10 9 8 7 6 5 4 3 2 1

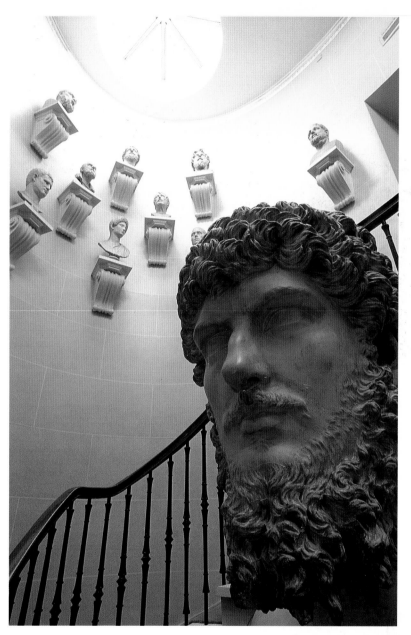

Gilbert **Summers** is a Scot in the happy position of living in Scotland and earning his keep largely by writing about his own country. As well as numerous texts for the Scottish Tourist Board and other tourism organizations, his published works include *Walk Loch Lomond and the Trossachs*, *Exploring Rural Scotland*, and *Traditions of Scotland*. He is also Scottish editor for Fodor's Gold Guides and is married with two young children who help test Scotland's visitor attractions.

Busts line the stairs of the National Gallery of Scotland in Edinburgh

How to use this book

This book is divided into five main sections:

❏ **Section 1: *Scotland Is***

Discusses aspects of life and living today, from the economy to festivals and events

❏ **Section 2: *Scotland Was***

Places the country in its historical context, and explores those past events whose influences are felt to this day

❏ **Section 3: *A to Z Section***

Breaks down into regional chapters, and covers places to visit, including walks and drives. Within this section fall the Focus On articles, which consider a variety of subjects in greater detail

❏ **Section 4: *Travel Facts***

Contains the strictly practical information that is vital for a successful trip

❏ **Section 5: *Hotels and Restaurants***

Lists recommended establishments throughout Scotland, giving a brief summary of what they offer

How to use the star rating
Most of the places described in this book have been given a separate rating:

▶▶▶ **Do not miss**

▶▶ **Highly recommended**

▶ **Worth seeing**

　 Not essential viewing

Map references
To make the location of a particular place easier to find, every main entry in this book is given a map reference, such as 176B3. The first number (176) indicates the page on which the map can be found; the letter (B) and the second number (3) pinpoint the square in which the main entry is located. The maps on the inside front cover and inside back cover are referred to as IFC and IBC respectively.

Contents

Quick reference

**This quick-reference guide high-
lights the features of the book
you will use most often: the
maps, the introductory features,
the Focus On articles, the walks,
and the drives.**

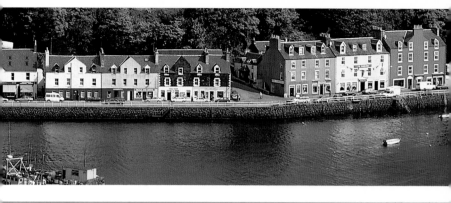

Walks

Drives

Travel Facts

Alex Salmond
Leader of the Scottish National Party, Alex Salmond wants Scotland to be an independent member of the European Union (EU), with its own parliament—and, like all other normal, small countries who are prospering in Europe, free to negotiate as equals. A fighter for all Scottish interests, he was first elected as a British member of parliament in 1987.

8

My Scotland

by Alex Salmond

One of the greatest joys for any Scot is to share with the world our nation's beauty and diversity. I am proud, therefore, to welcome you to Scotland at the beginning of your exploration. Prepare to discover a unique and varied land, molded by over a thousand years of history and nationhood. But before you begin your journey, you may ask, what is Scotland?

You will find that Scotland is a nation with its feet firmly planted in Europe, but with its mind open to the world. An *auld alliance* with the French, and strong trading links with the continent of Europe have left their mark on the language, architecture, and cuisine of the east coast. We look north and east to Scandinavia, and there is still a strong Nordic feel to the Northern Isles. In the west, Gaelic, the language of the original Scots, establishes a close cultural association with Celtic Ireland, and from the south comes the English language and the relationship with England which runs like a thread through so much of our past.

Throughout this land, history is brought to vivid and haunting life in the brooding shadows of mighty castles, the alleyways of medieval towns, and in the grandeur of royal palaces. Vibrant colors and breathtaking views await you in the towering majesty of the Highlands and the rolling fertility of the Lowlands—and, of course, the best of food and the finest of whisky, to give you renewed strength for the journey.

This is our Scotland. I know you will enjoy your stay.

My Scotland

by Dorothy-Grace Elder

My Scotland is many countries. There's the high and mighty Scotland from Perthshire upward where, in late summer, the giants go partying, spilling their claret down the mountains, splashing the purple of the high heather into the sapphire lochs. Hell, there's little need for heaven if you've seen, on this earth, the River Garry on a crystal morning when the mountains toss off their chiffon sleeping-jackets and you wake to the river's chatter, sit on a pink cushion of wild thyme, and let peace seep into your town-weary, trauchled, wabbit soul.

My Scotland is also the more douce, green and gold Borderland, with hedges scarved in honeysuckle by quiet lanes, or the knockout East Neuk of Fife, part Dutch in its architecture, with every wynd to the sea whispering of pirates and plunder past. And my Scotland is Orkney, with its unending brushwork of light, and Glasgow, with its unending laughs. See Glasgow in winter, with its sumptuous pantos. When home-grown stars take the stage and make tough audiences roll with laughter, the love for these comics is almost tangible, with audiences showing ferocious support for both their tongue and their humor.

We're not really a small country. We have a mere 5 million people birling around a landmass not much smaller than the space England shoehorns 50 million into. If we ironed out our crinkly west coast, it would stretch a few thousand miles. We count castles and islands in hundreds, revenue from oil and whisky in billions—though most is pumped straight past us. Who can say we're mean when we freely give away such wealth to anyone prepared to make the journey?

Dorothy-Grace Elder
The author of a top humorous newspaper column (in *Scotland on Sunday*), Dorothy-Grace Elder contributes articles on social issues to the *Daily Record*, Scotland's largest-circulation daily paper. She has fought campaigns for Scottish jobs, industry, and language, and has produced many documentaries for the BBC and other broadcasters.

Glossary

wynd	an alley
wabbit	tired
trauchled	weighed down
birling	spinning
douce	gentle

SCOTTS
ORANGE MARMALADE
MEDIUM CUT
WITH

TEACHER'S

HIGHLAND CREAM

ESTABLISHED 1830

Perfection of Old
SCOTCH WHISKY

Wm Teacher & Sons Ltd
GLASGOW SCOTLAND

NET 1lb
450g ℮

PRODUCE OF SCOTLAND

The names 'Teacher's' and
'Highland Cream' are
registered trade marks of
William Teacher and
Sons Limited.

5 000229 048000

The Scottish image

■ **Misty glens, lochs, mountains, tartan, bagpipes, and kilts: these are the most familiar images of Scotland. How these essentially Highland aspects came to represent the whole of Scotland—Highland, Lowland, urban, and rural—is one of the oddities of the nation's history ...■**

Tartan Today, you can cross the Border and hear bagpipes in a Southern Uplands town, eat shortbread from a tartan wrapper in the middle of Glasgow, and take in a Highland Games within easy reach of Edinburgh. All this is well before you reach the real Highlands. Scotland, at least those aspects of it dealing with tourism, embraces its kilted image wholeheartedly: tartan sells.

The glorious paradox is that if a tartan-clad Highlander had appeared in a Lowland town a few centuries ago, he would have been locked up, if not shot on sight. The Highlanders were regarded as barbarous thieves by Lowland Scots. After the crushing of the final rebellion against the Hanoverian dynasty on Culloden Moor near Inverness in 1746, the tartan was even banned by Act of Parliament. Tartan was associated

with revolt and lawlessness. Now the kilt and its associated paraphernalia represent the whole of Scotland, Highland or Lowland, Gaelic speaking or otherwise, to many of today's visitors.

Bagpipes The unmistakable cadences of the bagpipe or Highland war pipe form the soundtrack to the romantic image of Scotland. Perhaps originally a device for signaling across long Highland distances, the bagpipe survived partly through its use in Highland regiments, and now plays its role in many pipe bands. Most Scottish towns have at least one band, and the pipes create instant Highland atmosphere at all kinds of gatherings, from protest marches to weddings.

Scenery As for the misty glens (valleys) and bens (high hills), a love for this landscape grew out of the cult of the picturesque embraced by the Romantic poets (William Wordsworth, strongly associated with the English Lake District, made several tours of the Highlands). Today, a taste for wild scenery is for many the main reason for visiting Scotland.

The scenery is absolutely amazing, and it is possible to see some of Scotland's most rugged places without leaving a main road. This is why the name Glen Coe appears on the destination headboard of so many tour buses. The valley provides a matchless combination of awesome scenery and chilling tale of the Highlands of old: a massacre of the local clan by a clan militia took place there in 1692. Farther west, the island of Skye makes a startling impact when the Cuillin Hills etch themselves against a blue sky.

The new face of Scottish tradition?

Morning mist over Flanders Moss, from the edge of the Trossachs

With scenic grandeur like this, and the romance of kilts and other Highland paraphernalia, it is all too easy to forget the other aspects of Scotland. The country has some of the finest stretches of unspoiled coastline in Europe: on the east coast, both sheer cliffs and sandy beaches provide superb scenery. The Borders towns, with their textile traditions and strong sense of community, are full of character and do not need any dressing up in Highland costume. The Northern Isles, notably Shetland, are a world away from "Highlandry," and have a vivid Scandinavian heritage. Then there is the modern Scotland, as expressed in style-conscious Glasgow or cosmopolitan Edinburgh. Scotland can offer you ceilidhs (Highland-style evenings of song and dance) if you want them, but make the most of its wealth of other attributes as well.

❑ After the Battle of Culloden in 1746, many rebels were condemned to death by the authorities. One of these was a Highland piper. He pleaded for mercy on the grounds that he was a musician, but the judge defined his pipes as a weapon of war and the sentence was duly carried out. ❑

Many Scottish postcards tend to perpetuate the tartan cliché

■ **Perhaps the best-known Scottish festivity is Hogmanay—the last night of the year and its hungover aftermath. Until recent years, it was far more important than Christmas north of the border ...■**

Hogmanay Though none can agree on the word's origins (possibly dialect French *"au geux menez,"* "bring [gifts] to the beggars"), Hogmanay is still strong in Scotland. Until recent times, the night of December 31, Hogmanay Night, was the most important in the Scots calendar. Other deep-winter festivals, derived from early pagan fire rituals, survive in places, for example the swinging of fireballs, with the combustible material held in place by wire, in Stonehaven; or the "burning of the clavie," a kind of portable bonfire in a basket, at Burghead in Moray. Most famous of all is Up-Helly-Aa, a Viking celebration in Shetland when people go guising (dressing up in costume) and enjoy various shows, including the spectacular burning of a Viking longship. Beltane or May Day festivities can also be found in a few places in modern Scotland.

Other types of event are those comparatively modern ones, such as Highland Games and agricultural shows. Highland Games are very popular in many towns and have

Fringe Sunday in Edinburgh's Holyrood Park—truly cosmopolitan

spread beyond the Highlands. They are a combination of musical, dancing, and athletic skills all happening in the same arena, often simultaneously, held in towns and villages throughout the Highlands and far beyond.

Highland Games Clan societies and other promoters of Scotland's romantic martial image give the games an ancient history, arguing that they were originally held so that clan chiefs could select the most talented people for their retinues. However, most seem to have originated in early Victorian times, when a resurgence of interest in things Scottish resulted in the formation of various Caledonian clubs. Games gave the members an excuse to cavort in tartan finery. Yet another explanation is that the games were trials of strength by bored lumberjacks, busy cutting down the Highland forests. No matter what their origins, be prepared to enjoy parachute jumps and guest appearances by TV characters as happenings in the games "tradition" as well.

Rural events Agricultural shows are as entertaining as Highland Games,

On the festival cavalcade

and serve as a showcase for Scottish agriculture. They take place throughout the Lowlands. Great meeting places for the rural communities, they embrace not just the serious business of selling agricultural machinery and livestock, but also displays of just about anything else from trick cycling to terrier racing.

❑ Like the Mod, the Borders Common Ridings have strong regional associations. These ancient celebrations of horsemanship in the Borders towns owe their origins at least in part to a need to reaffirm town boundaries in the face of frequent cross-border raiding parties. Unlike Highland Games, they are definitely not held for the benefit of visitors. ❑

Cultural festivals The Edinburgh International Festival is the spectacular flagship of mainstream cultural events, from theater to comedy skits. In fact, the capital suffers from festival "overkill" in late August, partly due to the size of the Fringe, the less formal and more unruly younger brother of the "official" festival. This huge grab bag of performances spreads out of halls and theaters onto the streets of the capital. Nobody could visit Edinburgh during the Fringe and possibly miss it! Also adding to the throng

Highland events -the hammer thrower at the Pitlochry Games

❑ The Gaels, that is the Gaelic speakers of Celtic origin whose linguistic stronghold is in the far northwest of Scotland, have their own big cultural event for Gaeldom, the autumn National Mod, which is sometimes rather unkindly and unjustifiably described in the press as the "Whisky Olympics." ❑

is the Edinburgh Military Tattoo, and a range of smaller events such as the Book Festival and the Jazz Festival. Earlier in the year, rival Glasgow holds MayFest. This broad-based festival is international and eclectic in content, and delivered with all the panache and local support now associated with the city. Folk festivals are also held in many places at various times of the year, two of the most notable being in Shetland: the Folk Festival in April and the Accordian and Fiddle Festival in October.

■ **Three languages are spoken in Scotland: Gaelic, (Lowland) Scots, and English. All Gaels are bilingual. Some Lowlanders still tend to undervalue their native tongue, while the use of a broad Scots vowel by a child of English parents living in Scotland can sometimes be greeted with something near to horror ...■**

The first language Gaelic was once the principal language over much of Scotland, but has been in slow retreat for seven centuries. Today, Gaelic's stronghold is the far north and west, notably the Outer Hebrides islands. However, increased funding for Gaelic broadcasting in the early 1990s has resulted, ironically, in Gaelic being heard in parts of Scotland that have had virtually no Gaelic speakers for centuries. Gaelic enters the vocabulary of Scots and English speakers most often in anglicized or part-anglicized place-names or topographical features such as ben (high hill), loch

Lowland Scots In its late medieval heyday, the Scots tongue, which evolved from a Northumbrian form of Anglo-Saxon, had roughly the same relationship to "English" that Dutch has to German. Today, it is diluted and impoverished by its kinship with "Standard English," and has the further disadvantage of non-standardized spelling. However, its rich borrowings from Norse, French, German, and Dutch can still be heard, especially in the northeast, which most linguists consider to be its heartland. Even in its densest forms it roughly follows standard English in most grammatical forms,

This Gaelic sign in Fort William literally means "a hundred thousand welcomes"

(lake), strath (river valley or adjacent low-lying grassland), glen (valley), or cairn (heap of stones). Sassenach (Englishman), slogan (war cry), and ceilidh (a sort of Scottish hoedown) are other Gaelic words commonly encountered. As the panel at the top shows, many places on the west coast possess only a name in Gaelic.

but differs considerably in vocabulary and pronunciation.

Traps for the listener The linguistic nuances of Scotland are worth listening for. For example, there are Scots constructions using an everyday English vocabulary. "I'll see you the length of the bus stop," is all but opaque to many non-Scots, yet does not use any exclusively "Scots" words. It means "I will escort you as far as the bus stop." There are single

14

words that mean something different to Scots and English. "Messages" means shopping to most Scots (and French, for that matter), with the mysterious "going the messages," that is, doing the shopping, a further complication.

❏ If you are a non-Scot and your car breaks down—beware. A mechanic telling you "I doubt you'll need a new engine" is giving you bad news, not good. In Scotland "I doubt" often means "I regret that..." or "I am afraid that...." ❏

DINGWALL
Inbhirpheofharain

Dingwall in Highland Region also uses the traditional Gaelic welcome

Scots: a separate language?
Perhaps the listener will *skite* (slip) on a *creishy* (greasy) butter wrapper on a *dreich* (dull) day, accidentally *breenging* into (colliding with) the farm's *dour* (unfriendly) *orraman* (spare hand) *daundering* (walking slowly) down to the *roup* (auction)!

Language experts talk of "the great vowel shift," that is, the change in vowel qualities that took place in medieval times (and makes the works of English medieval writer Geoffrey Chaucer difficult for English speakers today). This shift did not occur in northern word forms. Thus "take" is "tak," "bowl" is "bool," "cow" is "coo," and "most" is "maist" (and so on) in northeast Scotland today. Then listen for a scattering of surviving weak Anglo-Saxon plural forms: "shoes" are "sheen," "eyes" are "een." Add Scottish constructions to the northern vocabulary and characteristic pronunciation, and it takes a brave linguist to say that Scots is just a dialect of English.

But do not worry—you will be understood everywhere, and might hear no Scots tongue at all. Bilingual Scots, in the sense of those who can still speak "dense" Lowland forms as well as English, modify their language into a near standard English (with a Scots accent, naturally) for the benefit of everyday conversation with the rest of the English-speaking world.

English in Scotland The overheating of the English real estate market in the mid-1980s saw many English people take advantage of the high selling prices in the south to move into rural Scotland, where property was much cheaper. It is possible to travel in many parts of the Highlands and hear no local native voices at all.

❏ The linguistic historian Billy Kay has memorably described Lowland Scots as being "a language spoken by consenting adults in private." ❏

Scottish food

■ **In the Scotland of old, diet and wealth were interrelated; the same is true today. But instead of trips to the supermarket to fill up the station wagon, the wealthy merchants and lairds, and the powerful clan chiefs, took advantage of direct trading links across the North Sea to acquire the dainty spices and French wines that went with their status ...■**

16

A meager diet It is significant that Scotland's most famous dish, haggis, is an ancient folk recipe using the cheapest cuts of meat, stuffed into tripe, then boiled. In a nation with an unpredictable climate and a history of economic uncertainties, everyday Scots cooking had much to do with eking out ingredients.

Today, poverty in the bleak housing projects of deindustrialized Scotland is a factor in health statistics that no amount of tartan packaging can totally conceal. In low-income households, a dependence on cheap and convenient high-cholesterol and otherwise unbalanced foods ensure Scotland is a poor performer in the healthy-eating league table: deaths through heart disease are the worst in Europe.

Paradoxically, Scotland today has

The Waterfront Wine Bar in Leith, near Edinburgh

numerous advantages when it comes to "local produce." Peterhead is Europe's largest whitefish landing port. Scottish seafood is sought out by top chefs south of the border and on the Continent. (In fact, locals grumble that the best is exported.) Aberdeen Angus beef, though eclipsed by overseas breeds in recent years, is making a comeback and still has considerable cachet. Scots farmers remind anyone who will listen that their beef is "grass-fed" on natural pastures. Meanwhile, Scottish farmed venison, with all its low-fat virtues, is widely available on restaurant menus.

The Scots as home bakers The largest soft fruit growing area in the E.U. lies within the hinterland of Dundee, in central Scotland. With the prevailing climate just right for raspberries and their cousins, as well as strawberries, it is no coincidence that Dundee is famous for its jams. The

Scottish food

Shortbread—distinctive product and unmistakable packaging

Scots sweet tooth not only sends some of its population to an early grave, but also is evident in a still sturdy tradition of home baking, including shortbread and other traditionally fattening goodies. Finally, the humble oat, until well into the present century still a staple of Lowland farmhands, has recently won new converts with the discovery of its role as a good source of soluble fiber.

Eating out today Food lovers will be able to find a high standard of cuisine north of the border. Some restaurants advertise "Taste of Scotland" menus, which means they belong to an organization dedicated to high standards and the fresh and creative use of Scottish local produce. However, an establishment offering "Scottish" cuisine will not automatically be of the highest order. In a few places there still exists the fake Scots menu, where catered foods masquerade as traditional dishes, and even the humble cup of coffee is translated into creaking mock Scots as a "tassie o bean bree."("Tassie" is "cup," "bree" is "soup," or brine.) There is much more to good Scottish food than "flambéing" the steak in whisky or coating the ice cream in oatmeal, and the discriminating diner will find plenty to please, not just an updated local tradition. Other styles, from Italian to Indian, are also well represented, notably, but not only, in larger towns.

❑ "The little Highland Mutton, when fat, is delicious, and certainly the greatest of luxuries. And the small Beef, when fresh, is very sweet and succulent…. Amongst the poorer classes in Scotland, beef is eaten only at Martinmas, when a Mart or Ox is killed; and the only other butcher meat they eat throughout the year is an occasional Braxy."

Edward Burt's *Letters from the North of Scotland*, 1730

A "mart" is an animal, such as an ox or sheep, killed for salting for winter.
A "braxy" is a sheep that has died of braxy, an intestinal illness. ❑

■ **To many people, especially from the more urban south, the appeal of Scotland lies in its "unspoiled" qualities: the silent hills and open skies of the northlands represent a near-mystical, changeless purity. But is the north really the untouched wilderness, a description so beloved of tourism brochure writers? ...■**

The fate of Scotland's woodlands

In environmental terms, the upland landscapes that cover 75 per cent of Scotland have a sad story to tell of destruction and forest clearance, started originally in the Southern Uplands and the Lowlands by Bronze Age man about 3,000 years ago. The needs of agriculture meant that by the Middle Ages much of the forest south of the Highlands had gone.

Harboring wolves and brigands, the Highland forests, too, were destroyed. Charcoal was used in early iron smelting, and the Highland oaks were used to make it. Queen Elizabeth I of England (1558–1603) decreed that English trees should be reserved for shipbuilding, so her smelters turned to the Highlands, aided and abetted by Scottish Lowland businessmen. Until coke replaced charcoal in around 1813, Highland forests were destroyed wholesale for smelting purposes.

By 1743 the last wolf had gone, following the brown bear, reindeer, elk, boar, and beaver into oblivion. Then the great flocks of sheep—still a feature of the Highlands today— arrived with flockmasters firing whole hillsides, eager to extend the grazings. The modern type of sporting estate seen today, encouraging red deer on an open hillside, also evolved. High populations of nibbling sheep and deer still prevent forest regeneration. In the eastern Highlands, the management of grouse on the moor involves annual burning of open hillsides, to encourage young heather growth.

When reforestation was at last tackled, much was at first in blocks of Sitka spruce or other alien species,

The Black Wood of Rannoch—a rare surviving example of Scotland's natural pine forest

now seen throughout the Highlands, even in traditional beauty spots such as the Trossachs. Elsewhere, it is the open "hillscape," burned and over-grazed, degraded for quick profit and described by some ecologists as a wet desert, that is the wilderness enjoyed by millions each year.

Finding the real wilderness Yet the picture is not all gloomy. Real wilderness, in the sense of an unchanged landscape, give or take a few ski resorts, lies above 2,800 feet. Meanwhile, on lower ground, there is a more sensitive attitude to forestry planting, at least in some places, and a wide range of habitats, many in the care of conservation organizations. Little chunks of high-grade landscape survive even in the Lowlands in the form of river gorge woodlands, Lowland raised bog, and also wetlands, notably at the Loch of Strathbeg in the northeast.

The oakwoods on the east side of Loch Lomond still ring with spring birdsong. An echo of the great wood of Caledon can be found in the Black Wood of Rannoch on the south shore of Loch Rannoch. Here the character-istic habitat survives: an open wood-land of great-limbed pines, with an undergrowth of juniper and heather. Crossbills call in the treetops, and it is still possible to see capercaillie, the big grouse of the woods. Around Rothiemurchus on Speyside, near Aviemore, and by Loch Maree in Wester Ross, on the Beinn Eighe side, wild country can be enjoyed in a comparatively "undegraded" state.

Finally, though land misuse is un-deniable, the paradox is plain: despite everything, the Highlands, with their vast stretches of open, man-made moorland, are hauntingly beautiful.

A remnant Scots pine in Glen Falloch. Overgrazing prevents its offspring from regenerating

❏ The unique survival of a feudal method of land ownership in Scotland—10 per cent of Scotland is owned by 13 individuals—has not always worked in favor of conservation and healthy land use. The financial worth of sporting estates is partly measured in deer numbers, so the incentive exists to keep stocks at artificially high levels, to the detriment of the Highland habitat. ❏

■ **Why do many Scots still write "Scottish" and not "British" in passports and hotel guest-register books? In 1992, about three-quarters of Scottish voters turned to parties with devolution or separatist policies. None of these will be implemented. In 1990s Scotland, some say that democracy has failed ...■**

Who feels British? In 1707, during the rounds of negotiations and bribes in Westminster, the London seat of government, that ended with the loss of Scotland's independence, the proposals for each day of negotiation were laid before the Scots, who were left to argue among themselves. The English Parliament continued its business. When the deal was concluded, nothing had changed for English parliamentary representa-

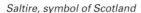

Saltire, symbol of Scotland

tives. There were new Scots faces at Westminster, but nothing was fundamentally altered to make the English feel British. Neither do many Scots, even to this day.

By the 19th century, the Liberal party and a succession of pressure groups had pledged themselves to home rule. They flourished and

withered over the decades. In 1928, the forerunner of what became the Scottish National Party (SNP) was formed. In 1974, it saw support translated into 11 government seats, though this figure was reduced to three later.

Meanwhile, Scotland had become a Labour Party stronghold, with the ruling Conservatives' policies deeply unpopular north of the border. A wave of well-off folk from the prosperous south of England who had capitalized on the mid-1980s property boom and snapped up desirable properties all over Scotland further increased resentment. Before the general election of 1992, the media, much of it London-based and supporting the Conservative government, hyped the Nationalists' chances, seeing them as the "second force" in Scottish politics. The SNP's breakthrough did not occur. Though increasing their share of the vote, they actually lost seats. Scotland in the early 1990s remained governed by a party with barely enough Scottish Conservative MPs to man the Scottish Office in Edinburgh.

20

The Scandinavian model

Nationalists argue that Scotland is self-sufficient in food and energy, while proportionately exporting 21 per cent more for every manufacturing worker than the United Kingdom as a whole. Of the 11 nations who have overtaken the United Kingdom in the world wealth league within the last 30 years, seven are small European nations. And of those, three—Finland, Iceland, and Norway—have become independent during this century. Scotland looks closely at the Scandinavian model of economic success, and points to the influence of Denmark, for example, with a similar population size, climate, resources, and economy, within the E.U.

Small wonder that a rallying cry from the SNP is "Britain's finished." The far older Auld Alliance (the historical tendency of Scotland to side with France against England) and the old trading alliances with the Low Countries (Holland and Belgium) are reminders that in pre-Union days Scotland looked to Europe.

However, in this unpredictable situation, the majority of Scots, either uninterested or unable to unite against Westminster rule, view the full-blown independence issue—as opposed to greater self-rule—with fear and uncertainty. Fiercely partisan in support of their national soccer or rugby team, they seem reluctant to translate this into political will. Only a minority within Scotland supports the Union as it stands, but the

Political message on a disused railroad viaduct, north of Montrose

The Vigil for a Scottish Parliament trailer, parked outside government buildings in Edinburgh

Scottish electorate seems unable to line up behind a single opposition party to gain greater freedom from Westminster. The Scottish politicians' tendency to squabble among themselves should preserve the United Kingdom for the foreseeable future.

❏ Linda Colley, a professor of history at Yale University, describes Scotland's situation: "the alienation of the Celtic fringe is not a recipe for a healthy democracy, nor for a happy and long-lasting union." ❏

■ **One fact is certain: Scotland as the "Workshop of the Western World" has gone forever, the nation's smokestack industries, dependent on coal and iron, mostly reduced to dereliction and the memories of old men ...■**

Harvesting in Fife; agriculture now plays a lesser role in the economy

Even as late as the mid-1960s, manufacturing made up 32 per cent of Scotland's GDP, while 35 per cent of its workforce was employed in it. By the early 1990s, manufacturing was down to 22 per cent, with only 20 per cent of the workforce in this sector, putting Scotland below the United Kingdom average. Today, seven out of 10 workers are now in the service sector and not manufacturing anything. However, Scotland is not quite yet a nation of waiters and tartan gift-shop assistants.

Electronics—the sunrise industry

Silicon Glen was the apt name coined to describe the sunrise industry of electronics, which currently employs 45,000 people north of the border and is reckoned to be the leader in Scottish manufacturing growth. More than a third of all personal computers sold in Europe are actually made in Scotland, thanks to financial incentives for inward-bound companies, plus a skilled workforce. The view from IBM's site (where all of its monitor research and development worldwide takes place) is out to the moors of Renfrewshire in the southwest. U.S. electronics giant Motorola is at East Kilbride, California-based Tandem Computers company prefers Stirling, while Digital, the second-largest computer manufacturer, is at Ayr (their European headquarters), Livingston, and South Queensferry.

Exports Scotland's most famous export, whisky, continues to be important, though the degree of Scottish control within the industry is limited, as most production is in the hands of multinationals based outside Scotland. About 71,000 direct or indirect jobs depend on it U.K.-wide, while exports per employee are six times the U.K. average. One other curious fact is that 55 per cent of production and 70 per cent of the workforce are in the Lowlands, in spite of the product's Highland associations.

Another of Scotland's famous products is textiles. This sector has had a tough time in recent years, but is still worth an astonishing £1.7 billion ($2.5 billion) annually to the Scottish economy. It employs 50,000 people and is centered on the Borders, where one of the nation's few homegrown multinationals, Dawson International, employs around 5,000. This concentration in the south of Scotland leads to some unusual statistics: the town of Hawick exports more than £110 million ($165 million) of knitwear annually, making it one of the largest exporting centers per capita anywhere in the United Kingdom. (All this in a town of over 16,000 people, which has the distinction of being the largest town in Scotland not to be served by the railroad.)

Black gold from the North Sea Oil made a substantial impact on the Scottish economy from the late 1960s onward, turning upside down the local economies of places like Aberdeen, often described as Scotland's oil capital, and Peterhead, a leading fishing port on the northeast coast, whose harbor of refuge found a new role sheltering and servicing oil supply vessels. More than 50,000 jobs in Grampian depend on oil. However, some say the boom has passed, not just because the easier finds have been exploited, but also because increasing offshore automation will require fewer workers, while onshore supply bases will also require fewer staff. Meanwhile, optimists point to the possibility of opening up a second exploration front in the waters west of Shetland, where initial surveys have revealed a huge and as yet untapped oil accumulation.

Other sectors The impact of tourism should not be overlooked: it contributes a hefty £1.74 billion ($2.6 million) annually to the Scottish economy and supports 178,000 jobs. Meanwhile fishing, fish farming, agriculture, the financial industry itself, plus the remainder of the surviving engineering sector (which still includes names like Rolls Royce,

Textile manufacture—still important in the Borders' economy

British Aerospace, Howden Group, and Motherwell Bridge) should continue to ensure a measure of prosperity north of the border.

❏ Oil experts estimate the recoverable reserves in the fields west of Shetland to be 5 billion barrels—roughly equivalent to the entire North Sea production for between seven and eight years. Rigs will have to combat heavy Atlantic swell, strong winds, and twice the water depth of the North Sea in order to gain this new oily bonanza. ❏

Ravenscraig—the heavy industry of yesterday?

■ **Scotland's position on the edge of continental Europe, surrounded by sea on three sides, helps explain her unpredictable weather. The country is a battleground between the continental climate of Europe and the weather systems coming off the Atlantic Ocean ...■**

Not truly tropical The Gulf Stream is often heralded as the saving grace of Scotland's weather. Much emphasized in travel brochures, this warming oceanic current reaches Scotland as the North Atlantic Drift. It hardly lends a "subtropical air" to the west coast (as you will sometimes see in print), but it is appreciated by tender tree ferns and cabbage palms at places like Logan Botanic Garden in Galloway in the southwest, and Inverewe Garden in Wester Ross (at the same latitude as Moscow).

weather is a risk worth taking. The popular tourism area of Lochaber is one of the wettest parts and July one of the wetter months, but also one of the busiest for tourists.

When it is not raining, the sparkling colors of the hills and sea lochs of the west make some of the finest landscapes anywhere in the world. Besides, the dreaded east coast *haar*, a summer sea fog, also complicates the picture. Scottish weather is a highly localized gamble, with few rules or generalizations—except to expect the worst and then be pleasantly surprised.

❏ The summit of Ben Nevis has a pretty generous mean annual rainfall twice that of Fort William (4 miles away), which gets 79 inches. But if you really want to test your rain gear, visit the head of Glen Garry, which offers a spectacular 200 inches every year. ❏

Glen Coe, one of Scotland's five ski resorts

Hebridean rain, Berneray, one of the smaller Western Isles

Where to find good weather
Sunshine in Scotland is most likely to be encountered away from the prevailing southwesterlies: the east coast "resorts"—Dunbar, St. Andrews, and Lossiemouth—all have encouraging statistics. The west is far wetter than the east. While Dunbar gets away with 22 inches of rainfall yearly, Inveraray on Loch Fyne enjoys 81 inches. For many visitors, wet

SCOTLAND WAS

■ **The scanty clues from "shell-middens,"
the garbage dumps of early man, suggest
that Scotland was first colonized about
8,000 years ago, after the last Ice Age. Over
the millennia, different races blended
together, leaving only their grave goods,
standing stones, and cairns (stone heaps) as
mysterious evidence for today's archeologists. Then Celtic invaders from Europe
arrived in about 500 BC with superior metalworking techniques. The Romans came and
failed to subdue the northlands, finally
withdrawing shortly after AD 212 ...■**

After the Romans, "Scotland" roughly comprised a British kingdom in Strathclyde and the southwest, with a capital at Dumbarton. ("Dun-Briton" means "the fort of the Britons," who had been the main Celtic tribe until pushed west by European invaders.) A Pictish confederation controlled the north. Within a couple of centuries a new wave of Celtic settlers arrived, this time from Ireland. These were the Scots who established the kingdom of Dalriada, with its center at Dunadd near Crinan in Argyll, in western Scotland.

The shape of Scotland The Angles arrived in the southeast in the 5th century. This Germanic tribe created a powerful Northumbrian kingdom, which took in the counties of East, West, and Mid Lothian (by present-day Edinburgh). Thus, along with the three Celtic ethnic groups (Britons, Picts, and Scots), a fourth, non-Celtic power base became important.

The northern expansion of this Anglo-Saxon grouping was checked at the Battle of Nechtansmere in Angus in AD 685, when the Pictish King Brude defeated the Angles under Egfrith, one of the important events that influenced the final form of Scotland. It also shifted the power base in England south from Northumbria to around the Thames, where it has remained ever since, so the shadowy northern Picts altered the course of English history as well.

Christianity played its part in

The Stones of Stenness, Orkney

Dun Troddan Broch, Glenelg

❑ The Roman historian Tacitus records a tantalizing tidbit on Scotland's first named battle, when red-haired warriors with painted bodies were defeated by a Roman force at Mons Graupius, a site as yet unidentified. There are traces of Roman marching camps as far north as the Moray Firth (estuary), but their greatest monument is the remains of the Antonine Wall (AD 142–3), which was built across the narrow waist of Scotland. ❑

Scotland's story. A Galloway-born Briton, St. Ninian, is the first recorded native Christian. However, the later St. Columba is better known. He came from Ireland to Iona in Dalriada in AD 563 to convert the northern Picts. As the Britons were already Christian by this time, this forged closer links between the two groups.

Yet another factor was at work in shaping Scotland. The ravages of the Vikings troubled both the northern Picts and also the Scots on the western seaboard. Some say the repeated pillaging of the Christian settlement and seat of learning at Iona set back the course of civilization for centuries. The Picts were so weakened by Norse raids that

Kenneth MacAlpin, King of Scots, was able to extend his kingdom north and east. He was crowned King of Scots and Picts in AD 844.

Thereafter, MacAlpin strengthened an alliance with the Britons, further extending his sway. However, only after the Battle of Carham (on the English side of the border near Coldstream) in 1025, when the Scottish King Malcolm I defeated the Northumbrians, did they give up the southeast so that the counties of Lothian became part of Scotland.

Finally, the marriage in 1070 of King Malcolm III to Margaret, a daughter of the English king, Edward the Confessor, set a pattern of intermarriage between the royal houses of Scotland and England that also was to influence strongly the fate of Scotland.

❑ Tacitus uses the word Picti—painted people—as well as Caledonii (hence Caledonian) to describe the northern tribes. Later, Alba (hence Alban and Albion) was the Gaelic word that described the combined Scot-Pictish kingdom north of the rivers Forth and Clyde. ❑

■ **The Wars of Independence refer to a period in Scottish history when Scotland's right to exist as an independent nation was threatened by the expansionist aspirations of the English Plantagenet kings. But it was not quite as simple as that. Nothing between Scotland and England ever was simple ...■**

The English overlords? In 12th-century Scotland, mainly in the time of King David I (1124–53), the Norman feudal system had taken root. David married the daughter of an English earl, gaining lands near Cambridge in southern England. In feudal terms, land meant an obligation to the over-lord, in this case the English king. This bowing of the knee as an English land-holder by David (and earlier kings) rein-

Bannockburn prelude—Robert Bruce kills Sir Henry de Bohun in single combat

forced a view that the Scots were under English command.This was strengthened by the Treaty of Falaise in 1174, signed by King William the Lion who, seeking territorial gains, joined a revolt by English barons against King Henry II of England. The barons were defeated; William was captured and forced to sign a treaty of allegiance, confirming the feudal over-lordship of England. (Scotland later bought its "independence" back when King Richard the Lionheart needed money for a crusade.)

A tragic fall King Alexander III of Scotland ruled a comparatively peaceful kingdom until 1286, when he died after falling from his horse. Through intermarriage, King Edward I of England was the great-uncle of the heir to the Scottish throne, Margaret of Norway. Acting as arbiter, he suggested she marry his son, thus securing close union between the two kingdoms. The Scots agreed but unfortunately the Maid of Norway died, leaving 13 other claimants with varying degrees of legitimacy.

Edward seized his chance in the power struggle and demanded acknowledgement of his own claim as overlord of Scotland. The claimants complied and Edward chose John Balliol, who became a puppet king, ever after known in Scotland as "Toom Tabard"—empty coat. However, even he was pushed too far by Edward, who demanded his services against the French. Balliol sided with France, and saw his army crushed at Dunbar by Edward's forces in 1296. Scotland was occupied by the English thereafter. The Scots aristocracy, spectacularly syco-phantic, secured their property by meekly swearing allegiance to Edward. He then destroyed many of Scotland's own records and carried off a variety of relics, including the Stone of Destiny, which has not yet been returned.

This was the background to the campaign called the Scots Wars of Independence. In the midst of Edward's policy of dismantling Scotland's administration and machinery of nationhood, there arose the first of her freedom fighters, William Wallace, who achieved some successes before his betrayal and death in 1305.

28

> ❏ William Wallace's most famous victory was at the Battle of Stirling Bridge in 1297, where, within sight of the English-held Stirling Castle, Wallace's men fell upon and defeated the opposing forces while they attempted to cross the narrow bridge. ❏

Stirling Castle—key to the kingdom

The Bannockburn campaign

Then Robert Bruce saw his chance. Bruce came from an old Norman family (de Brus refers to a Normandy place-name, and is often anglicized as "the Bruce"), and, like other Scots nobles, he played his part in the complex politics of English court life. His grandfather had been one of the original 13 claimants to the Scottish throne. He was crowned King of Scotland in 1307 and initiated a seven-year military campaign, which ended at the Battle of Bannockburn in 1314 with a (historically rare) Scots victory. Thereafter, though Scotland and England were certainly not at peace, Scotland won almost 400

years of independence from England.
Scotland's churchmen were unreservedly nationalist throughout the struggle. With the Pope still believing in England's right to rule Scotland, they met to prepare Scotland's most famous document, the Declaration of Arbroath, in 1320: "For so long as a hundred of us remain alive, we shall never accept subjection to the domination of the English..."

Robert Bruce, victor at Bannockburn

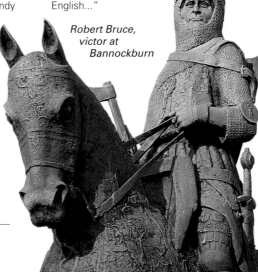

■ **She was queen for only seven years, but she played her part in a large-scale drama involving the royal houses of Scotland, France, and England. Since her death more than 400 years ago, she has become perhaps the best-known figure in Scotland's history ...■**

Mary, Queen of Scots (1542–87) was at the center of political upheavals even as a small child. The Stuart monarchs of Scotland had the inconvenient habit of dying when their offspring were too young to rule. Mary's father, King James V, died a week after hearing of his daughter's birth. Within three years this led to English attacks on Scotland—the destructive episodes known as the "rough wooing." This was King Henry VIII of England's less than subtle attempt to marry off his own young son Edward to the infant Mary. To get rid of the English invaders, the Scots called on the French for help. The price for this was the removal of Mary to France in 1548 for marriage to the Dauphin, the young French prince, in order to secure a Catholic alliance against England.

Scotland's tragic queen On her return to Scotland in 1561, Mary was a young and beautiful widow. The Dauphin had died, still in his teens. With Scotland in the throes of the Reformation and a widening Protestant–Catholic split, Mary was, politically speaking, hot property. Politicians (Scottish and English) soon worked out that finding Mary a Protestant husband might

Mary, Queen of Scots

offer the best chance of stability. However, Mary fell for the lanky young Lord Darnley. (Mary was very tall, and may have enjoyed the novelty of being looked down on.) Though at first she described him as the "lustiest and best proportioned lang man," the marriage proved a disaster. Darnley took to tavern life in solace, finding that Mary soon excluded him from any real authority.

The murder (by Darnley and others) of her secretary and favorite, David Riccio, witnessed by Mary while six months pregnant, indicates the ruthlessness of the conspirators against her in that age of political and religious instability. The birth of a son—the future King James VI of Scotland, James I of England—and his baptism as a Catholic at Stirling Castle was a cause for alarm among the Protestant factions.

30

FRANKLYN'S CIGARETTES

EXECUTION OF MARY QUEEN OF SCOTS

Plot and counterplot More controversy followed. The house in Edinburgh in which Lord Darnley was convalescing after an illness suddenly blew up one night. Darnley was later found strangled in the adjacent garden, his body strangely unmarked by the explosion. Exactly what happened that night in February 1567 remains one of Scotland's great historical mysteries, but suspicion still falls on the third man in Mary's life, the earthy James Hepburn, Earl of Bothwell. Before Darnley's death, it was well known both that Mary's reconciliation with him had failed, and that she was pregnant once again. Rumors were rife at court about the possible father of her child. In any event, Mary married Bothwell after his acquittal of Lord Darnley's murder. The last Scottish scenes in the drama saw the rising of a confederacy of the Protestant Lords of the Congregation against her new liaison, which eventually led to Mary's surrender and imprisonment in Loch Leven Castle. Her pregnancy subsequently ended with stillborn twins.

A few months later, in May of 1568, she escaped, gathered an army, and suffered defeat at Langside at the hands of the Protestant faction. Soon after she fled to England, crossing the border only 11 days after escaping from her imprisonment in Loch Leven Castle. There she remained a political pawn in the hands of Queen Elizabeth I, her cousin, who signed her death warrant in 1587.

Renaissance stonework on Falkland Palace, hunting lodge of the Stuarts

❏ Riccio was ugly, small, and hunched (though a fine lutenist), and it is unlikely that his role extended beyond that of musician and chief secretary to the Queen. Court gossip, however, suggested otherwise. ❏

■ **Nearly three centuries after the Union of 1707 between Scotland and England, the topic still surfaces in the correspondence columns of quality Scottish newspapers. The Union of Parliaments and the loss of independence is a live issue in a way it has never been south of the border** ...■

Scotland's foreign venture After the Union of the Crowns in 1603, when James VI of Scotland became James I of England, Scotland shared a monarch with England but had its own Parliament. Poorly developed Scotland assumed that this would mean sharing in trade with England's burgeoning colonies. When it became clear that England intended to keep the economic benefits to herself, the Scots decided to found their own colonies. The Darien Scheme, the establishing of a settlement on the disease-ridden isthmus of Panama in 1698, proved a financial catastrophe. Fever struck the colonists, and neighboring Spanish possessions rose against them. The Scots appealed to nearby English colonies for aid. This was refused for fear of upsetting Spain.

Everything was abandoned, ruining both the Scottish aristocracy and the ordinary folk who had put up funds. By 1701, anti-English feeling was running high. There was also a crisis of succession for Scotland and England. The Scots Parliament attempted blackmail. They stated that unless Scotland gained trading rights in English markets, they would not choose the same monarch as England. Instead of favoring the Protestant Hanoverian succession,

32

Christmas in Parliament Square, on Edinburgh's Royal Mile

❑ In 1707, the Lord Chancellor, who was instrumental in carrying forward the legislation, touched the written act with the royal scepter (symbolizing royal assent) and consigned independent Scotland to history. As he handed the scepter back to a clerk, he was heard to mutter to himself "Now, there's an end of an auld sang." ❑

they would turn instead to the exiled Catholic Stuart dynasty, waiting on the Continent for their chance. Once more for England the threat of a Scottish alliance with Catholic France presented itself.

Political horse-trading The foolish blackmail attempt caused England to retaliate with the Alien Act of 1705. This prevented Scots from holding property in England, and banned the purchase of all Scottish goods and services in England. England's parliament thus alarmed the now penniless Scots nobility, many of whom also had English properties, and also closed off Scotland's main market.

The price of peace was accepting the Hanoverian succession and the end of an independent Scottish parliament. As a trade-off, England offered access to her markets in the colonies. In addition, an English army stationed itself at Newcastle, close to the Scottish border. Discussions began in London, with the Scottish representatives aware that if agreement to England's terms was not secured, Scotland would be invaded.

Bought and sold for English gold?
When the final votes were taken, the nobility were heavily in favor and the popular representatives more evenly divided. This is hardly surprising. The Scottish landowners could recoup their losses after the Darien disaster, since bribes were standard parliamentary practices for moving through legislation. The Duke of Atholl was recompensed generously for not making trouble. The Duke of Argyll became a general, his brother Archie acquired a peerage. About

£20,000 ($30,000) in all was spent in buying off the Scottish aristocracy.

Later, the Scots said the deal was crooked, though the machinations were everyday parliamentary routine and only marginally less subtle than today's practices. Robert Burns wrote the song still widely sung in Scotland today:

We are bought and sold for English gold,
Such a parcel of rogues in a nation.

Echoes of 1707 When Scotland's degree of self-government is aired in the media, today's prime minister can rightly state that Scotland entered the Union voluntarily. Yet the echoes from the arguments of 1707 never quite die away. They surface, for example, when the Westminster parliament passes unpopular legislation applicable only to Scotland. The Earl of Seafield was wrong with his prediction in 1707. The siren song of freedom is still faintly heard today.

James Ogilvy, 1st Earl of Seafield, as portrayed by Sir John Baptiste de Medina

The Jacobites

■ **In about a century, the Jacobites went from feared political and military force to a suitable sentiment for Victorian drawing room song. Most celebrated of all is Prince Charles Edward Stuart, the Bonnie Prince Charlie of Jacobite hagiography ...■**

34

Who were the Jacobites? Decades of conflict between the monarch, the church, and the state (both in Scotland and England) came to a head with the exile of the Catholic King James VII (II of England) in 1689.

Though opinion on the matter was divided, a Convention of Estates (political representatives who formed a decision-making committee) in Scotland eventually went along with England and accepted William of Orange, husband of Mary, the daughter of the exiled King James VII. The Scottish supporters of the exiled James were furious. Thus originated the Jacobites (from the Latin Jacobus, for James). They rallied around John Graham of Claverhouse, the "Bonnie Dundee" of later Jacobite image-building.

He led them against a government army in the Battle of Killiecrankie in 1689. Fortunately for later tourism, he chose a most scenic location in Perthshire for his side's victory and his own demise, killed by a stray bullet. The Jacobites had created their first

saint, but, deprived of a figurehead, they were soon stopped in their tracks at nearby Dunkeld. There the grimly fanatical Cameronians, earlier persecuted by the Catholic faction, took their revenge.

"It was a' for oor rightfu' king..."
(It was all for our rightful king.) It is sometimes forgotten that the exiled Stuarts were actually the rightful bloodline. This belief in the justice of their cause was instilled into James Francis, the Old Pretender, King James VII's son, as he grew up on the Continent. In turn it was also fostered in the last Stuart king's grandson, Italian-born Charles, the Young Pretender, who as Bonnie Prince Charlie became the most famous Jacobite of all.

Uprisings Encouraged by Catholic France and Spain, this court in exile waited for the call, which came with an uprising in 1715. Its leader, John, Earl of Mar, was known even

Highlander statue on top of the Glenfinnan Monument

"THA 'S A DH'FHÀSAS FLÙR AIR MACHAIR MAIRIDH CLIÙ NA H-AINNIR CHAOIMH"
"THE PRESERVER OF PRINCE CHARLES EDWARD STUART WILL BE MENTIONED IN HISTORY AND IF COURAGE AND FIDELITY BE VIRTUES, MENTIONED WITH HONOUR"
JOHNSON

in his own lifetime as Bobbin John, from his habit of changing sides—an indication of the political complexities of the times. Mar led an army out of the hills to an inconclusive battle above Stirling on the hillslopes of Sheriffmuir. The affair had fizzled out by the time the Old Pretender "James VIII" landed on Scottish soil at Peterhead, so he did not stay long.

The 1719 rebellion was even more farcical. Spanish mercenaries were landed on the northwest coast near Dornie. They linked up with local Jacobites in Glen Shiel. Mortar fire from a detachment of government troops soon dealt with the matter. "Sgurr na Spainteach," Spaniards' Peak, in Glen Shiel, commemorates the incident. In between times, there were other plans and other invasion fleets that failed to materialize or were blown off course by storms.

The last rebellion Later, France and Britain went to war. Eager to encourage any destabilization of her island neighbor, France equipped the hotheaded, handsome Bonnie Prince Charlie and sent him off to Scotland in 1745 to raise support. After some successes, the mad escapade ended with Charles's army cut to pieces on the battlefield of Culloden. Charles was in Scotland for less than a year. The Jacobites were never a threat again. Soon the bloodshed had been sanitized and transformed into

romantic notions of exiled kings across the water and a huge number of maudlin songs.

When Charles first landed on Scottish soil on Eriskay on the Outer Hebrides, the northwestern islands off mainland Scotland, he was told by the local chief to go home. He said he had come home. Only about 6,000 of the 30,000 fighting men in the Highlands rallied to his cause.

❏ King James VII was the last of the Catholic Stuart dynasty, a line that had originated in the 14th century with the grandson of Robert the Bruce. ❏

Glenfinnan, where Bonnie Prince Charlie landed on the Scottish mainland some 250 years ago on August 19, 1745

■ **Far from being absorbed by the expanding greater Britain, Scotland retained its identity in the 18th century with an intellectual renaissance that tended toward a liberal-minded patriotism. It played an important role in the international movement known as the Age of Reason ...■**

Some people label the entire period between the Union of the Crowns in 1707 and the death of the influential writer Sir Walter Scott in 1832 as the Scottish Enlightenment. However, if Scotland did have a true post-Union Golden Age, then most commentators place it within the second half of the 18th century.

Edinburgh's greatness In its heyday, the movement was centered upon Edinburgh. The New Town was its architectural expression, but the Enlightenment embraced many other fields, from medicine to philosophy, agriculture to economics. This was the time of Edinburgh-born David Hume, one of the more influential philosophers of the Western world; of Kirkcaldy-born Adam Smith, who wrote the *Wealth of Nations* as the

Adam Smith, whose Wealth of Nations *was a masterpiece of political economy*

cornerstone of the new science of political economy; of Edinburgh's pioneering geologist James Hutton; of chemists such as Joseph Black, discoverer of carbon dioxide; and of many more who laid the foundations of a range of modern disciplines, many of them flowering out of the seedbed of Edinburgh University.

Intellectual life Edinburgh was the first university in the world to introduce a chair of English Literature, and it also led the way in important pioneering medical work. No less than three generations of Monros held the professorship in anatomy. Glasgow-born William Cullen not only established a tradition of chemical research work, but also became professor of chemistry at Edinburgh in 1756 and lectured in clinical medicine at the Royal Infirmary, exploring the links between the two disciplines.

Edinburgh between 1750 and 1790 was certainly a stimulating place to live. It was also a place where those creating the intellectual wealth were well aware of their role. They recognized the paradox that a lead in so many fields had been taken in a poor nation that had so recently lost status.

Even with New Town construction under way, the sheer proximity of many families of both high and humble birth in the tall, cramped

❏ Amyat, commenting on the intellectual life of Edinburgh society in the 1750s, remarked: "Here I stand at what is called the Cross of Edinburgh, and can, in a few minutes, take 50 men of genius and learning by the hand." ❏

A map of Scotland dating from 1797

tenements of Edinburgh's Old Town seemed to generate a special atmosphere, a cross-fertilizing of ideas that was widely commented upon by outsiders. They noted the debating and literary societies, the interest in written essays and stimulating conversation, as well as in the concrete forms of communication, such as building roads, bridges, and canals. Referring to this ready access to scientists, engineers, and all kinds of thinkers and writers, the English visitor Amyat (chemist to King George III) wrote that the philosophers in Scotland "tell us what they know, and deliver their sentiments without disguise or reserve."

By 1789 Thomas Jefferson, traveling in Europe on political business, wrote that "no place in the world can pretend to be competition with Edinburgh." Yet half a century later, the light had dimmed. An urge for rapid political change, embodied in the French Revolution and the Romantic movement, had overwhelmed the moderation and harmony that was the goal of the greatest Enlightenment thinkers.

Royal Society of Edinburgh, founded in 1783

❏ David Hume to Elliott of Minto in 1757: "is it not strange… that, at a time when we have lost our Princes, our Parliaments, our independent Government, even the presence of our chief Nobility, are unhappy in our accent and Pronunciation… speak a very corrupt Dialect of the Tongue… is it not strange… we shou'd really be the People most distinguish'd for literature in Europe?" ❏

The Highland Clearances

■ **The great mercantile cities of the Lowlands went about their business of making money. The powerful Highland landowners were similarly motivated. To improve their estates, they cleared their tenants from ground they had worked for centuries. Today this process might be called ethnic cleansing ...■**

The series of evictions and forced emigration known as the Highland Clearances did not happen immediately after the defeat of the Jacobite rebel forces at Culloden in 1746. Nevertheless, after Culloden, the old-style clan chiefs were stripped of their powers. The reality of hard economics asserted itself in the poor lands of the north.

meal. Also, kelp was gathered, dried, and burned, and the ash used in the manufacture of soap and glass. This made money for landowners with coastal properties.

The landowners raised rents to increase profits and altered leases to reduce individual landholdings, in order to compel tenants to spend more time fishing or kelp gathering.

An abandoned croft at Arnol, on the Isle of Lewis in the Western Isles

The improving landlords A program of improvements was implemented by new landowners, only some of whom were still of Highland stock, as they tried to make money from their property. The second half of the 18th century saw the founding of state-sponsored fishing stations such as Tobermory and Ullapool. The potato was first grown and soon became a staple. Better nourishment allowed the Highland population to expand.

A short-lived prosperity Britain's wars employed Highland manpower, and were also a market for Highland produce such as cattle, fish, and

Far from evicting tenants, the first decades of the 1800s saw land-owners, the majority of whom were absentees, actually requiring man-power to make money.

The slump came at the end of the Napoleonic Wars in the early 19th century, when the market for cattle collapsed. Agricultural improve-ments, successful in the Lowlands, just did not work on the thin, acid Highland soils. New chemical processes made kelp gathering unnecessary, and even the fishing became unprofitable. The landown-ers turned to sheep to make money. Unfortunately, the tenants' farming activities—the growing of potatoes and the pasturing of cattle—conflicted with the needs of the new-style Cheviot or black-face breeds.

❏ "Much the same thing is done today by town councils who uproot people from their old, shabby, but neighborly streets and place them in ultra-modern, clinically clean, but often inhuman high-rise flats [apartments], usually against their will." *Dunrobin Castle Guidebook*, 1991. Dunrobin was the home of the initiators of the Sutherland Clearances. ❏

Violence in the glens The people of the glens were evicted. The violence that accompanied the policy flared up in a now infamous list of Highland place-names, of which Strathnaver on the Sutherland Estates is perhaps the best known.

In 1785, the last Earl of Sutherland's daughter, Elizabeth Gordon, married one of the richest men in England, George Granville Leveson-Gower, second Marquess of Stafford. He had made a fortune in coal and wood, and owned a vast estate in England. With his marriage came most of the northern Scottish county of Sutherland, including Dunrobin Castle.

In the program of estate improvements, upward of 5,000 Highlanders were cleared up to 1821. They were either settled on narrow coastal strips or were forced to emigrate, mostly across the Atlantic. In Strathnaver, many of the tenants were unable to take out their belongings as their houses were burned before their eyes. The estate factor, Patrick Sellar, was even charged with arson and homicide, as some homes were set on fire with old people still inside them. He was acquitted.

The same pattern of evictions by landowners—titled aristocrats, entrepreneurs, and industrialists—stretched from Shetland to Perthshire. Many sincerely believed it was for the best. Today, in the Highlands, with their silent glens admired by city dwellers, visitors creep reverently around the treasures in the castles of the descendants of these "improvers."

Dunrobin Castle, Golspie, Sutherland

■ **The Scots have always been adventurers. Soldiers and merchants traveled in Europe from the very early days of the Scots nation. Then, when ships became large enough to undertake longer voyages, Scots left their homeland and became entrepreneurs and explorers, as well as simply colonists, all over the globe ...■**

In 1297, Sir William Wallace, the Scottish freedom fighter, wrote to the senators of Lubeck and Hamburg thanking them for helping Scottish merchants, and offering safe conduct for any of their representatives at Scotland's ports. This is an early reference to Scots entrepreneurs abroad. It is estimated that Poland had 30,000 Scots living and operating in business there in the 17th century.

Dunbar acknowledges its famous son, John Muir

To the four corners of the globe
Scots were prominent in the Far East. William Jardine, born in Dumfriesshire, in southern Scotland, was an independent China trader who joined forces with James Matheson to form the Hong Kong-based Jardine Matheson of today. Its early profits were amassed in the

unsavory opium trade. Hugh Falconer and William Jamieson were early Scottish pioneers of tea plantations in India. Fraserburgh-born Thomas Glover introduced modern technology to Japan, particularly in shipbuilding. He ordered Japan's first slip dock, which in turn led to the expansion of the now multinational company Mitsubishi.

Not only was Thomas Glover a trusted adviser and personal friend of Mitsubishi's founder, Yataro Iwasaki, he also imported the first steam locomotive and the first telegraph line. Incidents in his extraordinary life are said to have inspired Puccini's opera *Madame Butterfly.*

The Scots turned westward as well, building Glasgow's early wealth on plantations of Virginian tobacco and Jamaican sugar. Later developments such as the Prairie Cattle Company Limited, Texas's first major joint stock venture in cattle ranching, were actually Edinburgh based. More than half the Hudson Bay Company's senior staff were Scots. Even more significantly, at least 13 U.S. presidents claimed Scottish ancestry.

These emigrant Scots or their descendants became involved in every sphere. The son of a poor country tailor in an upcountry parish in Aberdeenshire went on to found *Forbes Magazine*, the still-successful financial journal. Bertie Charles Forbes (1880–1954) became a millionaire in the process. James Gordon Bennet (1795–1872) left his native Keith in Moray in the northeast, and went on to found the *New York Herald.* In industry, the best-known Scot is the steel magnate Andrew Carnegie from Dunfermline; his name has become a byword for philanthropy. The squalor of the

Glasgow slums of the early 19th century produced Allan Pinkerton, the founder of the oldest and largest private investigation agency in the world. In 1867, a young Scottish emigrant, John Muir from Dunbar, began to develop the idea of environmental conservation while walking in the Sierra Nevada. It was to lead to the founding of the conservation movement in the United States.

There were, naturally, the oddities: the Scots who suddenly popped up in unexpected places, like the businessmen who formed the African Lakes Corporation in 1878, or the Scottish lace workers in Spain who founded the first Spanish soccer team. Less surprising, perhaps, is a certain James Chisholm, who founded the first pub in Sydney, Australia, called the Thistle Tavern—presumably around the same time as another Scot, Lachlan Macquarie, brought order as the first governor of the former Australian penal colony of New South Wales.

Dunfermline-born Andrew Carnegie

The call of the homeland Whatever the reason—religious persecution, lack of opportunity, forced clearance, voluntary emigration, or just a sense of adventure—Scots men and women have been the country's leading export over the centuries. Small wonder the Clan Donald has over 100,000 members worldwide. For many the call of the homeland is still strong. Libraries throughout Scotland, carrying records on microfiche formerly only available at New Register House, do brisk business with genealogical inquiries.

❑ The word Scot in Polish also means a commercial traveler, and the Poles have a simile "as poor as a Scots peddler's pack." Evidently not all Scots were successful in business. ❑

■ The image of Scotland as a resourceful, industrial place sits uncomfortably with the more romantic notion of misty bens (hills) and glens. Yet, in times gone by, the output of heavy industry and, in particular, shipbuilding, ensured that Scottish products went around the world and that "Clyde built" (that is, a product of the many shipbuilding yards along the River Clyde) meant the very finest of its kind ...■

The Scottish industrial belt was formerly a diagonal corridor across the waist of Scotland, less than 30 miles wide from coast to coast. It took in the coalfields of Ayrshire and the south of Edinburgh, the Vale of Leven dyeing industries south of Loch Lomond, and Angus textile manufacturing (all now mere vestiges of their former size, if there at all). Paradoxically, it also included some of Scotland's best farmland.

The key to prosperity—coal and iron Among these activities, those based on locally available coal and iron had the highest profile, if only because of the effect they had on

The Clydeside birth of a Cunarder, the Queen Mary

the environment and landscape. It is arguable that the real cradle of the Industrial Revolution in Scotland lay east of Glasgow, in the Falkirk area, where the Carron Company was founded in 1760, close to iron mines.

However, by the early years of the 19th century, the easily workable blackband iron ore of Lanarkshire had been discovered. What had been the fruit garden of the west of Scotland was turned over in a search for this important mineral. The air of Lanarkshire filled with grime and smoke as ironworks sprang up, using local coal to fuel the furnaces. The stage was set for the Clyde area to become one of the world's greatest shipbuilding centers. Though England's River Tyne was also important, most of the developments in ship design and, in particular, marine engines and boilers, were made on the banks of the Clyde.

❑ The Carron Company's most famous product was the carronade, a short-barreled, large-bore cannon used in Britain's imperialist wars. ❑

The song of the Clyde Formerly, the shipyards stretched practically unbroken all the way downstream to Greenock, but these days most have long gone. Even as recently as 1929, the Clyde built 20 percent of the world's shipping. Then the so-called Clyde symphony or the "song of the Clyde" was at its height: the noise of thousands of riveters banging home the red-hot rivets that held together the locally made steel plates.

Sunset over the Clyde shipyards

The romance of ships Glasgow, of course, had all kinds of other manufacturing operations, including the production of railway locomotives. Dundee and the Angus hinterland thrived on textiles, Edinburgh had her printing and publishing industries, as well as shale oil extraction to the west. Even modest Aberdeen could claim a surprisingly large engineering sector, while the Borders were well-known for textiles.

Yet only shipbuilding and the proud and graceful products that sailed the waters of the globe acquired the romance and mystique that comes with the associations of distant places. Though the local coal and iron which helped build the ships have long been depleted, the hammers are not yet quite silent.

❑ During World War II, the Clyde shipyards still had the capacity to build 2,000 ships, repair more than 23,000, and convert hundreds more. To put it another way, the workforce built or repaired 13 ships every day for five years. ❑

The Clyde still sees the launch of large vessels—as ever, diagonally into the narrow river. But on the banks of today's Clyde there are also long stretches of landfill docks and redeveloped sites.

Only at places such as the Denny Ship Model Experiment Tank at Dumbarton (see page 140) are there echoes of the great, grimy days of the Clyde, the river that made Glasgow.

Edinburgh The city makes a stirring first impression: it is hard to avoid the initial visual drama. By road, only a couple of hours or less from the border with England, the A68 plunges over the edge of the Southern Uplands to reveal the Lothians, Edinburgh's countryside, spread out below: the sweep of the Pentland Hills stopping short at the edge of the city; farther around, the dark profile of Arthur's Seat dominating the other more gentle rises on which Scotland's capital is built; then the long reach of the estuary known as the Firth of Forth, with just a hint of the Highlands beyond. This is the setting for one of the world's most distinguished cities.

From the air, on the final approaches, the city map is plain: the castle on its high rock and the Palace of Holyroodhouse in its Royal Park, act as head and tail for the backbone of the Royal Mile, which runs through the Old Town. Across the green space of Princes Street Gardens, symmetrical patterns reveal the plan of the neo-classical New Town. Moments after this port wing view, and over the high spans of the Forth rail and road bridges, the traveler touches down.

By train, you reach the center at Waverley Station. On emerging, the skyline seems familiar: the profiles of castle and battlement, the Gothic-spired Scott Monument and Greek-porticoed art galleries are known worldwide through print and postcard, yet still excite.

From every angle, Edinburgh strikes theatrical poses. The neoclassical collection of monuments on top of Calton Hill seem about to frame some Greek tragedy. Above the rooftops of the Royal Mile, the long, red ridge

Edinburgh Castle dominates the city skyline

of Salisbury Crags skirts the rocks of Arthur's Seat—it could well be a painted backdrop for one of Sir Walter Scott's melodramas. At 1PM each day a cannon cracks out, puffing blue smoke over the castle battlements. Do not be alarmed: this is not another uprising, only Edinburgh squeezing extra drama out of a time check. Edinburgh generates excitement and a sense of expectation. This is where things happen…

Old Edinburgh Edinburgh's **Castle Rock** dates from the last Ice Age. An eastward-grinding glacier nibbled away at its hard, volcanic plug, leaving three steep sides and a ramp running down eastward. An archeological dig in the 1990s to establish the age of settlement on the Rock found some chewed herring bones, now carbon-dated to around 800 BC.

The Castle Rock was a Dark Age stronghold, fortified by the Saxon King Edwin in the 7th century. The oldest building in Edinburgh today is the 12th-century **St. Margaret's Chapel** within the castle, named after Queen Margaret. She married King Malcolm, whose Celtic court was at Dunfermline, then the capital. As a Saxon southerner, she persuaded the court to move to the Saxon-influenced Lothians. Edinburgh became the capital thereafter.

By the 12th century, the huddle of little houses protected by the castle had spilled down the ramp—the embryonic **Royal Mile**—perhaps as far as today's Tron Kirk ("kirk" is the Scottish word for church) on the High Street. Margaret's son, King David, founded **Holyrood Abbey**, another landmark in the shaping of the old city.

The castle was sacked by King Edward I of England in 1296, and many of the nation's records destroyed. After the English withdrew, Edinburgh became a royal burgh (town; see panel) in 1329, and faced the wars and vicissitudes of Scotland's long struggle under a weak monarchy with a powerful and ambitious neighbor on her southern border. The High Kirk of St. Giles was burned in 1385 by King Richard II of England, the Royal Mile torched in 1542 during Henry VIII's "rough wooing" (see page 30).

As a means of defense, Edinburgh was a walled town. Bits of wall survive today, near St. Mary's Street and above the Grassmarket. In the main, the community remained within its high walls until the mid-18th century.

Then it crossed the marshy defensive gap, now the site of Princes Street Gardens, to found the New Town.

New Edinburgh In the creative heat and spirit of optimism of the Age of Enlightenment, the city laid the foundations of the townscape of today. The first **New Town** comprises the rectangle bounded by **Charlotte** and **St. Andrew Squares** to west and east, and **Princes** and **Queen Streets** to south and north. Other development plans followed around Moray Place and, less successfully, along Royal Terrace.

The great public buildings and monuments that enhance the city environment so much today were built at the same time: the **Royal Scottish Academy** and the **National Gallery**, honey-colored, columned temples floating in garden greenery when viewed from the east; the fluted shapes of more columns of Calton Hill's unfinished National Monument, which block and change the views east along Princes Street from every angle.

Amid all this neoclassicism, the monument to Sir Walter Scott shoots out of the trees like a Gothic skyrocket. Architecturally isolated, Scott's immortalization in sandstone plays its part in the theatrical quality of Edinburgh, and has become an essential symbol of the city. Towering above Holyroodhouse, the impossible profile of **Arthur's Seat** looks like a backdrop for one of Scott's own theatrical melodramas—or an entirely appropriate setting for the cultural overkill generated annually through the Edinburgh International Festival, the Fringe, and other attendant festivals.

For all its expensive parking fines and crowds, as well as the proportion of well-meant but uninspiring productions that turn the Fringe into something of a grab bag, Edinburgh undoubtedly remains an exciting place. Away from the downtown cosmopolitan throng, life in the New Town goes on as it has done for more than two centuries, below the plasterwork in elegant drawing rooms or amid the shade of the private gardens overlooked by palace-fronted façades: all in all, a curious meeting of the past and present.

Scotland's burghs
A Scottish burgh, a term first used in the 12th century, was a town with certain rights; when these rights were granted by the monarch, a town became a royal burgh. The rights were mainly to do with mercantile matters, such as the granting of the right to hold fairs or markets, in order to raise money for the Crown, as well as for the community itself. Characteristics of a burgh usually included a mercat (market) cross, to indicate the place of the market and the town center, as well as a tolbooth, a civic building that served as an administrative center and, very often, a courtroom and prison, too. Burghs disappeared with the local government reorganization that took place in 1975.

47

Calton Hill

Visitors view the former Royal High School near Calton Hill

Edinburgh's unfinished Parthenon
The prolific architect William Playfair had a hand in many Edinburgh streets and buildings. He is also less happily associated with the National Monument, the columned façade on Calton Hill. Intended to be an exact copy of the Parthenon in Athens and a tribute to the dead of the Napoleonic Wars, it was started in 1822. Money ran out in 1829, and the work has been left unfinished ever since. It has become known as "Edinburgh's Disgrace," but it has a certain appeal even in its present state.

▶▶ **Calton Hill** 45D3

Robert Louis Stevenson's favorite view of Edinburgh was from this hill to the east of Princes Street. Even in Stevenson's day it carried its extraordinary neoclassical collection of buildings: the **Old Observatory** (the only surviving building by New Town planner James Craig), the **City** or **New Observatory**, the **Dugald Stuart Memorial** (loosely based on the temple of Lysicrates in ancient Athens), the unfinished **National Monument**, and the **Nelson Monument**, which ignores its neoclassical neighbors and instead is shaped like an upturned telescope. If the walk up the steps to the hilltop is too much, take the car. Look for the turnoff by the former Royal High School. The hill is open at all times.

■ **Camera Obscura** 44C1

594 Castlehill
This building has a varied history: the lower stories were built in the 17th century, and the upper, castellated stories added in 1853, when the building first became a camera obscura. As well as panoramic projections of Edinburgh, thanks to its revolutionary design and mirrors, the center offers a variety of Edinburgh-related exhibitions. It is one of only three such buildings in Scotland today, and is open daily.

■ **Canongate Kirk** 45D2

Canongate
This church was built in 1688 for the congregation when King James VII converted the abbey church at Holyrood into a chapel for the Knights of the Thistle. Of greater interest, though, is the adjoining **graveyard**. Graves include that of Mrs. McLehose, the attractive young woman abandoned by her husband and with whom the 18th-century Scottish poet Robert Burns conducted a passionate correspondence (just that and no more, since Burns was confined to his Edinburgh lodgings with a twisted knee). She outlived him by 45 years. Also here is the grave of Robert Fergusson, the brilliant Edinburgh poet who inspired Burns, though they never met. When Burns visited, he was shocked to find Fergusson's grave unmarked, and paid for his headstone.

Itinerary

A long weekend in Edinburgh

Day 1 Rampart views from **Edinburgh Castle** aid orientation in this fairly simply laid-out city, and a self-guided castle tour, taking most of a morning, is worthwhile. Then go downhill, diverting for **Victoria Street** shopping. (Use the steps at West Bow.) Try, say, Jacksons on the **Royal Mile** for lunch, or head to the Kalpna by Nicholson Street, or take on a chance with a pub lunch anywhere on the Mile.

Be selective if time is short. The **Museum of Childhood** is fun, or continue to **Huntly House**. The **Palace of Holyroodhouse** is also popular or instead make your way over to **Calton Hill** for city views, en route to the **National Gallery** at the foot of the Mound. You should just catch it before closing.

Day 2 Yesterday the Old Town, today the New. Start at the **National Portrait Gallery**, then go on to the **Georgian House**. In between, try Jenners on Princes Street for shopping. For lunch, choose from the many options nearby: La Lanterna on Hanover Street if on a budget, or **Martin's** on Rose Street if you have reservations, or a Rose Street pub. In the afternoon, explore northward through the New Town to reach the Royal Botanic Garden, then return via Stockbridge and shops. In the evening, check out Leith's choice of eating places, or, if the weather is fine, walk in the Royal Park to enjoy great views from Arthur's Seat, followed by a beer in the Sheep's Heid in Duddingston.

Day 3 The **Waverley Market** shopping mall is useful for last-minute souvenir shopping. If you have time, revisit the Royal Mile. The **Scotch Whisky Heritage Centre**, the **Writers' Museum**, and **Gladstone's Land** are all within easy reach of the city center.

Timekeeping
The firing of the 1PM gun from the ramparts of Edinburgh Castle originated from a request by the Leith Dock Commission in 1861 to locate a time ball on top of the Nelson Monument (which was visible from the docks). Punctually every day since then (except in wartime and on Sundays), an audible signal has boomed out across the city, and simultaneously the time ball has dropped down its pole on the monument, enabling mariners of old to check their chronometers and nowadays making tourists jump visibly as they stroll along Princes Street at lunchtime.

49

*Edinburgh Castle
from Calton Hill*

EDINBURGH

▶▶▶ **Edinburgh Castle** *44B1*

Possibly Scotland's most famous landmark, Edinburgh Castle dominates the center of the city with its silhouette of ramparts and rooftops. Almost a million visitors every year swarm over its buildings, from the 12th-century chapel to its latest addition, a restaurant with one of the finest views anywhere in the city.

Edinburgh Castle was an important royal court from at least the 11th century. Through the Middle Ages, its buildings were mainly around the highest point of the Castle Rock. King David II built the first strong defensive line across the eastern neck after 1356.

Little of the very early works survive. Today's **Great Hall** of King James IV dates from the early 16th century, but has been greatly altered. The massive **Half Moon Battery** dates in part from the latter half of the 16th century. As the castle's royal role became less important than its military one, successive waves of buildings and defenses were dictated by military needs and warfare, which severely damaged the castle on many occasions.

The castle fired its last shot in anger in 1745 at Bonnie Prince Charlie's men, who failed to take the high rock. Thereafter, as well as a barracks and administrative center, the castle also became a military prison. It still serves as a military headquarters, and not all areas can be visited.

Start your tour by the **Esplanade**, the mid-18th century parade ground. Beyond the Victorian gatehouse, you find yourself below the vast walls of the **Half Moon Battery** and **Forewall Battery**. Beyond the **Portcullis Gate** the upper levels are reached, with cannon much in evidence and fine views over Edinburgh beyond the barrels.

Reminders of a constant military presence include the handsome **Governor's House**, dating from 1742, now the Officers' Mess, and the **New Barracks**, whose bold blocking has dominated the skyline since the 1790s. The former hospital, to the right (beyond tiny **St. Margaret's Chapel**), is now part of the Scottish United Services Museum, a place of monosyllabic attendants and immaculate uniforms. (The main historic collection is in the Queen Anne Barracks.)

The Vaults, beside the Victorian prison, are more atmospheric. These dripping, dank corridors of naked rock have been barracks, stores, bakehouse, and, as memorably described in Robert Louis Stevenson's *St. Ives*, a prison for French soldiers (look for their graffiti). The most famous inhabitant today is the great cannon known as **Mons Meg**: she squats evilly on a spotlit plinth beside her audiovisual introduction.

Back above ground, on Crown Square, is the **Scottish National War Memorial**, an emotional ambush of gray light, tattered flags, and endless names. Opposite is the anticlimax of the **Great Hall**. Like the small room in the palace in which Mary, Queen of Scots gave birth to the James who was to rule both Scotland and England, this just fails to grab the imagination. However, also here is a very illuminating display on the story of the castle, plus

The Scottish United Services Museum, Edinburgh Castle

the **Honours of Scotland Exhibition**. This is a highlight, where you can view the oldest regalia in Europe: the Scottish crown, scepter, and sword of state. In close-up, the royal crown seems a bit like the castle itself: a little battered and frequently repaired over the centuries, yet the pride of a poor nation. The castle is open all year.

► **City Art Centre**　　　　　　　　　　*44C2*

Market Street
The city's own art gallery is housed in a six-floor former warehouse. It stages a changing program of exhibitions, and displays the city's collection of Scottish paintings. It has a track record of bringing world-class exhibitions to the city, from the Chinese Warriors to the Pharaohs, and is open all year.

► **Craigmillar Castle**　　　　　　　　　　*45D1*

Off A68
If Edinburgh Castle were less of a magnet, and if Craigmillar Castle were not situated quite so near one of Edinburgh's less salubrious housing developments, then the impressive Craigmillar would have many more visitors. In Mary, Queen of Scots' time, the imposing fortress was held by Sir Simon Preston, one of her staunchest allies. Behind the massive curtain wall, somewhere amid the 16th-century buildings, the plot to murder her husband, Lord Darnley, was hatched (see pages 30–1). The castle is open all year, but is closed Thursday afternoons and Fridays in winter.

City Art Centre

The Scottish Regalia
On June 24, 1953 the Regalia of Scotland were taken from the castle to St. Giles Cathedral, where they were presented to Her Majesty the Queen. The galaxy of lords and earls who guarded the Honours of the Nation were dressed in ermine and grand costumes. The Queen, however, wore a simple coat and hat. Still clutching her handbag, she touched the oldest crown in Europe. The incongruity is still remembered in Scotland to this day, though in the official portrait of the event, by Stanley Cursiter, now in the Royal Collection, the handbag has been carefully painted out.

51

Mons Meg
This siege gun or bombard was made in Mons in the 1440s and sent by its owner, the Duke of Burgundy, to his nephew by marriage, King James II, in 1457. The gun had a firing rate of, at the most, one cannonball every 30 minutes. Though cumbersome to move over the rough roads of its day, it did take part in sieges before finally bursting while firing a salute in 1680. It was later displayed in the Tower of London, before its return to Edinburgh Castle.

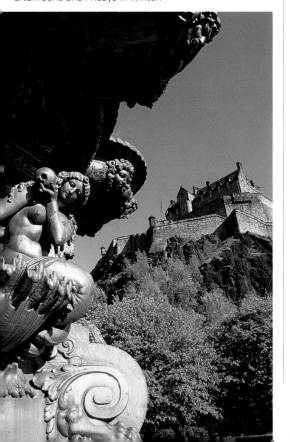

Edinburgh Castle from Princes Street Gardens

Walk **A flavor of old Edinburgh**

This pleasant stroll takes in attractions on the Royal Mile, before heading to the Grassmarket and a fine view of the castle. Allow two hours. *See map on page 44.*

Looking east down the Royal Mile in the direction of the Palace of Holyroodhouse

Amid the general crush of visitors on Castlehill at the very top of the **Royal Mile**, look for the **Witch's Well** (on the wall), which recalls the last witch burned here in 1722. Nearby is **Cannonball House,** which has a cannonball embedded in the gable with a variety of expla-

nations as to how it got there. Farther down the hill are the **Camera Obscura** (see page 48) and the **Scotch Whisky Heritage Centre** (see page 63). Continue down the hill to the traffic circle.

The Lawnmarket has numerous souvenir shops to distract you, but for a hint of old Edinburgh, turn right just after the traffic circle into the short Upper Bow. Go to the end of the truncated street, and look over the railings to see Victoria Street curving down below. Now imagine the shape of the town before Victoria Street was built: Upper Bow plunged steeply down to join the lowest point of Victoria Street, called West Bow, which leads into the Grassmarket. The insignificant lane you have just come down used to be the main road into old Edinburgh from the west.

Return to the Lawnmarket on the Royal Mile. Opposite is **Gladstone's Land** (see page 54), one of a number of restored 17th-century properties in this area.

Lady Stair's House (the Writers' Museum; see page 57) is also on the north side of the street—cut through a small square to reach it—with **Deacon Brodie's Tavern** occupying the corner site. Deacon Brodie, a respectable locksmith by day and a villain by night, inspired Robert Louis Stevenson's story, *The Strange Case of Dr. Jekyll and Mr. Hyde.*

Turn right onto George IV Bridge and right again to reach Victoria Street, which has a good selection of shops and cafés. West Bow leads into the **Grassmarket**. The right to hold regular markets here was granted by King James III in 1477. The area gained notoriety as the hanging place of common criminals, as well as Covenanter martyrs (see page 55). **St. Andrew's Cross**, railed and set into the cobbles, marks the gallows' site.

For an impressive view of the castle, cross over the Grassmarket, go halfway along and follow The Vennel up in a series of steps to a well-preserved portion of the city wall. This is **Telfer's Wall**, 1628–36, which now defines the boundaries of George Heriot's School beyond. From here, there is an excellent view of the castle, to the north. Return to the Grassmarket, then bear right, passing **Mr. Wood's Fossil Shop,** which offers souvenirs with a difference (very small trilobites are a bargain). Then go up **Candlemaker Row,** where tourists risk life and limb standing in the middle of the road to photograph the statue of **Greyfriars Bobby** (see page 55) at the top. Make your way back to the Royal Mile along George IV Bridge.

❏ Beneath Edinburgh City Chambers in the High Street, site of the former Royal Exchange, lies Mary King's Close. This narrow street was abandoned after the plague of 1645, and sealed off to prevent the disease from spreading. It was subsequently covered by the foundations of the later buildings on the High Street. The 17th-century time capsule survives today and is used for storing council documents. It can be visited by prior arrangement. ❏

❏ The Old Town right up to the 18th century, and even later, was a pretty smelly place. This fact was recorded by numerous visitors. Household wastes of every description were emptied from the tall tenements into the narrow High Street with a warning cry of "gardyloo" from on high (the phrase comes from the French *gardez l'eau*— "beware, water"). This was the cause of great embarrassment to biographer James Boswell as he escorted the distinguished man of letters, Dr. Samuel Johnson, up the Royal Mile before they set off for their Hebridean Tour in 1773. The odor is also remembered by a famous fiddle tune, somewhat ironically entitled "The Floo'ers (flowers) o' Edinburgh." ❏

The City Chambers, built as the Royal Exchange

The Georgian House, Charlotte Square

Greyfriars Bobby, Edinburgh's best-known dog

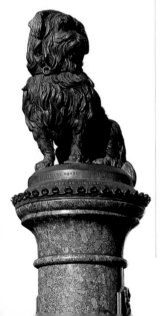

►   **Fruitmarket Gallery**   *44C2*

Market Street

Another of Edinburgh's high-profile art showcases, the Fruitmarket emphasizes contemporary art and design with a strong international flavor. Combine it with a visit to the City Art Centre opposite (see page 51). The gallery is open daily, except on Sunday mornings and Mondays.

►►   **Georgian House**   *44A2*

Charlotte Square

In the middle of revered English architect Robert Adam's palace-fronted block, at No.7 Charlotte Square, the conservation body known as the National Trust for Scotland has re-created the look of 1796, when the building was new. From the magnificent drawing room with its glittering candlesticks, to the well-scrubbed pantries and kitchen, this is an authentic peek at the past, and a starting point for appreciating the impact the New Town made on Edinburgh life for those who could afford it. The house is open from April to October.

►   **Gladstone's Land**   *44C2*

477 Lawnmarket

When the local merchant Thomas Gledstanes acquired the property that now bears his name in 1617, it had a wooden front and a timber gallery overhanging the ground floor, a typical 16th-century building that would have resembled John Knox House farther down the street (see page 57). Gledstanes modernized it by adding a stone front and stone arcading. Like so much of the

Royal Mile, this ancient tenement was scheduled to be swept aside, but instead a purchaser presented it to the fledgling National Trust for Scotland in 1935. The Trust restored it and uncovered its by then hidden arcades, now unique in Edinburgh. Some fine painted ceilings also survive from Gledstanes's time, and are set off by period room settings. The house is open from April to October.

▶ **Greyfriars Kirk** 44C1

Greyfriars Place

King Charles I's attempt to introduce the English Episcopal service book to Scotland in 1637 was widely opposed. The following year, a large crowd gathered in the churchyard of the Greyfriars to sign the National Covenant. This important historical manifesto professed loyalty to the king, but warned him not to interfere in the affairs of the kirk. It can be seen to this day within the church. Thus were born the Covenanters, who played their part in the bloody religious wars of the 17th century. The churchyard itself, where 1,400 Covenanters were imprisoned in 1679, is on the site of a 15th-century Franciscan friary and has a good range of 17th-century grave monuments.

The Covenanters Prison in Greyfriars Kirkyard

55

It was also the burial place of John Gray, the policeman owner of Greyfriars Bobby, a dog who refused to leave his master's grave. The kindhearted graveyard attendant fed him at first. Soon the faithful terrier was a well-known phenomenon, cared for by the locals. He soon adopted a local restaurant, delighting the eating place's owner, who did extra business because of the publicity. People came from long distances to see the dog arrive each lunchtime.

When a law was passed forbidding ownerless dogs, Bobby's supporters appealed to the Lord Provost (the Scottish equivalent of a Lord Mayor), who gave the dog immunity by way of an inscribed collar. Bobby died in 1872, but the tale did not end there. A baroness erected a fountain at the top of nearby Candlemaker Row. Later still, Bobby was featured in a Walt Disney film, which explains his appeal to many visitors today. Dog artifacts are on display in **Huntly House** (see below). The churchyard is open daily, the church in summer only.

▶▶ **Huntly House** 45D2

Canongate

This 16th-century building houses the city's museum of life over the centuries. Local silver, glass, pottery, shop signs, and a host of other artifacts are all displayed in a maze of interconnecting rooms. It helps to know a little about the history of Edinburgh before you browse around so that, for example, the artifacts connected with King George IV's visit, or the original New Town plan signed by James Craig, are more significant. The museum is open daily except Sundays.

Register House

Record-keeping in Scotland has had a troubled history. King Edward I of England vindictively destroyed the country's earliest records in the 13th century. Register House was situated in the castle by the mid-16th century, and then in the Tolbooth a century later. Only in 1774 was a foundation stone laid for a custom-built Register House, designed by Robert Adam, and partly financed by funds raised from the sale of estates forfeited by Jacobite lairds (see page 38). The building, at the east end of Princes Street, is still in use today, guarded by a statue of the Duke of Wellington, who defeated Napoleon at Waterloo.

Literary Edinburgh

JOHN
KNOX
HOUSE

■ **From its earliest days as capital of Scotland, Edinburgh has always had strong literary connections. Thomas Nelson, J. Bartholomew, Oliver & Boyd, and W. & R. Chambers are some of the famous publishing houses with origins in Edinburgh ...■**

Scotland's poetic golden age

Medieval Edinburgh was a literary place. Gavin Douglas, *c.*1474–1522, Dean of St. Giles, translated the *Aeneid*, the first translation of a Latin poet ever printed in English.

William Dunbar, *c.*1460–*c.*1520, was a court poet whose work was in print by 1508, the earliest example of Scottish typography. Sir David Lyndsay of The Mount scandalized the courtiers with his *Satyre of the Thrie Estatis* in 1540. The piece returns regularly to the Edinburgh Festival.

56

Originally a wig-maker in the Grassmarket, 18th-century poet Allan Ramsay later set up Britain's first circulating library, and is the first of the "modern" names associated with literary Edinburgh. Then came Robert Fergusson, who captured the spirit of the Enlightenment in Edinburgh and inspired a later generation, among them Robert Burns.

A vibrant literary community Conspicuous in the 19th century was Sir Walter Scott, writing of "mine own romantic town" from his house on Castle Street. As a teenager, he had once met Burns at a local literary gathering. Edinburgh's literary life, with its publishers, tavern life, and buzzing creativity, attracted writers from all over the world. It was the first city to recognize the achievements of Charles Dickens by making him a citizen. Charlotte Brontë was also enthralled by the place. Her brother Branwell wrote to the influential Edinburgh-based *Blackwood's Magazine* asking for a job when he was 15. His letter was ignored at the time but is now in the National Library.

Edinburgh in its prime Robert Louis Stevenson was a native of Edinburgh, and became one of its most famous Victorian writers. Stevenson wrote of the city not just in romantic terms, but in a style that still brings its taverns and low life alive. Scotland's most influential 20th-century poet, Hugh MacDiarmid, also had strong Edinburgh connections through a variety of publishing enterprises. British novelist Muriel Spark was educated at James Gillespie's High School for Girls, the real-life Marcia Blane School of her novel *The Prime of Miss Jean Brodie.*

Today, it is still possible to rub shoulders with poets and writers, even moderately famous ones, in one of the city's "literary" pubs such as Milne's Bar on Hanover Street. The bohemian life survives in Edinburgh, perhaps as a reaction to the city's Calvinistic and prim outlook.

Burns' memorabilia, The Writers' Museum

ROBERT LOUIS STEVENSON
CENTENARY CELEBRATIONS

RLS 100

▶ **John Knox House**   45D2

45 High Street

Nobody seems to know if John Knox (see panel) really did live in this house on High Street. There is absolutely no documentary evidence, only a folk tradition. However, this was enough to save it when threatened with demolition as long ago as 1849. The late 15th-century building with its projecting second-floor gallery is a reminder of what the Royal Mile would once have looked like: narrow and lined by tenements, with their projecting floors virtually shutting out the light. The house was damaged by the English Earl of Hertford's men in 1544, when it was owned by Mariota Arres and James Mossman. Their initials are on the wall above the shop door. Mossman was the keeper of the Royal Mint to Mary, Queen of Scots, and was eventually hanged for his allegiance. Today, there is an exhibition on the lives of both Mossman and Knox within the property, which is closed on Sundays (Knox would have approved).

▶ **Lady Stair's House
(The Writers' Museum)**   44C2

Off Lawnmarket

This building bears the date of 1622, and was only later associated with the widow (died 1759) of the first Earl of Stair. The close on which it was built was at one time the main communication between the Old Town at the Lawnmarket and the New Town, and it is still possible to walk through to the top of The Mound. The house was given to the city in 1907, and it is now a museum of Burns, Scott, and Stevenson memorabilia. It is open daily except Sundays.

▪ **Lauriston Castle**   44A2

Off Cramond Road South

Slightly removed from the main tourist thoroughfares, Lauriston Castle makes a worthwhile excursion, perhaps combined with a walk by the River Cramond. Built in 1593 on the site of a tower destroyed in 1544, the castle's original owner was John Napier (1550–1617). This Scottish mathematician was the inventor of logarithms. The castle was presented to the city in 1926, and its turn-of-the-century interiors are carefully preserved. It is open daily except Fridays in summer (closed lunchtimes), and open on weekend afternoons in winter.

Lauriston Castle near Cramond

57

John Knox
Born at Haddington (see page 115), John Knox (1513–72), architect of the Reformation in Scotland, became filled with Lutheran reforming zeal in 1544 and was called to the ministry in 1547. He led an adventurous life, including a spell as a French galley slave, following capture at St. Andrew's Castle. He preached in England and on the Continent, as well as making his mark in Scotland, where his views were uncompromisingly antagonistic to those of Mary, Queen of Scots.

Edinburgh's oldest house
Moubrey House, next door to John Knox House, is probably even older than its more famous neighbor and can therefore claim the distinction of being Edinburgh's oldest dwelling, built by Andrew Moubrey *c.* 1472.

The National
Gallery of Scotland

A museum for adults?
The founder of the Museum of Childhood, Patrick Murray, an Edinburgh town councilor, insisted it was a museum portraying a specialized field of social history. A bachelor, he did not actually like children—or at least he pretended not to. He formerly displayed in the museum entrance hall a design for a memorial window to "good" King Herod!

►► **National Portrait Gallery, Scottish**   44C3
Queen Street

The Scottish National Portrait Gallery was built with much Caledonian zeal after funding was provided by John Ritchie Findlay, who owned *The Scotsman* newspaper. At the gallery's opening in 1889, it was stated that "a gallery such as this is...the highest incentive to true patriotism we can possibly have." Since then, the images of the famous Scots who stare down from the walls have become part of Scotland's fabric, reproduced both in scholarly books and on shortbread cans, so that the viewer coming upon Nasmyth's Robert Burns may find it quite familiar—a veritable icon of Scotland.

Take time to look at the setting of these famous Scots. the architect, Robert Rowand Anderson, was an Endinburgh native, but amid the orderly neoclassicism on the very edge of the first phase of the New Town, he created a Gothic palace, now one of Edinburgh's few monuments to Gothic revivalism. Inside, the late Victorian fashion for mural painting found expression in a processional frieze of famous Scottish figures—a kind of miniature portrait gallery in itself—with other wall-sized scenes from Scotland's story, set between the sandstone columns. Stained glass and Scottish heraldry make their contribution to the general ambience.

The Stewart monarchs are here, including the only portrait of Mary, Queen of Scots made in her lifetime—a small bronze bust of Mary, around age 17. Flora Macdonald, who played a role in Jacobite schemes, is also on view, as is King George IV entering Holyroodhouse in 1822. This visit of the monarch marked the rehabilitation of tartan, which is much in evidence in many other works.

Poets, painters, novelists, engineers, philosophers, and famous fiddlers are all here—and not only from distant times. Though the heyday for the medium of portraiture has gone, there are many powerful figures from nearer our own time, such as Hugh MacDiarmid, Norman MacCaig, and Murial Spark. Some of the more recent pictures are the result of a survey that asked gallery users, which natives they would most like to see on the walls. So

Sean Connery has also entered this hall of fame. A visit here is an insight into the qualities of "Scottishness" and how we perceive them. The gallery is open daily.

▶▶▶ Museum of Childhood   45D2
High Street

If you have never really forgotten your last train set or the day your dollhouse was packed into the attic, then the Museum of Childhood should appeal to you. There is a collection of older material such as the Victorian dolls, and German automata; the eerie part is the objects half recognized from one's own childhood. There, behind glass, is that even larger construction set to which you always aspired. If you have children, then you should consider visiting, though the younger members may be overwhelmed by the massed ranks of historic teddies. Even without children, this museum should still be on the "must see" list—it is really just an excuse for grownups to indulge. The museum is open Monday to Saturday.

▶▶▶ National Gallery of Scotland   44B2
The Mound

William Playfair's National Gallery was completed in 1857, and rates among the top two or three classical designs in Edinburgh. Its sparingly ornamented length, honey colored in the thin Edinburgh sunlight, has a simple dignity entirely in keeping with its role as a repository for Scotland's finest art.

Inside, its human scale makes it easily accessible. There are no vast and intimidating halls, but controversy raged in the conservative Edinburgh art world of the 19th century when the present display was first opened. Against a rich red background, many of the paintings are hung very high and close together. Visit it for some of the best old masters in the United Kingdom outside London, for its Impressionists and, naturally, for its Scottish paintings. There are also important collections of prints, drawings, and (notably by J.M.W. Turner) watercolors. The gallery is open daily.

A great architect
William Henry Playfair (1789–1857) not only designed the National Gallery (which was finally completed in the same year that he died), but is also associated with many other buildings in and around the New Town, which still lend distinction to the city's profile. These include Donaldson's Hospital, St. Stephen's Church and, on Calton Hill, National Monument, the New Observatory, and the monument to Scottish philosopher Dugald Stuart (1753–1828).

59

Roman treasure in the Royal Museum of Scotland collections

The Museum of Childhood, a top attraction on the Royal Mile

![Looking over Hillend Ski Centre toward Edinburgh]

Walk **From Swanston to Colinton Dell**

A rural walk to the south of Edinburgh in the footsteps of Robert Louis Stevenson, with spectacular views back toward the city. Allow about three hours for the walk (one way).

Take a bus or car to the southern edge of the city. Bus travelers can alight at the Hillend Ski Centre on A703 and cross Lothianburn Golf Course by a path to reach the attractive little hamlet of Swanston to the west. Those with a car can take it all the way to the hamlet, where there is a parking lot.

Swanston is associated with Robert Louis Stevenson—his family had a summer cottage there—and is part of the setting for his unfinished novel *St. Ives*. The former Stevenson family home (private) is still there as described in the work: "It had something of the air of a rambling, infinitesimal cathedral… grotesquely decorated with crockets and gargoyles, ravished from some medieval church." (In real life, these were salvaged from the restoration of St. Giles.)

The Hermitage of Braid, on the way from Edinburgh to Swanston

Looking over Hillend Ski Centre toward Edinburgh

For a longer expedition (more than just to Swanston)—one that requires good footwear and the best part of a morning or afternoon — follow the track into the Pentland Hills south of Swanston. The objective is the broad ridge, seen to the south, of Caerketton and Allermuir Hills, two of the Pentland tops. Alternatively, Caerketton (the rocky one) can be reached by missing Swanston entirely and going up toward the ski center at Hillend, striking upward on a path to the left of it. Either way, you join a skyline path westward along the heathery hilltops, enjoying superb city views. Take in Capelaw Hill before descending an easy path and track to Bonaly Country Park. (There is a parking lot for those making a separate excursion.) Follow Bonaly Road down into the suburb of Colinton to reach Spylaw Park. Turning right (toward town) soon brings the walker to Colinton Parish Church above a bend in the Water of Leith, another place which Stevenson knew well; his maternal grandfather, the Reverend Dr. Lewis Balfour, was minister here. It is childhood memories of this leafy dell, with its mossy banks and river, that Stevenson recalls in his lines "Here is the mill with the humming of thunder./Here is the weir with the wonder of foam." Buses run from Colinton back into the city center.

►   **Palace of Holyroodhouse**   *45E2*

As late as the 1890s, Robert Louis Stevenson in his *Picturesque Notes on Edinburgh* observed that "The Palace of Holyroodhouse has been left aside in the growth of Edinburgh, and stands gray and silent in a workman's quarter among breweries and gasworks." This was the low point in the story of what is still the official residence of the Royal Family in Scotland. The palace evolved from the guest house of the adjacent Holyrood Abbey, now a ruin.

The first palace, started by King James IV, was damaged during the English raids of 1544, part of the "rough wooing" (see page 30), though the northwest tower (or the King James V Tower—the left-hand tower on the frontage) survived the flames to be rebuilt. It is this tower that contains the rooms associated with Mary, Queen of Scots.

Holyrood was ablaze again in 1650, the same year as Oliver Cromwell and his troops stayed there while occupying the north. He ordered some repair, but the main work seen today is primarily the result of a major remodeling in 1671–80, during the reign of King Charles II. His brother, King James VII (James II of England), was sometimes in residence there.

However, it is most strongly associated with Mary, Queen of Scots (see page 30), though the site of the murder of her secretary Riccio is no longer marked with red paint but instead by a discreet plaque. After such highlights as grand receptions held by the transient Bonnie Prince Charlie and later by King George IV in his 1822 visit, it fell into decline, though Queen Victoria and her consort, Prince Albert, used it in 1850. Much restoration work in the present century has restored its dignity. As well as portraits of monarchs (some of them mythical), there are tapestries and fine furniture from the royal collections. It is open daily, but closes to visitors and transforms itself from a tourist center to a high-security establishment whenever a member of the Royal Family comes to visit.

Palace of Holyroodhouse— detail of entrance gates

The Law Courts
Behind St. Giles, Parliament House, the seat of Scottish government until 1707, is now the Supreme Law Courts of Scotland. There are portraits by Sir Henry Raeburn among other artists, as well as a hammerbeam (ornate wooden-beamed) ceiling to admire.

Royal portraits
Jacob de Witt, a Dutchman living in Edinburgh, signed a contract with His Majesty's Cash Keeper in 1684 to deliver 110 portraits of Scottish kings within two years at £120 ($180) per year. These ran from the possibly mythical King Fergus I to the then contemporary King Charles II—so at least in one case de Witt had a likeness to work from. The painter fulfilled his contract at more than one a week, and at least 80 of the portraits can be seen today.

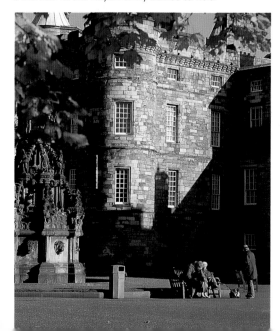

Palace of Holyroodhouse

EDINBURGH

The Old Physic Garden
Few of the train passengers arriving at Waverley Station notice the plaque that records the site of the first public botanic garden in Edinburgh. The Old Physic Garden was in the hollow now occupied by the station and post office. The area saw many changes, not the least of which was the draining of the Nor' Loch, which once provided Edinburgh Castle's defenses to the north (in part of today's Princes Street Gardens). The partial draining of the ancient loch flooded the Old Physic Garden in 1689, and many of its precious plants were lost.

Royal Botanic Garden—an all-weather, all-year attraction

A Presbyterian protest
A humble cabbage stall owner called Jenny Geddes earned her place in history on July 23, 1637. King Charles I had declared St. Giles a cathedral and had ordered the use of the Episcopal service book. No sooner had the Dean of Edinburgh started this unfamiliar service to the staunchly Presbyterian congregation, than Jenny Geddes threw her prayer stool at him, screaming "Daur ye say mass in my lug! (Dare you say mass in my ear?)." More missiles followed, and a full-scale riot ensued. Her great gesture over, Jenny quietly returned to cabbage selling.

▶▶ **The People's Story** 45D2
Canongate
The People's Story is just that—a museum recording the experiences of the ordinary folk of Edinburgh through the generations from the 18th century to the present day. As such, it does not portray a sanitized and romantic view of a city in which bad housing and poor working conditions coexisted with a genteel preoccupation with middle-class respectability. It is overtly political in its cameos of the local trades and the workers who put in long hours for small rewards. The overwhelming impression is of generations of drudgery from all kinds of people, from skilled craftsmen making barrels for the local brewing industry, down to humble servants whose first job was to polish the steel in the grate until it shone, then light the mistress's fire to blacken it again. It certainly puts today's Royal Mile, with its quaint gift shops and affluent visitors, in a new light. Open all year, closed Sundays.

▶▶▶ **Royal Botanic Garden** 44B3
Inverleith Row
The Botanic Garden provides a welcome escape from the city-center bustle. One of Edinburgh's most precious recreational assets, it is "strollable" from Princes Street via Stockbridge, though you may wish to take the bus back up the hill. It is especially suitable for children as it is dog free—though the squirrels can be persistent. In addition to the largest rhododendron collection anywhere, and a magnificent rock garden (best in May), there are substantial areas under glass, making this a worthwhile wet-weather place as well. Make sure you locate the panorama information board near the café on the highest point of the garden for a fine view of the city skyline. The garden is open all year, and worth a visit in any season.

▶▶ **Royal Museum of Scotland** 44C1
Chambers Street
This lofty Victorian building, with its soaring columns and

62

galleries, houses the national collection of scientific, natural, historical, geological, archeological, and other objects. In fact, it does exactly what a traditional museum should do, except that it offers its endless browsing potential in a spacious and airy ambience. It is a pleasant and stimulating place. Be sure to check out the program of special talks and lectures. Open all year.

John Knox in St. Giles

▶ **St. Giles: the High Kirk of Edinburgh**   *44C1*
High Street
Often called St. Giles' Cathedral, though purists argue it only achieved this status briefly, St. Giles was at one time the only church within the walls of old Edinburgh. The tower of St. Giles, whose crown was completed in 1500, is one of the few remaining examples of 15th-century work to be seen in the High Street today. Much of the church has been altered and reworked over the centuries. Today's dull exterior is the result of the "restoration" by William Burn in 1829. Only the tower and crown escaped this gray stone.

Once the venerable church even had a long arcade of booths, the "krames," leaning against the north side. These were removed in 1817, along with the "luckenbooths," other small shops that contributed to the crowded narrowness of this part of the High Street. Just to the west of the church is the site of the Old Tolbooth, also removed in 1817. Now stones mark the spot in the shape of a heart—a reference to Scott's description of the Tolbooth as the "Heart of Midlothian."

▶ **Scotch Whisky Heritage Centre**   *44C1*
Castlehill
The problem with whisky-making (note the Scots spelling) is that it is not in itself a visually dramatic process, much of it consisting of waiting until the enzymes do their job. The Scotch Whisky Heritage Centre injects a dose of fun into the subject by taking a high-tech approach, with talking tableaus and commentary all viewed while riding along slowly on a hollowed-out whisky barrel. Whisky's story is told from its ancient origins via tales of smuggling and prohibition to modern marketing methods. There is also a well-stocked shop. Both center and shop are open all year.

The story of Scottish whisky is told on the Royal Mile

■ **The Scottish patriot, Fletcher of Saltoun, wrote in 1698: "As the happy situation of London has been the principal cause of the glory and riches of England, so the bad situation of Edinburgh has been one great occasion of the poverty and uncleanliness in which the greater part of the people of Scotland live....." ...■**

Top: an ornate ceiling inside the head office of the Royal Bank of Scotland at 36 St. Andrew Square

The Mound

In the great building spree that went on in 18th-century Edinburgh, somewhere had to be found for the material dug out for foundations. In the case of the Royal Exchange (today's City Chambers), the rubble became the Castle Esplanade. Meanwhile, Geordie Boyd, a local tailor, started dumping earth into the quagmire of the old Nor Loch. So did everyone else, and "Geordie Boyd's mud brig" grew and grew. Two million cartloads later, in 1830, it became The Mound, the elegant roadway linking the Old and New Towns.

An 18th-century vision Many stories of the squalor of the Old Town of Edinburgh are documented. As the more peaceful 18th century began in Scotland, improvements began within the Old Town itself. But the long-term solution was for the city's inhabitants to escape entirely from the rocky ramp running down from the castle.

George Drummond, Lord Provost of Edinburgh, had a clear vision of a new Edinburgh rising on what was then only a low ridge between the castle and the sea. A competition to design a new town was organized, which was won by a young and unknown architect, James Craig. His 1767 design shows a simple grid of streets balanced by a square at either end. This is the Princes Street to Queen Street area, with Charlotte Square and St. Andrew Square at either end.

Princes Street If you stroll along Queen Street today, you can see how it echoes Princes Street: it is built up on one side only, and has gardens (still private) opposite. Down amid the hubbub and main street shop fronts on Princes Street, it is hard to believe that in Craig's original plan the area was meant to be entirely residential. He designated today's Thistle and Rose streets, lesser byways between the grand thoroughfares, as the abode and business place of tradesmen and shopkeepers. The use of the lanes behind Thistle and Rose streets to reach the back doors of the wealthier residents was a clever element in his deceptively simple plan.

Princes Street did not remain residential for long. The main tide of commercial developments began to flow from east to west by the mid-19th century. Before that, the residents with their grand drawing rooms looking out to the castle over the trees in the gardens had fought another battle. A speculator wanted to build along the south side of Princes Street, and the indignant citizens,

Period atmosphere in elegant Charlotte Square

determined to preserve their views, had to take their case to the House of Lords before the project was stopped. (The city fathers of the day were quite happy to allow the speculator to build.) Today's low-profile Waverley Market is a reminder of those far-off legal battles.

String-pulling Stand on what used to be the bare ridge, and is now George Street, about halfway along, and look up and down the street. In Craig's plan the two squares, Charlotte and St. Andrew, at either end of the view, also had churches. While the green copper dome of the former St. George's (now West Register House) is plain on the western skyline, to the east in St. Andrew Square there is a fine town house instead of a church.

A place of worship was never built there because of civic string-pulling by Sir Laurence Dundas. Rich, power-

Princes Street
Princes Street was to be called St. Giles Street, but King George III objected as it reminded him of the St. Giles district of London, which was notorious for its low life at the time. So the most famous street in Scotland became Prince's Street after the Prince Regent, before assuming its plural form in 1848.

ful, and onetime Commissary General of the army in Flanders, Dundas acquired the site and altered the plan to suit himself. He employed Sir William Chambers to design the magnificent façade that is seen today, and this fine town house is now the headquarters of the Royal Bank of Scotland. It has ornate ceilings in its main hall, well worth looking at, even if you do not have an account there. The city fathers got their church eventually, built on a less satisfactory site, around the corner on George Street. This is St. Andrew's, still in use today and open to visitors.

By the end of the 19th century, the first New Town was complete, paving the way for further phases to the north, east, and west, and creating Edinburgh's unique neoclassical ambience.

The grand façades of Edinburgh's New Town

Walk The New Town

Discover the surprisingly intact second phase of the New Town in the streets to the north of Charlotte Square. Allow three hours.

Starting from the **Floral Clock** on Princes Street, opposite the Royal Scottish Academy, walk north to George Street, turning left at the **statue of King George IV**. Go past the **Assembly Rooms**, now a major Festival Fringe showcase, where Sir Walter Scott publicly admitted to writing the Waverley Novels during a grand dinner in 1827.

Continue down George Street to **Charlotte Square** at the west end, which balances **St. Andrew Square** at the east. The Robert Adam-designed north façade of Charlotte Square is impressively harmonious, while intrusive modern additions detract from the other three sides.

Continue downhill to **Moray Place**, typical of the New Town with its private gardens, cobbled roads, and grand façades. Leave by **Doune Terrace**. Cross the **Water of Leith** to shop in Stockbridge, otherwise turn left along undistinguished India Place. Keep going to enter the wooded valley of the Water of Leith, and go down steps by the bridge. **St. Bernard's Well**, half hidden in the greenery, is a former mineral spring in the shape of a Grecian temple with a statue of Hygeia, designed by Alexander Nasmyth in 1789.

The footpath continues to **Dean Village**. Overhead is Thomas Telford's road bridge, built in 1832. A 1643 Baxters (Bakers) "coat-of-arms" survives on the abutment of the original bridge below. Climb back to the busy streets by cobbled Bell's Brae, the former main road.

St. Bernard's Well, a pleasant walk by the Water of Leith

▶ **Scottish Agricultural Museum** *44A1*

Ingliston, 7 miles west of Edinburgh
This is Scotland's national farming museum, situated adjacent to Scotland's premier agricultural showground site. It covers all aspects of rural life in the past, including the old trades associated with farming, and social and home life in the countryside. There are good displays of equipment and artifacts, and evocative photographs. It would probably be much more popular were it not a little awkwardly situated. It is close to Edinburgh Airport, and open daily all year.

▶ **Scottish National Gallery of Modern Art** *4466*

Belford Road
Housed in former school premises, an excursion here could be made via a stretch of the Water of Leith footpath, joining it perhaps at Dean Village. Scotland's own collection of moderns includes works by Derain, Matisse, Picasso, Giacometti, Hockney, and Hepworth, among many others. Scotland's own artists are not neglected, with the Scottish colorists—Peploe, Cadell, Fergusson, and Hunter—well represented. The gallery also has a popular cafeteria much patronized by locals. The gallery is open daily.

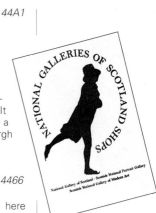

An adaptation of The Rev. Robert Walker Skating by Raeburn—symbol of Edinburgh art

▶ **(Edinburgh) Zoo** *44A1*

Corstorphine Road
The zoo once suffered all the problems of financing a traditional, wide-ranging animal collection in a time when a variety of other leisure attractions were siphoning off visitors. Now it has slimmed down. The sad, solitary elephant has gone, and, along with some new and spacious enclosures, there is a very substantial gift shop with an animal theme (a good place for children's presents). Just a few of the fairly primitive enclosures still remain—for the tigers and some of the other big cats, for instance—but the penguins and gorillas (awesome in close-up through the glass) certainly look happy enough. Young children will undoubtedly appreciate it, though parents may get a backache lifting them up to see into some of the enclosures. Also, the zoo is built on a slope, which makes stroller pushing something of an endurance test. There is a breeding program for endangered species. The zoo has excellent educational facilities, and it is open daily.

Penguins on parade
Edinburgh Zoo's "Penguin Parade" is an old-established institution. The penguins are shepherded out of their modern, spacious enclosure daily in the summer months, and they trundle around a grassy area nearby. Formerly, they were walked right out of the zoo, but their appearance on the pavements by Corstorphine Road caused traffic accidents as drivers were distracted. Their perambulations these days are less extensive.

67

Accommodations

There really are "accommodations to suit all pockets" in Edinburgh. Sit on the top deck of a bus coming in on the main road from Cameron Toll, through the district of Newington, and you can get some idea of the selection of accommodations. The hotels and guest houses are lined up as far as the eye can see—and that is just one street, though it changes its name as it heads toward The Bridges and central Edinburgh.

However, do not be misled into thinking that finding the right place to stay will be easy, since Edinburgh is a hugely popular destination. If you are visiting specifically to "do" Edinburgh at festival time, then make reservations well in advance. Otherwise, late August–early September is best avoided altogether. Finding somewhere at a reasonable rate will be much easier outside that period, and easier still out of season. If you do find yourself in the city during the festival and need somewhere to stay, it's worth persevering with the Edinburgh and Scotland Information Centre, 3 Princes Street (tel: 0131-557 1700), who will certainly assist. It would be misleading to suggest that finding accommodations is impossible, more that things are *very* busy.

Hotels Many of the international chains are represented in Edinburgh, for example, the Edinburgh Sheraton, with its views of the castle, or the Hilton, down by the Water of Leith. Then there are the former railway hotels: the grand-style Caledonian, with its sumptuous Pompadour Restaurant, and, dominating the skyline at the other end of Princes Street, the equally luxurious Balmoral. (This used to be called the North British, taking its name from the other pre-1923 railroad company that ran into Edinburgh.)

Also in the expensive bracket are the Old Town-style Holiday Inn Crown Plaza on High Street, the popular George on George Street, the Roxburghe in Charlotte Square, the Carlton Highland on North Bridge, and the King James Thistle off Princes Street at the east end.

Quality can be enjoyed without overspending your budget. Notable for its personal service and country-club atmosphere

Reserving accommodations
The Edinburgh and Scotland Information Centre (see page 272) helps visitors find accommodations, though the lines can be very long. Try the advance central reservation service (tel: 0131-557 9655), but note that it cannot be used to reserve accommodations at Festival time.

68

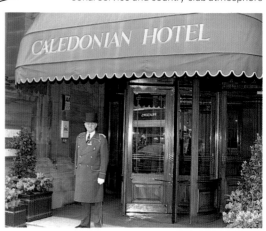

Echoes of the great railroad age—the Caledonian Hotel

*A Princes Street land-
mark—the clock tower
of the Balmoral Hotel,
formerly the North
British, at Princes
Street, east end*

in the city is Channings, on South Learmonth Gardens. Mrs. Sibbets Edinburgh Holidays is an equally personal and individualized small establishment tucked into the heart of the New Town in Northumberland Place.

Guest houses There is a wide choice of guest houses. Off-season rates at the Galloway Guest House in Dean Park Crescent offer outstanding value for money. This is also an exception to the general rule that the smaller establishments tend to be some distance from the down-town area—though this should not be a problem as Edinburgh bus services are adequate. Remember, if coming by car, to enquire about parking at the establish-ment of your choice, since Edinburgh traffic wardens strike without mercy after 8AM.

In all cases, off-season rates are cheaper, and there are often special weekend rates or other kinds of deals from the larger hotels.

Parking
If you are bringing a car to Edinburgh, it is best to check exactly what the parking arrangements are, especially if you wish to sleep late in the morning. Parking laws are rigorously enforced after 8AM.

Hostels There are two permanent Edinburgh youth hostels, at 7 Bruntsfield Crescent EH10 4EZ, tel: 0131-447 2994, and 18 Eglinton Crescent EH12 5DD, tel: 0131-337 1120; these are supplemented in summer by additional hostel accommodations using university student residences. For advance bookings, contact the District Office, 161 Warrender Park Road EH9 1EQ, tel: 0131-229 8660. All are within easy reach of the main visitor attractions.

Out of town Another option is to choose accommoda-tions outside the city. The Norton House Hotel and the Royal Scot are on the west side of the city, within easy reach of Edinburgh Airport. Rural locations within easy reach of Edinburgh include Silverburn, where farmhouse-type accommodations are offered by Mrs. Taylor at Silverburn Steading.

Edinburgh's colorful pub signs

Edinburgh sees itself as a cosmopolitan city, and features most of the world's main styles of cooking. However, restaurants come and go, and chefs move around, so it is always best to take up-to-the-minute local advice if you want a meal to remember.

Restaurants In addition to a wide choice of independent restaurants, the main hotels all have good restaurants, with the Grill Rooms at the Balmoral and the Sheraton, and the Pompadour at the Caledonian, particularly notable if you want to treat yourself. On the other hand, the area around the university, especially around Nicolson Street, has a number of eating places offering particularly good value for money. Leith, Edinburgh's seaport, has in recent years been the setting for a number of enterprising restaurant developments and should not be overlooked. This is a place to head to in the evening to eat, drink, and be noticed in one of the trendy wine bars.

For consistent reliability, Martin's on Rose Street North Lane and The Vintner's Room down in Leith are examples of well-prepared, imaginative cuisine, but it is almost unfair to single them out as the city has so many possibilities: Merchant's, Vito's, Kelly's, The Indian Cavalry Club, L'Auberge, Denzler's, Le Marché Noir, Shamiana, and more. Pierre Victoire's offers Franco-Scottish cuisine and is a favorite for lunches with the business community. If you want quality on a budget, try The Kalpna on Nicolson Street, with its inspiring Indian vegetarian cooking; for a

70

In the haggis season... Haggis (boiled, meat-stuffed tripe) may be Scotland's national dish, but it can be dull, dry, greasy, or gritty—though it can also be spicy and delicious. If you want to try it, you will sometimes find it on Scottish themed restaurant menus as an appetizer.

Plenty of atmosphere at the Café Royal Oyster Bar

Scotland's sweet tooth—Casey's candy shop

cross section of the natives enjoying an evening out, try the Waterfront Wine Bar in Leith.

The only thing that is really hard to track down in Edinburgh is an easily identifiable local cuisine, though the surrounding East Lothian countryside is market garden country, supplying plenty of local produce. The other name for Edinburgh's eastern hinterland is "Scotland's Granary," which has in turn helped develop a tradition of fine baking, though probably no more so here than in other parts of Scotland. Local gourmets are more likely to whisper reverently about the near-legendary Valvolla and Crolla delicatessen in Haddington Place, with its authentic Italian ambience.

Healthy eating Edinburgh's fairly enlightened attitude to food can be deduced from the success of Henderson's on Hanover Street. This vegetarian, organic food self-service restaurant is not a new place, capitalizing on the current trend for healthy eating. Instead, it has survived and prospered on the same site for decades—since long before the notion of health food reached the rest of high-cholesterol Scotland.

The heavyweight traditional Scottish breakfast is still available in most guest houses and bed-and-breakfast establishments, but you can skip it and linger over a croissant and coffee in any one of a number of café bars instead. Home-baked cakes for afternoon tea are easily found, and the Sheraton offers traditional Scottish shortbread, though you need not go so far upscale.

Edinburgh rock candy The quintessential Edinburgh souvenir is sold at any number of tourist shops, and could be just the gift for someone with a (very) sweet tooth. If you would prefer a food souvenir posing less danger to teeth, perhaps a better idea would be some authentic Scottish shortbread from one of Edinburgh's many delicatessens or gift shops.

Roll play
An Edinburgh bakery is a good place to note the regional differences in the names for various baked goods. Muffins describe at least two types of bun. Pancakes are even more of a problem. Are they the same as crumpets, or even pikelets? Aberdeen rolls in most Edinburgh bakeries are butteries, sometimes rowies. And what exactly are Jap cakes and German biscuits? If you think this is complicated, try ordering a pound of potted hough from the butcher next door.

Shopping

Main shopping areas Do not make the mistake of assuming that Edinburgh's shopping ends with Princes Street. Far from it. With the exception of Jenners, which is the city's last independently owned major store, and a very few other places, Princes Street has little more to offer than can be found on a dozen other British main streets. This is not to say that the shops are necessarily bad—just that there is not a huge choice of unique or characterful Scottish wares along its length.

Within a few moments' walk of Princes Street are two covered malls. The St. James Centre was built on the site of part of the New Town, and offers nothing more than an assortment of clothing retailers and the like. The Waverley Market beside the Scott Monument is much more interesting.

Tartan umbrellas—practical souvenirs of Edinburgh

Open for business
Especially in the height of the season, many shops catering to visitors are open every day. Off-peak, the city has late-night hours on Thursdays, and supermarkets stay open late right through the week, all year round.

The elegant interior of Jenners

Scottish goods Shopping in Edinburgh is worthwhile, but the best shops are not all in one place. The city offers a good range of Scottish products. Stores selling imported souvenirs abound along the Royal Mile, but there are several high-quality outlets as well. The Royal Mile Living Craft Centre, at 12 High Street, offers a good cross section of Scottish wares made on the premises, including bagpipes and kilts. Farther on, at No.361, Giles of Edinburgh is a high-quality gift shop (the teddy bear golfers are delightful). Judith Glue, just below St. Giles Kirk, has an excellent selection of Orkney knitwear and Scottish gifts.

Specialty shops Small, individual businesses still survive on Victoria Street, along with Byzantium, an interesting antiques and crafts market. A little farther on in the Grassmarket, among the odd mixture of down-and-outs and exclusive designer shops, is Mr. Wood's Fossils. As its name suggests, it sells all kinds of fossils. Also within easy reach of Princes Street is the William Street/Stafford Street area, with a number of smaller specialized fashion and gift shops, of which Studio One on Stafford Street is a long-established example.

Shopping out of the center Farther afield, the districts of Bruntsfield and Morningside are worth a stroll along the main streets, down the high canyons of the Edinburgh tenement blocks. Stockbridge, toward the Water of Leith, is also worth a look, and only minutes from the heart of

A Royal Mile souvenir shop—tartan all the way

the city. Edinburgh Crystal at Penicuik, nearly half an hour away by car, runs factory tours showing the glass-blowing process and has hand-cut products. (You can also buy this selection in the city.)

Bookstores Edinburgh's literary leanings are confirmed by the large number of bookstores scattered around, many of which are secondhand stores. Among new book retailers are James Thin, The Edinburgh Bookshop, Waterstones, and many more, some with late hours, make the city a browser's paradise.

Art and antiques Antiques shops seem to come and go, but try Bruntsfield Place or Causewayside, where they gather in clusters. It is best to ask around for up-to-the-minute information. Some antiques shops usually have a good selection of Scottish paintings, but Edinburgh is exceptionally well-endowed with specialized galleries, with excellent selections of both contemporary and antique material. The Firth Gallery on William Street specializes in living Scottish artists; the Edinburgh Gallery on Dundas Street tends toward contemporary figurative and landscape work; while Stills on High Street exhibits photography by both Scottish and international artists. For those who hunt around, bargains and high-quality work can be found in the city. If tracking them down takes you off Princes Street, then that is all the better—the real Edinburgh can be found en route.

Jenners
The last independent store on Princes Street, Jenners has been an Edinburgh institution since 1838. It offers a good selection of items, from Edinburgh Crystal to exclusive fashions and a large toy department. This traditional department store is housed in a handsome building of 1895, with lots of baroque detail outside and a mock-Jacobean galleried interior.

It may not be Paris or Las Vegas, but the city of Edinburgh belies its sober and respectable image with a vibrant and varied nightlife.

The annual flurry of Fringe posters

Theater and concert halls The Traverse Theatre on Cambridge Street (tel: 0131-228 1404) puts on the most stimulatingly experimental material, while the Royal Lyceum Theatre on Grindley Street (tel: 0131-229 9697) stages more "middle of the road" plays. The Kings Theatre on Leven Street (tel: 0131-229 1201) has a varied lightweight program, including variety and pantomime. The Usher Hall on Lothian Road (tel: 0131-228 1155) is the city's old-established concert hall, now sharing prestige with the Festival Theatre on Nicolson Street (tel: 0131-529 6000). The Queen's Hall on Clerk Street (tel: 0131-668 2019) is a more intimate concert setting, while The Playhouse, Greenhouse Place (tel: 0131-557 2692) sees a lot of big showbiz names.

74

Festival nights
Remember that Edinburgh's nightlife, like the city itself, moves up a gear in Festival time. Everywhere is crowded and full of visitors. This is the season when Edinburgh appears truly cosmopolitan.

Film The independent Dominion on Newbattle Terrace in Morningside (tel: 0131-447 2660) is particularly good, while the Filmhouse on Lothian Road (tel: 0131-228 6382) is the place to see off beat, less commercial, or foreign language films.

Other kinds of nightlife The city's casinos include the Stanley Berkeley in Rutland Place (tel: 0131-228 4446) and Stanley Martell on Newington Road (tel: 0131-667 7763). Both offer free membership with 48 hours' notice.

Alternatively, treat yourself to a Scottish evening, with lots of songs and dancing. Several of the downtown hotels hold these on a regular basis. Try the Carlton Highland Hotel on North Bridge (tel: 0131-556 7277) or the King James Hotel, Leith Street (tel: 0131-556 0111).

There are at least half a dozen disco clubs, offering something for fans of Techno, rave, chart sound, mainstream and/or the gay scene, where you can dance till dawn. A couple of examples are Minus One at the Carlton Highland Hotel (tel: 0131-556 7277) and Red Hot Pepper Club on Semple Street (tel: 0131-229 7733).

Listings
For up-to-the-minute events information in Edinburgh, try *The List,* available from all downtown newspaper stalls, or *The Scotsman* on Saturdays, whose weekend section is very strong on entertainment events throughout Scotland, but emphasizing Edinburgh. The latter is a useful place to find information on folk music in the capital.

Fringe actors—an encounter at every street corner

Airport transfers Edinburgh Airport, Edinburgh EH12 9DN (tel: 0131-333 1000) is 7 miles from the center of the city. Airport buses run at peak times every 30 minutes between the terminal building and Waverley Bridge. The ride lasts about 30 minutes (45 minutes in the rush hour) and costs roughly a quarter of the taxi fare.

Arriving by train or bus Waverley Station could hardly be closer to the city center, and there is a taxi stand right within the station. The main bus station is at St. Andrew Square, moments away from Princes Street, along which run the principal city bus services (see below).

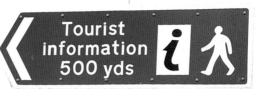

Tourist information For the main Edinburgh tourist information center, see page 272. For information about Edinburgh at the airport, check with the Tourist Information Desk (tel: 0131-333 2167).

Getting around by bus Edinburgh has an extensive bus network, with two main companies covering most of the routes in and around the city.

On Lothian Region Transport (LRT) maroon and white buses, you pay the driver when you get on with the exact fare. LRT offers a variety of unlimited travel tickets to visitors. Further information from the LRT information office at 27 Hanover Street (tel: 0131-555 6363).

On SMT Eastern Scottish green and cream buses, you pay the driver when you get on, and change is given. Some of these services are small buses known as Citysprinters. Further information from The Bus Shop, St. Andrew Square Bus Station, Edinburgh, (tel: 0131-558 1616).

Taxis Black taxis are widely available within the city. There are a number of taxi stands, and taxis showing an illuminated "For Hire" sign can be hailed in the street. Black taxis cannot be picked up at Edinburgh Airport, but a fleet of other licensed cabs (usually ordinary cars) is available there.

75

Travel to the airport
Both main rail lines converging on Edinburgh, from Glasgow and from the north, pass the airport practically adjacent to its perimeter. So far, nobody has thought to build a station. Airport to city center connections are by road, through the suburb of Corstorphine, which can get very busy at peak times, to Princes Street. Allow a good hour before check-in time if you are catching a plane.

If time is short, take a bus tour

GLASGOW

Botanic Gardens
Hunterian Art Gallery
UNIVERSITY AVE
GIBSON ST
PARK ROAD
GREAT WESTERN ROAD
MARYHILL ROAD
GEORGE'S
Queen's Cross Church
GARSCUBE ROAD
Forth & Clyde Canal
CRAIGH...

St Mary's Episcopal Cathedral
ELDON ST
WOODLANDS ROAD
SAINT
PHOENIX RD
ROAD

Hunterian Museum
4 Glasgow University
Kelvingrove Art Gallery and Museum
KELVIN WAY
Kelvin
Kelvingrove Park

WEST GRAHAM ST

Museum of Transport
SAUCHIEHALL STREET
ARGYLE STREET

Tenement House
Museum of The Royal Highland Fusiliers
Glasgow School of Art
Royal Scottish Academy of Music & Drama
RENFREW
The Roy

KELVINHAUGH STREET
3
Fossil Grove Victoria Park
Summit Centre Ice Rink
ELDERSLIE STREET
BERKELEY ST
SAUCHIEHALL ST
ROSE ST
King's Theatre
Third Eye Centre
McLellan Galleries
BATH STREET
Pavilion Theatre

Mitchell Library
M8
Charing Cross Station
DOUGLAS ST
BLYTHSWOOD ST
WEST
GEORGE

Exhibition Station
ST VINCENT STREET
St Vincent St Free Church
Regional Police HQ
CAMPBELL ST
WELLINGTON ST
HOPE ST
RENFIELD ST
WEST

CLYDESIDE EXPRESSWAY
STOBCROSS ROAD
Clydeway Centre
Hollywood Bowl
ST VINCENT ST
BOTHWELL ST
WATERLOO ST
The Anderston Centre
GORDON ST

Scottish Exhibition & Conference Centre
North Rotunda
FINNIESTON ST
STOBCROSS STREET
Anderston Station
Arts Centre
Central Station

Daily Record and Sunday Mail Offices
ARGYLE
JAMES WATT ST
YORK ST
ROBERTSON ST
OSWALD ST
JAMAICA ST
St En...
Cen...

2
The Dome of Discovery
GOVAN DALE
Clyde
LANCEFIELD QUAY
ANDERSTON QUAY
BROOMIELAW
KINGSTON BRIDGE
GEORGE V BRIDGE
GLASGOW BRIDGE
CLYD...

PAISLEY
ROAD
CLYDE PL
KINGSTON
St Andre... Cathedr...
Footb...

PAISLEY ROAD WEST
News Scotland Ltd
SEAWARD ST
MORRISON ST
NELSON ST
COMMERCE ST
BRIDGE ST
BOXFORD ST
CARNOUSTIE ST
GLOUCESTER ST
WALLACE ST
COOK ST
WEST ST
TRADESTON ST
NORFOLK ST

1
Plantation Park
M8
SCOTLAND STREET
SHIELDS RD
SALKELD ST
EGLINTON STREET
CUMBERLAND ST
GOR...

Burrell Collection, Greenbank Garden
Scotland Street School (Museum of Education)

A
B
C

Springburn Museum

SPRINGBURN ROAD

Sighthill
Park

M8

PINKSTON ROAD

BBIES LOAN

KYLE ST

BAIRD STREET

STIRLING ROAD

ROYSTON HILL

CASTLE

M8

ALEXANDRA PARADE

gow
lege

WCADDENS ROAD
ottish
Centre

HANOVER STREET

NORTH FREDERICK STREET

New Royal
Infirmary

CASTLE ST

NISHART STREET

ERMONT ST

Glasgow
ternational
oncert Hall

Strathclyde
University

CATHEDRAL STREET

CATHEDRAL ST

Royal
Infirmary

GLEBE ST

ATHEDRAL
ST

Strathclyde
University

Cathedral

ueen St
Station

Royal
Maternity
Hospital

Provand's
Lordship

St Mungo Museum

Necropolis

GEORGE

City
Chambers

GEORGE ST

JOHN KNOX ST

SQ

FREDERICK ST

COCHRANE ST

Hutchesons'
Hall

STREET

7 tirling's
Library

INGRAM STREET

Ramshorn Theatre

High Street
Station

DUKE STREET

VIRGINIA ST

GLASSFORD ST

WILSON ST

HIGH STREET

CANDLERIGGS

City
Hall

TRONGATE

STOCKWELL

Argyle
St Sta

Tron
Steeple

Tron
Theatre

Tolbooth
Steeple

KING ST

Mercat
Cross

Barrowlands
Ballroom

GALLOWGATE

BRIDGEGATE

SALTMARKET

The Barras

BAIN ST

ICTORIA
BRIDGE STREET

GREENDYKE ST

Merchants
Hall Steeple

Glasgow

LONDON ROAD

ALBERT BRIDGE

sgow
ntral
sque

People's Palace

Clyde

Green

ABERCROMBY ST

zens
eatre

BALLATER STREET

Footbridge

ARCADIA ST

RIESTON

Dolphin
Arts
Centre

JAMES ST

200   400 yards

D   E

Glasgow Not so long ago, the idea of down-to-earth
Glasgow becoming a serious rival to Edinburgh in the cultural and entertainment stakes would have been dismissed as impossible (especially by the complacent
capital). But, throughout the 1980s, Glasgow ran a broadly based campaign to change its image. The native
Glaswegians' friendliness, adaptability, and innate loyalty
to their native city was harnessed to turn Glasgow into
one of the most exciting places in the United Kingdom.
Today, a thousand cameos of downtown Glasgow with
its fine civic buildings rival the grand panorama of
Edinburgh. The buoyant enthusiasm of the folk of the
west make Edinburgh's standoffishness seem all the

Look up for the best details on Glasgow's buildings

more absurd. Glasgow's choice of cultural, entertainment, eating, and shopping attractions matches anything the capital can offer, except perhaps at Edinburgh Festival time. In short, Glasgow has arrived.

The story of the city is essentially one of trade, though long ago it was a religious center of some importance. St. Kentigern, or Mungo (c. AD 518–603) is said to have built its first church on the site of the present cathedral, founding the settlement later to become a royal burgh (town), in 1611. This status gave certain trading rights, though the prosperity of the city's traders grew slowly at first, their activities hindered by the shallow, silty river. Only after the Protestant Reformation, which ended Glasgow's role as a religious seat, did commerce really get under way. By 1688, the first pier had been built on the Broomielaw, on the riverside.

After the Union of 1707, the pace accelerated as it became easier to trade with the English colonies in America. Set on the western seaboard, Glasgow was well placed for this trade, and it soon began to rival the English port of Bristol in importance. In came rum, cotton, and tobacco; out went manufactured goods such as hats, shoes, and linen. One group of merchants in particular came to rival the aristocracy because of their wealth and power: Glasgow's Tobacco Lords.

"Workshop of the Western World" The Glasgow talent for adaptability and resourcefulness showed itself in the way that new markets were founded after the collapse of the tobacco trade when America became independent in 1776. Using the nearby resources of coal and ironstone, Glasgow was soon a city with a heavy manufacturing

Typical Glasgow street scene: St. George's Tron Church closes off the view west down George Street

base in the throes of the Industrial Revolution. At its height it became the "Second City of the British Empire," and was the "Workshop of the Western World" throughout the 19th century. This confidence expressed itself in fine civic buildings, both in the Merchant City—that part of Glasgow lying west of the old High Street—and farther west in the streets that were built on a relentless grid, disregarding local topography. It is in this inner city that the finest architecture can be seen today.

However, the ores and the coal that formed the backbone of the heavy industry, particularly around Lanarkshire immediately to the south, gradually became depleted. Even by the early years of the 20th century, Glasgow was losing touch with the shifting patterns of the world economy. By mid-century, many of the shipyards were uncompetitive, and its locomotive works were finding it difficult to compete for orders.

Glasgow today is a post-industrial city, now emerging from a phase of urban renewal, with something of the spirit of the enterprising Victorians playing a part in the city's rebirth.

Not that the recovery, or the effect, is uniform. The city still has some problem peripheral housing projects (but then, so has Edinburgh). There are still holes in the Merchant City, a few building sites with grand plans still unfulfilled. But anyone strolling through the fashionable Italian Centre (an 18th-century warehouse conversion) or the sophisticated Princes Square (everything that a modern shopping mall ought to be, but more often than not isn't) can see that the new Glasgow has something rather special.

The River Clyde
Mention the River Clyde to the locals and soon the phrase "doon the watter" (down the water/river) will be heard. This refers to the now all-but-vanished summer vacation tradition of the toiling masses in the Clydeside area, who escaped from the shipyards, foundries, engineering works, mills, and offices, on a trip by steamer down the Clyde to the playground of the lower estuary—to Rothesay, Dunoon, Helensburgh, or any one of the other Clyde resorts (see Bute, page 231).

A clean river
Salmon returned to the River Clyde in 1983. Because of pollution, they had not been found there for the previous 120 years.

Medieval stained glass at the Burrell Collection (see page 81)

An exploding myth
One enduring Glasgow myth is that the Kelvingrove Art Gallery and Museum was built back to front, and that the architect committed suicide by jumping from the tower. It isn't, and he didn't!

The 18th-century elegance of Pollok House, in whose grounds stands the Burrell Collection

▶▶ Art Gallery and Museum — 76A4

Kelvingrove Park

This arresting, turn-of-the-century building in red sandstone sits in Kelvingrove Park. Often known as the Kelvingrove Art Gallery, it houses one of Britain's finest civic art collections. Within, individual galleries or wings lead off from its high, cold, and echoing central hall. French paintings of the Barbizon, Impressionist, and post-Impressionist periods are here in plenty, as well as the old masters, with 17th-century Dutch work particularly prominent. "Home-grown" work is likewise strong, with The Glasgow Boys, a late 19th-century artistic flowering, represented by Hornel, Henry, Guthrie, Walton, and others. Also featured are works by the Scottish colorists—Peploe, Cadell, Hunter, and Fergusson.

The museum is strong on European arms and armor, with good displays of silver, pottery, glass, and porcelain, as well as archeological and ethnographic materials. The Natural History section has an important taxidermy department. The gallery and museum are open daily.

▶ Botanic Gardens — 76A4

Great Western Road

The original botanic collection was in a physic garden of the university, which moved to its present site on Great Western Road in 1842. The centerpiece of the garden today is the magnificent Kibble Palace of 1863, a sort of glass "big top" originally built for a well-to-do Glasgow merchant named John Kibble at his Clyde coast home. He decided to give it to the city, provided he could use it for 20 years, and it was reassembled in the garden in 1871. It has been a warm and ferny refuge ever since, with its bleached statues reflected in the ponds of colorful water lilies. Exterior features include an herb garden and an arboretum. Other specialties are an internationally renowned orchid collection, and the national collection of begonias. The gardens are open daily.

▶▶▶ Burrell Collection   76A1

Pollok Country Park, 4 miles southwest of Glasgow

Sir William Burrell was a wealthy Glasgow shipowner with a wide-ranging taste for *objets d'art*. He started collecting as a boy, and was still acquiring pieces at the time of his death in 1958, aged 96. Even by 1901, when the city staged the Glasgow International Exhibition, Burrell was the largest single lender for the displays, which included medieval tapestries, ivories, wood and alabaster sculpture, stained glass and bronzes, Roman glass, 16th- and 18th-century Dutch, German, and Venetian table glass, plus silver, furniture, Persian rugs, and many paintings, including works by Manet, Whistler, and Monticelli. He acquired his first Degas just a little later, an indication that his eclectic tastes were already fully formed when he still had more than half a century of collecting ahead of him.

In 1944, he gave the whole collection of 8,000 or so items to the city, along with almost half a million pounds ($750,000) to build a suitable home for them. As one of the conditions attached was a rural and pollution-free setting, matters languished for some years, but a site was found by 1967 and, after a competition and a 12-year building phase, the magnificent Burrell Collection opened in Glasgow's Pollok Park in 1983. It is open daily.

At the Art Gallery and Museum, Kelvingrove

▶▶▶ Gallery of Modern Art

Royal Exchange Square   77D2

The Gallery of Modern Art (opened 1996), started life as a tobacco baron's mansion of 1780, then became a bank, an exchange or meeting and entertainment place for businessmen, then a library. It is one of Scotland's major contemporary art venues, on four floors, each identified by one of the elements: fire, earth, water, or air. It displays Glasgow Museums' collection of art, craft, and design from 1950 to the present. Artists who have become internationally known since the 1980s are emphasized, and the gallery actively acquired works from beyond Scotland, for example, from Papua New Guinea and Ethiopia. Crafts and design also play an important role both in displays and as an integral part of the building. The gallery runs a wide-ranging program of temporary exhibitions, events, workshops, and performance art and dance. It is open daily.

The Kibble Palace, Glasgow Botanic Gardens

Pollok House
Pollok Park, the setting of the Burrell, comprised the former policies (grounds) of Pollok House, donated to the city in 1967. Nearby Pollok House, built *c*. 1750 with later additions, now houses a further European painting collection as well as furniture, ceramics, glass, and silver.

►► Glasgow Cathedral   77E3

Cathedral Street

Now a little isolated from the main thrust and vigor of the modern city center, Glasgow Cathedral, open daily, is one of the most ancient and historic sites in the city. The short trip eastward is well worth making, and is an easy walk from the Merchant City. The site has been occupied since the early Christian era, and is associated with Glasgow's patron saint, St. Kentigern, or Mungo. He founded a church here, possibly in the early 7th century. The earliest identifiable work dates from the 13th century.

There are five elements in the cathedral, which has an unusual shape: the nave, the choir, the upper and lower chapter houses, the lower church, and the Blacader Aisle. The late medieval roof, towering 99 feet above the nave, incorporates 14th-century timber, while the choir and nave are separated by a 15th-century screen or pulpitum. The unique lower church, below the choir, was a 13th-century extension on the sloping site, and contains St. Mungo's tomb. The Blacader Aisle, where spotlights pick out the

Glasgow Cathedral

ceiling bosses (ornamental studs), is the "youngest" part of the cathedral, built by Archbishop Blacader (1483–1508). Monuments to the great and good of Glasgow, battle honors of various regiments, and some excellent modern stained glass are also here. The Necropolis behind the cathedral is also worth a visit.

► City Chambers   77D2

George Square

The exterior of the City Chambers is exotic enough, with its turreted, colonnaded façade in Venetian style, topped by a tower and festooned with carving. Inside, it verges on the outrageous, with a mosaic basilica of an entrance hall, marbled staircases, and galleries, epitomizing the excessive exuberance of full-blown Victoriana. The building was intended to restore confidence after the City of Glasgow Bank collapse, and was opened by Queen Victoria in 1888. Weekday tours are available (subject to council functions).

The Merchant City

■ Glasgow's transformation from religious seat to commercial center resulted in the original community expanding westward from its High Street, cathedral, mercat (market) cross, and other trappings of a market town. It was this "new town," at the heart of Glasgow today, that became the Merchant City …■

The growth of trade Glasgow's expansion could only be funded by trade, but the shallow, silty nature of the river at first hindered the aspirations of the traders and burgesses (borough citizens). The first pier was built on the nearby Broomielaw by 1688, and over the years the river was deepened. Gradual commercial expansion meant that the rural grazings west of High Street were required for commerce. Various manufacturing concerns, as well as vast warehouses and the grand mansions of the successful traders sprang up in successive waves. The development picked up steam in the 18th century as a planned development of gridded streets.

Glasgow became one of Europe's most important tobacco ports, with its nerve center within the Merchant City. The ships that came in with the golden leaf from Virginia, sailed out again with cargoes ordered by the planters on the far side of the Atlantic. Thus the Merchant City prospered, even surviving the economic disruption of American Independence.

Architectural style The city developed urban characteristics unique in Scotland. Most notable of these is the compact Glasgow square, usually enclosing a church: one example is at Nelson Mandela Place, west of Queen Street Station. Another feature is the deliberate placing of prominent buildings to close off vistas.

The Victorians, with their emphasis on civic pride, brought other styles to the Merchant City. However, decline set in during the 20th century, when the 18th-century warehouses sat empty and the old tobacco exchanges were outmoded. The area became a little rundown until the design-led, late 20th-century renaissance. Now the Merchant City is again the focus of innovation, though this time it is the small, specialized (and very exclusive) retailers of fine clothes, furniture, and other upscale supplies who have brought new life to this fascinating and historic area.

Top: chimney pots are numbered for each tenement apartment

Cotton
One way the business community of the Merchant City diversified after American Independence was by investing in cotton. Glasgow became second in importance only to Manchester, England in this industry.

83

The Duke of Wellington *by Marochetti*

MERCVRY

Glasgow City Center

A walk that takes in the architectural riches, past glory, and modern regeneration of the Merchant City area. Allow two and a half hours. *See map on pages 76–7.*

Near Queen Street Station, admire the early French Gothic style of the **Glasgow Stock Exchange** (1875). Go down Queen Street, with its views across statue-filled George Square, to the **Gallery of Modern Art**, in the former Royal Exchange. Originally a grand mansion, it had a colonnaded classical façade stuck on later to enhance the view from Ingram Street.

Go through **Royal Exchange Square** (there is a good tearoom here) for the shopping delights of pedestrians-only **Buchanan Street**. The modern charms of the discreet **Princes Square** shopping development, airy yet compact, contrast with the **Argyll Arcade** below, built in 1827 as Scotland's first shopping arcade. The arcade opens into Argyle Street itself.

The shops move generally downscale the farther east you go, so, unless you intend a weekend visit to the flea market at the **Barras** farther

Glasgow offers the best shopping choice in Scotland

yet to the east (see panel, page 86), turn up Candleriggs to reach the heart of the old **Merchant City**. Some 18th-century warehousing survives. The Italianate-style City Hall (1817) is still a concert hall, though only the façades of the markets remain. The Merchant City is still in the throes of regeneration: note the **Café Gandolfi** on Albion Street, around the corner, an example of the new Merchant City enterprise.

Thread through Wilson Street, past more interesting new shops on **Ingram Square** and the massive, classical, old **Sheriff Court**. Continue west to Virginia Street, named after the New World trade. **Virginia Court**, halfway along, has ancient cart ruts in its cobbles. Nearby is the former **Tobacco Exchange**, now a collection of bookshops and antique stalls. Then make your way through to **George Square**, with Robert Adam's **Trades House** (his only surviving work in Glasgow) in the near vicinity, and, to the north, **Hutchesons' Hall** on Ingram Street.

▶ **Greenbank Garden** 76A1

Flenders Road
Greenbank is 6 miles south of town, in fairly plush Clarkston. Set around a fine Georgian house, originally built for a Glasgow merchant, the 12-acre policies (grounds) include a big walled garden. Greenbank is run as a demonstration garden, with a variety of small-scale features. It is in the care of the conservation body, the National Trust for Scotland, and is open every day.

▶▶ **Hunterian Museum and Art Gallery** 76A4

University Avenue and Hillhead Street
William Hunter (1718–83) trained at Glasgow University and became a famous physician in London. He bequeathed substantial scientific collections to his parent university, and the Hunterian opened in 1807 as Scotland's first public museum. The emphasis is now on geology, archeology, coins, and art. Exhibits include the fossil of the Bearsden shark (named after a suburb of Glasgow), as well as the city's own meteorite!

The Hunterian Art Gallery has existed as a separate (but practically adjacent) entity since 1980. It includes European works from Rembrandt to Sir Joshua Reynolds, as well as Scottish 19th- and 20th-century work. The Print Gallery exhibits works from the largest print collection in Scotland, from Dürer to David Hockney. Also prominent is the American-born painter James McNeill Whistler, whose estate was made a gift in 1935. Charles Rennie Mackintosh is well represented, too. Furniture and fittings from the architect's home are displayed in the arresting Mackintosh House—a reconstruction of the principal rooms of his own home. The Museum and Art Gallery are closed on Sundays.

▶ **Hutchesons' Hall** 77D2

158 Ingram Street
Hutchesons' Hall was built in 1802 to a design by David Hamilton, one of the city's most talented local architects. It is now the west-of-Scotland headquarters of the National Trust for Scotland, and has a visitor center and gift shop. The Hall is open, daily except Sundays.

Charles Rennie Mackintosh (1868–1928)
Mackintosh gutted the end of the town house at 78 Southpark Avenue, Hillhead, Glasgow and refitted it in his own unique style. It came into the hands of the university in 1945 and was demolished in 1963. Prior to demolition a detailed survey was carried out and much was salvaged, ultimately to be lovingly rebuilt almost 20 years later in the Mackintosh section of the Hunterian Art Gallery.

85

Charles Rennie Mackintosh

Buildings Tours & Exhibitions

Mackintosh style in the Hunterian

St. Mungo

Barras Flea Market
If it is a weekend, a visit to the People's Palace can be combined with a browse around the Barras, Glasgow's flea market. It lies within easy walking distance north of Glasgow Green.

Glasgow Green
In the days when Glasgow was a hotbed of Communism and the struggle for workers' power, the Clydeside area orators used Glasgow Green as an important speaking platform. The authorities retaliated in the 1930s by planting flower beds in strategic positions to discourage crowds from gathering.

At the Museum of Transport

▶ **St. Mungo Museum**   *77E3*
Cathedral Square
With picture windows that reveal the skyline of the soaring cathedral and the knobbly monuments of the Necropolis, this museum of religious life and art (open daily) also takes a broad overview of human ways of dealing with big issues: life, death, the hereafter, and how they are treated across the world.

Salvador Dali's *Christ of St. John of the Cross* is here, just around the corner from a many-limbed Shiva as Nataraja, the Lord of the Dance. Dali's masterpiece is hung so high that it is best viewed from the gallery on the other side of the room. From Japanese shrines to Aboriginal paintings, the religious art and artifacts of all kinds of cultures are brought together here. A separate gallery shows material from human rites of passage—birth, marriage, and so on—more anthropological, perhaps, than religious in the strict sense. Take time to read the comments boards, where visitors are asked to write a few notes on what they think of the museum experience and pin them up for public consumption. Quite a few note the close relationship between religion and conflict.

▶ **Museum of Education**   *76B1*
Scotland Street
Housed in a Mackintosh building of 1904, the former Scotland Street School now pays homage to education in Scotland and gives a sense of how it felt for pupils, right down to the squeak of chalk on slate. Inside are period classrooms from various eras, and changing exhibitions. The museum is closed on Sunday mornings.

▶▶▶ **Museum of Transport**   *76A4*
Kelvin Hall, 1 Bunhouse Road
This spacious site around the back of the Kelvin Hall holds all kinds of historic transportation exhibits. It is fun, and not just for children, with huge steam locomotives, brooding and awesome, tramcars and buses, Hillman Imps (Scotland's fairly awful last home-produced automobile), and other gleaming vehicles from past eras. The fire engines and ship models are hugely popular, and there is also a very evocative 1938 Glasgow street

scene. The Museum of Transport is just across the road from the Art Gallery and Museum at Kelvingrove, with the Hunterian within easy reach. It is open daily.

▶ ▶ ▶ People's Palace   77E1

Glasgow Green

In the heart of the ancient park known as Glasgow Green, the People's Palace, as the name implies, is for and about the "ordinary people" of Glasgow. This late-Victorian sandstone edifice has a museum at the front and a huge, glass conservatory, known as the Winter Gardens, at the back. This is heated so that palms and other tender plants can flourish, and there is also a café, which makes it a popular place for idling and for posing for wedding and other photographs. To go from the clear light and bustle of the Winter Gardens, through the swing-doors to the museum, is an odd experience, a little like discovering someone's attic.

The story of the Tobacco Lords is told in the museum, together with those of the radical weavers, the temperance and Co-operative movements, and women's suffrage, alongside the ephemera of countless everyday lives, from tram tickets to wartime ration books, as well as reconstructions of typical Glasgow working-class tenement housing. The Palace is open daily.

Just down the road, off the Green, is the former **Templeton's Carpet Factory**, another of Glasgow's exuberant examples of Victoriana, sometimes called the Doge's Palace. Multicolored brick and tile have been used to create an extraordinary Venetian-style façade (the building can only be viewed from the outside). Also on Glasgow Green, which, in spite of renewals, still has a faintly neglected air, is the Doulton Fountain, a 43-foot-high terra-cotta creation, formerly an exhibit at the 1888 International Exhibition at Kelvingrove.

Shop-front display in the Museum of Transport

Provand's Lordship, one of only two remaining medieval buildings in Glasgow

Charles Rennie Mackintosh, architect, designer, and leading exponent of art nouveau in Scotland

▶ Provand's Lordship   77E3

High Street

Close to the cathedral is Glasgow's only other downtown medieval building, Provand's Lordship. The word "Provand" is the same as prebend, a clergyman who is paid from cathedral revenue, and who officiates there. The Provand or Prebend of Balornock once inhabited the house.

It was built in 1471 as a manse (minister's house) for the long-vanished hospital adjacent. With its characteristic steeply pitched roof with crow-stepped gables and armorial panels, it was, in its day, a suitably dignified residence for churchmen. Later in its long history, it had less distinguished occupants. Glasgow's hangman occupied a one-story lean-to cottage next door. Now a lone survivor, Provand's Lordship has become a city museum housing period furniture. The dark rooms, with their low doorframes, small windows, and worn steps, have a curious musty atmosphere about them (yes, the house is said to be haunted). As well as the interesting furniture, there are displays on the many changes of use the building has undergone in its 500-year history. It is open daily.

▶ Queen's Cross Church   76C4

Garscube Road

This is the only church designed by Charles Rennie Mackintosh. Built in 1897–9 it is now the headquarters of the Charles Rennie Mackintosh Society, with a small exhibition area, library, and shop. It is open on Tuesdays, Thursdays, Fridays, and Sundays, but check with the tourist information center.

▶ (Glasgow) School of Art   76C3

Renfrew Street

This is Mackintosh's masterpiece, a work of world stature, though crowded by later developments, and is still a breathtaking design. The School of Art is sometimes described as the first and finest architectural work of the modern European movement. Here all of the Mackintosh characteristics are seen to good effect: the sinuous swirls of the forms of nature, the bold and uncluttered lines, the detailing and supreme awareness of the effect of light and shadow. Entry to exhibitions is daily except Sunday, with tours Monday to Friday at 11AM and 2PM, and Saturday at 10:30AM.

▶▶ Springburn Museum   77E4

Atlas Square

Springburn was a hamlet with a few weavers and quarrymen on the north side of Glasgow until the railroad came in 1842. Thirty years later, it was the center of a railroad empire. Most of the 27,000 Springburn folk were at one time connected with the railroad in some way. The workshops of the Caledonian and the North British Railways were here, as well as two more builders, one of them, Hyde Park, the largest in Europe. Their products went all over the globe. Now almost everything is gone, and the shriek of the steam dinosaurs has long been silenced. This is the theme of the Springburn Museum, set up to record a vanished way of life and the industrial heritage of the community. It is open Monday to Saturday.

►► The Tenement House 76B4

145 Buccleuch Street

A young girl moved into the tenement building with her mother in 1911. They were pleased to have such a well-appointed apartment. The young girl was a Miss Toward. She never married, and after her mother's death lived there alone until 1965. A relative who bought the apartment realized that it was a "time capsule" of Glasgow life, because Miss Toward had never thrown anything away, and had never changed the layout of her home. Here was a complete slice of tenement life from the early years of the century.

The apartment has a hall and four rooms: the bedroom (reserved usually for the lodger in Miss Toward's case); the parlor or best room, used when, for example, the kirk elder (church minister) called; the bathroom—a sure sign that this was a very well-appointed tenement for its date (it was built in 1892); and the kitchen, complete with a large black cooking range with coal bin. It is open on weekday afternoons in summer between March 1 and October 31: check with the Tourist Information Centre or the National Trust for Scotland in Hutchesons' Hall in advance of your visit.

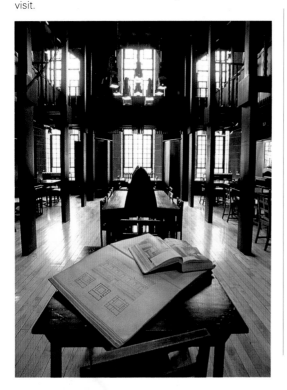

Glasgow School of Art, a remarkable example of Mackintosh design

The coal bin
Miss Toward of the Tenement House had a kitchen coal bin that held half a ton when full, and would have been typical of its time. Pity the poor coalmen on the Glasgow tenement stairs!

Fossil Grove
Among Glasgow's many green spaces, Victoria Park is notable for its Fossil Grove. This is a roofed area in which excavations have exposed the fossilized stumps and roots of trees that grew here 330 million years ago.

Accommodations

As befits Scotland's largest city and one where tourism is increasing, Glasgow has a reasonable choice of accommodations at all price levels. Recent years have seen an increasing number of quality hotels opening up close to the center, mainly to serve the business and conference market, partly because of the Scottish Exhibition Centre down by the Clyde. Another trend has been the arrival of a few smaller, intimate, town house–style establishments, set among the city's rows of Georgian houses. Lodging in the university residence halls should not be overlooked at the budget end of the market. The city's Tourist Information Centre (see page 272) can also organize special short stays in the city.

Out of town It is easy to get into the countryside from Glasgow—Loch Lomond is only half an hour away—so it is also worth considering out-of-town accommodations if exploring the city. Organizations such as the Farm Holiday Bureau, National Agricultural Centre, Stoneleigh, Warwickshire, England CV8 2LZ, tel: 0103 696909, offer farmhouse accommodations in the silence of the moors and upland grazings of the Campsie Hills, for example, which are well within an hour of the city center.

Though Glasgow does not have anything like the accommodations bottlenecks as Edinburgh, it certainly gets very busy. Remember that there are tourist information centers that can find accommodations both in Paisley and at Glasgow Airport, as well as the main downtown office.

Top hotels Starting at the top end, the newish Glasgow Hilton made an impact on opening, with all the international style (and prices) you would expect from this international chain. (Driving here is tricky, though the tall building is visible enough. The hotel thoughtfully pro-

The Devonshire Hotel

Stained glass—the Devonshire

vides a little map in order to help you find your way to the parking lot.)

The Moat House International, the Glasgow Marriott (right in the center), and the Hospitality Inn and Convention Centre (likewise in the thick of things) are all worth considering if you are looking for the no-nonsense professionalism of the larger establishment. The Kelvin Park Lorne is a moderately priced hotel—ideal for the Art Gallery at Kelvingrove, and large enough to have good facilities, yet still small enough to be friendly. (The locals' "genius for instant friendship" is most noticeable in the service industries—receptionists sometimes genuinely remember guests.)

For those who want to be pampered, the Devonshire Hotel at 5 Devonshire Gardens, is a town house of deluxe standard near Great Western Road. (Do not confuse this with One Devonshire Gardens, a couple of doors down, which is equally luxurious and slightly more expensive.)

Also at the top end and out of town is Cameron House and Country Club, on the banks of Loch Lomond, with superb leisure facilities. Other possibilities if you want a country base with easy access to the heart of the city are the areas around Balloch (at the south end of Loch Lomond), Helensburgh (a Clyde resort), and Drymen, which is located east of the loch.

Residence halls For travelers on a budget, as well as a good selection of all manner of bed-and-breakfast establishments and guest houses, there are university residence halls available. Locations include Sauchiehall Street, ideal for the city-center shops, Clyde Street, a good base for the Merchant City, and Cathedral Street, and all offer reasonable value for money. Glasgow also has a youth hostel, at 7/8 Park Terrace, G3 6BY, tel: 0141-332 3004.

Campus lodging
For details of Glasgow's on-campus lodging—there are at least six residence halls for Glasgow University alone—contact Glasgow University's Conference and Vacation office at 52 Hillhead Street, Glasgow G12 8PZ (tel: 0141-330 5385), or Strathclyde University's Residence and Catering Services at 50 Richmond Street, Glasgow G1 1XP (tel: 0141-553 4148).

Package deals
Glasgow is now a popular destination for English-based bus companies and other operators, who offer a complete package of travel and accommodations. For more details, contact the Greater Glasgow Tourist Board—address in Travel Facts, page 272—and ask for their latest list of package tours.

Food and drink

As in any other big city, fashionable places to eat and drink in Glasgow come and go, as do chefs. You need to strike up a conversation with a local or follow a recommendation in the press (see panel page 96) for up-to-date news. Glasgow has ambience in plenty when it comes to eating and drinking: that is all part of its downtown vibrancy and its newfound confidence—it is probably the most exciting place to be in Scotland for an evening out.

The city also has a core of long-established, well-loved restaurants that are easy to track down.

Glasgow seems to specialize in the kind of place that offers competent cuisine along with plenty of atmosphere, so that any minor shortcomings are easily forgiven. Another characteristic is the many pubs and restaurants that now occupy buildings originally designed for other commercial uses—you can catch yourself staring upward from your glass of beer at the fine old woodwork of a former bank, or the decorated tiles of a Victorian insurance office. There are themed places as well, which are very popular with locals and have an element of theatricality. Yet another category is the restaurant with a pub or café attached, offering two different styles for an evening out.

Scotland's patriot on a pub sign

Recommended restaurants The well-loved Ubiquitous Chip off Byres Road offers a menu that is probably as near as you can get to a local cuisine, with a pronounced Scottish flavor. Much the same can be said about the Buttery on Argyle Street, with its Victorian décor. Another favorite with a loyal clientele is the long-established Rogano in Exchange Place, which first opened its art-deco doors in 1935. Seafood is a specialty here.

Also to be relied upon is the upstairs restaurant at Babbity Bowsters in the Merchant City; its downstairs bar is also a popular spot. (A babbity bowster can be either a country dance or a children's game.) The nearby Café Gandolfi serves interesting food in an informal setting, and is probably the best place to take in the upbeat air of the revived Merchant City. Another successful bistro-style establishment is Whistler's Mother on Byres Road, which divides itself neatly into two in order to cater to students in one half and slightly better-off youngish professionals in the other.

The previously Edinburgh-based phenomenon of Pierre Victoire has been successfully transplanted to Byres Road in Glasgow. Pierre Victoire specializes in authentic French cuisine in an atmosphere of Gallic chaos. It is not unknown for customers to be asked to answer the phone when the staff are busy. Informality definitely rules. There is another branch on Miller Street.

Pubs Glasgow's pubs vary, but the centrally placed ones can be very upscale. Typical of this kind is the Drum and Monkey, formerly banking premises on St. Vincent Street. It is popular with businesspeople, who have lunch in its small and intimate back room with its dark wooden pews, and has a more boisterous main hall. Not far off on West Regent Street, a similarly successful transformation can be seen at De Quinceys. At one time the Moorish tiles that brighten the premises looked down on the main business hall of an insurance company; now they provide an impressively stylish background to a scene of cheerful drinking.

Tearooms Glasgow's tea-rooms have always been something of an institution. The Willow Tea Room is a surviving, though restored, typical Mackintosh design on Sauchiehall Street. These days, tea and coffee are also served throughout the day in any of a number of bistro-style establishments. The Victoria and Albert on Buchanan Street serves tea or coffee with homemade shortbread in the morning in its bar, and the Jenny Tearoom beside the Gallery of Modern Art on Exchange Square has a reputation with the serious tea drinker.

The Rogano, an old-established part of Glasgow's restaurant scene

A street name
Sauchiehall Street is really sauchie-haugh street: "sauchies" are willows, and a "haugh" is a watery field. The willow reference is echoed in the Willow Tea Room on the street.

For shoppers
Princes Square has a variety of places to eat. Try the Café October, right on the top floor, with its noticeably bright atmosphere—perhaps an effect of being so near to the glass roof.

Byres Road pub

Shopping

St. Enoch Square
Built on the site of the old St. Enoch Station, St. Enoch Square is now a massive under-cover shopping mall, a touch better than most 1990s malls thanks to its interesting architecture, with exposed girders and pipes. Another attractive feature is an open-to-view skating rink. However, it is not as upscale and intimate as Princes Square.

There are more shops in Glasgow than anywhere else in Scotland. All the usual chain stores can be found, but, thanks partly to Merchant City enterprise, there is also a very good selection of smaller specialized outlets. Glasgow is style- and fashion-conscious, so clothes shops proliferate, though not all of them survive.

Main areas The main shopping streets are found from Argyle Street northward as far as Sauchiehall Street, taking in streets on both sides of pleasingly pedestrianized Buchanan Street, northwest of which is a grid of streets well worth exploring. The Merchant City lies to the east of it, and should be trawled through. There is a further cluster of shopping possibilities around Byres Road to the west, which should not be overlooked. Except for Byres Road, most of Glasgow's shops are within easy walking distance of Buchanan Street. The best of the new-style malls are likewise found around Buchanan Street: Princes Square, which opens directly off it, and the St. Enoch Centre, moments away just across Argyle Street and less upscale in feel, but worth exploring if only for its design.

Outlets for Scottish goods If you are looking for high-quality Scottish wares, then Geoffrey (Tailor) Highland Crafts, quite far along Sauchiehall Street (but worth walking) is just the place for Scottish knitwear or tweed souvenirs, or for an entire Highland outfit. Hector Russell, Kiltmaker, on Renfield Street will also oblige in much the same market niche.

Old-established John Smith's, Glasgow's own bookshop, has a huge selection of material on Scotland and Glasgow. Postcards home could be written with something exclusive picked up at the Pen Shop in Princes Square, which is a useful shopping mall for gifts as well as fashions, including reasonably priced knitwear at a branch of the Jumpers chain.

Designer shops If you ask about designer shops in Merchant City, locals may well point you toward Ichi Ni San on Bell Street, which has exclusive (mostly) women's collections. Another Merchant City treat for shoppers is the Glasgow Needlewoman on Candleriggs, with every sort of embroidery and needlework accessory imaginable. If antiques are your interest, then the Virginia Galleries is well worth a browse. The galleries comprise a number of small antiques businesses, with prices surprisingly reasonable considering their location. Baguette, on Renfield Street, is a little more sophisticated, and has some excellent antique jewelry. Catherine Shaw, on Gordon Street and in the Argyll Arcade, has giftware in Charles Rennie Mackintosh style.

Typifying the new Glasgow style is the Italian Centre, just off Ingram Street, of which the city is inordinately

Jewelers are plentiful in the Argyll Arcade

Paddy's Market
Do not confuse the Barras with Paddy's Market, near the river. Paddy's Market gets its name from the penniless Irish immigrants of a century ago, who would literally sell the shirts off their backs, so desperate was their poverty. Something of the same air of desperation still hangs around today. This little lane of stalls belies Glasgow's upbeat new image.

95

proud, particularly because this gathering of fashion shops includes labels seen nowhere else in the United Kingdom outside London.

Flea market If you tire of the chic shops of Merchant City, then a trip to the Barras flea market will prove a refreshing antidote—though remember that it is open on weekends only. The Barras is a reminder that Glasgow has not yet become too precious in its new image. The name may have been translated into "Barrowland" in an attempt to prettify and anglicize it, but it still remains a boisterous flea market in a hodgepodge of sheds and warehouses. There at least, the prospect of a real bargain flits just ahead at the next stall, and even if it remains out of reach, the market nevertheless provides great entertainment.

Princes Square— modern shopping at its most sophisticated

Nightlife

Glasgow has a huge selection of pubs and bistros, plus a range of clubs offering musical entertainment from proper ceilidhs (not fake affairs for tourists) to new wave.

Theater and concert halls The city's cultural flagship is the Royal Concert Hall, Sauchiehall Street (tel: 0141-227 5111), a first home for the Royal Scottish Orchestra, who, along with Scottish Ballet and Scottish Opera, have their headquarters in the city. The Royal Scottish Academy of Music and Drama, Stevenson Hall, Renfrew Street (tel: 0141-332 5057) offers a varied program of international performances. The Tramway, Albert Drive (tel: 0141-227 5111), is an exciting showcase for opera, drama, and dance performances. The Tron Theatre, Trongate (tel: 0141-552 4267), offers the best of contemporary Scottish and international theater. The Pavilion Theatre, Renfield Street (tel: 0141-332 1846), puts on variety shows, rock, and pop concerts, while the Kings Theatre, Bath Street (tel: 0141-227 5111), has drama and various popular productions. With the Citizens' Theatre, City Hall, and the Henry Wood Hall, these are just some of the performing spaces Glasgow has to offer.

Film An alternative to the regular movie theaters, the Glasgow Film Theatre, Rose Street (tel: 0141-332 6535) is an independent concern, offering new releases, classic revivals, and popular reruns.

Other nightlife These are some examples from the broad spectrum:Glasgow's "Grand Ole Opry," Paisley Road West (tel: 0141-429 5396), is where the local cowboys and Indians hang out (and dress up) for the country and western music. King Tut's Wahwah Hut, St. Vincent Street, is a nationally acclaimed club for new bands. The Tunnel Club, Mitchell Street (tel: 0141-204 1000), is an award-winning "designer" club for the ultra-trendy, with state-of-the-art dance music. Victoria's, Sauchiehall Street (tel: 0141-332 1444), is a popular upscale nightclub with a supper bar: the hunting ground of professional soccer players, off-duty air crew, and models, with several floors to suit all musical tastes. The Riverside Club, Fox Street (tel: 0141-248 3144) is *the* ceilidh place in town, like an upstairs barn with a tiny stage. The Renfrew Ferry, Clyde Place (tel: 0141-552 0767), looks like a floating conservatory but is actually the former Renfrew ferry: another great ceilidh place with other kinds of music as well (best to check the local papers for details). The Scotia Bar, Stockwell Street (tel: 0141-552 8681), is an old-fashioned little pub with lots of impromptu performances, mostly of folk music.

Listings
The List, available from all central newspaper stalls, gives information on events in Glasgow and Edinburgh. *The Herald* newspaper on Saturdays lists entertainment activities with a Glasgow emphasis.

The groundbreaking Citizens' Theatre

Airport transfers Glasgow Airport, Paisley PA3 2ST (tel: 0141-887 1111), is 8 miles from the center of the city, with an express bus service that takes 30 minutes at a very reasonable fare. These buses connect with the hourly service to downtown Edinburgh. There is also a railroad station at Paisley Gilmour Street, about 2 miles away. Metered taxis are available, with fares upward of £12 ($18) to the center. The Airport Tourist Information Centre (tel: 0141-848 4440) can reserve accommodations, though the main information center is in the city center (see addresses page 272).

Arriving by train or bus Glasgow Central is the central train terminus for services from the south (London's Euston Station is about five hours away). Glasgow Queen Street is the terminus for services from Edinburgh (45 minutes by rail) and the north and west (Aberdeen and Fort William, for instance). Glasgow's main bus station is Buchanan Bus Station, Killermont Street, though some services use Anderston Bus Station, Argyle Street.

The Drum and Monkey

Public transportation within Glasgow Glasgow is the only Scottish city with a subway network, a modernized and useful service open 6:30AM–10:45PM daily, with trains every six–eight minutes all day. Flat rate tickets are on sale at all stations on the subway, which takes the form of a large circle. For information contact St. Enoch Square Travel Centre (tel: 0141-226 4826). This important source of travel information is centrally located beside the St. Enoch Centre, and also has details of Glasgow's extensive suburban rail network.

There are many bus companies operating within the city. Several different types of multi-journey or flexible tickets are available, some combining train, bus, and subway. The Family Day Tripper ticket, allowing travel as far afield as Loch Lomond, is good value.

Taxis Black cabs are widely available throughout the city, and main taxi stands are located at the stations. A fleet of airport taxis operates the service from the airport.

Grid rows: 4, 3, 2, 1 — Columns: A, B, C

ARGYLL & BUTE
Lochgair
Otter Ferry
Ardentinny
Benmore
Cowal
Hill House
Garelochhead
Loch Lomond
Drymen
Killearn
Fintry
STIRLING
Stirling
Alloa
Cowdenbeath
Kincardine
Dunfermline
Culross
Bo'ness
Hopetoun House
Dunoon
Gourock
Helensburgh
Alexandria
Balloch
Strathblane
Campsie Fells
Denny
Kilsyth
Falkirk
Polmont
Grangemouth
Linlithgow
Broxburn
Kilfinan
Kyles of Bute
Colintraive
Milngavie
Lennoxtown
Cumbernauld
Bathgate
M80
M9
M8
WEST LOTHIAN
Livingston
Kames
Greenock
Port Glasgow
INVERCLYDE
Clydebank
Renfrew
Kirkintilloch
GLASGOW
Airdrie
Coatbridge
Whitburn
Tarbert
Rothesay
Bute
Johnstone
RENFREWSHIRE
Paisley
Rutherglen
M8
M73
M80
Shotts
Skipness
Sound of Bute
Largs
Gt Cumbrae I.
Kilbirnie
Barrhead
Bothwell
Hamilton
Motherwell
Wishaw
Carluke
Pentland Hills
Wester
Kilchattan
West Kilbride
Beith
East Kilbride
Chatelherault
Larkhall
Carnwath
Dolphinton
NORTH AYRSHIRE
Dalgarven Mill
Dalry
Stewarton
Strathaven
Falls of Clyde
Lanark
New Lanark
Biggar
Nether
Castle
North Arran
Arran
Ardrossan
Saltcoats
Scottish Maritime Museum
Kilwinning
Irvine
Dean Castle
Cunninghame
Lesmahagow
Dawyck Botanic Garden
SOUTH LANARKSHIRE
Upper Tweedale
Machrie Moor
Brodick
Lamlash
Holy I.
Firth of Clyde
Kilmarnock
Galston
Douglas
M74
Abington
Crawford
Tweed
Broughton
Blackwaterfoot
Whiting Bay
Troon
Prestwick
Tarbolton
Mauchline
Auchinleck
Murkirk
Crawfordjohn
Leadhills
Wanlockhead
Devil's Beeftub
Moffat
White Coomb
EAST AYRSHIRE
Ayr
Alloway
Coylton
Cumnock
New Cumnock
Dunure
Kyle
Nith
Culzean Castle & Country Park
Maybole
Crosshill
Dalmellington
Sanquhar
Drumlanrig Castle
Carronbridge
Thornhill
Border
Turnberry
Doon
Carsphairn
Moniaive
Nith
Dalswinton
Lochmaben
Locke
A74M
Ailsa Craig
Dailly
Loch Doon
Galloway Forest Park 842m
Merrick
Southern
DUMFRIES AND GALLOWAY
Newbridge
Dumfries
Girvan
SOUTH AYRSHIRE
Pinwherry
Dalry
New Galloway
Ballantrae
Barrhill
Clatteringshaws Loch
Cree
Galloway
Raider's Road
Loch Ken
Crossmichael
Sweetheart Abbey
Glencaple
New Abbey
Caerlaverock Castle & Nat Nature Res
Belfast & Larne
Kirkcolm
Castle Kennedy Gardens
Newton Stewart
Threave Castle
Castle Douglas
Dalbeattie
Kippford
Arbigland Garden
Stranraer
Glenluce
Creetown
Fleet Valley
Threave Garden
Gatehouse of Fleet
Palnackie
Rockcliffe
Orchardton Tower
Portpatrick
Auchenmalg
Wigtown
Mill on the Fleet
Kirkcudbright
Logan Botanic Garden
Sandhead
Bladnoch
Borgue
Dundrennan
East Stewartry Coast
Solway Firth
Port Logan
Luce Bay
The Machars
Garlieston
Wigtown Bay
Port William
Whithorn
Drummore
St Ninian's Cave
Isle of Whithorn
Burrow Head
Mull of Galloway
Rhins of Galloway
Loch Ryan
Knapdale
Kintyre
Kilbrannan Sound

The South Unless indulging in the souvenir shops, and tartan frolics of Gretna or Gretna Green—"Joke Anvil Weddings Performed Here," crossing the border from England is a low-key affair. Sometimes a piper plays at Carter Bar, where A68 enters Scotland, but otherwise at first sight things look much the same.

However, Scotland is distinct from England, even in its southern sector—from the look of the money to buying beer in pubs, a subtly altered culture is all around. Geographers call the area the Southern Uplands—blue waves of hills, resonant with tales of ancient skirmishes in these fought-over lands—a dramatic sight from Carter Bar. Farther west, in the Galloway Forest Park north of Newton Stewart, the end of the park road is within walking distance of The Merrick, at 2,613 feet the highest mountain in southern Scotland, with a vista of dark lochs, birch woods, and purple slopes.

THE SOUTH

Ayrshire Continuing north from Galloway, the sheep-cropped moors and conifer woods blend into Ayrshire, another area with a highly characteristic landscape. There is a lushness in the river valleys, woods, and hedgerows which is highly reminiscent of South Wales, a parallel sustained by the signs, in places, of now vanished heavy industry, coal and ironworks, backed by green hills. Farther north, the typical Ayrshire view is across hawthorn hedge and pasture to a long horizon dominated by the blurred profile of Arran (an island) and Kintyre (a peninsula), a setting more Highland than Lowland.

Beyond the geological edge of the Southern Uplands, and into the southern part of the central corridor across Scotland, the scenery changes again. The summery yellow grainfields of East Lothian have red-roofed villages with hills as a backdrop, or even the sheer unexpectedness of the vista from the prehistoric site on the top of Cairnpapple Hill behind Linlithgow, with the Forth Valley spread out in front of you like a geography lesson.

100

As well as its fine landscapes, southern Scotland has highly individual townscapes and communities. The characteristic pastel-washed frontages and wide streets of the Galloway towns are surprising for anyone with preconceptions of dour, gray Scottish communities. No one who accidentally stumbles upon a Common Riding in one of the Borders towns can fail to notice the groundswell of loyalty to place and culture.

Marking the border at Coldstream

Borders landscape near Galashiels

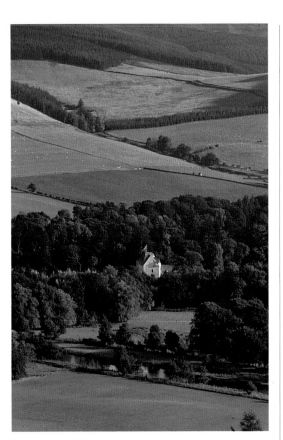

Typical river valley scenery near Walkerburn

The rival county towns
After Berwick became English, Greenlaw saw its chance to become the county town of the Scottish county of Berwickshire. However, nearby Duns also wanted this status, and managed to achieve it several times. Each time it did so, little Greenlaw built another fine civic building. A 17th-century courtroom and prison, an 18th-century hotel to accommodate visiting lawyers and officials, and a 19th-century town hall all add to the fine townscape of today's Greenlaw. It was superseded by Duns for the last time in 1903.

These are mainly modern revivals of the ancient customs of marking out the boundaries of the community, as well as great celebrations of horsemanship—another Borders specialty. (A Scottish Borders MP—member of parliament—once requested that the date of a general election be changed so that it did not clash with the Selkirk Common Riding, which he enjoyed attending.)

Land of Burns Similarly, in Ayrshire, where you cannot turn a corner without finding a signpost pointing to some aspect of the life of Robert Burns, there is a genuine and unique regard for Scotland's poet. This is not something that tourism promoters have foisted upon reluctant communities, but instead an affection for the plowman poet and pride in his achievements.

From bards to model villages by the tumbling cataracts of New Lanark, from stern Borders towers to the softness of East Lothian, from the faded Victorian resorts of the golf-mad Clyde coast to the breathtaking bird cliffs of St. Abbs, the south of Scotland offers a slice of the real Scotland without too much tartan ribbon (even if you can find a pipe band in a Borders town just as easily as farther north). In fact, the region's variety and complex character may ultimately satisfy much more than that of the weather-dominated north. It is not an area to hurry through.

Ayrshire electric illusions
At a point within sight of Culzean Castle, 9 miles south of Ayr, A719 is called Croy Brae, or more familiarly, Electric Brae. Because of a particularly effective optical illusion, the road gives the impression of going downhill when it is actually going up. The site got its name as it was formerly thought that electricity had some part to play in the phenomenon, though this is not the case. Take care when traveling this road, as you are likely to encounter puzzled motorists freewheeling "uphill" to satisfy their curiosity.

THE SOUTH

The Edinburgh Light Horse
Sir Walter Scott was a
countryman at heart, with
the landowner's ideal of an
ordered society where
everyone knew their place.
He and some friends
founded the Edinburgh
Light Horse, a kind of
"Home Guard," in
response to a threatened
Napoleonic invasion in
1797. They galloped around
enthusiastically, but saw
little real action. However,
in the troubled times when
workers began to protest
about working conditions,
Scotland's champion did
manage to threaten to
saber some mill workers at
Moredun Mill and take a
few pot shots at dissenting
miners at Cross Causeway,
both in Edinburgh.

▶▶▶ **Abbotsford House** 99D3

Sir Walter Scott's creation of his own version of Scotland
and its heroic past is embodied in the house that was his
life. Abbotsford is the masonry equivalent of a book of
Scottish quotations. Here is the door from the Old
Tolbooth in Edinburgh, there is the desk made with wood
from a Spanish Armada ship. Look at Rob Roy's gun,
Bonnie Prince Charlie's quaich (cup), James IV's hunting
bottle (did he club game with it?), the keys of Lochleven
Castle, and other treasures. You may get the feeling that
Sir Walter himself left only a few moments ago. *It is open:*
daily, mid-March to October.

▶ **Ayr** 98B3

A preference for a two-week stint in the Mediterranean
sun instead of a traditional seashore vacation, plus the
demise of traditional industries such as coal mining, have
left Ayr and its hinterland facing a challenging future.
Nevertheless, it is a bustling place (but take care with the
parking system, which needs vouchers from local shops
and garages). It makes a good base if you are keen on
playing golf.

Non-golfers can pursue the life of Burns. There seem to
be so many places in the vicinity in which Burnsiana are
displayed that after a day or two you will recognize his
handwriting from several paces off. In fact, as you stare

*Scottish memorabilia,
Abbotsford House*

through the glass at a lock of Highland Mary's hair (she
was a blond), it all becomes slightly eerie, as well as sad.
Take your pick from the **Auld Kirk**, the church where
many of Burns's contemporaries are buried, the **Twa
Brigs o Ayr**, the older of which is 15th century or earlier, plus a statue or two, then follow signs to Alloway.

Alloway▶▶, a leafy suburb of Ayr, is disturbed only
by incessant tour groups from all nations on their way
to the shrine of Scotland's national bard. **Burns
Cottage**, with a museum adjacent (*open:* daily
all year) is an excellent starting point. Down the
road the **Tam O'Shanter Experience** has a
10-minute presentation on Burns, then the
poem "Tam O'Shanter" springs to life in a three-
screen theatrical event (*open:* daily all year).

Nearby, the Burns Monument's neoclassical columns rise from a clipped garden, one of many contrasts with the poet's life of poverty and struggle. Also moments away are the **Auld Brig o Doon** and **Alloway Kirk**, both immortalized in the poem "Tam O' Shanter," a tale of drunkenness and orgy in a setting now taken over rather incongruously by respectable suburbia.

On the Burns trail Incurable romantics will pursue the poet east to **Mauchline**, a village sitting dourly on a grassy ridge in the hinterland of hawthorn-hedged fields. There they will find **Burns House Museum** (*open*: daily in summer) and—even better—a breathtaking view from the **Burns Memorial Tower** just up the road. Burns signposts are everywhere. You can even follow them to the grimly workaday town of **Kilmarnock**, where in a haven of greenery (a country park) stands **Dean Castle** (*open*: daily, afternoons). A rare volume, the first or Kilmarnock Edition, of Burns poetry is on display, but just as interesting are the early musical instruments and European armor collections.

Elsewhere in Ayr's hinterland, **Dalgarven Mill**—the Ayrshire Museum of Countrylife and Costume (*open*: daily in summer, closed Monday to Tuesday in winter), just north of Kilwinning—is in a restored water-powered flour mill. Also within easy reach of Ayr are the **Magnum Leisure Centre**, much trumpeted for its modern approach to recreation now that the traditional Clyde Coast seashore vacation is out of favor; the **Scottish Maritime Museum** (see page 117); and **Culzean Castle** (see page 110).

Dalgarven Mill

The Southern Uplands Fault
The Southern Uplands Fault, where the midland plain gives way to the high ground of southern Scotland, is most conspicuous in the east. Running into East Lothian and prominent from A68 south of Dalkeith (Midlothian), the ancient tough rocks of the Lammermuir Hills form an escarpment above the soft sandstones to the north. A convenient stopping point on A68 at Soutra Hill offers superb views back to the Pentlands, Edinburgh, the Firth of Forth, and beyond.

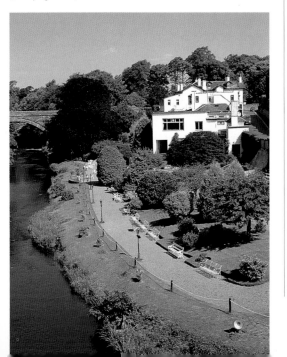

The gardens beside the Brig o Doon in Ayr

■ **Robert Burns (1759–96) is the best-known figure in Scottish literature, though whether for his poems or his pursuit of the lasses is perhaps another matter. Large tracts of Ayrshire, and the area around Dumfries, have plenty of signposted places of interest associated with his passionate life ...■**

Satirical observations
As an observer of others' follies, Burns wrote plenty of scathing and satirical observations of both people and state. A poem to the "Scotch Representatives in the House of Commons" contains the line, often quoted by the distilling industry "Freedom and Whisky gang thegither" (go together). It also contains this observation on the Scots army regiments:

"But bring a Scotchman
frae his hill
Clap in his cheek a
Highland gill
Say, such is royal George's
will And there's the foe,
He has nae thought but
how to kill Twa at a blow."

[A gill is a measure of whisky; royal George means King George III.]

Robert Burns

Ayrshire beginnings With his farming background and his daily toil, Burns might have lived and died anonymously as just another Ayrshire farmer, struggling with poor soil and the primitive agricultural practices of the day. Instead, his immortality was assured through poetry filled with shrewd observations on human nature, with lyricism and with optimism, and above all, belief in the brotherhood of man.

His father was a farmer who moved to Ayrshire from Kincardineshire, on the east coast, and built a cottage on some land he had acquired. This "auld clay biggin" still stands, a shrine to the thousands who have flocked there since the beginning of the 19th century. Burns's father was a hard worker determined to educate his family. Robert and his brother Gilbert acquired a reasonable, if sporadic, education. Robert read avidly when he was not helping on the farm. He had committed "the sin of rhyme" by the time he was 15 years old, while on the farm of Mount Oliphant.

Poems and passion After his father's death in 1784, he and his brother rented the farm of Mossgiel near Mauchline. Robert soon gained a local reputation as a maker of rhymes (among his other vices). In a period when passion and poverty went together with fierce creativity, Burns wrote some of his best-known works. This culminated in the publication of the famed Kilmarnock Edition of *Poems, Chiefly in the Scottish Dialect* in 1786. Around the same time there were writs from Jean Armour's father, livid at his daughter's association (pregnancy, to be precise) with Burns, the poor farmer; penance in the local church (for fornication); thought of emigration—only "the feelings of a father" kept him in Scotland; and also an affair with Highland Mary, which ended in mysterious circumstances. Highland Mary (Mary Campbell) is a figure about whom very little is known. She died in October 1786, possibly after bearing him a child. Certainly, Burns felt terribly guilty about her in later years. It is said she consented to be his wife, but he was already committed to Jean Armour, whom he later married.

Through the success of the Kilmarnock Edition, Burns gained sudden fame. He was soon lionized by the literary classes of Edinburgh, and welcomed as a plowman poet into genteel drawing rooms. He went along happily with the image.

The Songwriter Burns was also a maker of songs. In 1787, he started his completely unpaid contribution to James Johnson's *Scots Musical Museum*, reworking and improving many songs and fragments, a huge body of work still popular to this day. By 1788, he was back once again with Jean Armour. He married her and gave up the hopeless struggle of farming at Mossgiel, deciding instead to move to Ellisland Farm, not far from Dumfries. He took up employment with the Excise (taxation bureau), although he was still determined to succeed as a farmer. The farm at Ellisland failed in 1791.

In between his commitments to the Excise and the needs of the farm, he worked on with further volumes of *The Scots Musical Museum* as well as his own poetic

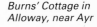

outpourings. Illness and low spirits dogged him as the 1790s progressed. Rheumatic fever took its toll in 1795 as he struggled to maintain the output for *A Select Collection of Original Scottish Airs for the Voice*. By July 1796, at the age of 37, he was dead.

Memories of Burns The Burns "industry" followed on thereafter. The first of many biographies was published by 1797, the year after his death, and the Irvine Burns Club, started in 1826, claims to be the oldest continuously operating club of its kind. Today, his birthday (January 25) is celebrated throughout Scotland—and far beyond, wherever Scots gather—with Burns Suppers, a unique format of haggis, whisky, poetry, and song. No other British poet has achieved anywhere near the same kind of popular appeal. On Burns Night even buttoned-up Scots have a good time, with their stern Calvinistic streak temporarily obscured by the outlook that, at least for one evening

"…man to man, the warld o'er
Shall brithers be for a' that."

Burns would certainly have approved.

The Brow Well
Though places associated with Burns are scattered throughout Ayrshire and Galloway, perhaps the saddest lies adjacent to B725 southeast of Dumfries. The Brow Well is a rock-cut well close to the sea. It was once famed for its mineral properties, and the poet, desperately ill with rheumatic fever and possibly bacterial endocarditis, visited it while sea-bathing nearby, in a last attempt to recover his health. He died three days after he returned from Brow.

Burns' Cottage in Alloway, near Ayr

Ae Fond Kiss
The curious affair by mail (see page 48) that Burns had with Mrs. Agnes McLehose in Edinburgh resulted in a great deal of correspondence, some frigid literary exercises in neoclassical idiom, and one great, truly great, love poem and song of parting—"Ae fond kiss and then we sever," with its haunting fourth verse:
Had we never lov'd sae kindly,
Had we never lov'd sae blindly!
Never met—or never parted,
We had ne'er been broken hearted.
This was written in 1791, as "Clarinda," as Burns addressed her, was preparing to rejoin her husband in the West Indies. Burns never saw her again.

▶ **Biggar** 98C3

The town of Biggar, equidistant from Glasgow and Edinburgh, has retained its own character and a sense of heritage. The original settlement is associated with 12th-century Flemish immigrants who arrived under the patronage of the Scottish kings. (The Fleming family is associated with much of Biggar's story—Mary Fleming was one of Mary, Queen of Scots's attendants, known collectively as the "Four Marys"). The incomers built "mottes," earthen mounds once topped with wooden castles. A motte survives behind today's High Street.

Biggar is essentially a center for a rural hinterland, and the **Corn Exchange**, with its clock tower, still dominates the wide main street, scene of former markets. **St. Mary's Kirk** dates from 1545—the last church built before the Reformation—and is open to view. It is a collegiate church, founded by Lord Fleming, Mary, Queen of Scots's uncle, to support teaching priests. All this can be taken in on a few minutes' walk from the main street. (Keep an eye out for knitwear bargains, if you are window-shopping.) The town also has a puppet theater—not a common feature of Scottish towns—as well as several worthwhile museums.

Gladstone Court Museum, a tribute to the energy of the local museum trust, is an indoor "street" of shops with a good selection of nostalgia-inducing artifacts. The **Greenhill Covenanter's House**, downhill toward the Biggar Burn behind St. Mary's, is a 17th-century farm relocated stone by stone. It sheds some light on the Covenanting movement (see page 55) and the complexities of the Scottish religious wars by way of artifacts and displays. For a total contrast, visit **Biggar Gasworks Museum▶**, which is unique. Thanks to North Sea Gas,

Biggar Gasworks

An old-fashioned pharmacist's shop in Gladstone Court Museum, Biggar

the traditional gasworks have vanished from most places, but not from Biggar. Sometimes they fire it up, creating an olfactory trip down memory lane for some. **Moat Park Heritage Centre** tells of Biggar's early history, and also focuses on geology and on embroidery, with samplers and patchwork coverlets. All museums in Biggar are closed in winter.

▶▶▶ Caerlaverock Castle and National Nature Reserve   98C1

Caerlaverock Castle is unique in Britain. No other castle builder employed this odd triangular moated design. The castle is worth visiting for this feature alone. It sits in its moat, massive and menacing in red sandstone, and offers another puzzle. Nobody knows who built Caerlaverock, which is of late 13th-century origin. It was taken by King Edward I of England around 1300 and regained by the Scots by 1312, only to suffer further in later Anglo–Scots conflicts. Unexpectedly for this frontier fortress, there is an ornate 17th-century range within: Nithsdale's Building, built by the Lords Maxwell. But all is scarred and ruinous—a troubled history in stone. *Open*: daily.

Caerlaverock National Nature Reserve▶▶▶ Combine a castle visit with deluxe bird-watching on the marshes. Particularly good away from high summer, best of all on a calm winter's day, they have plenty of wildfowl to spot. Among the birds here are 13,000 barnacle geese from Spitzbergen, with superb views possible of the flocks from the visitor center or from the conveniently placed hides. This is one of Scotland's major wildlife spectacles if you time it right. It is open all year.

▶▶ Castle Kennedy Gardens   98A1

The Earl of Stair built these pleasure grounds. As a field marshal, instead of toiling with a wheelbarrow and a shovel, he used the troops that he commanded to build the main landscape features. (They were supposed to be chasing Covenanters.) The result is gardening on a grand scale, with superb vistas down the monkey puzzle avenue, woodland walks and lakes, and masses of rhododendrons in spring. May is probably the best month to visit. It is undoubtedly worth the excursion to the west of Galloway, and could easily be combined with a visit to Logan Botanic Garden (see page 120). *Open*: April to September.

Castle remains
Within Castle Kennedy Gardens is the shell of Castle Kennedy, burned down in 1716, but now lending an antique air to the parklands. The Victorian Lochinch Castle on the grounds is strictly private.

The Debatable Land
The Debatable Land was the name given to disputed territory between England and Scotland, between the rivers Sark and Esk, not far from Carlisle, England. Grazing was its only use, as buildings were forbidden. In 1552, it was split in two and a settlement agreed.

107

Caerlaverock Castle

In Chatelherault

The past uniform of
the famous
Coldstream Guards

► **Castle Douglas** 98C1

This is a cheerful sort of place, with its busy main street at the center of a simple grid. The town's designer, Sir William Douglas, was a rich local merchant who rebuilt the old village in 1792. Now bypassed by means of A75, Castle Douglas has plenty of shops to make strolling worthwhile, and is the sort of stopover where you can watch the local community going about its daily business.

Adjacent Carlingwark Loch was once a source of marl, the limey clay used as fertilizer that originally made the town prosperous. To the northeast is the Motte of Urr, the largest man-made castle mound in Scotland. The former 12th-century administrative headquarters of the de Berkeleys is now an impressive green mound by the river, visible from B794. In the fields hereabouts, look for the handsome belted Galloway cattle, more common as stuffed animals in gift shops than in real life.

A few minutes to the southeast of Castle Douglas, **Threave Garden►►** is the training ground for the National Trust for Scotland's gardeners. There are always fresh plantings and new ideas to see within its 64 acres. Early spring (April) has spectacular drifts of daffodils, with over 200 cultivars. Later, the peat garden—that specialty of the cool, moist, Scottish climate—is a high point. Most aspects of Scottish gardening can be seen on trial here, from the traditional flower border to the Victorian hothouse. *Open*: daily.

Threave Castle►► This gaunt 14th-century tower rising out of the watery scenery on an island in the River Dee was once owned by Archibald the Grim. It is an appropriate setting for the name. The Lord of Galloway built his fortress with the intention of intimidating. Formerly the main power base of the Black Douglases, the strongest of the Scottish nobles until they overreached themselves in a conflict with King James II, Threave was successfully besieged in 1455 by the king's forces. Excavations have revealed a lot about medieval defensive buildings, as well as the most complete medieval riverside harbor in Scotland. There is a pleasant walk, though wet in places, from the farmyard parking lot to the riverside. Ring a bell for the boatman. The castle is closed in winter, but the walk is still worthwhile, with close-up views from the bank. Threave Wildfowl Refuge is nearby.

▶▶ Chatelherault 98B3

The wealthy Duke of Hamilton asked William Adam to design a hunting lodge and kennels within the pleasure grounds surrounding Hamilton Palace. Chatelherault was part of one of the most ambitious landscaping works in 18th-century Britain. Nothing remains now of the 3-mile avenue, the lake, or the canalized River Clyde. Even Hamilton Palace was demolished in 1927 after the family had sold off most of the ground for mining. Today there is only dipping parkland, now a country park—plus the result of a breathtaking $11 million worth of public funds spent in restoring Adam's one-room deep façade, part of which is a visitor center telling the extraordinary story. It is well worth the diversion from M74. *Open*: daily.

▶ Coldstream 99E3

A pleasant village just north of the border, Coldstream, like Gretna Green, once did a brisk trade in runaway marriages. This is recalled on a plaque by the handsome

little tollhouse on the Scottish side of John Smeaton's elegant 1760s bridge. Coldstream is also associated with the Guards regiment of the same name. Items from their glorious past can be seen in the Coldstream Museum (*open*: summer only, closed Friday).

North of the village is **The Hirsel▶**, once the home of Sir Alec Douglas-Home, Lord Home of The Hirsel, who was prime minister in 1963–4. There are walks in the estate through varied habitats of woodland (with rhododendrons in spring), farm, and lake, which are enjoyed by bird-watchers in particular. A craft complex and visitor center in a converted farm building sheds light on the life of a Borders country estate. *Open*: daily.

COLDSTREAM
Birthplace of the Regiment

109

Found in the loch
Not only valuable marl came out of Carlingwark Loch by Castle Douglas. Among other historical artifacts, a forge was once recovered from the lakewaters. It is thought to have been used by King Edward I's forces as they passed this way during one of their forays in around 1300.

The Coldstream Guards
The primacy of the Grenadier Guards as the senior regiment in the Guards Division of the British Army is disputed by the Coldstream Guards. Both regiments share 1660 as their official founding date. When on parade the Coldstreamers will not stand next to the Grenadiers, instead taking the left of the line. Their motto is *Nulli secundus*—second to none.

Threave Castle

THE SOUTH

National Guest Flat
In 1946, the top floor of the main part of Culzean Castle was put at the disposal of General Dwight D. Eisenhower as a token of the Scottish people's gratitude for his role as Supreme Commander of the Allied Forces in Europe in World War II. It has become known as the National Guest Flat, and its story is told in the Eisenhower Room in the castle today.

An Italian influence?
The unique studded façade of Crichton Castle dates from the 1580s. The Palazzo Steripinto in Sciacca, Sicily (1501) is a possible source of inspiration, as the 5th Earl of Bothwell was in exile in southern Italy.

▶▶ **Crichton Castle**   99D3

This forbidding, brooding, atmospheric castle is easily missed if you hurry along A68, intent on Edinburgh. It is worth stopping, not least because of the fine Lothians countryside in which the castle is set. Built between the late 14th and late 16th centuries, it is associated with the Earls of Bothwell. Mary, Queen of Scots was here in January 1562, attending the wedding of her half brother to Lady Janet Hepburn. The son of that marriage, the 5th Earl of Bothwell, frequently in exile, commissioned the castle's unique feature: the diamond-faceted façade of the north range. (*Open*: daily in summer.) Beyond the castle a pathway leads through some pleasant scenery to Borthwick Castle (a private hotel).

▶▶▶ **Culzean Castle and Country Park**   98A2

Culzean, pronounced "Kul-*ain*," is the National Trust for Scotland's most popular attraction. Set on its cliff-top perch, it has been associated with the Kennedy family since the 14th century. The present building was commissioned by the 10th Earl of Cassillis, and is one of Robert Adam's most famous designs, taking 20 years to reach completion in 1792. The structure itself, with its ornate plasterwork, oval staircase, and round drawing room, plus 570 acres of policies, came into the hands of the National Trust in 1945, to be held for all time. Now the once-private grounds behind their high walls swallow up more than half a million visitors every year, though fewer visit the castle itself. Stabilizing the wind and salt-eroded sandstone of the structure and the outbuildings was only one problem for the Trust to solve. Simply running the estate is a huge operation in itself. This is conservation and countryside education on a large scale. Within the extensive policies are woodland walks, a walled garden, swan pond, deer park, and aviary, as well as a ranger service to help interpret it all, based in a reception and interpretation center. The castle is open daily from April to October, the country park is open all year-round.

Culzean Castle

► **Dalbeattie** 98C1

Dalbeattie presents an uncharacteristic Galloway townscape of silver granite, like a little detached chunk of Aberdeen, but its granite has brought prosperity—even the Grand Harbor of Valletta in Malta used it. The town is a good base for exploring the coastline, especially around

Rockcliffe and Kippford, two little communities dozing quietly by the estuary. Kippford is favored by sailing enthusiasts, Rockcliffe has more the air of a retirement haven. Farther up the Water of Urr is Palnackie, where a flounder tramping festival is held annually in the muddy creek. Also nearby is Orchardton Tower, a 15th-century tower house unique in Scotland because it is circular.

►► **Dawyck Botanic Gardens** 98C3

On B712 southwest of Peebles, this specialist garden of the Royal Botanic Garden in Edinburgh is often overlooked as it lies a little off the main tourist routes. It is worth seeking out, especially in late spring and early summer when the garden is ablaze with rhododendrons. The plantings here are on a large scale, with grand conifers and shrubs, and woodland walks. The garden closes in winter.

►► **Dirleton Castle** 99D4

Overlooking the village green (square) of the village of Dirleton, this ancient fortress dates back in part to the early 13th century, when its great circular towers, now overlaid with later work, were built by the Anglo–Norman de Vaux family. The strategically important castle, commanding east–west routes around the Lammermuirs, was captured by King Edward I of England in 1298. It also has a pit-prison, a dungeon cut from the solid rock. The castle was eventually left in ruins by Cromwell's troops in 1650, and became part of the Archerfield estate. The site lies within a much later wall, enclosing a 17th-century bowling green and ancient yews as well as a fine garden. This last feature is a good enough reason to visit the castle, especially in high season when the flower border is at its colorful best, (*castle open* daily). Historic Scotland, the organization that cares for the castle, has re-created a Victorian garden here. Combine a visit with a walk at Yellowcraigs, for fine coastal scenery. An access road is signposted just east of the castle.

The Jubilee Path
Rockcliffe is joined to Kippford by the Jubilee Path, through the scrub by the sea edge with views to the blue shallows of the Water of Urr estuary. It makes a very pleasant stroll, with a drink to follow at the local hotel in Kippford. Note that though only a mile apart by the Jubilee Path, the two places are 5 miles apart by road.

The beach at Yellowcraigs, Dirleton, with Fidra offshore

111

Literary connections
Conspicuous offshore at Yellowcraigs (by Dirleton) are the island of Fidra and its lighthouse. This is one of the places said to be the inspiration for the topography of Robert Louis Stevenson's *Treasure Island*. Certainly, Stevenson knew this part of the coastline well, using other nearby coastal features in *Catriona*.

Eyemouth, an active fishing port

A stabbing at the altar
In assessing his chances of securing the throne of Scotland, Robert the Bruce (see page 28) had to deal with other powerful families with Scottish interests at the English court. For this purpose the encounter was typical of the murky politics of the day. He met with John Comyn (the Red Comyn) at Greyfriars Kirk in Dumfries. Most historians believe that they had been jointly plotting against King Edward of England, and that Comyn had let the English know about this. Bruce had been warned and left England in great haste. At his meeting with Comyn he accused him of treachery, and the fatal stabbing followed. The game was up. To return to King Edward was impossible. Bruce had to declare his intention: to win Scotland's crown.

A Dunbar shop

▶ **Dumfries** 98C2

With its old bridges, museum, and Camera Obscura, a reasonable range of shops, and plenty of Burns strands to follow, Dumfries is a pleasant rather than a breathtaking town. It is known as the Queen of the South, and it is the largest center for some distance around, with a good mix of light industry and commerce, tourism and historic sites. Now that it is bypassed by terrifyingly busy A75, the

town environment has greatly improved. The prevailing street color is the distinctive pink of the local sandstone. Dumfries has a long past, the settlement which grew up around the ford on the River Nith becoming a royal burgh in the 12th century. The now-vanished Greyfriars was the scene of the stabbing of the Red Comyn by Robert the Bruce, an incident that led to the Scottish Wars of Independence (see panel). Much later, and flying in the face of Jacobite romantic myth, Dumfries wanted no dealings with the adventurer Bonnie Prince Charlie, though he helped himself to town funds as well as the lead off the roof of St. Michael's Church.

Like Ayr, Dumfries has capitalized on its Robert Burns connections (see pages 104–5). He moved here in 1791 to take up his post as an excise officer, and now lies buried in a grand mausoleum in St. Nicholas's churchyard. The house in which he died is also a museum (closed Sundays and Mondays in winter), and the Globe Inn, known to Burns, is still a pub, complete with the chair he used and the window on which he scratched some radical verses.

Robert Burns Centre▶ Modern input to the Burns cult takes the form of this handsome former mill building by the River Nith. The center offers refreshments as well as an exhibition on the Dumfries Burns connection. *Open*: daily, except Sundays and Mondays in winter.

▶▶ **Dunbar** 99D4

Boasting high sunshine records—when the coastal "haar" (sea fog) stays away—and low rainfall, Dunbar is a curious mix of traditional resort, decayed port, and elegant Georgian sea town. Down by the harbor are the shattered and eroded fragments of one of medieval Scotland's most important fortresses, controlling an important coastal route used by the English invaders. The

A natural first
Dalswinton Loch lies 6 miles north of Dumfries. The first steam-powered boat ever built was tested on it in 1788. The designer was William Symington, an engineer who was born not far off at Leadhills. His engine developed 0.45 horsepower (0.34KW), barely enough to turn the cranks.

Burns' Mausoleum, Dumfries

An unfortunate name
The former county town of Duns is recalled in the uncomplimentary "dunce." This is ironic, as it refers to John Duns Scotus (1266–1308), a philosopher and leading divine said to have been born in the town. The modern usage came about through later criticism of his teachings.

Scots were defeated here in 1296. Much later, the Covenanting army met the same fate at the hands of Oliver Cromwell in 1650.

Today, the townscape owes its origins partly to funds generated by intense trading activities in the 18th century, which included, briefly, whaling. The handsome 17th-century town house predates these times, though Dunbar or Lauderdale House, blocking the eastward High Street view, was built by one of the powerful trading families in the town. There are other elegant buildings to be admired, but a stroll will inevitably lead seaward, past the Cromwellian Old Harbor to the New or Victoria Harbor, dating from 1842. In spring, gulls nest on the old castle and other harbor-front buildings.

Dunbar lies adjacent to the John Muir Country Park▶▶, 175 acres of excellent coastal habitat, varying from salt marsh to sea buckthorn, around the estuary of the River Tyne. It offers plenty of walks at all seasons, and has the further attraction of completely altering its character at high tide.

▶ **Eyemouth Museum** 99E3

A converted Georgian church in the fishing port of Eyemouth is the setting for this successful community venture. Eyemouth Museum was set up in 1981 to record the centenary of the Great East Coast Fishing Disaster of October 1881, when 189 fishermen lost their lives in a sudden hurricane. As well as telling the tale of the disaster, commemorated in a magnificent tapestry, the museum also touches on other aspects of folk life in the area, including agricultural developments. The museum is closed in winter. A visit here could be combined with bird-watching around St. Abbs' Head.

▶ **Galashiels** 99D3

A sturdy, respectable mill town, rather than a picturesque place, "Gala" has lots of shops to browse in for knitwear bargains. In fact, the textile theme is inescapable, notably at **Peter Anderson Cashmere Woolen Mill▶▶**. Their museum, with its traditional spinning and weaving artifacts, tells the story of the town's development as an important textile manufacturing center. There is also a factory tour and a mill shop. *Open*: daily; closed Sundays, October to May. Tours available Monday to Friday only.

▶▶ **Galloway Forest Park** 98B2

Between the Rivers Cree and Ken, the open moors below the gray hills of Galloway lost their original tree cover long ago. From 1922 onward, the Forestry Commission reclothed many of the slopes using alien species, designating the 240-square-mile area a forest park in 1943, and leaving a third of it as open land. Like all Forestry Commission properties, it offers unlimited access to the public unless areas are closed for tree felling. There are numerous marked forest trails and opportunities to fish or camp, and the park is also bisected by the Southern Upland Way (a long-distance footpath). Among the many points of interest are the 10-mile forest drive near Clatteringshaws Loch; the Raider's Road, linking A712 and A762; and the peerless views from the road end at Glen Trool. The Bruce's Stone, commemorating the first victory in the Independence Wars, can also be found here.

▶▶ **Gatehouse of Fleet** 98B1

Peaceful in pastel colors, Gatehouse of Fleet, on the edge of the hills, was founded in the 1760s as a mill community, competing with others in the English counties of Yorkshire and Lancashire. Looming over the access road (A75) just southwest is the 15th-century **Cardoness Castle**, a typically austere tower house. B796 north out of Gatehouse offers a flavor of the empty hinterland and high hills of Galloway, as well as a long view to the viaduct over the Big Water of Fleet (part of the now abandoned "Port Road," the Dumfries–Stranraer railroad). Use this road if you are visiting the Gem Rock Museum at Creetown; it is a much more attractive drive than A75.

Peter Anderson Woolen Mill

An old bridge
Haddington's picturesque Nungate Bridge is a bridge with a past. Referred to as early as the 13th century, it has seen many alterations over the years, as the different colors of its stonework suggest.

114

The Queen's Way
A712 between Newton Stewart and New Galloway, as it passes through the Galloway Forest Park, is known as the Queen's Way. The original Queen's Way was the old pilgrim road used by Mary, Queen of Scots, among many other monarchs, which led down to Whithorn (see page 120).

Outdoor refreshments by the Tyne, Haddington

Mill on the Fleet▶▶▶ A visitor center in a former bobbin mill tells the tale of Gatehouse's cotton spinning, offering a high-tech interpretation. Visitors are given hard hats, inside which are tiny loudspeakers activated at various points in the displays to provide commentary. This can be a little disconcerting, but the home-baked scones (tea biscuits) in the café downstairs more than compensate. *Open*: April to September.

Galloway landscape

▶▶▶ Haddington 99D4

One of the most pleasing towns of the Lothians, the counties surrounding Edinburgh, Haddington was the former administrative headquarters of the old county, and for centuries played an important part in Lothian affairs. A 12th-century royal burgh (town), it also lay at the center of one of the most favored agricultural regions of Scotland, and had continental trade through the now silted-up port of Aberlady to the north.

Today, it retains its triangular medieval street plan, and the fine, mainly Georgian, buildings in the center of town have been preserved and carefully painted to create a coordinated and harmonious façade along High Street rivaled by few other Scottish towns. The air of a prosperous old community is enhanced by other trappings of a Scottish burgh: the impressive town house originally built by William Adam, the market cross, the courthouse, and the 14th- to 15th-century St. Mary's Church, with its warm, red stones reflected in the river. This is a town to study at a slow pace, admiring the detailing of wrought-iron balconies, ornamental urns, cornice decoration, and so on. Note also the small passageways running off the main thoroughfares. Tucked around a corner in Sidegate, a plaque at eye level records the exact heights of the River Tyne floods: the last big one was in 1948.

Scottish tweed
The traditional explanation for the name "tweed" is that a merchant in London received a consignment of Scottish cloth and misread the word "tweel" (twill). Because of the River Tweed, the name stuck. This is probably a myth, though at least two Scottish tweed mills claim they sent the consignment. There is a written reference from Aberdeen in 1541 to "small twedlyne"—tweedling. According to philologists, the words tweel and tweeling, tweed and tweedling have been around a long time, and have nothing to do with rivers. Besides, the traditional version does not explain Harris tweed, given that Harris in the Outer Hebrides islands in the northeast is so far away.

A long ride
Mary, Queen of Scots rode from Jedburgh to Hermitage Castle and back in a day, just over 50 miles, to visit the wounded Earl of Bothwell. Though this is sometimes romantically described as a foolhardy venture undertaken on her own, it was not in fact unusual to cover such a distance in a day, and besides, the queen was in company with many members of her court and a squad of soldiers. Far from mad with love for Bothwell, Mary undertook the journey for good political reasons, as he was a trusted lieutenant on border matters.

▶ **Hawick**   99D2

Hawick is the largest of the Borders towns. Perhaps workaday rather than handsome, it is a kind of no-nonsense place getting on with its own affairs. Its long and bustling main street is worth a browse for woolen shops with keenly priced cashmeres.

At one end is **Drumlanrig's Tower**, above the tourist information center. It portrays the local history of the area. A few minutes' walk away, **Wilton Lodge Park** is also attractive, with Victorian walled gardens and its own museum and art gallery.

▶ **Hermitage Castle**   99D2

Off B6399 in bleak and lonely Borders country, the grimness of Hermitage Castle echoes the emptiness around. High in atmosphere, reeking of the violence of the medieval Borderlands, Hermitage is particularly impressive if the clouds are low on the hills. One of the tales about this 14th-century keep, or fortress, concerns the wicked Lord Soulis, who was so cruel that the locals eventually revolted, wrapped him in lead, and boiled him to death in a cauldron. *Open*: daily, but only on weekends in winter.

▶ **Innerleithen**   99D3

A compact mill town by the confluence of the Leithen Water with the mighty Tweed, Innerleithen is home to some famous knitwear names, notably Ballantynes. Sir Walter Scott used it as the setting for his novel *St. Ronan's Well* (1821).

Robert Smail's Printing Works▶▶▶, run by the National Trust for Scotland, is perhaps the main attraction within the town. The local printers, which served the community for well over a hundred years, remained in the original family hands until purchased by the Trust in 1986. The Victorian office, paper store, composing room, and machine room all survived as a unique time capsule. Most importantly, so did 50 "guard books"—the complete record of every item ever printed at the works, as well as endless ephemera from the past. There are now print demonstrations and a shop (all closed in winter).

Just minutes away to the south is one of the most interesting grand homes in the Borders. **Traquair House**▶▶▶ boasts that it is the oldest continuously inhabited house in Scotland, and that it has been associated with the Stuarts or Maxwell-Stuarts, the Lairds (lords) of Traquair, since 1491. Before that it was a hunting lodge used by Scottish monarchs. Over the centuries it has been transformed from a grim Borders keep to a stately mansion, and has remained practically unchanged since the end of the 17th century. Curiously, for a house occupied by frequent holders of high office during Scotland's troubled past, the mansion only once

A Borders' time capsule

St. Ronan's Well
The sulfurous waters of St. Ronan's Well were said to be particularly effective for "ladies desirous of becoming in an interesting condition." According to local legend, the sulfur content is the result of the local holy man, St. Ronan, catching the Deil (Devil) with his shepherd's crook and immersing him in the waters.

Traquair Castle

Traquair coat of arms

The closed gate
Traquair House has two parallel drives, one of them ending at permanently closed gates. When Bonnie Prince Charlie rode out after a visit to Traquair in the autumn of 1745, the 5th Earl wished him success and closed the gates behind him, vowing they would never be opened again until a Stuart was on the throne.

saw violence—in 1688, when a mob from Peebles stormed the building and destroyed religious artifacts.

The lairds were staunch Catholics, which is why the house has a secret staircase intended as a quick escape route for priests. As Catholics, they were also Jacobites. A total of 27 Scottish and English monarchs have been guests at Traquair, and Bonnie Prince Charlie is said to have visited. Family lore and the paraphernalia and treasures of generations, including notable Mary, Queen of Scots's relics, are further attractions of the house, which is also pleasantly unintimidating in scale. If there is only time for one Borders house, then make it Traquair. *Open*: daily in the main tourist season.

Irvine   98B3

Scattered around the riverside area of the New Town of Irvine, the **Scottish Maritime Museum**▶ has a variety of craft, including a lifeboat, a tug, and a puffer (an inshore supply boat) moored in the harbor by floating pontoons, an undercover exhibition, a typical shipyard worker's cottage, and a Victorian boat shed, the largest of its kind ever built. This latter used to be on the Clyde, and was reconstructed here, brick by brick. (*Open*: daily from April to October.) A ferry runs from nearby Ardrossan to Brodick on the Isle of Arran (see page 230).

A historic heckler
In the old part of Irvine is the Glasgow Vennel, formerly the main road out of town. Robert Burns came here to learn to dress flax, a process known as heckling. (Hecklers tended to be politically argumentative types, hence the modern usage.) The venture came to an end when Burns's partner's wife dropped a candle during a drunken Hogmanay Party. The dried flax caught fire and the business was burned down. The thatched Heckling Shop has been restored, along with Burns's lodgings nearby.

Mercat (market) Cross, Jedburgh

Kelso Abbey

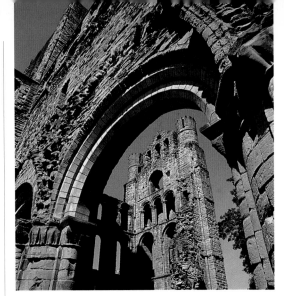

►► Jedburgh   99D3

Jedburgh, on A68, is the first Scottish town at which many visitors pause. It is a typical Borders town, with a history of tweed making. The local weavers were the first to combine two colors in their weave, thus inventing the cloth. Even the tourist information center and parking lot is on the site of a former mill. The original woolen developments were centered around the activities of the monks in the Borders' abbeys, of which Jedburgh's abbey is the best preserved.

The shell of the once great building of **Jedburgh Abbey►►►** still dominates the town skyline, though it was destroyed by English forces during the "rough wooing" (see page 30). The Abbey Visitor Centre makes an excellent introduction to the vanished monastic life of the Borders. Also of note in the town is Mary, Queen of Scots' House, a near-contemporary fortified or "bastel" (like the French *bastille*) house, now a museum (*open*: daily, Easter to mid-November). The former prison, on the site of the vanished castle (Castle Jail), was once a Georgian model prison, but is now another museum (*open*: daily in summer). The town has further associations with Sir Walter Scott and Bonnie Prince Charlie—actually, every historic figure who crossed over the border seems to have stopped at Jedburgh, including the Wordsworths.

A flattering description
With its long waterfront, Lord Cockburn described Kirkcudbright as "the Venice of Scotland." Clearly, he never saw it with the tide out.

The Union Canal
Linlithgow is a good place to discover the Union Canal, ideal for strolls along the towpath. There is an impressive aqueduct about 2 miles to the west. Linlithgow has a canal museum and cruising opportunities. Inquire on weekends in summer.

►► Kelso   99E3

When the writer H.V. Morton passed this way in the 1920s, he was struck by the appearance of the main square in Kelso. "Surely I was in France! An enormous *grande place* paved with whinstone forms the heart of the town. Round it rise those tall, demure, many-storied houses, which seem to know almost as many stories as a concierge." Little has changed in the intervening years, except the traffic in this market town. Stroll from the square past the poignant fragment of **Kelso Abbey**, which was severely damaged by the Earl of Hertford's forces in 1545. All 112 inhabitants were slaughtered. The tourist information center and the local museum are almost opposite. Rennie's handsome bridge of 1803 spans the Tweed just a little farther on. From the parapet there is a fine view to **Floors Castle►**, the largest inhabited house in Scotland. It offers glittering excesses of fine French furniture, porcelain, paintings, and tapestries, as well as extensive parkland and walks. *Open*: daily, from Easter until end September.

Mellerstain House►►, an attractive Robert Adam mansion with fine views, to the northwest of Kelso, has typically ornate Adam plasterwork and decoration (*open*: daily, except Saturdays in summer).

►►► Kirkcudbright   98B1

Pronounced "kir-*coo*-bree," Kirkcudbright has a typically spacious Galloway layout, and its genteel, brightly painted Georgian streetscapes give it a dignified and harmonious air. The 16th-century **Maclellan's Castle** is a ruined turreted mansion conspicuous on the skyline, and an exception to the prevailing 18th-century work.

There are a few antiques shops to browse around, as well as the Harbour Gallery, though the main artistic connection is **Broughton House**, with its collection of the works of Edward Hornel (1864–1933) of the artistic set known as the "Glasgow Boys." The picturesque Tolbooth and mercat (market) cross complete the harmonious groupings within this Solway town, which has one other pleasing feature: **The Stewartry Museum►►** is a traditional museum with no high-tech embellishments. Visitors can discover the Dorothy L. Sayers connection (see panel) and find out why the founder of the American navy was once locked in the local tolbooth. *Open*: Monday to Saturday from March to October, also Sunday afternoons from June to September; open Saturdays only in winter.

Five Red Herrings
The renowned English detective novelist Dorothy L. Sayers had two aunts and an uncle in Kirkcudbright. She used the local area as a setting for one of her Lord Peter Wimsey novels, *Five Red Herrings*, published in 1931. Another and more famous work set in Galloway—at least in part—is John Buchan's *The Thirty-Nine Steps* (published in 1915).

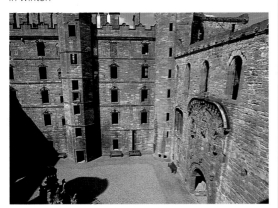

Linlithgow Palace

►   Linlithgow Palace   98C4

Birthplace of Mary, Queen of Scots, this once magnificent royal palace is now a cold shell. It was burned, probably accidentally, by Hanoverian troops during the last Jacobite rebellion in 1745. It is worth a diversion from M90, and a visit can be combined with a look at nearby St. Michael's Church, the largest surviving pre-Reformation church in Scotland.

THE SOUTH

Logan Botanic Garden

►► **Logan Botanic Garden**   98A1

Galloway trumpets its prevailing mildness to persuade visitors to stay. Nowhere is the benign influence of the North Atlantic Drift more apparent than in Logan Botanic Garden. This specialist garden of the Royal Botanic Garden in Edinburgh specializes in tender plants that would not survive in other parts of Scotland. It has a great deal of success with the arrestingly exotic Australasian tree ferns, as well as cabbage palms and a whole range of temperamental Southern Hemisphere species. *Open*: daily, mid-March to October.

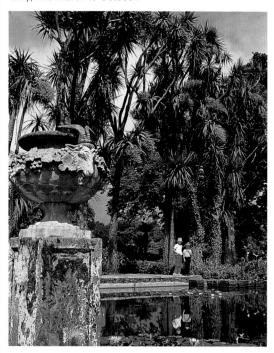

►► **The Machars**   98B1

Lush green is the key color of the Machars, to which are added the black and white of cattle in the pasture and the yellow splash of gorse on the little rough hillocks. This is gentle, rolling countryside, with the big hills of Galloway receding to the north. A triangle lying between Wigtown Bay and Luce Bay, the Machars are sometimes overlooked but have a curious serenity. Perhaps this echoes their early religious links. Here, at Whithorn, not at Iona, is the cradle of Christianity in Britain.

Whithorn Dig and Visitor Centre►► This archeological attraction is on the site of the first Christian community in Scotland, and displays material dating from AD 400 that was dug up on the site. The ruined Whithorn Priory and a museum are adjacent. Whithorn became a place of pilgrimage for the Scottish kings. The complex is open daily from April until the end of October.

Whithorn is associated with St. Ninian. His chapel on a grassy headland at Isle of Whithorn (not actually an island) is an anticlimax, though his cave makes a worthwhile walk down a lane and along the pebbly shore. The town of Wigtown is also attractive, with a wide main street. It is associated with the drowning of two Covenanter martyrs, tied to a stake before the incoming tide in 1685. You can visit the site, down by the endless mudflats of the shore.

►►► Melrose 99D3

Melrose is cozy and handsomely rustic, almost too neat to be true. It has an abbey, romantically ruined in red sandstone, visible from the road (*open*: daily, all year). Next door, the National Trust for Scotland sells various gifts and dried flowers grown in Priorwood Garden (*open*: garden, April to December; shop open all year). There is also a car museum, and plenty of gift and clothes shops. Melrose is overshadowed by the beautiful Eildon Hills, where an energetic walk (starting across the golf course) offers outstanding views.

Trimontium Exhibition►► This is a fascinating account of one of the Romans' main forts in Scotland, just a few fields away at Newstead, though unfortunately nothing is apparent on the site. The exhibition is closed in winter. Alternatively, there are a number of excursions from Melrose, including Dryburgh Abbey and Scott's View (see page 126).

A grim reminder of the Covenanters

121

Near Wigtown, River Bladnoch

A good location
Why did the Romans build their main fort at Trimontium? According to the Trimontium Exhibition in Melrose, when the legions came over the Cheviot Hills, they made for the most conspicuous landmark, the triple-peaked Eildon Hills, instantly recognizable from any angle, and right in the center of southern Scotland.

► Moffat 98C2

The ram statue on the Colvin Fountain in the middle of the town square is a reminder of Moffat's origins in the wool trade, though it also had a reputation in the 18th century as a spa town. The woolen bargains at Moffat Weavers at the southern end of town are popular with tourists. Moffat is on A701, a scenic route to Edinburgh known as "the Beeftub road." As well as the **Devil's Beeftub**, a hollow carved out by a glacier at the head of the valley, there are more glaciation features to be seen to the northeast, up the Moffat Water by A708. This passes the Grey Mare's Tail, a geologically classic waterfall pouring over the lip of a hanging valley. Hardy walkers can penetrate beyond the waterfall, either to circle around Loch Skeen or to reach the broad rounded summit of **White Coomb**, at 2,550 feet one of the highest hills in the whole of the Southern Uplands.

► ► **New Abbey**   *98C1*

New Abbey is a little village on A710, dominated by the red ruins of Sweetheart Abbey. This religious seat was found- ed in 1273 by Devorgilla, wife of John Balliol (see page 28). On his death she had his heart embalmed in an ivory and silver casket, hence the abbey's name. The abbey suffered from its proximity to the border in the Wars of Independence. During the Protestant Reform- ation its riches were disposed of, and the building gradually deteriorated. Today, visitors can enjoy a peaceful stroll through the pointed Gothic ruins. The 18th-century **New Abbey Corn Mill**► is moments away from the abbey. The great grinding stones, powered by water via an impressive set of gearing, produce oatmeal of various grades. You can visit both

attractions (*open*: daily in summer, closed Thursday after- noons and Fridays in winter). Walk a bit farther to reach the **Shambellie House Museum of Costume**, an outstation of the Royal Museum of Scotland. It shows material from the National Costume Collection (*open*: daily in summer, closed in winter).

Shambellie House Museum of Costume

► ► ► **New Lanark and the Falls of Clyde**   *98C3*

The River Clyde seems a world away from its down- stream industry here amid the farms and orchards of Lanarkshire, on the edge of the hills. It roars through a wooded gorge over spectacular waterfalls ("linns") in a setting unique in Scotland. This alone would be well worth the detour, but it is only one part of the experience. The river was harnessed to power cotton mills in an unusual experiment in workers' welfare. The model village of New Lanark has survived intact, and there is a visitor center within the mill complex, open all year.

New Abbey Corn Mill

New Lanark

■ **A remarkable industrial and social experiment took place in the upper reaches of the River Clyde in the late 18th and early 19th centuries. Two hundred years later, there is still a great deal for the modern visitor to see ...■**

In 1783, a successful Glasgow businessman, David Dale, bought this wooded bowl with its roaring river as a potential site for a spinning mill. Before the end of the century, New Lanark had become the single largest industrial enterprise in Scotland. Some of the river's force was diverted, a little way downstream, to turn giant waterwheels that, with belts and drives, powered noisy cotton looms housed in vast mill buildings. In 1793, over 1,100 employees tended these machines, of whom 800 were young boys and girls.

Social benefits Dale the master was no despotic employer. Hours were long, but substantial housing was provided as well as educational facilities. Many of his child workers were orphans who were, by the standards of the day, well fed and cared for. Another source of workers was Highland emigration: New Lanark employed people who would otherwise have headed for the New World because of repression and depressed economic conditions in their native lands to the north.

The Falls of Clyde
The waterfalls that comprise the Falls of Clyde are in a delightful wooded river gorge, and are well worth the walk upstream. (Go through the gap in the wall at the far end of the village.) Some of the water is diverted through tunnels to run a hydroelectric power station. When this is not operating, for example during station maintenance work, the falls are at their best. However, even with a reduced flow, they are still extremely impressive.

Bell tower on New Buildings, New Lanark

Robert Owen

123

Robert Owen This Welshman was born in 1771 (32 years after Dale), and also made his way in the spinning industry. He had strong ideas about equality and social welfare. In 1799, he married David Dale's daughter. Along with two partners, he then bought New Lanark and assumed management in 1800. Already embodying principles of welfare and worker care, the model village became the setting for Owen's own social experiments and even more benevolent management style.

After some business vicissitudes in the early years of the 19th century, Owen was able to put his principles into practice with new Quaker backers. To the four great mills and blocks of workers' houses were added the New Institute for the Formation of Character (1816) and Robert Owen's School (1817), as the first steps in the creation of his vision of a society without crime, poverty, or misery—the fundamentals of "Owenism."

No care for trees
Neidpath Castle eventually came into the hands of the Douglas Earls of March. The 3rd Earl inherited it but cared little for this country property, instead leading a spendthrift life in London. He even sold for timber a fine stand of ornamental trees planted by his father and grandfather. This vandalism was subsequently condemned by William Wordsworth's *Sonnet Composed at Neidpath Castle.* "Degenerate Douglas! oh the unworthy Lord!"

Traditional iron-mongers, Peebles

▶ **Newton Stewart** 98B1

A kind of gateway between the Machars and the Galloway Forest Park, Newton Stewart has a good range of shops (including antiques shops) along its long main street. Nearby, the Wood of Cree is a Royal Society for the Protection of Birds nature reserve, preserving in its 525 acres the largest oak wood left in the southwest. Species include several summer warblers, plus dippers and gray wagtails. The scenically outstanding Glen Trool road (see page 114) is easily reached from the town.

▶▶ **North Berwick** 99D4

Within easy commuting range of Edinburgh, North Berwick has developed from a small fishing port into a resort. Its little harbor is jammed with pleasure craft, its harbor-front granary is converted to apartments, and its Victorian and Edwardian architecture likewise suggest prosperity. The golf course reaches almost to the center of town. Behind the town is the conspicuous cone of the North **Berwick Law**, a 580-foot volcanic plug. Views from the top are excellent and take in the Bell Rock Lighthouse, off the fishing port of Arbroath in Angus, east Scotland. North Berwick gives easy access to some fine coastline, notably westward along the sands toward Yellowcraigs (see page 111). East of the town, on the way to Tantallon, is another good beach at Seacliff. Other nearby attractions include the historic aircraft collection at the **Museum of Flight** at East Fortune (*open*: daily in summer only).

Tantallon Castle▶▶▶ This 14th-century former Douglas stronghold straddles a headland, a grim, fortified wall of eroded red sandstone, with the Bass Rock as a backdrop beyond. *Open*: daily all year, except Thursday afternoons and Fridays in winter.

▶▶ **Peebles** 99D3

Respectable, well-scrubbed Peebles is well within day-trip range from Edinburgh, and is accordingly busy throughout the year. There is a good choice of shops for antiques and fashions, and probably the best old-fashioned ironmonger (hardware store) in Scotland. The town was the birthplace of William and Robert Chambers, compilers of *Chambers Dictionaries*. After making their fortune in Edinburgh, they endowed their hometown with the impressive municipal buildings on the main street, now housing a library and museum.

Neidpath Castle▶▶ A few minutes west of the town, this stronghold can be reached on foot along the River Tweed as a pleasant alternative to going by car. An L-plan tower house, originally built by the Hayes family, Neidpath has survived remarkably intact. It was "modernized" for comfort in the 17th century, though retaining its medieval outward appearance, but fell into decay by the early 19th century. It was restored by the present owners, the Earls of Wemyss (*open*: daily in the main season).

▶▶ **Rosslyn Chapel** 99D3

The best example of medieval stone carving in Scotland (if not Britain) can be found a few minutes' stroll beyond the former mining village of Roslin. Perched above the wooded Roslin Glen, Rosslyn Chapel was founded in 1446 by William Sinclair, 3rd Earl of Orkney. The church, still used as a place of worship, is really only the choir of a much larger design, which was never completed. It is associated with Scott's romantic poem *The Lay of the Last Minstrel*. There are fine wooded walks from the site, with both Rosslyn Castle and Hawthornden (both private) hidden in the glen below. The chapel is open daily (restricted hours in winter).

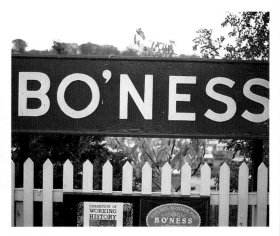

▶▶ **Scottish Railway Preservation Society (Bo'ness and Kinneil Railway)** 98C4

At Bo'ness on the River Forth, a typical Scottish branch line has been re-created, offering a 4-mile trip uphill to Birkhill (with extensions likely) where a former clay mine can be visited. It captures the feel of a vanished age, and could be tied in with a trip to Linlithgow. It is open every weekend in the summer, plus "bank holiday" Mondays (public holidays), with other openings in peak season and "Santa Special" weekends in December.

"Maude" (former Class J36) at Bo'ness

Literary visitors
Rosslyn Inn (now a private house), adjacent to the chapel, was the main lodging for many famous folk who came to see the wonders of the place. The Wordsworths stayed here, leaving very early to visit Sir Walter Scott at his first marital home at nearby Lasswade (the Scotts were still in bed when they arrived). Before that, Robert Burns stayed, and English lexicographer Dr. Samuel Johnson and his biographer James Boswell took lunch and tea here.

A branch line— re-created

Bass Rock birds
The gannet's Latin name, *Sula bassana*, recalls its long association with the Bass Rock. Gannets occupy about 14,000 nest sites on the Bass. There are smaller numbers of kittiwakes, guillemots, razorbills, and puffins. Boat trips go from North Berwick.

Drive **Border views and abbeys**

The river valleys and rounded hills of the Borders make rewarding country for touring. This route is 40 miles long, and easily driven in a day if no diversions are taken.

Smailholm Tower for Borders views

Take A68 north from Jedburgh, then B6400 heading east. The unmistakable high tower of the **Waterloo Monument**, which can be seen on an ancient earthwork, was raised in 1815 on the instructions of William Kerr, 6th Marquis of Lothian.

Continue past the modern village of Roxburgh, to reach **Kelso** with its ruined abbey.

Take B6364 northward, and soon you will see a dark square of battlements rising ahead. Take a minor road to Hume. Built by Lord Hume in the 1790s on the site of the original **Hume Castle**, the site offers one of Scotland's best views.

Travel west to cross A6089 at a staggered crossroads for the view from **Smailholm Tower**, a 16th-century fortified Borders keep (fortress) associated with Sir Walter Scott. Then drop gently down westward to find signs for the peaceful riverside **Dryburgh Abbey**.

Scott's View, Scott's favorite viewpoint for the Eildon Hills, is signposted. The minor road leads to A68 and Melrose, with its abbey. You can either detour to Selkirk, or return to Jedburgh on A68.

▶ **Scottish Mining Museum** 99D3

The former Lady Victoria Colliery (coal mine and associated works) is in the former mining village of Newtongrange, at one time the largest of its kind in Scotland. Pit and village were under the sway of domineering pit managers, a story told by tableaus that follow the career of a typical miner. There is also an impressive steam winding engine. Industrial heritage enthusiasts can also take a coal trail down to Prestongrange on the coast near Musselburgh, where there are other mining artifacts. The museum is closed in winter.

A vanished way of life at Newtongrange

▶▶ **Selkirk** 99D3

Sir Walter Scott presided as sheriff in Selkirk, and his **Courtroom** (*open*: daily in summer, except Tuesday) tells of his life, writings, and time as a judge. **Halliwell's House**▶▶ was once an ironmonger's; it is now a museum with plenty to be learned, especially about the Common Ridings. Ask to see the excellent videos giving an insight into this important Borders tradition (*open*: April to October). **Abbotsford House** is nearby (see page 102).

▶ **South Queensferry** 98C4

South Queensferry makes a pleasant evening excursion from Edinburgh to view the great bridges that dominate the skyline upriver and downriver. Alternatively, tie it in with a day visit to the overblown opulence of **Hopetoun House**▶ to the west, where the architects William and John Adam created a spectacular mansion that is now filled with valuables (*open*: daily in summer). South Queensferry is also only minutes from **Dalmeny House**, where porcelain from the Rothschild Mentmore collection is among an impressive range of items on display (*open*: on summer afternoons, Sunday to Tuesday).

"King Coal" now a museum

Open everyday
April - September 11.00-4.00
Guided tours, exhibitions
shop, cafe.

The Forth Rail Bridge

■ **The estuary of the Forth was the last great challenge of the Victorian railroad age. In 1873, the railroad companies of the east coast trunk route oversaw the laying of a foundation stone for a Forth Bridge designed by Sir Thomas Bouch. But then the Tay Bridge—which he had designed—fell, and his plans for the Forth were abandoned ...■**

Maintenance costs
The phrase "painting the Forth bridge" has passed into common usage to describe a never-ending job. The painting area has been estimated as 146 acres, and 8,403 gallons of Forth Bridge oxide of iron brushing paint are needed to coat it from end to end. Originally, many of the bridge painters were ex-sailing ship crew, accustomed to shinning up and down holding only a rope. Today, hydraulic lifts and cradles are used. In 1993, the press reported that because of cutbacks, British Rail would no longer be able to paint the bridge continuously.

The Forth Bridge, impressive from every angle

A new design was supplied by Benjamin Baker of the engineering company Fowler and Baker. This was based on the cantilever principle, invented in the Far East, and used steel instead of the treacherous cast iron of the first Tay Bridge. The contract for the work was signed in 1882, with William Arrol as the main contractor.

Building progress The next four years were taken up with building the cofferdams, sinking the caissons (water-tight chambers used for laying foundations underwater), and building the piers on which the immense weight of steel would rest. The superstructure was built in the following four years. While the first Tay bridge has sometimes been described as an optimist's bridge, the Forth is a pessimist's bridge. The engineers were all too aware of the effects of lateral wind pressure, which had been the downfall of the Tay design. Exhaustive scale-model tests were carried out, and all the various calculations were based on a "worst-case scenario"—the freakish situation in which a hurricane blew up one side of the Forth and down the other.

Facts and figures The bridge was opened in March 1890. It cost 57 lives during construction (and still proves an endless source of astonishing statistics, not the least curious of which is the fact that the bridge is almost a yard longer on a hot summer day than in midwinter). It had consumed 60,346 tons of steel, 194,273 cubic yards of granite (on the approach viaducts), 23,463 tons of cement, and almost 7 million rivets. The last one was banged into place by the Prince of Wales at a spot marked by a plaque. It was the monument of the age.

128

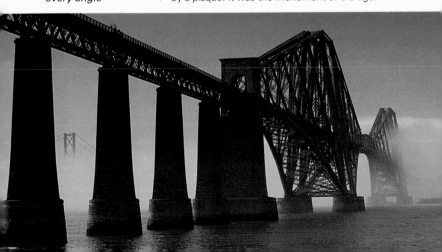

▶▶▶ St. Abbs   99E4

The great seabird colonies of northern Scotland, particularly Shetland, are justly famous. But there is one place in southern Scotland where, for very little effort, in May and June in particular, a spectacular "bird city" can be seen that rivals anything the north can offer. The cliffs and stacks of St. Abbs Head are favored by 10,000 guillemots alone. This portly, penguin-like auk is just one of the many species that make the experience a cacophony of noise, sound, and, not least, smell (a distinctly fishy one). Razorbills, fulmars, and kittiwakes add to the din. The cliffs can be viewed with relative ease, as some of them are offshore stacks. If time permits, walk the whole length of the path from the Northfield Farm parking lot to the lighthouse, starting at the eastern end to walk counterclockwise around the reserve. There are magnificent sea views all the way, with the biggest seabird colonies bursting into view by the lighthouse itself. Bird-watchers haunt the spot at autumn migration time as well. There are lots of rare birds—ask the warden for details.

Bird species
St. Abbs Head specialties in autumn migration include sooty and manx shearwaters, and arctic and great skuas. Summertime sees plenty of gannets going to and from the Bass Rock breeding grounds near North Berwick.

Early charity
More than one grand duke made money from the lead mines at Wanlockhead. The Hopetoun estates were involved at nearby Leadhills. In the early 19th century, the Wanlockhead proprietor, the Duke of Buccleuch and Queensberry (owner of Drumlanrig Castle), passed through and gave £5 ($7.50) to the miners to drink to his health. Instead they "considered they should testify their respect and gratitude by making the £5 the commencement of a charitable fund for the relief of miners when sick, or rendered unfit for work by age, as also for the benefit of their widows." Whether or not this gave the duke food for thought is not recorded.

St. Abbs, mecca for divers

▶ Wanlockhead   98C2

Wanlockhead is Scotland's highest village, though it is a considerable distance from the Highlands. It stands among the bald, bleak domes of the Lowther Hills, a strange, almost claustrophobic, gathering of steep-sided glaciated hills buffering Strathclyde and Galloway. The Lowthers are cut by impressive road passes, notably the Dalveen and the Mennock, the latter leading to Wanlockhead and its neighbor, Leadhills.

Britain's most important nonferrous metal mining area used to be there, in the endless winds and open moors. Gold was found as early as the reign of King James IV, but lead made fortunes for the local landowners. The mine closed in the 1930s, a story told in the **Museum of the Scottish Lead Mining Industry** (*open:* April to October). There are several other historical threads to follow, ranging from the vanished branch line, once Britain's highest railway, to the Covenanters, whose strongholds were in these lonely heights.

Gulls on offshore rocks, St. Abbs

129

CENTRAL SCOTLAND

130

Nicoll Moncrief's gratitude seems to be as much to King James (VI of Scotland, I of England) as to God. This carving is in the village of Falkland

Central Scotland This region has two distinct characters because it bridges the Highland Line, or, more accurately, the Highland Boundary Fault. This is not just a geological distinction but a real divide between two cultures, Highland and Lowland, separated by a mountain barrier and, formerly, also by language and traditions.

It was in the Highland part of Central Scotland that the cult of the picturesque first took root. From the cities of the central belt, the first tourists admired the beauties of the Trossachs and Loch Lomond—not just because they were attractive, but also because they were the first bit of wild Scotland that was accessible from the Lowlands. This led to the growth of resort towns that still cater to visitors today: places such as Callander, Crieff, Dunkeld, and Pitlochry, all of which have long-established reputations as vacation spots in or near the Highlands.

The feeling of entering or leaving different cultures is an important element in the Central Scottish "experience." Ben Ledi looms at the end of Callander main street as a reminder that there is real grandeur beyond the cut-rate woolen mill sales. At Dunkeld, there is a strong sense of passing between the Highland portals. Alternatively, drive up any of the Angus glens—or follow back roads beyond Alyth—for a full flavor of the openness in the silent, rounded hills of the Grampian edge. From the unexpected drama of the Reekie Linn waterfall near Kirriemuir, Scotland's mini-Niagara smoking its way over a high

Romantic prospects
Though Sir Walter Scott is often said to have put the Trossachs on the tourist map, he was certainly not the first to discover them. As early as 1794, the Statistical Account of Scotland noted under the heading "Romantic Prospects" that "The Trossachs are often visited by persons of taste, who are desirous of seeing nature in her rudest and most unpolished state."

The heart of Scotland
Breadalbane is an ancient name for the heart of Scotland in central Perthshire. Crianlarich, Killin, and farther east, Aberfeldy, with all the high hills around, are considered to be within it. The name is derived from two Gaelic words: *braghaid*, the upper part, and *Alban*, Scotland, hence Breadalbane means "the uplands of Alban," an appropriate enough name for this wild country.

Viewing the fault line
Perhaps the best vantage point for viewing the Highland Boundary Fault is from the top of Conic Hill behind Balmaha on the shores of Loch Lomond. The climb can be made along a bit of the West Highland Way. From the hilltop, the fault line runs out and through the main Loch Lomond islands to the west, while it disappears eastward toward Callander. The pink and pebbly conglomerate rock is characteristic of the geology of the edge of the Highlands.

ledge, to the heights of Ben Lawers, Central Scotland's much trampled upon highest mountain, scenic drama can be found in abundance.

Yet Central Scotland is not without a very attractive Lowland character. Northeast Fife, with its long beaches backed by finely trimmed golf courses, seems a long way both from the Highlands and from the legacy of the Industrial Revolution. This portion of Fife missed out on the effects of industry, so plain in other parts of the Lowlands. Instead, it kept its essentially rural character. Its European heritage from its early trading links with the Low Countries is seen today in architecture, especially on the coast. Thus St. Andrews and the East Neuk of Fife have very distinct personalities, being Scottish without being either tartan or grimy. Angus, below the Grampians, is almost wholly rural, though here the hills are always a backdrop, forming one side of Strathmore, the long rural corridor that leads northeastward from Perth up to the Mearns on the edge of the old county of Kincardineshire.

Central Scotland's industrial background includes linoleum at Kirkcaldy, Dunfermline's specialized damask ware, and also industries based on the city of Dundee,

Rural Perthshire

still noted for its jam and its journalism. Brewing is still associated with Alloa in the old county of Clackmannan below the Ochil Hills. Perhaps the most interesting chunk of industrial heritage can be found at Culross overlooking the Forth, where a small Scottish burgh (town) seemed to be passed over by progress for more than two centuries until restoration.

Just as the shipyard workers of the industrial Glasgow of old would escape on weekends to the mountainous beauty of the Trossachs and the mill workers of Dundee would go northwest to the long Angus glens, so it is still the hills and mountains that inevitably call to visitors today. To take in the essence of Central Scotland, find a high point near the Highland edge: Callander Crags behind Callander, the highest section of the Duke's Road in the Trossachs, Dumyat (pronounced "De-_my_-att") behind Stirling, the delectable Duncryne Hill on the southern edge of Loch Lomond, or the Caterthun hill forts on a Grampian shoulder in Angus. Northward, waves of hills roll on to the end of Scotland. Southward is all the grit and liveliness of the Lowland towns. That is the essence of Central Scotland.

The Signal Tower
The Bell Rock lighthouse by Robert Stevenson was built on the Inchcape Rock, a reef submerged at high tide, about 11 miles southeast of Arbroath. It was first lit in 1811 and was a magnificent achievement for its day. To facilitate rock-to-shore communication when the lighthouse was under construction, a signal tower was built, which was also the shore base for the light. This is today's Signal Tower Museum, where the story is told in full.

▶▶ **Aberfeldy** 130B2

The largest settlement in the area known as Breadalbane, Aberfeldy is a pleasantly peaceful place, far enough removed from the rush of A9 to the east. It makes a good center for exploring the local walks and trails, notably along the Moness Burn (Creek) to view the "**Birks of Aberfeldy**" in the wooded den. These birch woods were made famous by Robert Burns, who penned the lyrics of the Scottish song of the same name after his Highland tour. Aberfeldy itself has a water mill and a distillery to visit. **Castle Menzies** is nearby to the northwest on B846 (*open*: daily, in the main season). This 16th-century fortified Z-plan tower is in the care of the Clan Menzies. To reach it by road means crossing the River Tay by the finest of General Wade's bridges (see panel). This handsome, five-arched, humpbacked structure was designed by the architect William Adam and built in 1733.

Arbroath 131D2

A salty, seagull-strafed, seacoast town, Arbroath in Angus is handsome in a workaday kind of way. It gave its name

Blair Castle

Wade's bridges
General Wade, the military road builder, built many fine bridges in Scotland, but none were so grand as his work at Aberfeldy. It was not to everyone's taste. Dorothy Wordsworth toured with her brother William in 1803 and, among many carping comments on things Scottish in her journal, she described how the party "crossed the Tay by a bridge of ambitious and ugly architecture. Many of the bridges in Scotland are so...."

to the Arbroath smokie, a smoked, split haddock. Smokies can be bought from several merchants in the narrow streets of the "fishing quarter." Arbroath mixes its fishing activities with the slightly time-warped air of a 1950s traditional Scottish holiday resort—not as dire as it sounds as there is very fine coastline to explore north of the town, as well as the hinterland of Angus within easy reach. In the center of the town stand the soft red sandstone walls of the 12th-century **Arbroath Abbey▶**, (*open*: daily), scene of important events in Scotland's history (see panel, page 135). Other aspects of the town's history are portrayed in the curious **Signal Tower Museum▶**, close to the harbor. By way of a change from maritime themes, the museum has a display on one of Arbroath's specialist industries: the manufacture of lawnmowers. The museum is open throughout the year, but is closed Sundays except in July and August. Contributing to the holiday air is **Kerr's Miniature Railway▶▶**. This ride-on track, open in the summer, running parallel to the high embankment of the adjacent main Edinburgh–Aberdeen railroad, has delighted generations, as photographs on the entrance kiosk reveal.

► **Balquhidder** *130B2*

The Braes (slopes) of Balquhidder and Balquhidder Glen, in which lie the long reaches of Loch Voil, are often missed by those rushing north on A84 from Callander. Once a place in which desperate men from broken clans fetched up and settled—though it was also the stronghold of the MacLarens and the Macgregors—the area around Balquhidder has glorious scenery that is worth exploring. Many people visit the **grave of Rob Roy** (see pages 136–7), in Balquhidder churchyard, something of an anticlimax, while others make their way to the end of the public road, in order to climb the choice of **Munros** (see panel, page 149 for definition) within easy reach. Another worthwhile walk is to hike up through the trees to the windy heights of Kirkton Glen (start by the church) where the little jewel of **Lochan nan Eireannaich** (loch of the Irish) sits below the crags of an old hill pass to Glen Dochart. Listen for the ring ouzel (the mountain blackbird) that sings here in summer.

► **Blair Atholl and Blair Castle** *130B3*

Blair Atholl is famed chiefly for **Blair Castle**►► whose white painted turrets are conspicuous from A9. The old established settlement that grew up near the castle also has a mill and a folk museum to visit. Blair Castle itself, the ancestral seat of the earls, then the dukes of Atholl, dates from at least 1269. There are many stories associated with it, particularly concerning its role in the Jacobite rebellion of 1745, and many rooms filled with the accumulated furniture and artifacts of centuries of continuous occuption. It is the archetypal Scottish castle, though you may tire of hearing that the Duke of Atholl, Chief of Clan Murray, was the only person in Britain allowed to keep a private army. The castle is closed in winter.

The Declaration of Arbroath
In the Scots Wars of Independence, the country's leading churchmen were firmly nationalist. In 1320, they met in Arbroath Abbey to write a famous document in Scotland's story, the Declaration of Arbroath. Its most widely quoted passage is: "For so long as a hundred of us shall remain alive we shall never accept subjection to the domination of the English. For we fight not for glory, or riches or honour, but for freedom alone which no good man will consent to lose but with his life."

135

The Falls of Bruar
North of Blair Castle, accessible from the old A9, these falls are within the extensive landholding of the Blair Charitable Trust. Robert Burns visited on his Highland tour and suggested to the Duke of Atholl that he might plant more trees to create even more beauty around the falls. The suggestion was taken up and the falls today are noted for their mature larch trees. A fairly steep uphill walk to a bridge with a commanding view makes a refreshing break from the awful driving often experienced on A9.

Fishing the River Tay by Aberfeldy

Detail, Castle Menzies, near Aberfeldy

The Bracklinn Falls

For a wager, Sir Walter Scott once rode a pony across the rickety old bridge that used to span the rocky gorge below the Bracklinn Falls. The bridge at the same point today is a much more substantial structure. Take care with children, however, on the slippery rocks and tree roots near the farther edge of the gorge, beyond the bridge.

Mill machinery, Keathbank Mill

▶ **Blairgowrie** *131C2*

A busy center with a good range of stores, Blairgowrie first prospered from the River Ericht as it powered its way out of the Highlands. Flax mills were built on its bank and by the early 19th century the town was booming. A second wave of prosperity followed after raspberry growing on a commercial scale was introduced. Today, the soft fruit (berries) crop is still important, with the long rows of raspberry canes in the surrounding fields looking a little like vineyards.

The old **Keathbank Mill**▶▶ (on the north side of the town off A93) has been converted into a visitor center. The waterwheel and machinery still turn to impress visitors with their awesome scale. Also on display is the largest model railroad in Britain—a complete "O-gauge" model of Norton Fitzwarren junction on the old Great Western Railway. There is a heraldry workshop, too, carving huge coats of arms. The center is open daily in the main season.

En route to the town, A93 is bordered for 1,700 feet just beyond the River Isla by the 100-foot high **Meikleour Beech Hedge**.

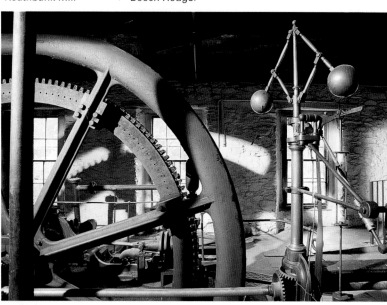

Berries

Around Blairgowrie and up into Strathmore is the largest berry growing area in the E.U., though under threat from Polish competition. Raspberries, as well as tayberries and loganberries and also strawberries, appreciate just the right combination of sunshine and moisture.

▶▶ **Callander** *130A2*

Right on the Highland edge, with Ben Ledi looming at the end of the main street, Callander seems busy throughout the year. The town's bustle is a reminder of its role as a gateway not just to the Highlands but specifically to the beauties of the Trossachs. The old village of Callander was rebuilt and extended after 1763, when the authorities took over the land of the Drummonds, the previous owners who forfeited them after the 1745 Jacobite rebellion. It is an example of early town planning, and soon took on its role of serving visitors which it has had ever since. Escape from the tartan wares of the shopping street to discover the **Bracklinn Falls**▶▶, a picturesque spot sign-

Walk The Bracklinn Falls

Only minutes from Callander's busy main street lies an escape on the very edge of the Highlands. Allow one hour to the Falls, or three hours for the Callander Crags circuit.

The Bracklinn Falls are signed north (right if coming from Stirling) up a street near the Roman Camp Hotel sign. If traveling by car, drive up this road, soon entering attractive mixed woodland for a short way until the Falls car park is seen on the right.

Take the level path running east from the parking area. Soon the pines flanking the path end, revealing a pleasing green vista back across the Lowlands. Continue through a double kissing gate, with the Falls sounding close at hand. Descend steps to a bridge over the white water. The path peters out on the far side, among the oak trees.

Retrace your steps. The energetic can walk uphill along the road from the car park, into open country with views north of an attractive glen. It is possible to circle back to Callander via the Callander Crags on the skyline, but you will need good walking shoes.

posted from the east side of the town (see the walk on this page). Slightly more demanding (for pedestrians) are the **Callander Crags►►**, overlooking a dense bowl of woodland immediately behind the town and threaded by sheltered paths. Waterfall and woodland can be combined in a single excursion by continuing farther up the signposted road into an attractive Highland glen.

Rob Roy and the Trossachs Visitor Centre►►, a modern tourist orientation center, interprets the life of Rob Roy Macgregor, Scotland's Robin Hood, by means of audiovisuals and fairly high-tech displays (including a talking cow). It also sets the folk hero firmly in the Trossachs landscapes (see page 160). *Open*: March to December and weekends in February.

►► The Caterthuns *131D3*
These 2,000-year-old ramparts are Scotland's prehistory at its best. To stand in the center of a great ring of broken stone with only a curlew call for company is certainly atmospheric. It is well worth the effort of seeking out this breezy high place on the shoulders of the Grampians near Edzell in Angus, with superb views to the Lowlands. The builders of the White and the Brown Catherthun hill forts must have been capable of organizing manpower in plenty to quarry and build such defenses, impressive even in ruin.

Callander's Rob Roy and Trossachs Visitor Centre is housed in a former church

Crieff Visitors' Centre, paperweights

Early industry
Throughout the 17th century, Culross claimed the monopoly through its trade guild on the manufacture of baking girdles (griddles). These are said to have been invented by the local smiths after King Robert the Bruce ordered them to provide iron plates so that his soldiers could cook their oatcakes.

The Palace, Culross

▶▶ Crieff 130B2

A town at the edge of the Highlands with a resort and retirement air, Crieff seems all hills. Until 1770 it was an important cattle market. It has also been a spa. At the lowest point of the town, by the River Earn on A822, is a cluster of commercial developments open to tourists. **The Crieff Visitor Centre▶** offers on-site manufacture and sale of, in one section, pottery and, in the other, glass paperweights. Opposite, **Stuart Crystal▶** is a shop aglitter with potential wedding presents of Stuart, Waterford, and Wedgwood wares. Both stay open throughout the year. Down the road a short way is the sunken Italian garden of **Drummond Castle▶**, where the formal terracing is ideal for leisurely strolling in the summer. A similar distance north of the town is the **Glenturret Distillery▶▶**, one of Scotland's oldest, offering the usual whisky (to use the Scots spelling) experience: tour, audiovisual program, and shop. *Open*: all year.

▶▶▶ Culross 130B1

Because of its very early involvement in coal mining and salt pans, Culross ought to have been just another nondescript industrial community on the banks of the Forth. Instead, after the town's early economic prosperity, the Industrial Revolution bypassed the town for a variety of economic reasons, and it was all but forgotten. Thus Culross entered the 20th century with many 17th- and 18th-century domestic buildings intact. This was appreciated by the infant National Trust for Scotland as early as the 1930s. Today, the streetscapes have been preserved, and the attractive dwellings with their red pantiled roofs restored. Cobbled streets and the old mercat (market) cross give the place the air of a movie set (which indeed it is on occasion), but this is a lived-in community. There are some interiors to see, notably the Culross **Palace** (really the town house) of Sir George Bruce, Culross's 16th-century entrepreneur. *Open*: April to October.

▶ Cupar 131C2

Cupar is a handsome enough, typical Lowland Scottish town, simply getting on with its business in the center of a rural and agricultural area, the Howe (hollow) of Fife. Cupar once made money with its linen manufacture and still maintains its role as the administrative headquarters of the old county of Fife. As well as exploring a network of pleasantly out-of-the-way rural roads, including a fine ridge route to Falkland (see page 145), it is worth visiting **Hill of Tarvit House**▶▶, an Edwardian mansion in the care of the National Trust for Scotland. The house opens at Easter, then, daily afternoons from May to September, and weekend afternoons in October. The grounds and garden are open all year.

▶▶ Deep Sea World 131C1

In this fishy panorama of a visitor center in North Queensferry, a moving walkway carries you unnervingly along an underwater transparent viewing tunnel where large sharks swim by. This is probably as close as you will ever get to knowing how a fish feels in an aquarium. There are also coral reef displays, rock pools to fumble in, and a variety of other marine exhibits. *Open*: daily.

▶▶ Doune 130B1

Doune was once the Scottish center for manufacturing pistols. Today, this little place with winding streets is chiefly visited by those going to **Doune Castle**▶▶▶, the finest surviving medieval castle in Scotland. Built in the 14th century by the powerful regent of Scotland, Robert Stewart, Duke of Albany, the fortress is built to a simple and strong plan: a formidable range of buildings surrounding an inner courtyard. Note the security features, such as a separate stairway for each main hallway and the duke's bedroom's emergency exit. As well as allowing the main quarters to be sealed off if intruders gained entry to the courtyard, the design acknowledges the need for some comfort: the guest bedrooms are built directly above the kitchen with its 18-foot-wide fireplace. *Open*: daily in summer, closed Thursday afternoon and Friday in winter.

Drove roads
The Crieff tryst ,or cattle market, was an important affair in the days when the Highland black cattle were walked from their pastures in various parts of Scotland to an annual autumn fair. Throughout the north there was a network of "drove roads" used by the cattle drovers. These old ways through the glens flowed together like tributaries and converged on major markets such as Crieff. The trade ended when railroads arrived and could move stock more quickly.

Doune Motor Museum houses the world's second-oldest Rolls Royce

The Doune Motor Museum
If you thought a MacPherson Strut was a kind of Highland fling, then a visit to one of Doune's attractions will clarify matters. The Doune Motor Museum is essentially the private collection of a car enthusiast, the Earl of Moray. The 40-odd vehicles in this custom-built museum include the second-oldest surviving Rolls Royce. The museum opens daily from April to November.

► **Dumbarton** 130A1

This town on the Clyde estuary is associated with ship-building, but is worth visiting for two very different features. The first of these, **Dumbarton Castle►**, is built on the natural defensive site of Dumbarton Rock, a volcanic plug. Though little remains from its early defensive days, the fortress is associated with Mary, Queen of Scots. She was held there in safety before her departure for France at the age of five. (*Open*: daily in summer, closed Thursday afternoon and Friday in winter.) The **Denny Ship Model Experiment Tank►►** was the world's first commercial experimental tank for ship-builders' scale models, built in 1882 by the local builders William Denny. The hulls of many famous vessels were designed and tested here, including the P & O's *Canberra*. *Open*: Monday to Saturday all year.

► **Dunblane** 130B1

The little town—or city, strictly speaking—of Dunblane on the Allan Water has winding streets and little shops and, thanks to a bypass, it is a peaceful kind of place, especially around the **cathedral►►**. The seat of the bishop of the Diocese of Dunblane since the 13th century, this place of worship is the usual Scottish mix of very early architecture and more recent restoration work. (The nave was roofless for 300 years until 1893.) It demands a slow walk around to examine the 15th-century misericords, early effigies, and other points of interest (*open*: daily).

Doune Castle (see page 139) is a few minutes to the west.

Dundee 131C2

Dundee is a puzzle. It sits on slopes facing south over the estuary of the River Tay, which is spanned by road and rail bridges. Its center is an uneasy mix of Victorian edifices, slashed by new roads and partly overshadowed by a covered shopping mall (neither better nor worse than those in other British cities). It is nearly as big as Aberdeen, but without the granite personality that makes Aberdeen instantly identifiable.

Dumbarton Castle
This is reckoned to be Scotland's oldest continuously fortified site. It was the capital of the kingdom of the Strathclyde Britons by the 5th century AD, and was later attacked by the Vikings. The name is derived from Dun-breattan—the fort of the Britons.

140

An ancient walk
The Darn Road is an ancient route (used by the Romans) that links Dunblane with Bridge of Allan for foot traffic. It makes a pleasant afternoon's walk. On the way, the path passes a cave overlooking the Allan Water, which is associated with Robert Louis Stevenson. He used to vacation nearby as a boy.

In Claypotts Castle, Dundee

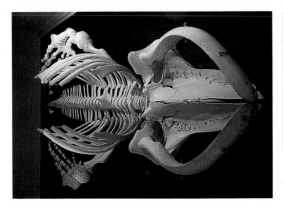

The great Tay whale in Dundee's Barrack Street Museum

The doggerel poet
William McGonagall (1830–1902), the Scottish doggerel poet, is strongly associated with Dundee. His uniformly bad verse soon met with acclaim, notably from the student and legal fraternity. His eulogies to the Tay Bridge and the stranding of the great Tay whale are just two occasions when his special talents (a complete disregard for meter in particular) were brought to bear.

141

Dundee is Scotland's fourth city, and promotes itself under the banner "City of Discovery." Yet it is not a natural visitor magnet. The "Discovery" part of its slogan is a reference to RRS (Royal Research Ship) **Discovery▶▶**, berthed permanently at the Discovery Point floating exhibition (*open*: daily). This was the vessel used by Captain Scott (of Antarctic fame) and built in Dundee in 1901 because of that city's expertise in building vessels for the whaling industry. The nearby frigate **Unicorn** is the oldest British warship still afloat. (She was built in Chatham, England in 1824.) Then there are Dundee's museums to investigate: the **Barrack Street Museum▶** (*open*: Monday to Saturday) with its natural history collection including the famous Tay Whale eulogized by the notorious William McGonagall, and the

Dunblane Cathedral, stained glass

McManus Galleries▶ (*open*: daily except Sundays), the city's municipal museum and art gallery focusing on local history.

Within the endless coastal suburbia that ends at the golf courses at Carnoustie is **Broughty Castle Museum▶** (*open*: daily, except Fridays and Sundays; also Sunday, July to September), with more tales to tell about whales and other local historical matters. Then there are the **Mills Observatory** (*open*: daily except Sundays), opened in 1935, and a candy factory in the style of the 1940s, also open to visitors, and country parks in the attractive Angus hinterlands. Yet the city still seems in transition—not quite embracing its heritage as an industry in itself, but uneasy that its odd historical mix of whaling, textiles, jam-making, and journalism will necessarily fire the imagination.

CENTRAL SCOTLAND

▶ Dunfermline *131C1*

"What Benares is to the Hindu, Mecca to the Mohammedan, Jerusalem to the Christian, all that Dunfermline is to me." Thus eulogized Dunfermline's most famous son, Andrew Carnegie. The Dunfermline of today is still full of Carnegie associations—it even has a Carnegie Hall—but this "auld grey toun" above the Forth goes much further back. It was the capital of Scotland in the time of the 11th-century king, Malcolm Canmore (the Gaelic *ceann mohr* means great head or chief). This Celtic warlord married Margaret of the English royal house after she was shipwrecked nearby while fleeing the Norman Conquest in 1070. Margaret was later canonized and under her good influence, Dunfermline became the religious center of Scotland.

Dunfermline Abbey▶, with its adjoining monastery and the royal palace, still survive, though both have been rebuilt over the centuries. Today, there is a strong sense of layers of history around the historic heart of the town, though sorting them out takes time. There are plenty of explanatory panels and models within the palace complex to clarify matters. (*Open*: daily except Sunday mornings; closed Thursday afternoon and Friday, October to March). The 12th-century work in the abbey church has been described as the finest surviving Scottish-Norman architecture in Scotland. King Robert the Bruce is buried here: the Victorians spelled out his name in great stone blocks on top of the church tower.

Andrew Carnegie Birthplace Museum▶▶ Dunfermline soon turned to commercial matters: brewing and weaving. Andrew Carnegie (1835–1919) was the son of a weaver who emigrated to the United States. In due course, Carnegie's business acumen in the steel industry made him rich enough to give away $350 million. Exactly how is told in this museum, which starts off modestly enough in the cottage of his birth. The adjacent Memorial Hall is filled with an extraordinary assemblage of Carnegie memorabilia, including a whole display case filled with "freedom caskets"—the ornate boxes in which grateful communities gave him the metaphorical keys to their towns and cities. (*Open*: daily, all year.)

Dunfermline's Carnegie Library was the first of nearly 3,000 worldwide. This and other amenities, including the

Andrew Carnegie in his Pittencrieff Park, Dunfermline

Industrial espionage
Dunfermline was already engaged in spinning when, at the beginning of the 18th century, some Huguenot master weavers set up in business in Edinburgh using a secret process which made attractive patterns on plain linen cloth. The new damask linen was a huge success. Dunfermline weaver James Blake masqueraded as a witless laborer, got himself a job cleaning the Huguenot looms, and memorized the process. The spy then built his own loom, laying the foundation for the Dunfermline damask linen industry.

Dunkeld "Little Houses" (private)

local museum, the Music Institute, the Carnegie Center (complete with ornate Turkish baths), and the substantial Pittencrieff Park all indicate the generosity of this extraordinary "local boy made good" who transformed his hometown from a gray workaday place into a well-resourced community. Dunfermline may not be the most picturesque of Scotland's towns, but it has an interesting story to tell. The abbey and museums are under cover, so it could be a place to visit on a rainy-day trip.

▶ 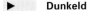 **Dunkeld** 131C2

A classic Highland edge community, Dunkeld has benefited environmentally (if not commercially) from the A9 bypass. As well as some shopping (including antiques) and the picturesque 18th-century "Little Houses," it also has Thomas Telford's handsome bridge, opened in 1809. This was a toll bridge, and the imposition of the toll caused riots in 1868. Downstream by a footpath is the Birnam oak, last

Carnegie's initials on Pittencrieff Park gates, Dunfermline

Literary inspiration
It was while vacationing in the Dunkeld area in 1893 and studying fungi that Beatrix Potter wrote an illustrated letter about a naughty and adventurous bunny to a young friend. The bunny became the famous Peter Rabbit, and an expert local amateur naturalist, Charles Mackintosh, the retired postman, is suspected of being the prototype for Mr. McGregor the gardener.

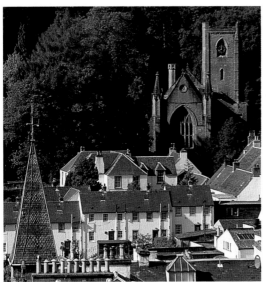

relic of Birnam Wood ("Macbeth shall never vanquished be until/Great Birnam wood to high Dunsinane hill/Shall come against him," prophesy the witches in Shakespeare's *Macbeth*). Dunkeld also has a cathedral, founded in the 12th century and wrecked at the Reformation. Its choir has been restored as the parish church. Walk up the wooded valley of the River Braan (on the opposite side of A9 to Dunkeld) to **the Hermitage▶▶**, the pleasure grounds of the dukes of Atholl. On the way, what might be the tallest tree in Scotland can be seen, a 200-foot-high Douglas fir. It grows in a hollow by the river at the foot of a slope, but it still looks impressive. The Hermitage is open at all times.

Loch of the Lowes▶▶ Accessible off a minor road on A923 above Dunkeld, this Scottish Wildlife Trust reserve is a gem of Highland-edge scenery and has ospreys in summer. The visitor center is open in summer only, but the observation blind is open all year.

Dunkeld Cathedral and "Little Houses"

The Hermitage Folly
Also known as Ossian's Hall, this was built in 1758 by the 2nd Duke of Atholl's nephew. The curious belvedere overlooks the roaring waters of the River Braan. By 1783, it had acquired a set of mirrors within: a pulley slid back a partition (a painting of Ossian) to reveal them and give the illusion of water pouring in from all directions. This aristocratic toy was not to everyone's taste. William Wordsworth visited and was appalled, and the place was vandalized in 1821 and again in 1869. The restored shell survives to this day.

Maintaining the fishing fleet, Pittenweem

East Neuk sign, Pittenweem

▶▶▶ East Neuk of Fife · 131D1

The chief attraction of the East Neuk of Fife, a land of well manicured golf courses, lush hedgerows, and rich barley fields and woods all set by a glittering sea, is its little string of coastal communities. The area can easily be reached from Edinburgh, and it makes a very worthwhile excursion in a day from St. Andrews (see page 154).

The eastern tip of Fife, Fife Ness, is not one of Scotland's most dramatic headlands, though bird-watchers enjoy it at migration time. However, nearby **Crail▶▶**, easternmost of the villages, is a pretty place with one of the most frequently photographed harbors in Scotland (wait for high tide). Old trading links with the Low Countries are echoed in the architecture, with crow-stepped gables and a Dutch-style town house whose bell, cast in 1520, has a Dutch inscription. There is also a good local museum.

Moving west, next comes **Anstruther▶**, with its sea-front stores selling colorful fishing nets and beach balls as a reminder of the traditional vacation trade. The **Scottish Fisheries Museum▶▶▶** overlooks the harbor, with a comprehensive presentation on the development of fishing in Scotland, from open boats right through to the most awesome modern catching machines. There are plenty of ship models, as well as the real thing (historic vessels float in the harbor). Children should enjoy the marine aquaria and tableaus full of authentic details, right down to the smell of tarry rope. This museum gives a very strong sense of the endless struggle, frequent tragedy, and foundations of prosperity of many east-coast communities. It is open all year.

Pittenweem▶▶ has a waterfront that has been tidied without being made overly pretty. It also offers plenty of challenge to the photographer torn between bright-hulled fishing boats and red pantiled houses. Up a lane near the harbor, the cave-shrine of St. Fillan can be found. The damp abode of an ancient saint is referred to in the name Pittenweem ("place of the cave").

Continuing west, you reach **St. Monance**, another community tied to the sea—its kirk could not stand any closer to the waves. In between these communities is a varied coastline of sand and rock.

Kellie Castle▶▶ is a short way inland. This National Trust for Scotland property dates mainly from the 16th and 17th centuries and was restored in Victorian times. Its walled garden is a peaceful scented haven in high summer and is worked organically. The grounds are open all year-round, though the castle itself is closed in winter.

▶ **Edzell**   *131D3*

Edzell slumbers happily behind its ornate arch commemorating Queen Victoria's visit, and is one of those out-of-the-way places where little ever seems to stir along the wide main street. However, there are a number of points of interest nearby. **Fasque House▶**, home of the family of the 19th-century prime minister W.E. Gladstone, is within easy reach, as are the **Caterthuns** (see page 137). **Edzell Castle▶▶** is also worth exploring, and is signposted from Edzell along a minor road. The early 16th-century red-stoned tower was a former Lindsay stronghold and features an unusual pleasance, or walled garden, with unique heraldic and symbolic sculptures. *Open*: throughout the year, except Thursday afternoon and Friday in winter.

Scots names
Howe in "Howe of Fife" means hollow. *Neuk* as in East Neuk, is the Scots for corner (hence nook).

An educational visit
Visit the Scottish Fisheries Museum and learn the difference between fifies, zulus, and scaffies (they are all different kinds of early fishing craft).

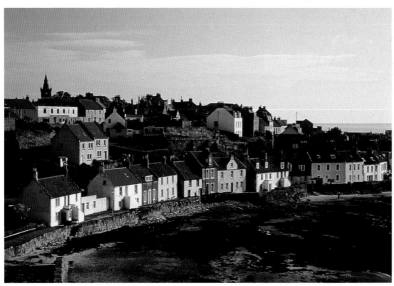

▶▶ **Falkland Palace**   *131C1*

The façade of this impressive Renaissance-style former hunting lodge (1501–41) of the Stuart monarchs dominates the main street and the handsome little cottages of Falkland, tucked below the Lomond Hills. Behind the castle are small but attractive gardens and a real (royal) tennis court dating from 1539 (said to be the oldest in Britain). The castle closes in winter.

Pittenweem

▶ **Fife Folk Museum**   *131C2*

Set in Ceres, the very essence of a rural northeast Fife village, this growing collection of artifacts showing Fife's rural past is housed in a 17th-century weigh house and adjoining former weavers' cottages. (*Open*: daily except Fridays in summer). In the village watch for "The Provost," a curious "toby-jug" carving, set in a niche in a gable wall by the crossroads.

A simple plaque over a cottage door in Crail, Fife

CENTRAL SCOTLAND

The first steamship
Henry Bell was provost of Helensburgh in 1812. Owning a hotel there, he decided to drum up trade and hit on the revolutionary idea of taking a boiler and engine and installing it in a wooden seagoing vessel in order to take potential customers from Glasgow to Helensburgh. He called his vessel the Comet and thus became the first to operate commercial steam navigation in Europe, 13 years before the opening of the first public steam railroad. An obelisk in Helensburgh recalls this entrepreneur.

Devil on the dormer, facing a Helensburgh church

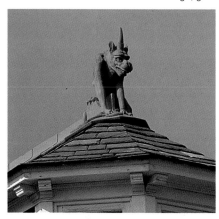

▶ **Glamis Castle and Angus Folk Museum** *131C2*
Glamis (pronounced "Glahms") is an ancient castle site. Its present appearance dates from the 17th century, but the main tower is in part much older. The building is closely associated with the present royal family. It has fine collections of china, tapestry, painting, and furniture. The other end of the social scale is represented at the **Angus Folk Museum**▶, a National Trust for Scotland property. A row of 19th-century cottages with stone-slabbed roofs have been knocked through to form a continuous passage with rooms, tableaus, and display cases covering, in suitably sanitized form, everyday life in the rural Angus of old. Both museum and castle are closed in winter.

▶ **Helensburgh** *130A1*
Sir James Colquhoun, eighth baronet of Colquhoun and Luss, had plans for the little *clachan* (the Gaelic for "village") near his castle, since it was the fashion of the Georgian age to improve. He bought the land and advertised for weavers but failed to attract any. Then he went upscale, promoting the new town of Helensburgh (named after his wife) as a residential place. This plan worked, thanks in part to the later improved communications by rail and sea. Ever since, Helensburgh has retained its properous character, its wide streets and grand properties (built by well-to-do Glasgow commuters), earning it a reputation as a "museum of villas."

Hill House▶▶ Finest of all the villas is Charles Rennie Mackintosh's masterpiece, now in the care of the National Trust for Scotland. His design was so comprehensive that he even included detail for light fixtures, carpet patterns, and window *snibs* (Scots for "catches"). It was built in 1904 as the family home of the wealthy Glasgow publisher Walter Blackie (*open*: afternoons daily, April to October).

▶ **Hillfoots Towns** *130B1*
The Hillfoots towns of Menstrie, Alva, Tillicoultry, and Dollar are strung out below the steep scarp face of the Ochil Hills east of Stirling. They formed the second-largest textile manufacturing area in Scotland, using the streams running steeply off the Ochils to power the mills, and the high, green, open pastures on the heights to raise the sheep whose wool was processed. Most (but not all) of the manufacturing has gone now, leaving impressive mill architecture at places such as Alva. The hill country above the towns is quite unspoiled and offers a good selection of walks into the Ochils, notably from the **Ochil Hills Woodland Park** between Alva and Tillicoultry.

Dollar▶▶, to the east, is the most attractive of the towns, while Blairlogie, to the west, is a pleasant village. (The others are rather dour, their attraction lying in the countryside of the Ochils above them.) Behind Dollar, on a high shoulder above a darkly wooded glen, is **Castle**

Ben Cleugh
The highest point in the Ochil Hills is Ben Cleuch (2,362 feet). If the clouds are high its summit offers superb views of the hills of the Central Highlands. But do not underestimate these exposed broad slopes, especially in winter: use proper footwear and walking equipment. The Ben Cleuch path starts from Tillicoultry or Alva.

Adam Smith
The Adam Smith Centre, Kirkcaldy's civic center and theater (built in 1889 and refurbished in 1973), is named after Adam Smith, who was born in the town in 1723. A plaque near Kirk Wynd marks the site of the house where the economist wrote his influential treatise *An Inquiry into the Nature and Causes of the Wealth of Nations*.

Campbell▶▶▶. This impressive stronghold is accessible by car or by a very picturesque (and quite dramatic) walk, at one stage through a narrow gorge. The fortress was owned by the first Earl of Argyll, Chancellor of Scotland to King James IV, and comprises a basic 15th-century tower house with later additions, including a notable loggia—an arcade with arches. Rearing above the trees at the head of the valley, it is one of the more impressively situated castles in Scotland and well worth a visit—especially on a clear day, for the views from the ramparts. It could be tied in with a trip to Culross, an easy distance away (*open*: daily, except Thursday afternoon and Friday in winter).

*Typical Wemyss
ware cats*

Kirkcaldy   131C1

The "lang toun" (long town) of Kirkcaldy (pronounced "Kircoddy") may not be the most scenic of Scottish towns, but it has good stores and amenities, including a fine park and a theater. Visit its Art Gallery and Museum, both for a fine collection of Scottish artists (notably Peploe) and its displays of local Wemyss ware pottery (*open*: daily).

Northwest of town is **Ravenscraig Castle**, an austere and ruined fortress overlooking the Firth, founded by King James II in 1460 and later owned by the Sinclair earls of Orkney. Also close at hand is the picturesque **Dysart**, where the National Trust for Scotland has attractively restored properties around a tiny harbor.

Loch Lomond

■ **One of Scotland's most famous stretches of inland water is the result of a glacier dumping its gouged-out gravels, thus creating a dam at the southern end of the deep trench it had dug. This took place 10,000 years ago, leaving Loch Lomond 26 feet above sea level, in contrast to the long narrow sea loch of Loch Long immediately to the west ...■**

The Banks of Loch Lomond
By yon bonnie banks and
 by yon bonnie braes,
Where the sun shines
 bright on Loch Lomond
Where me and my true love
 were ever wont to gae
On the bonnie bonnie
 banks o Loch Lomond.

Chorus
Ye'll tak the high road and
 I'll tak the low road
And I'll be in Scotland
 afore ye
But me and my true love
 will never meet again
On the bonnie, bonnie
 banks o Loch Lomond

Musical connections
The song "The Banks of
Loch Lomond" is thought to
have been written by a
condemned Jacobite
prisoner while in jail in
Carlisle, in England, after
the 1745 rebellion. His lines
about "yon bonnie banks"
have gone round the world,
though the unknown
lyricist is not the only one
to make reference to the
loch. Alan Jay Lerner's
1947 hit "Almost Like Being
in Love" has the lines:
"Maybe the sun gave me
 the pow'r,
But I could swim Loch
 Lomond and be home in
 half an hour.
Maybe the air gave me the
 drive
For I'm all aglow and
 alive."

Accessibility Loch Lomond is Scotland's largest loch in surface area. Famed in song, it has exerted its pull on visitors since the late 18th century. The "bonnie banks" are indisputably bonnie—but probably no more so than those of many a Highland loch lying farther north. Loch Lomond's attraction really lies in its accessibility, a characteristic it shares with the Trossachs.

Its Lowland southern end is only half an hour (sometimes less) from central Glasgow by road. This makes it commuter and also weekend-cottage country, as a stroll around neat little Drymen, with its exclusive shops, will confirm. The nearest point of the loch to Glasgow is at Balloch, at the head of the surprisingly industrialized Vale of Leven. Though Balloch is hardly picturesque, **Balloch**

Castle Country Park (open all year) has a visitor center at the castle (which is also the ranger service headquarters).

To grasp how this loch was made, climb little **Duncryne Hill** south of Gartocharn, for a sublime view of the receding loch, narrowing northward and squeezed by the hard shoulders of Highland hills. The Highland Boundary Fault with its tough rocks confined the land-shaping glacier. When it reached the soft rocks of the Lowland edge, it widened out, just as Loch Lomond's waters do today.

The eastern side Take B837 (no through road) up the eastern bank of the loch. **Balmaha**, with humpy Conic Hill behind it marking the geological line where the Highlands begin, is the stepping-off point for boat excursions around Loch Lomond's islands. These come in various shapes and sizes, though **Inchcailloch** (Scottish Natural Heritage), with its ruined 13th-century chapel and fine woodlands, is particularly outstanding. Cruises land there from Balmaha.

Rowardennan is the end of the road for car explorers, though it is pleasant to continue eastward on foot up the track which forms part of the **West Highland Way**. This officially signposted 98-mile long-distance footpath from Milngavie, by Glasgow, to Fort William drops to the lochside at Balmaha for its journey northward. The parking lot at Rowardennan is also the favored starting-off point for the climb up Ben Lomond, Scotland's most southerly (and probably most popular) "Munro" (see panel).

Tourists in cars can also sneak up on the loch via Aberfoyle to reach Inversnaid, where the road drops steeply out of the "hanging valley" of **Glen Arklet** and down to the water. This scantily populated place with its ferny banks and waterfalls is recalled in a poem by Gerard Manley Hopkins. The northern tip of Loch Lomond tails away in the marshy fields at the end of Glen Falloch.

The western side The main A82 road takes the west side of the loch, slicing away at the bonnie banks with road improvements in order to carry the tourists north at ever higher speeds. Thus many visitors miss tiny Inveruglas, from where a private road (walkers only) leads to **Loch Sloy**, the old homelands of the Clan MacFarlane, tucked behind the high hills known as the Arrochar Alps. Farther south is **Tarbet**, its name meaning a place of portage: the Vikings once carried their longships from the head of Loch Long and pillaged Loch Lomond's settlements. Also on A82 is **Luss**, with pretty cottages that are part of the planned estate village originally built by the Colquhouns.

Munros
A Munro is a mountain in Scotland over 3,000 feet high. Munro-bagging is a popular sport north of the border. The name recalls the first compiler of Scotland's heights, Sir Hugh Munro, who published a list of 277 peaks in 1891. The actual number of Munros in Scotland changes sometimes as surveys add or eliminate certain peaks. In addition, there can be problems of definition of what qualifies as a discrete mountain. For example, when does a subsidiary top of a Munro become a separate Munro? However, the current agreed figure is 277.

Luss
The village name Luss is explained by a charming legend concerning the death of a local girl married to a high-ranking French officer during the 14th-century Anglo-French wars. She died in France but was buried by Loch Lomond. Fleurs-de-lis (a species of iris and a heraldic device of the Bourbons) were scattered on her grave and, it is said, grew there ever afterward. Though the story is romantic it is equally likely that Luss is from the Gaelic word lios, meaning "garden."

The Stone of Scone

The Stone of Scone, or Stone of Destiny, was the traditional coronation throne of the Scottish monarchs until it was stolen by King Edward I of England in 1297. It can be seen today in Westminster Abbey in London. Controversy still surrounds this stone. Some Scots believe it is a fake, and that the real Stone of Destiny was hidden before Edward's arrival and briefly found again in the early 19th century, though it subsequently vanished. Whatever the truth, the Stone of Scone remains a powerful nationalist symbol in Scotland.

Scone Palace

►   **Montrose**   *131D2*

A typical east coast Lowland town, Montrose looks both to land and sea, with a maritime past, an involvement in North Sea oil, and one of Angus's main livestock markets. It is also something of a resort, with long beaches and a choice of old established golf courses. Bird-watchers flock to the basin of the River Esk, which hems in the town to the west, as this Scottish Wildlife Trust reserve is an important and decidedly muddy habitat for waders and wildfowl.

Coastal scenery is impressive with further natural history interest at **St. Cyrus** (Scottish Natural Heritage) to the north. A visitor center here interprets the formerly important local activity of salmon netting, as well as the nearby bird and plant life. Close by to the south are the long sands of **Lunan Bay**, guarded by the ruined Red Castle above the dunes—an idyllic spot for beach strollers.

The House of Dun►►► Close to the town, this National Trust for Scotland property was originally built in 1730 to a William Adam design, and has seen extensive and expensive restoration work, especially to its spectacular plasterwork. In one of the courtyard buildings, Angus weavers can be found weaving real linen napery (table linen) on traditional hand looms—a rare survivor of an industry once widespread in the area. *Open*: daily in the main season.

►►   **Perth**   *131C2*

Though known as a site still prone to flooding, Perth's strategic position as a major Lowland town with easy access to the Highlands has always given it an important role. It was the cradle of the Reformation in Scotland, after John Knox's preaching sparked off a riot in the town—and it also had bleaching and dyeing industries because of the softness and power of the River Tay's waters.

Rebuilding and renewal mean that very little is left of the ancient town. Instead, there is a grid of handsome streets completed by the early 19th century. They obliterated much of the earlier medieval plan, but include neo-classical buildings such as Perth Academy (1807), the

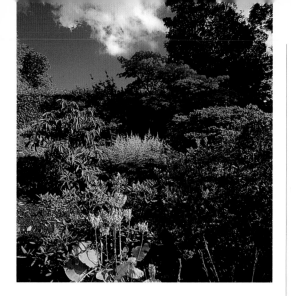

Roads from Perth
Perth offers the choice of the fast (possibly too fast) A9 heading for Speyside and Inverness, the slow A92 taking the high route over Glenshee for Royal Deeside, and the fast divided highway, the new A90(M) via Dundee for Aberdeen. Beware if driving on A92 in the skiing season. It leads to the ski developments at Glenshee, and the bends south of the Spittal of Glenshee are too often treated as a slalom course by car-borne skiing enthusiasts.

County Buildings (1815–19)—Perth was a former county town—and the unique waterworks (1832), built as a classical temple with monumental column, and now a picture gallery. Meanwhile, amid these stately civic surroundings, Perth gets on with its role as a center for a mainly rural and fairly well-off hinterland. It has a wide range of specialist shops for antiques, crafts, jewelry, outdoor and sports equipment, a museum, and art gallery (in George Street, *open*: daily), and a thriving repertory theater. The **Regimental Museum of the Black Watch** at Balhousie Castle on the North Inch tells the story of the Highland regiment founded in 1740. *Open*: Monday to Friday all year.

On the edge of town, the small-scale **Branklyn Garden►►►** has outstanding late spring color from azaleas and blue poppies (*Meconopsis*), and many other horticultural treasures. *Open*: daily except in winter. **Fairways Heavy Horse Center** is another popular excursion only a few minutes farther on the Dundee road. This center for working and breeding horses has working Clydesdales, with dray rides, vintage horse implements, and video shows. It is open throughout the main season.

Off the Blairgowrie Road, **Scone Palace►►** is one of Scotland's grandest stately homes. Scone (pronounced "skoon") was the traditional crowning place of Scottish monarchs. The site was actually the Moot Hill, within the palace grounds. Scone Palace as seen today dates mainly from the early years of the 19th century. It has magnificent collections of porcelain, furniture, ivories, 18th-century clocks, and 16th-century needlework as well as a coffee shop, restaurant, gift shop, playground, and fine gardens. *Open*: daily in the main season.

Branklyn Garden, Perth

151

Shopping for antiques, Perth

Gates at Scone Palace

Clan skirmish re-enactment by Loch Achray, Trossachs

The Soldier's Leap

The Battle of Killiecrankie in 1689 was the first attempt by the Jacobites to restore the exiled king, James VII. They won after the government forces were unable to resist the wild charge of the Highland clans. However, in his victory, the Jacobite leader, John Graham of Claverhouse, Viscount Dundee, was killed by a stray bullet. Without "Bonnie Dundee's" charismatic leadership, the rebellion fizzled out. Also in this battle, a certain Donald MacBean, a government soldier, leapt 20 feet across the River Garry to avoid being impaled on a Highland claymore sword. The spot is known as the Soldier's Leap.

►► Pitlochry 130B2

Pitlochry claims to be the geographical center of Scotland. Its situation among the Perthshire hills was noted by Queen Victoria's personal physician when she stayed along the road at Blair Castle. His recommendations on the wholesome air led to many of the well-to-do subsequently building large mansions in this previously quiet weaving village. The Perth to Inverness railroad's arrival in 1863 accelerated the growth of the fledgling resort. New hotels were built, including the Pitlochry Hydropathic, and Pitlochry developed a popularity it has retained ever since. Statistics suggest that the population of 2,500 offers 6,700 beds and plays host to nearly a million visitors a year.

Hydro-Electric Visitor Centre. Not as dull as it sounds, this attraction overlooking Loch Faskally, only moments from the main street, has a fish ladder—a stepped series of pools enabling fish to get upriver—and an explanation of the complex Tummel Valley hydroelectric project. You can see the fish jumping or swimming past the viewing chamber—if you are lucky—at any time except winter. Another highlight of the town is the Pitlochry Festival Theatre, which features popular productions right through the main season.

Killiecrankie►►► is a dramatic battle site set amid a very scenic river gorge with woodlands and steep rocks. The National Trust for Scotland visitor center tells the story of both the battle and the gorge itself, where there are superb walks among the tall pines and larches planted by the dukes of Atholl. Combine a trip here with the Queen's View of Loch Tummel, a little way to the west. The visitor center closes in winter.

►► Queen Elizabeth Forest Park 130A1

The poorly drained, infertile uplands of Scotland have defeated many a landowner. After World War I, many of these unprofitable areas, for example, around the Trossachs and Loch Lomond, were bought by the state for forestry. In 1953, the 65 square miles (approximately) owned by the Forestry Commission in some of the most attractive landscapes of the Central Highlands became the Queen Elizabeth Forest Park. At least 60 miles of forest roads are open to foot traffic. The starting point is the Queen Elizabeth Forest Park Visitor Centre above

Aberfoyle, with its magnificent views back to the Lowlands. As well as well-marked trails in profusion for walkers, right across the area, there is a forest drive by Loch Achray for those who cannot bear to leave their cars, as well as dedicated bicycle routes. The amenity value of the forests around Loch Lomond and the Trossachs is heavily emphasized, and even though this is Scotland's best-known tourist area, it is perfectly possible to escape from people.

► **Rumbling Bridge**   *130B2*

Rumbling Bridge is a geological curiosity. The phenomenon that brought generations of tourists was the sinister rumbling of boulders grinding in a deep pot called "the Devil's Mill," in a gorge that the River Devon has cut into the soft rock of the Lowland edge. The place even had its own station, though the railroad has long vanished, and excursionists would picnic by the steep and ferny banks and wander the narrow footpaths and viewing points. They also admired the quaint little bridge of 1713, which spans the gorge and is spanned in turn by a later, higher bridge of 1816, which carries today's A823. These days, there are fewer visitors as the Rumbling Bridge gorge lies in a kind of tourist no-man's land, bypassed by travelers rushing up M90 for Perth or M9 for Stirling, but it is a curious spot and makes a pleasant extension to, say, an excursion to Castle Campbell or the Hillfoots towns.

Loch Faskally, by Pitlochry

Loch Venachar

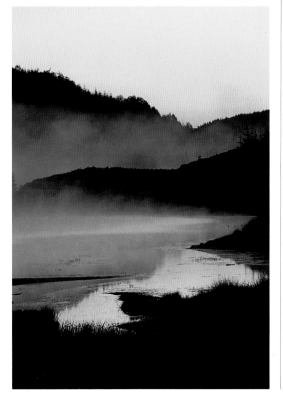

Tree types
The dominant tree species in the Queen Elizabeth Forest Park, in common with most other commercial forests in Scotland, are the alien sitka and Norway spruce, with some Scots and lodgepole pines in the drier areas. There are also some oak and beech plantings, supplementing the seminatural oakwoods (whose bark was once harvested for tannin) as well as birch scrub—a reminder of the natural regeneration that would take place if there were fewer sheep and deer.

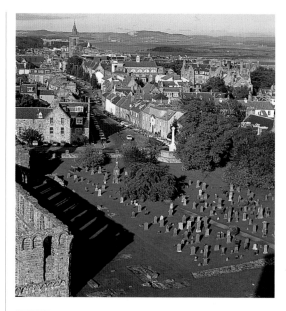

St. Andrews from St. Rule's Tower

Scotland's largest church
Some say that the design of St. Andrews Cathedral was in advance of the building technology of its age. It was by far the largest church in Scotland and one of the longest ever built anywhere in the U.K., with a length of about 350 feet.

A beach walk
For a change from the town, take a stroll along the beach at Tentsmuir, north of Leuchars near St. Andrews, where the pinewood-backed sandy beach goes on forever. En route, admire the fine Norman architecture of the parish church at Leuchars. Craigtoun Country Park, also near the town, is great for children.

▶▶▶ **St. Andrews** *131D2*

St. Andrews is unique: an ancient ecclesiastical capital, the oldest Scottish university town, and a world golfing Mecca. According to legend, a Greek monk, Regulus (or Rule), carrying relics of St. Andrew, one of Christ's disciples, was shipwrecked here and founded a church. Thereafter the cult of St. Andrew was focused on this part of Fife. The monk's name survives as St. Rule's Church (or tower), still standing near the ruined cathedral and probably from the early 12th century. Its topmost point makes a good place to view the town's medieval street plan.

Founded in 1160, **St. Andrews Cathedral**▶ is today a mere ruined fragment of what must once have been awesome architecture. It was damaged by natural disasters and then laid low by the Reformers. The cathedral's stonework was ultimately pillaged for use elsewhere in the town. Its on-site museum (*open*: daily) is well worth a visit for the glimpses of vanished magnificence. The ruins are open any time.

Teetering on the sea's brink, **St. Andrews Castle**▶▶ tells a tale of drama and religious conflict, and boasts an impressive bottle dungeon. A claustrophobic underground experience can be had following the route of sappers as they counter-mined during an attempt to tunnel under the castle during a 16th-century siege. The tunnel is electrically lit now. *Open*: daily, with a visitor center adjacent.

There are other local museums and the **Sea Life Centre** (*open*: daily all year) to visit, plus a golfing museum and excellent long beaches on either side of the town. Visitors can stroll around the many college precincts of Scotland's oldest university (founded in 1411), before sampling some of the finest shopping of any provincial town in Scotland. (The combination of university, visitors, and a prosperous farming hinterland ensures that high-quality wares are for sale.)

■ **Scotland is often called "the home of golf" and, brushing aside any suggestion that the game probably originated in the Low Countries, claims it for her own. Certainly, Scotland has a number of very old established courses, often lying close to town centers, where, had it not been for the early rights of golfers, the land would have been swallowed up by developments long ago. Nowhere is this better seen than in St. Andrews ...■**

Seaside pastime It is quite possible that golf came over when the medieval trading links with the Low Countries were strong. By the time of the early Stuart monarchs, a game with sticks and balls was taking up the time of both king and commoner alike. In 1457, King James II decreed that soldiers should not play golf. In 1503, King James IV treated himself to a new set of clubs.

Some say the sport originated with a piece of driftwood, a sea-washed pebble, and a rabbit burrow—all three are found on the Fife coast among the turf, links, and dunes. In the days before mowing machines were invented, golf had to be played where grass was naturally short. Usually only on seaside links did the exposure, poor soil, and nibbling rabbits all combine to keep the turf close-cropped. Bunkers developed from natural hollows into which a golf ball would frequently roll. Wind erosion on the thin grassy skin already damaged by players' efforts to hit out would soon create a sandy hazard.

The Old Course All this substantiates St. Andrews Old Course's claims to 15th-century origins. The Old Course is still the ultimate dream of many, which may explain why, for instance, Japanese visitors have acquired a reputation for slow play over it—they want to savor every moment. It represents traditional design at its very best. However, remember that there are other courses, both adjacent to the Old Course and right along the Fife coast.

A golfing hazard
One of the former hazards of the Old Course was the storage shed of the nearby railroad yard on the Fife coastline from Leuchars. This demanded a high approach shot on the 17th to clear the roof. Though the railroad has gone in one of the more short-sighted closures of the 1960s, the outline of the old shed has been preserved as the golf school of the nearby luxury hotel, which now occupies the site of the former sidings. Meanwhile, a campaign continues to reopen the line.

155

St. Andrews, the Old Course

CENTRAL SCOTLAND

A Jacobite battle
The Battle of Sheriffmuir, on the open slopes of the Ochil Hills above Stirling, was fought in 1715 between the rebellious Jacobite forces under the Earl of Mar and the government army under the Duke of Argyll. Unusually, it ended in a draw, with each of the opposing wings pushing back the other but neither side gaining overwhelming advantage. Argyll took his forces off to Dunblane, while Mar's men withdrew to Perth. As it was November, many of the Highland rebels wanted to go back home for the winter, and the rebellion fizzled out.

▶▶▶ **Stirling** *130B1*

Whoever controlled Stirling, controlled the Scotland of old. For centuries it was the lowest bridging point of the River Forth running east. There were marshes to the west, the Campsie Hills to the south, and the Ochil Hills (and the Highlands) northward.

Stirling Castle still preserves its impregnable air, rising out of the "carselands," former marshlands. Downhill from the castle, the Old Town has the air of an old Scottish burgh (town), with its mercat cross, tolbooth (town jail), and Church of the Holy Rude (c. 1456) as the ancient symbols of commerce, the law, and the church. Farther down, Victorian developments begin with handsome shopping streets and a railroad station, and spread into the suburbs.

Stirling Castle▶▶▶ Everyone who comes to Stirling gets at least as far as the Esplanade with its breathtaking panorama, but it is well worth entering the castle complex itself. This former royal court with its fine Renaissance work was sadly misused after Scotland's James VI deserted it to become King of England as well. Much has been restored, including the Renaissance palace of James V, the Chapel Royal of 1594, and many other buildings. *Open*: daily.

The National Trust for Scotland tells the story of one of Scotland's very few victories against the English at the **Bannockburn Visitor Centre**▶, 2.5 miles southeast of

Walk Old Stirling

See map opposite.

Fragments of an old Scottish townscape survive in this walk through the historic heart of Stirling below the castle. Allow two hours.

Follow the impressively rough-hewn old town wall opposite the tourist information center uphill past the old school, now an attractive hotel, to the historic buildings of St. John Street. These include the **Erskine Marykirk**, a classical church (1842–6), now

fronting a modern youth hostel; and the old **Detention Barracks** (1847), now the Old Town Jail museum.

The **Church of the Holy Rude** lies beyond, with Cowane's Hospital (the Guildhall, a summer ceilidh venue) nearby. A gate between them leads to the cemetery, with a fine view of the castle from the Ladies Rock. Steps and a gate lead to the Esplanade, next to the castle. The distant views here include the Arrochar Alps to the west, Ben Chonzie northward, and the Pentland Hills behind Edinburgh.

After visiting the **castle,** go downhill past **Argyll's Ludging**, Scotland's finest surviving Renaissance mansion (open to visitors), and pass the façade of **Mar's Wark**, a Renaissance palace damaged during the '45 rebellion. Broad Street, complete with cannon and tall 18th- and 19th-century tenements, gives way to Victorian developments and the main shopping streets.

King Robert I on Stirling Castle Esplanade

Stirling (see panel). The informative displays are housed in a modern building (*open*: daily, March to December).

The National Wallace Monument►► recalls Scotland's first freedom fighter (William Wallace), and has an audiovisual presentation as well as views from the top of the tower after 246 steps in a spiral staircase. *Open*: daily, March to October, and weekends in February and November.

Look for the summer program of costume drama set in historic halls within the castle and in the atmospheric streets. Changing exhibitions at the Smith Art Gallery and the performance programme at the MacRobert Arts Centre are further choices for visitors.

The view from the ramparts of Stirling Castle toward the Church of the Holy Rude

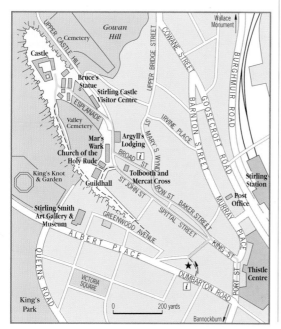

The reasons for Bannockburn
The Battle of Bannockburn was not what King Robert I (the Bruce) wanted. He was forced into this confrontation with the might of the English knights after his brother, Edward, besieging Stirling Castle, accepted an offer from its English governor that "if by midsummer a year thence he was not rescued by battle, he would yield the castle freely." This committed King Edward II of England to rescue his governor and fight the Scottish forces in a pitched battle.

Drive Perthshire's glens

A drive around some typical Highland glens with ribbon lochs and characteristic glaciated U-shaped profiles. This is a good autumn drive, when the roads are quiet and the colors spectacular. The trip totals 114 miles via Glen Lyon but not including the Loch Tummel extension. Allow one long day, or alternatively stop overnight in the Kenmore area.

Take A85 west from Perth, noting 15th-century Huntingtower on the outskirts of the town. On this section, south of the Highland Boundary Fault, the green landscape of well-worked farmland and woods rolls out across the shallow bowl of Strathearn, the

The Queen's View, Loch Tummel

Falls of Dochart, Killin

valley of the River Earn, as far south as the Ochil Hills.

Continue through **Crieff**, keeping on A85. The town has plenty of stores, and a cluster of visitor attractions on the edge of town (see page 138).

Because of its position on the Highland Boundary Fault, the village of **Comrie** farther along A85 is known as the earthquake center of Scotland. **Earthquake House**, built as a recording station in 1874, lies just west of the town. The hills close in toward St. Fillans, on the eastern end of **Loch Earn**, a popular loch for water sports. There is a major water-sports center at Lochearnhead. Note, en route, the fine views south to the bulk of Ben Vorlich.

At Lochearnhead, turn north up **Glen Ogle**. This grand glen, according to Queen Victoria's diaries, reminded her of a print of the Khyber Pass. The old railroad (closed 1965), with its decaying viaduct, is now a walkway, though not totally peaceful, because of the roar of peak season traffic in the confines of the hills. Try the turnoff at the head of the pass for views of the **Meall nan Tarmachan**

and **Ben Lawers** ranges.

After turning right at Lix Toll, on reaching Killin, watch out for pedestrians peering into cameras on the narrow bridge over the **Falls of Dochart**. There are friendly little shops in this attractive community, which, during winter, has an alpine flavor when there is snow on the slopes above.

Continue eastward, then take the unclassified road north toward Glen Lyon, unless it has recently snowed on the tops—this road traverses high ground. The National Trust for Scotland's visitor center blights the bright green flanks of **Ben Lawers**. The Trust is a conservation body, but ironically Ben Lawers' mountain flora is threatened by too many visitors, so pass on into Glen Lyon.

Turn east down this typical Highland glen, with a "big hoose" behind its wall, warning notices to keep off the hills during stalking, forestry on the slopes, farming on the river flats, and a hydroelectric project at the head of the glen. Note the Fortingall Yew where Glen Lyon opens out. This is reputed to be more than 3,000 years old, possibly the oldest tree in Europe. The Fortingall yew is said to be the birthplace of Pontius Pilate, whose father is supposed to have been a legionnaire stationed in

Schiehallion and Loch Rannoch

Scotland. Victorian guide book writers were notoriously imaginative.

Continue the tour by going north to **Loch Tummel** and then circling back by way of Pitlochry, or rejoin A9 east of Aberfeldy for the return to Perth.

■ **H. V. Morton, in** *In Search of Scotland*, **sums up the Trossachs. He complains how a traveler can wander around for months looking for essential Scotland "enduring heat, cold, fatigue, high teas, Sabbaths, kirks, and at the end comes suddenly on the whole thing in concentrated form, boiled down to the very essence..." Even more exasperating, as he points out, the place is conveniently near Edinburgh and Glasgow ...**■

Wordsworth in the Trossachs

Among the many poems inspired by his Trossachs visits, Wordsworth composed *Stepping Westward* after exploring Loch Katrine. *The Solitary Reaper*, with its lines "Breaking the silence of the seas/Among the farthest Hebrides," owes its origins not to some west coast lass, but to a fieldworker the poet heard singing as she worked near Balquhidder.

160

SS Sir Walter Scott, *steam power on Loch Katrine*

Definitions The Trossachs phenomenon is a curious one. For a start, nobody can quite agree on where it is. It certainly centers on the narrow pass that leads from Loch Achray through to the huge parking lot at the east end of Loch Katrine. Usually it goes over the hills and knolls southward to take in Aberfoyle and Loch Ard. Ben Ledi is a part of it to the east. Sometimes the Trossachs is taken to mean all of this area as far as the Braes of Balquhidder and the banks of Loch Lomond at Inversnaid.

Then nobody can agree on what the word Trossachs means. Generations of writers have accepted an early explanation that it means "the bristly country" in Gaelic—yet no Gaelic word in current use supports this. The standard work for Victorian travelers, *Murray's Handbook* of 1894, dismisses it as the rugged country, while another possibility is that it derives from an obsolete Gaelic word *trasdaichean* meaning a transverse glen joining two others.

Popularity in the Romantic age Wherever it is and whatever it means, it was thoroughly on the tourist trail before the end of the 18th century, thanks to the

The Trossachs

Romantic movement with its cult of the picturesque. A Callander minister, writing in the *Old Statistical Account* for 1794, states that "The Trossachs are often visited by persons of taste, who are desirous of seeing nature in her rudest and unpolished state." Before then, shaggy landscapes were considered uncouth and vulgar, without order or harmony—as well as being downright dangerous and probably filled with savages as well.

The Romantic poets came to admire the wooded peaks mirrored in shimmering lochs. William and Dorothy Wordsworth, accompanied by Samuel Taylor Coleridge, passed through in 1803. Though the scenery hardly needed the extra attention, Sir Walter Scott took the landscapes around Ben Ledi and Loch Katrine (as well as Stirling Castle) in *The Lady of the Lake* (1810), and peopled them with heroes, knights, hermits, and fair ladies. This dramatic verse narrative was an overnight sensation (though little read today) and helped propel the Trossachs toward becoming the very byword for Scottish scenery. New inns were built, and roads opened up. At the eastern gateway, Callander's shopkeepers prospered.

Modern visitors The Trossachs are just as popular today, and a few new visitor attractions have opened. The **Rob Roy and Trossachs Visitor Centre** in Callander (closed January and weekdays in February) tells the Trossachs story through the eyes of the local hero and popular rogue Rob Roy Macgregor, who knew these Highland-edge landscapes well. (His clan found them convenient for hiding cattle stolen from Lowland farms.) At Aberfoyle, the **Scottish Wool Center** offers a worthwhile variation on the Scottish combination of large giftware shop with attractions attached. The "Story of Scottish Wool" from prehistoric times to the present is told by way of a presentation in a 150-seat arena, and there are live demonstrations in summer of shearing and working sheepdogs, as well as a chance to try carding and spinning (*open*: all year). These modern developments add a wet weather dimension to the attractions of the Trossachs.

However, the best way to understand the place is to walk—up **Ben Aon** overlooking Loch Achray; around the head of Loch Katrine in Glen Gyle to discover the old Macgregor graveyard; up Ben Ledi in the heart of the Trossachs. After all, visitors have had so much enjoyment doing just that for two centuries.

Hilltop rituals
Ben Ledi, tallest of the Trossachs hills, is associated with Beltane rites, ancient fire ceremonies on hilltops formerly practiced by the Celts. The coming of their summer was May 1. A folk memory of this lingers on but has attached itself to midsummer eve instead, when the uphill path to this 2,883-foot high hill can be quite busy as people gather to watch the sunset at its most northerly point.

The ferryman who takes visitors to the atmospheric Inchmahome Priory, on an island in the Lake of Menteith, near Callander

Far right: Macduff harbor
Right: whisky is exported from Scotland across the world—this bottle ended up in Australia

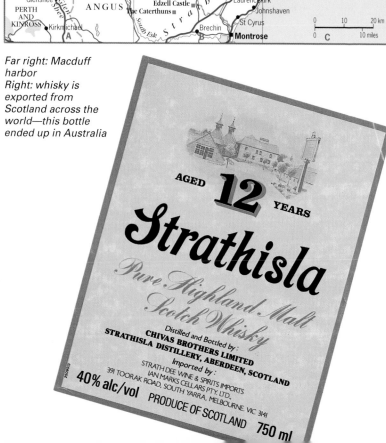

AGED **12** YEARS

Strathisla

Pure Highland Malt Scotch Whisky

Distilled and Bottled by :
CHIVAS BROTHERS LIMITED
STRATHISLA DISTILLERY, ABERDEEN, SCOTLAND
Imported by :
STRATH DEE WINE & SPIRITS IMPORTS
IAN MARKS CELLARS PTY. LTD.
391 TOORAK ROAD, SOUTH YARRA, MELBOURNE VIC 3141

40% alc/vol   PRODUCE OF SCOTLAND   750 ml

THE NORTHEAST

The Northeast This region lies, strictly speaking, north of the Highland line, the geological fault that runs from Helensburgh in the west to Stonehaven in the east. Yet the Northeast has good Lowland farmlands and the densest forms of the Lowland Scots tongue. It used to be described as "the Grampian cocoon"—the land beyond the Grampian hills, isolated from developments in Central Scotland. This may explain the vigorous survival of its old tongue, as well as a kind of independent spirit and attitude among many of the locals. But modern communications, as well as new settlers and the impact of North Sea oil, have made their mark in this essentially rural area.

The Northeast is different: not like the empty, wet, and rugged deserts of the Highlands with their original inhabitants in exile; nor even like the brisk and busy central corridor of Scotland, which spawned the industrial revolution. It is a community tied together by the twin bonds of its seagoing and its farming heritage. Its main center, Aberdeen, the third largest city in Scotland, sometimes seems to operate like a very large market town, in spite of all the peripheral industrial estates that grew up in the wake of the oil finds in the shallow seas to the east and north.

Geographically, the Northeast can be interpreted as a series of shelves, running down from the frost-shattered granite heights of the Cairngorms to the gently rolling, well-farmed Lowlands. These descending steps end

THE NORTHEAST

Oil supply vessels in Aberdeen harbor

spectacularly in a coastline whose beauty is hardly matched in the United Kingdom—preserved partly by remoteness, partly by the unglamorous workaday fields behind it, and also because it is usually very chilly.

Castles The "cocoon" effect means that many great castles have survived, away from the destructive mainstream of Scotland warfare and safely tucked out of sight behind their stone walls and woodland "policies" (grounds). Some still control farms and grand estates, others are now in the care of bodies such as the National Trust for Scotland and open to the public. If you travel in the Northeast, there seem to be signposts with castle logos at every turn.

Distinct areas The Northeast splits into a number of areas. There is the city of Aberdeen itself, with its wide commuter belt, taking in places from Ellon in the north, Inverurie, Alford, Banchory, and other little country towns that expanded in the oil boom. North from this area to Kinnaird Head, the northeast tip, is Buchan, built on fishing and farming, with granite towns and villages tucked into the folds of open farmland. The old county of Banff, at least in its lowland stretches, is transitional, softening the bleak edges of Buchan and merging in turn with the softer airs of Moray, in the rain shadow of the high hills in the inner Moray Firth.

Running west of Aberdeen is the valley of the River Dee, given royal approval by Queen Victoria and still, at least in part, a playground for the wealthy, not just aristocrats on hillground and forested estates, but also the occasional foreign millionaire. Deeside eventually runs into the great whalebacks of the Cairngorms, whose northwestern slopes face Speyside and the upper reaches of Moray. North and northeast of the Cairngorm plateau

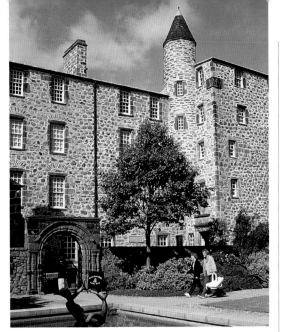

The Turra Coo
One tale of Northeast thrawnness (stubbornness) is that of the (locally) famous Turra Coo. Turra is Turriff, a small market town, and a coo is a cow. In 1912, a local farmer refused to cooperate with the new National Insurance Act. He was fined but refused to pay. The Sheriff Officer poinded (seized) a cow. After a failed attempt to auction it in Turriff—before a crowd of 1,500 intent on merriment—it was sold in Aberdeen, but bought by sympathizers. The coo was taken back home to its first owner, watched by another large crowd and the local brass band. This spawned a minor industry in Turra Coo commemorative postcards, pottery, glassware, etc. A memorial was erected in 1971.

are the lonely glens of former upper Banffshire, once hazy with the smoke from illicit stills.

Whisky Today the whisky (note the Scots spelling) industry, centered on the River Spey, is big business. Grand malt whisky names—Macallan, the Glenlivet, Glenfiddich, Glenfarclas, and so on—stretch all the way to the sea, sounding every bit as distinguished as the famous wines noted as place-names in France's Rhône valley.

Provost Skene's House, Aberdeen

King's College, Old Aberdeen

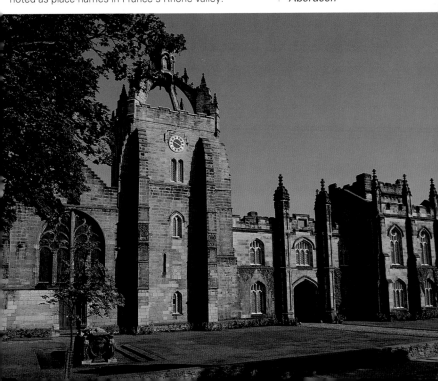

The Northern Lights

"The Northern Lights of Old Aberdeen" is a Scottish anthem sung worldwide by Aberdonians. However, the Northern Lights are certainly not confined to the city—where street lights make viewing difficult anyway. The *aurora borealis* (to give the Northern Lights their proper name) is a not uncommon phenomenon in the north of Scotland, illuminating the sky with (usually) greenish waving curtains and beams of light at any time of year when there is enough darkness to view it.

Granite detail from the entrance to St. Nicholas's churchyard

Aberdeen city center

▶▶▶ **Aberdeen**   *162C2*

With its population of well over 200,000 and its glittering granite and spacious streets, the United Kingdom's most northerly city makes an impact on first-time visitors. Built between the river mouths of the Dee and the Don, this old established place—a royal burgh (town) since 1124—once had strong trading links with Europe, while serving its agricultural hinterland and developing other industries such as textiles.

Before the end of the 18th century, it was exporting its characteristic silver-gray granite to London among other places and also build-ing the distinc-tive townscape that is still seen today around Union Street (the main shop-ping thorough-fare).

Unlike the soft sandstones of Edinburgh and Glasgow, tough granite does not suit ornate carv-ing. Instead it was used boldly in buildings, parapets, and spires. In sunshine, the mica chips become a million mir-rors; in rain, the stones reflect only the gray sky.

Many of Aberdeen's places of interest are within walk-ing distance of each other. The east end of Union Street is the former center of the early settlement, indicated by the **mercat cross**. Aberdeen's is one of the most splendid in Scotland, dating from 1686, and arcaded with heraldic panels and portraits. Opposite is the 17th-century **Tolbooth** or **Old Town House**. (It once held prisoners before trial, and tours of the old cells are available.) Note the Flemish medieval-style turrets on the adjacent **New Town House**, a reminder of old trading links. The Shiprow opposite, one of the oldest streets in the city, leads down to the harbor.

Aberdeen Maritime Museum► The 16th-century **Provost Ross's House** is a unique survivor on the old Shiprow, between the marketplace and quayside. The museum portrays the city's seagoing past, from early times via fishing boats and tea clippers right up to the oil boom (*open*: daily except Sunday).

Marischal College►► was founded in 1593 by the Earl Marischal as a Protestant alternative to the Catholic King's College in Old Aberdeen (see page 168). The two combined to form Aberdeen University in 1860. Marischal's arresting façade was built from 1891 onward, breaking all rules about granite and its severity. The spectacularly ornate work is set off by the gilded flags, and this giant granite wedding cake is still the second-largest granite building in the world. (Only El Escorial, near Madrid, Spain, is larger.) The Marischal museum (*open*: daily except Saturday) is within.

Provost Skene's House► Past the eye-catching façade of Marischal College and almost underneath the ugly modern building of St. Nicholas House, this steeply gabled rubble-built structure is the remnant of a once closely packed area of town houses. It dates in part from 1545. It is now a museum of civic life with restored furnished period rooms and a painted chapel, as well as a café (good for afternoon tea). *Open*: daily except Sundays.

Royal castle inspiration
By late Victorian times the east end of Union Street, called the Castlegate, was downright seedy. Even today, respectable, upright native Aberdonians are a bit uncomfortable about it. The 19th-century city planners had the answer. Right in the middle they built a Salvation Army Citadel (1893–6). It survives as such today, with a handsome baronial tower. This castle-like design was inspired by another symbol of strength and righteousness: Balmoral Castle. The resemblance is purely external.

167

"Education, Salvation, and Damnation"
One of the finest groupings of granite architecture in Aberdeen overlooks Union Terrace Gardens. St. Mark's Church of 1892, with its handsome dome and colonnaded portico, is flanked by the central library, inspired by Renaissance styles, and on the other side by the exuberant Edwardian flourishes of His Majesty's Theater. Together they form a trio which was dubbed "Education, Salvation, and Damnation."

An Aberdeen saying
There is an old saying still current among Aberdonians: "Tak awa Aiberdeen and twal mile roon aboot—an far are ye?" ("Take away Aberdeen and 12 miles round about and where are you?"), meaning that without Aberdeen the area would be lost and worthless.

THE NORTHEAST

168

A traveler's tale
Thomas Pennant, the Welsh traveler, visited Aberdeen in 1769 and took in St. Machar's. He describes how the Reformers took the lead off the roof of St. Machar's and stole the bells. Then they "shipped their sacrilegious booty with an intention of exposing it to sale in Holland; but the vessel had scarcely gone out of port, but it perished in a storm with all its ill-gained lading." Others tell the same story of Elgin Cathedral.

Right: one of the colorful exhibits from the Aberdeen Maritime Museum

Old Aberdeen

Along Schoolhill and past the faceless shopping malls, **Aberdeen Art Gallery▶▶ has** excellent collections of 18th- to 20th-century work. The gallery is open all year, closed Sunday mornings. Close by is **St. Nicholas Kirk▶**, the first place of worship in Aberdeen, founded in the 12th century.

Old Aberdeen▶▶, once a separate community near the River Don, lies north of the main city near the precincts of **King's College▶**. The university was founded in 1494: and its cobbled streets, and artisans' cottages make it an atmospheric campus. **King's College Chapel▶▶**, with its crown spire, is a very fine example of an early collegiate chapel (c. 1500). The tall oak screen and the ribbed wooden ceiling and stalls have ornate medieval wood carving. The King's College Visitor Centre (*open*: all year) is a good starting point for a tour.

Beyond the handsome Georgian **Old Aberdeen Town House▶▶**, is the Chanonry, leading to St. Machar's Cathedral and Seaton Park. The River Don curves around this park, then flows under the picturesque 14th-century Brig o'Balgownie.

St. Machar's Cathedral▶ St. Columba sent St. Machar to build this church near the sea, where a river flowed in the shape of a shepherd's crook. The nave was possibly rebuilt in red sandstone by around 1370, then finished in granite by the mid-15th century. The building was damaged during the Reformation and in the 17th century, but extensively restored in the 19th century (*open*: daily).

Aberdeen for children

■ Aberdeen has sandy beaches, a fun fair, leisure centers, swimming pools, and spacious parks—in short, many of the trappings of a resort town. It also has a large number of indoor sights specifically geared for children. If all else fails, you can always lose them for awhile in the large maze in the city's Hazlehead Park ...■

The Satrosphere, open all year and signposted from the west end of Union Street, is undoubtedly Aberdeen's top children's attraction. Do not be put off by the "interactive science and technology exhibition center" description: it is a hands-on, absorbing experience for any child with imagination. There are endless experiments and demonstrations for children. They can play with mirrors and light, create a giant bubble a yard wide, play tunes on 6-foot pan pipes, whisper into a parabolic reflector and be heard across the hall, become a TV newscaster, balance balls in streams of hot air, build a waterwheel, and become involved in dozens of other activities. This is unique in Scotland. Allow plenty of time to make the most of it. *Open*: daily except Sunday morning.

Other Aberdeen attractions Jonah's Journey in Rosemount Place takes its theme from life in Bible times—here children can visit a nomad's tent, dress up, and grind grain (*open*: Monday to Saturday in the morning, and Sunday afternoon).
James Dun's House, just by the art gallery in Schoolhill, sometimes has special exhibitions with children's themes, so is worth checking out. Older children might enjoy the ship models at the Maritime Museum (closed Sunday) and some of the exhibits (probably the shrunken heads!) at the Marischal College Museum.
 The Winter Gardens at the **Duthie Park** are popular with families. (Children love eyeballing the giant carp and spotting the terrapins.) **Hazlehead Park** (pictured at the top of this page) also has a domestic animal zoo, as has **Doonies Farm**. Most of Aberdeen's parks have good playgrounds—try the one on the Beach Esplanade, where there is also a traditional fairground (in summer). Out of town, **Storybook Glen** near Maryculter is a sheltered valley where fiberglass models of cartoon and fairy-tale characters loom disconcertingly out of the undergrowth. Nothing interacts, which can disappoint youngsters who have patted their umpteenth dwarf without response.

Floral facts
Seaton Park is only one of the city's open spaces. Aberdeen puts special emphasis on flowers and is a frequent winner of the "Britain in Bloom" award. Aberdeen's flower displays were initiated using 60 tons of daffodil bulbs and 600,000 crocuses in one phase alone. Rosebushes outnumber the locals by nine to one.

A ghoulish exhibit from the Marischal College Museum

Balmoral
Balmoral Castle is the private vacation home of the Royal Family and only opens its grounds and ballroom to the public for a short time each year. (Usually the ballroom houses a painting exhibition from the Royal Family's own private collections.) It is vital to check the opening days in advance—usually in May, June, and July daily except Sunday. Except for these months, Balmoral is transformed from a visitor attraction into a high security playground for royals and various heads of state. The royals are in residence in August.

Treasure Island
One wet day in Braemar in 1881, a man and his stepson were bored by the weather on their summer vacation and took out a paintbox to paint a map of an imaginary island. Suddenly, as the man later recalled, the island came alive and figures seemed to peer out of the jungle fronds. He set down to write their story at once. Thus Robert Louis Stevenson's *Treasure Island* with its tropical setting was born amid the cool piny greenery of Deeside.

Braemar

Corgarff Castle

▶▶ **Ballater**   *162A1*

Well-scrubbed and handsome Ballater has profited greatly from the needs of the royals at Balmoral for everything from bread to rubber boots. With Balmoral just westward, there are more "By Royal Appointment" signs here than anywhere else in Scotland.

Local excursions include the not-to-be-missed **Glen Muick** (pronounced Mick), with red deer sightings all but guaranteed. Also worth exploring are the birch woods around Dinnet, notably **Loch Kinord** and the **Burn o Vat**, and a good network of trails around **Glen Tanar**, near Aboyne. Hardy walkers can explore the **Mounth passes**— a series of high-level ancient trails leading across the massif of The Mounth. Northward is 16th-century **Corgarff Castle**, with its star-shaped defenses added in 1748.

▶ **Banff**   *162B3*

Pressure from a local conservation group saved some of Banff's attractive Georgian domestic architecture from redevelopment into the retail anonymity that blighted so many other Scottish towns. So this old seacoast town is worth a stroll in its own right. However, its main attraction is **Duff House** ▶▶, an Adam mansion massively restored and now the principal outstation of the National Galleries of Scotland. This country house gallery displays Scottish portraiture of the 18th and 19th centuries, as well as fine period furniture. *Open*: daily except Tuesday in summer, closed Monday to Wednesday in winter.

▶▶ **Braemar**   *162A1*

A93, coming west up Deeside, climbs out of the Dee valley and turns southward, seeking a pass over the Grampians. Braemar sits on the turn. It can feel a little transitory, yet it is an old established resort, benefiting like Ballater from the royal presence at Balmoral. The **Highland Heritage Centre**, open all year, takes up the theme of the royal connection and the Braemar Highland Gathering. There is an excellent selection of local excursions, including the **Linn of Dee**, a picturesque rocky cleft, west of Inverey. Also nearby is the **Devil's Punchbowl**, a water-worn rock feature among the pines at the Linn of Quoich. The **Colonel's Bed** is yet more rock and water: a narrow gorge with slippery shelves in Glen Ey. For the ambitious walker, **Glen Derry** gives access to the eastern end of the Cairngorms, as well as the pass of the Lairig Ghru leading through to the Spey. But beware—these are hills on a large scale.

The Picts and their art

■ **The northern Picts lived in and around the Grampians between the 4th and 9th centuries AD. The Mounth, the hill ground between Deeside and Angus, was an important barrier. Moray was their final stronghold before defeat and gradual absorption by the ascendant Scots, whose union with them formed the first kingdom of Scotland, known as Alba (see page 27)** ...■

Burghead The most important Pictish center was Burghead, on the coast near Elgin. A great promontory fort survived until a "new" town of Burghead was built on a grid plan in 1805–9, destroying much of the Pictish ramparts, and timber-laced walling that had stood there for more than a millennium. Six Pictish bull carvings survive from that time, outlined boldly in stone.

The bull is just one of the symbols that tantalize modern archeologists and historians. The Picts left earthworks such as coastal headland forts in the Northeast and inland sites like Bennachie, a hill near Inverurie, but it is their symbol stones that are the most vivid evidence of this far-off culture. A few stones are still in their original locations, some have been re-erected or placed in museums, others have been built into walls or lost entirely.

Standing stones The **Picardy Stone** near Insch is typical, a whinstone pillar with, among other subjects, a clearly executed double-disk and Z-rod (a recurring symbol

in Pictish art), serpent, and mirror. The **Maiden Stone** near Pitcaple is an impressive red granite monolith of considerable presence, especially when slanting light highlights the curious so-called "Pictish elephant," one of the most mysterious of the designs. This is a late (9th-century) work.

Most magnificent of all is **Sueno's Stone** on the outskirts of Forres, with its many figures galloping on the face of an 8-foot monolith. Theories abound on the meaning of this and other stones. Some suggest that Sueno's Stone is war reporting on a grand scale—recording, ironically, the Scots' victory over the Picts. Some see the other stones as monuments, others as proclamations. Nobody knows, but the designs have both power and inspiration. Tracking them down can make for interesting excursions in this northern corner.

The meaning of the stones
The Picts were divided into two realms, the northern and southern. Many of the finest symbol stones belong to the northern grouping. Their language was ousted by the arrival of the Scots from Ireland and they left no written records. It is known that inheritance was through the female line—though Pictish kings reigned, their sons did not succeed them. Do the symbols carved on the stones indicate lineages, alliances, and power within the leading Pictish families?

Left and below: the Maiden Stone, near Pitcaple

■ **Whisky is one of Scotland's top exports, worth £2.1 billion in 1993, and is important in the economy of many communities. There are more than 40 distilleries in Moray alone, the greatest concentration anywhere in Scotland. More than just distinctive plumes of steam in the attractive wooded river valley, these distilleries sustain engineers, coppersmiths, painters, plumbers, maltsters, and specialists in many more trades ...■**

Dallas Dhu
Amid all the live distilleries, busy bubbling, frothing, and producing odd aromas, you can also visit a distillery of the past. In the care of Historic Scotland, Dallas Dhu near Forres is a time capsule and allows a more intimate inspection than working distilleries. It is open all year (closed on Thursday afternoons and Fridays in winter).

Copper stills at the Glen Garioch Distillery, Oldmeldrum

For centuries *uisge beatha* (the Gaelic for "water of life") has been produced in Scotland from the simple ingredients of barley, water, yeast, and, usually, peat smoke. There are two main distinctions: malt whisky and grain whisky. Most drinkers would say that malt has a more complex flavor and bouquet. Certainly, modern marketing techniques have given it more cachet and a higher price! Malt whisky uses only malted barley. Grain whisky may use malted barley but also other cereals, notably corn. A single malt is the product of a single distillery, while a blend, as its name suggests, is a blend of malt and grain whiskies—the higher the proportion of malt whisky, the better (or more expensive) the blend.

Experts broadly classify malt whiskies into Highland, Lowland, Islay, and Campbeltown types. This can be generalized into eastern, notably from Speyside, and western, from the islands, mainly Islay. Of the two, the western malts are noticeably "peaty." The malt, which is the basis of malt whisky, has usually (but not necessarily) been bought from local maltings. Malt is germinated barley that has been killed off and then dried (sometimes with peat smoke).

The whisky-making process To make whisky, grind a large quantity of malted barley and add hot water to it in a large circular vat of several thousand quart capacity called a mash tun. Eventually, the result will be wort, a sweet-smelling liquid. Hold this in a worts receiver or underback below the mash tun. Use the solids in the mash tun, called draff, for winter cattle food.

Take the wort and add it with yeast to another enormous vessel, known as a wash-back, where it will ferment. Then pump this liquid, called the wash, via a wash charger into a wash still, which is a large copper container. Heat it, using gas if available. Condense the vapors in a worm—

172

coiled copper, water-cooled tube. Repeat this process at least twice. Then run the distillate into a spirit safe. This is the part that needs most expertise. Both beginning and end of the distilling process produce impurities. The whisky is, so to speak, in the middle.

Next, procure casks. Old sherry casks are particularly recommended. Add water to the whisky and place in the casks. Leave for several years before bottling as a single malt. Then sell worldwide as a prestige product!

The angels' share
This is the name given to the whisky that was definitely there when the distillery staff put it into the cask but has gone, five or more years later, when the casks are broached for bottling or blending. Nothing untoward has taken place. There is a natural evaporation through the wood of the casks.

173

Casks—and their contents—maturing at the Glenfiddich Distillery, Dufftown

Distillery tours The process of producing whisky is closely monitored by the British government. It is strictly commercially licensed and takes place only in Scotland's distilleries (and, in Scotland, the product is most definitely spelled "whisky," without an "e"). Many distilleries place strong emphasis on visitor facilities and attempt to inject some drama and excitement into a process that is visually undramatic but nevertheless requires skill, method, and large-scale investment.

A typical visit includes some kind of audiovisual presentation, with the malt whisky company describing its brand as the "true taste of Scotland" and laying great store on historical roots. (Awkward facts detracting from "Scottishness," such as the owning company being an overseas-based multinational, are skipped over.) Then there is a tour, of varying degrees of liveliness, depending on the guide; and afterward a return to the hospitality area where a dram is usually offered. There will often be some kind of historic exhibition and nearly always a shop. No tour of Speyside is complete without taking in at least one distillery.

Dolphins
The Moray Firth contains the largest inshore colony of bottle-nosed dolphins in Britain. (The species otherwise tends to favor offshore waters.) Leaping dolphins can be seen anywhere at any time in the Firth. The entrances to the inner firths can be rewarding for dolphin watchers, as can the mouths of the Rivers Findhorn and Spey (Spey Bay is particularly good for seals as well.) The bottle-nosed dolphin can be recognized by its uniform gray with a paler underbelly and a tall dorsal fin.

Crathes Castle, painted ceiling

► **Craigellachie**   *162A2*

A typical Speyside community dependent on the whisky industry and visiting anglers, Craigellachie is noted for its cooperage, now the **Speyside Cooperage Visitor Centre►►**, where the age-old skills of barrel making are demonstrated. *Open*: daily except Sunday, or Saturday in winter). Also nearby is **Craigellachie Bridge►**, a handsome design by Thomas Telford which crosses the Spey with an iron span cast in Wales.

►► **Crathes Castle**   *162B1*

This 16th-century L-plan tower house has many rare original features, notably four rooms with painted ceilings, as well as a ghost of a green lady and fine old furniture, locally made. Crathes is also noted for its gardens, made into compartments by close-clipped yew hedges and containing many unusual species. This makes a very worthwhile high summer excursion when in the Aberdeen area. The castle is open daily in summer, the gardens are open all year.

► **Dufftown**   *162A2*

A planned town founded in 1817, Dufftown has wide streets which center on a square and landmark **clock tower** (which houses the local museum). The little town is bound up with distilleries, including famous malt whisky names such as Glenfiddich, which is overlooked by the ruins of the 13th-century Balvenie Castle (itself a malt whisky name). The **Glenfiddich Distillery Visitor Centre►►►** offers one of the very best audiovisuals and tours, showing all of the stages from malting through to bottling (*open*: daily, except weekends in winter). Though

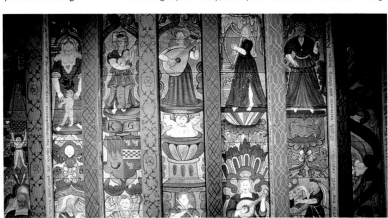

a planned town, Dufftown has a pedigree as a settlement that goes as far back as AD 566, when Mortlach Church was founded, one of the earliest religious sites in Scotland. There are Pictish stones and a "leper's squint," a hole through which lepers could observe proceedings inside the church.

► **Elgin**   *162A3*

Moray's commercial and administrative center, Elgin has reworked and rebuilt its townscape over the centuries yet retained fragments of early times. A medieval street plan can still be made out, with narrow alleyways leading off the broad main street, and some arcaded façades from 18th-century shops also survive. Take in the view from the top of the Lady Hill at its west end. This was the site of the castle—a little of the wall remains—occupied by King Edward I of England in the Wars of Independence.

Elgin Cathedral► ("The Lantern of the North") was founded in 1224 and burned in 1390 by the notorious Wolf of Badenoch, the black sheep of the royal Stewart family (following excommunication by the local bishop). The cathedral was rebuilt and in use till the Reformation, when it suffered the usual fate of great religious seats in Scotland. Much of its stonework was pillaged and used elsewhere, though the historic structure was taken into the care of the nation in 1825. *Open*: daily, except Thursday afternoons and Friday in winter.

"Acorn to Cask," the story of whisky barrels at Craigellachie

Elgin Cathedral

175

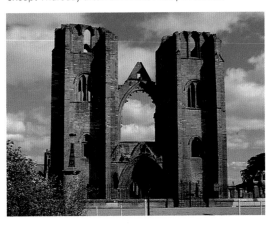

Elgin Museum► is reckoned to be one of the finest museums in the north. Among other exhibits it features the oldest dinosaurs found in Britain—though, like the museum itself, they are quite small. *Open*: daily, from April to October.

Other attractions in town include **Johnstons of Elgin►**, a woolen mill specializing in cashmere, with a visitor center and mill tours. The town also has a motor museum and a preserved meal mill. Nearby, out on the levels of the Laich of Moray, is **Duffus Castle►**, the impressive remains of a medieval castle with a 14th-century tower. Unusually for Scotland the moat is still water-filled.

Spynie Palace►, the ruin of a former bishop's mansion with good views from the tower, is to the east.

Elgin's former port is **Lossiemouth►**, now a resort and fishing town, with a busy airbase nearby. A beautiful coastline stretches out to east and west. Also within reach of the town is **Pluscarden Abbey►►**, originally a 13th-century foundation, suppressed at the Reformation. In 1948, monks from Prinknash Abbey, in Gloucester, started restoration. Visitors are welcome daily.

The Battle of Mons Graupius
The Roman historian Tacitus tells how Agricola's forces, ranging north in the summer of AD83, finally brought to battle and defeated the Caledonian warriors by a hill within sight of the sea in the north of Scotland. This was the Battle of Mons Graupius, which also gave the name Grampian, possibly due to a 1470s printing error when "n" was substituted for "u." Many historians favor a Grampian location for the battle, possibly Bennachie near Inverurie. The real battle site has never been found.

The Mounth

The Mounth, from the Gaelic *monadh*—("moorland" or "mountain"), is the name given to the hillmass south of Deeside. The Mounth passes were once important through routes to the north. Today, they survive as hill tracks marked on maps: the Capel Mounth, the Firmouth, the Fungle, and many more, now mainly the haunt of leisure-time walkers and mountain bikers. The motorable passes include A93 over Glen Shee and B974 Cairn o Mount.

▶ **Fettercairn** 162B1

Car travelers who tire of the fast A90 divided highway should try an interesting route to the Northeast via Fettercairn, a little place on the southern edge of the Grampian Hills. Fettercairn has an 1861 Gothic arch recalling the visit of Queen Victoria, and a malt whisky visitor center (*open*: May to September, except Sunday). The Fettercairn diversion leads on to the start of a scenic hill road, B974 to Banchory, which reaches its highest point at the **Cairn o Mount**. This hilltop cairn gives excellent views southward over Angus and is typical of skyline cairns (heaps of stones) which have been altered by generations of travelers. It dates from the 2nd millennium BC.

Fasque House▶ near Fettercairn has been the home of the Gladstone family for six generations (none of whom seemed to have thrown very much out). The most famous of them was William Gladstone, Victorian prime minister. Fasque (1809) is a castellated mansion in Georgian Gothic style, with a pleasingly mellowed, lived-in air (*open*: daily in summer).

▶ **Fochabers** 162A3

Worth visiting for its choice of antiques shops, this handsome little planned town was built by the Duke of Gordon in 1776. He thought the old village was too near his castle, so he knocked it down. He did not think of building a bypass for the A96, which makes the main street very noisy today. Fochabers is the home of Baxters canned-food processors, whose factory dominates the western approaches. There is an excellent view of the River Spey from a viewpoint south of the town, signposted **The Earth Pillars**, where eroded columns of red conglomerate rock form the foreground to a striking river panorama seen through the pinewood.

Fochabers Folk Museum▶▶ is housed in a converted church and is filled with artifacts of a bygone rural life, from horse-drawn carts to a turnip-chopping machine (*open*: daily).

Fyvie Castle

177

Forres' Falconer Museum is a good example of a small museum with a strong local collection

An early name
Some think that the "Varris" on the map of Ptolemy, the 1st century AD geographer, refers to today's Forres.

Randolph's Leap
Randolph's Leap, a beauty spot on the River Findhorn where the river narrows among rocks and woodlands, is unfairly named. The Randolph was Thomas Randolph, Earl of Moray. He was in hot pursuit of one Alastair Cumming who had just raided his Darnaway Castle. It was Cumming who escaped by leaping the river at this point. Judge for yourself the relative ease of choosing between a downward leap of around 10 feet or being skewered on a 14th-century broadsword.

► **Forres** 162A3

Like Elgin, farther east, Forres also maintains its medieval street plan in part. The main street bulges out at the former marketplace in the town center, though the buildings are mainly Victorian. The **Falconer Museum** (closed Sunday in winter) explores local history. Forres places great emphasis on its floral displays, winning awards year upon year.

Brodie Castle►► is a National Trust for Scotland property, a little to the east of Forres. Brodie is based on a 16th-century Z-plan with later additions, and houses fine French furniture, porcelain, and a painting collection. It closes in winter. Well worth visiting at any season is the **Califer Braes** viewpoint, with a broad view of the Moray Firth stretching out to the east and meeting the Highland Hills westward.

► **Fraserburgh** 162C3

Fraserburgh in itself is a fishing port with little merit in its townscape. However, it has a superb beach and a most interesting visitor attraction. **Scotland's Lighthouse Museum►►►** portrays the story and traditions of lighthouse service, now ending with automation. There are fascinating displays as well as a tour of Kinnaird Head lighthouse itself (*open*: daily).

►► **Fyvie Castle** 162B2

Five-towered Fyvie Castle epitomizes Northeast castles: a rambling, overbearing pile, imposing when viewed, yet hidden away behind its endless walls and tall trees. The oldest part of the building dates from the 13th century. This original quadrangular fortress evolved over the centuries into a magnificent stately home. Famous families in the Northeast, the Prestons, Meldrums, Setons, and Gordons, held it in turn, each adding substantially to the building. Then it was bought by Alexander Forbes Leith, a local boy made good in America. He substantially refurbished it in parts, adding Edwardian opulence to the mix. The castle has sumptuous interiors and fine furniture, and displays a magnificent painting collection (including a dozen Raeburns). The castle is closed in winter, the grounds are open all year.

Falconer Museum, Forres

►► Glen Shee
162A1

Climbing to over 2,000 feet at the Cairnwell, the A93 between Bridge of Cally and Braemar is the highest main road in the United Kingdom (though not the highest drivable road). Surrounded on both sides by Munros (see panel, page 149), it has been a prey to ski developers and is very popular when snow conditions are right. The solitude of the high tops in the immediate vicinity has been invaded by vast parking lots, snow fencing, chairlifts, tows, and catering facilities. With the highest hills just under 3,000 feet, the downhill runs are not very long, however. The chairlift operates outside the winter season. On the steep south side of the pass is the Devil's Elbow, a once fearsome hairpin bend now bypassed, but still visible.

► Grampian Transport Museum
162B2

Alford (pronounced aa-furd) offers plenty for children, in particular the Grampian Transport Museum with its extensive collection of historic vehicles (*open*: daily April to October) and the adjoining narrow-gauge railroad— built on the site of the long-vanished "real" railroad— which runs to Haughton Country Park. Take the road north to **Suie Hill** for a peerless view over rural Aberdeenshire. If it is a summer weekend, continue over to the community hall of the enterprising village of Clatt, where the locals serve a real home-baked afternoon tea.

►► Haddo House
162C2

There is quite a concentration of National Trust for Scotland properties in the Northeast. Haddo House, with its country park, is on the **Castle Trail**, the signposted route that takes in the best of them, though this William Adam design of 1731 has an elegance far removed from

Near Inverurie

the bold and battered fortresses typical of the trail. Haddo's interiors are mostly "Adam revival" from about 1880, and the overall impression is light and cheerful, inside and out, with curving wings on either side of a harmonious façade. The house is closed in winter, the grounds open all year. Combine this excursion with a visit to Pitmedden Garden (see panel, page 178).

▶ Huntly · *162B2*

A substantial (for Grampian) town serving a rural hinterland, Huntly was the power base of the influential Gordons, who built their castle here on a defensive site between the rivers Bogie and Deveron. Today, **Huntly Castle** stands as an imposing ruin, with heraldic adornments on its walls. (*Open*: daily, except Thursday afternoon and Friday in winter—though still highly visible even from outside.) Huntly is also worth visiting for its shops—small businesses, including outdoor wear, fishing, antiques, hardware, and so on, not yet charging city prices. It also has an all-weather cross-country ski track down by the river, with equipment for rent, giving novices an opportunity to try out the sport.

▶ Inverurie · *162B2*

Now bypassed by the busy A96, Inverurie is a locally important administrative center in the prosperous farming area known as the Garioch (pronounced "geerie"). It is overlooked by one of the Northeast's landmark hills: **Bennachie**, with its hilltop vitrified Pictish fort. There are other prehistoric sites in the vicinity (see page 171), including the atmospheric and enigmatic **Loanhead Stone Circle**, near Daviot, 5 miles to the northwest.

Keith · *162B3*

Another planned town on the main Aberdeen–Inverness road, Keith is also the gateway to the **Malt Whisky Trail**. This is a signposted drive—presumably for non-drinkers—around seven malt whisky distilleries, one of which, Strathisla, is in Keith, though the others lie in more picturesque settings in the attractive hinterland of the River Spey and around Ben Rinnes.

Gordon Bennett
Few places can claim to be the hometown of an expletive, but Keith was the birthplace of "Gordon Bennett." This mild British oath refers to James Gordon Bennett, born in the town in 1795. He was the founder and editor of the *New York Herald*, and is sometimes described as the father of lurid journalism because of his innovative sensationalist style.

Drive **The northeast coast**

The section of coast between the mouths of the rivers Don and Spey remains comparatively unexplored. Aberdeen to Sandend is 86 miles, the return along the main road 50 miles. Allow a full day.

Starting from Aberdeen, A92 is set back from the coast until the Ythan (pronounced <u>eye</u>-than) estuary at Newburgh on A975. The northern bank of the estuary is a wild habitat of dune and coastal heath, which is explained at the **Forvie Nature Reserve Visitor Centre** (run by Scottish Natural Heritage).

Continue north, diverting to tiny Whinnyfold, which has a view of the Bay of Cruden and the village of Cruden Bay. Bram Stoker used to vacation here, and the nearby ruin of Slains Castle reputedly inspired his *Dracula*.

At the gloomy **Bullers of Buchan**, the sea has burst through the cliff in a deep, tide-filled, kittiwake-haunted hollow. Beyond, **Peterhead**, the largest whitefish landing port in Europe, and also a North Sea oil servicing center, has a maritime museum.

After St. Fergus comes the austere

Peterhead's harbor—busy with fishing boats

and lonely coastline around **Rattray Head**. The **Loch of Strathbeg**, Scotland's largest landlocked coastal lagoon, is an important wintering ground for thousands of wildfowl.

Off B9033 the fishing villages of St. Combs and Cairnbulg huddle with gable ends to the sea. **Fraserburgh**, dour in gray granite, has **Scotland's Lighthouse Museum** on Kinnaird Head and a fine beach (see page 177).

Turning west, the sands are left behind for gray rocks which rear up beyond Rosehearty and reach impressive heights around Pennan. Seabird colonies are spectacular around the fearsomely precipitous **Troup Head** (not suitable for young children). **Gardenstown** has an attractive little harbor, as well as a fine walk to the west, to the ruin of the 11th-century Kirk of St. John the Evangelist.

180

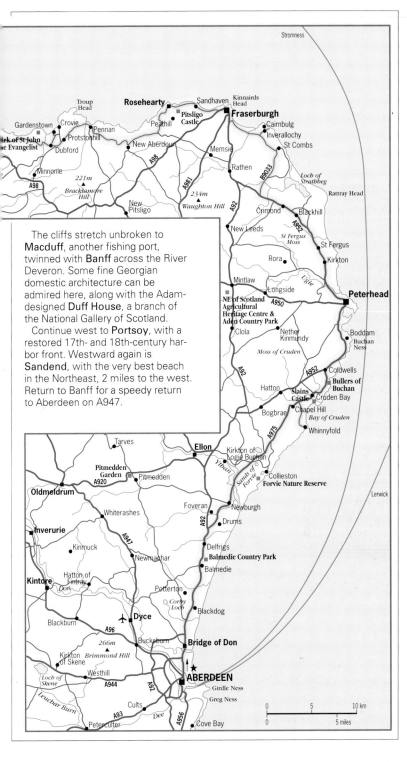

The cliffs stretch unbroken to **Macduff**, another fishing port, twinned with **Banff** across the River Deveron. Some fine Georgian domestic architecture can be admired here, along with the Adam-designed **Duff House**, a branch of the National Gallery of Scotland.

Continue west to **Portsoy**, with a restored 17th- and 18th-century harbor front. Westward again is **Sandend**, with the very best beach in the Northeast, 2 miles to the west. Return to Banff for a speedy return to Aberdeen on A947.

181

Kildrummy Castle

A traitor's reward
Kildrummy was besieged by the English in 1306. Sir Nigel Bruce (King Robert's brother) held out but was betrayed by Osbarn the smith, who had been promised gold by the besiegers. After the castle fell he got his reward—poured molten down his throat. Or so the story goes.

▶▶ **Kildrummy Castle and Gardens** *162B2*

Founded in the 13th century, Kildrummy is one of the best-preserved medieval castles in Scotland—though far from complete, as one glance at the shattered walls will confirm. Built in an unusual shield-shape plan, and echoing the fortresses at Caernarvon and Harlech in Wales, Kildrummy controlled the routes through Donside to the north. It withstood many sieges and was finally dismantled after its role as Jacobite headquarters in the 1715 rebellion. *Open*: daily in summer.

Kildrummy Castle Gardens are a separate concern from the castle, though the two make a good combined visit. They occupy the adjacent quarry from which the castle rock was cut. In this sheltered bowl are many unusual varieties of rock plant and shrubs, as well as a water garden designed by a Japanese engineer. The gardens are open daily in summer and there is often a chance to buy surplus plants.

▶▶ **Leith Hall** *162B2*

The archetypal "big hoose," Leith Hall was occupied by the Leiths, later the Leith Hays, for 300 years. They were a military family, and the National Trust for Scotland, which has been here since 1945, has made the most of this with an exhibition within the grand mansion. There are fine walks within the grounds and a pleasant garden. The house is closed in winter; the grounds are open all year.

An eccentric bird
Among the Leith Hall soldiers was Colonel Alexander Sebastian Leith Hay, who became laird in 1862. He was in the Thin Red Line at Balaclava and also helped crush the Indian Mutiny. He returned home with a white cockatoo named Cocky, which spoke Hindustani and lived for 50 years at Leith Hall. On its death it was given a burial with full military honors.

▶▶ **North East of Scotland Agricultural Heritage Centre** *162C2*

Anyone navigating the hinterland of the old county of Aberdeenshire, a bleak rolling landscape of fields and farmed slopes, will realize that the forefathers of today's rural communities must have been a hardworking lot. They were the ones who turned a poorly drained, boulder-strewn, exposed shoulder into a fertile and prosperous landscape. Their story is told in the North East of Scotland Agricultural Heritage Centre, housed in the old home farm of the former Aden (pronounced "aa-din") estate. The center's displays include an award-winning exhibition "*Weel Vrocht Grun,*" defiantly entitled in the Northeast's own speech and meaning "the well-worked ground." The estate is now a 232-acre country park, well sheltered by trees and proving that not all of this corner is exposed to all the winds that blow. *Open*: daily in summer.

► **Stonehaven** *162C1*

While Aberdeen's growth has turned many nearby places into dormitories, the center of Stonehaven appears to have retained its character. Originally a fishing settlement, it was extended in 1795 by the local laird (lord) who built spacious streets around a main square a short distance from the old harbor. Today, there are only a few working boats. The local museum is housed in the old town's 16th-century tolbooth, hard by the harbor edge (*open*: Wednesday to Monday, June to September).

Dunnottar Castle►► A few minutes down the coast, this 14th-century fortress is worth visiting for its spectacular setting on a rocky headland. Dunnottar was a stronghold of the Earls Marischal of Scotland. In the wars of the Commonwealth, the Scottish crown jewels were hidden here from Cromwell's army. *Open*: daily, except for winter weekends.

The Earls Marischal
The title of Marischal originally meant "the keeper of the king's mares." The Keith family of Dunnottar were the hereditary Earls Marischal until their extinction in the 18th century.

Stonehaven harbor

183

Tomintoul *162A2*

Near the southern end of the Malt Whisky Trail, Tomintoul lies among the uplands of Moray, with the Cairngorms on the far horizon. It was founded by the Duke of Gordon in 1779. The village makes a good base for exploring the Glenlivet Estate (part of the Crown Estate), which offers a variety of outdoor activities among the high moors and forests. Tomintoul also has a local museum, part of the tourist information center (closed in winter). It lies on A939 to Cockbridge, which rises to 2,000 feet, giving access to the Lecht skiing area, and has gained a certain notoriety as it is usually the first road in Scotland to be blocked by snow. However, it is an important link for tourists between Speyside and Deeside.

Scottish heights
Tomintoul is the highest village in the Highlands at 1,161 feet: the highest village in Scotland is Wanlockhead (1,381 feet) in Dumfries and Galloway.

THE GREAT GLEN AND THE WESTERN HIGHLANDS

REGION HIGHLIGHTS

184

Carrbridge: the arch across the River Dulnain dates from 1715

Braemore 109m
Loch Glascarnoch
Ballchraggan
Balintore
ur Mòr
1045m
Loch Glass
Invergordon
Cromarty
Moray Firth
Cromarty Firth
Burghead
Findhorn
Elgin
Loch Fannich
Ben Wyvis
Garve
Falls of Rogie
Dingwall
Black Isle
Rosemarkie
Fort George
Brodie Castle
Forres
Dallas Dhu
Loch Luichart
ath
Strathpeffer
Conon Bridge
Fortrose
Ardersier
Cawdor Castle
Nairn
Randolph's Leap
hnasheen
Muir of Ord
North Kessock
Culloden
Ferness
MORAY
Beauly
Beauly Firth
Battlefield
Glen trathfarrar
Aigas Dam Fish Lift
Inverness
Clava Cairns
Dava
Struy
Daviot
Lochindorb
Strathspey
Cannich
Milton
Drumnadrochit
Dores
Tomatin
Grantown-on-Spey
Cromdale
ardoch
Urquhart Castle
Glen Affric
Carrbridge
Nethy Bridge
Boat of Garten
Invermoriston
Foyers
Landmark Visitor Centre
Strathspey Railway & Loch Garten
Whitebridge
Loch Mhor
Aviemore
Glen Moriston
Monadhliath Mountains
Loch an Eilean
Glen More Forest Park
Caledonian Canal
Fort Augustus
Kingussie
Kincraig
Cairn Gorm 1245m 1309m
Loch Oich
Invergarry
Newtonmore
Ben Macdui
Loch Garry
Parallel Roads of Glen Roy
Laggan
Loch Laggan
Badenoch
The Cairngorm Mountains
Braemar
ABERDEENSHIRE
Loch Lochy
haber
Dalwhinnie
arlochy
Spean Bridge
une's aircase
Glen Spean
Loch Ericht
Pass of Drumochter
Grampian Mountains
1067m
3m
Nevis & n Nevis &
Loch Treig
Atholl
Spittal of Glenshee
Kinlochleven
Rannoch Station
Killichonan
Kinloch Rannoch
Tummel Bridge
Loch Rannoch 1081m
Loch Tummel
Blair Atholl
Killiecrankie
Pitlochry
len Coc
Loch Laidon
Tummel Forest Park
Schiehallion
Tay
Garry
Loch Tulla
Achallader Castle
Loch Rannoch & Glen Lyon
1214m
Kenmore
Aberfeldy
Dunkeld
Blairgowrie
Bridge of Orchy
1074m
Glen Lyon
Ben Lawers
Loch Tay
River Tay
Amulree
PERTH
Tyndrum
Dochart
Killin
929m
Ben Chonzie
Almond
Scone Palace
Stanley
nally
Ben Lui
1171m
Ben More
Lochearnhead
River Earn
Methven
AND KINROSS
Crianlarich
Balquhidder
985m Ben Earn
Loch Earn
Comrie
Crieff
Perth
Ardlui
Ben Vorlich
Strathyre
Braco
Earn
Bridge of Earn
STIRLING
Callander
Kinbuck
Auchterarder
Gleneagles Hotel
Arrochar
Tarbet
Loch Katrine
The Trossachs
973m
Aberfoyle
Doune
Dunblane
Ochil Hills
M90
Kinross
Ben Lomond
Queen Elizabeth Forest Park
Bridge of Allan
20m
Rumbling Bridge
Loch Leven
Lomond
Luss
Loch Lomond
Kippen
Forth
M9
Stirling
Alloa
Cowdenbeath
Dunfermline
Garelochhead
Balmaha
Kincardine
FIFE
elensburgh
Drymen
Killearn
Fintry
Campsie Fells
M80
Denny
Grangemouth
Kilsyth
Bo'ness
South Queensferry
Gourock
Alexandria
Strathblane
Lennoxtown
Falkirk
M9
Linlithgow
Livingston
eenock
Port Glasgow
Dumbarton
Milngavie
Kirkintilloch
Cumbernauld
M8
Renfrew
Clydebank
M80 M73
Airdrie
WEST
Malleny
Johnstone
M8
GLASGOW
Coatbridge
Whitburn
LOTHIAN
Largs
Paisley
Rutherglen
Motherwell
Barrhead
Hamilton
Wishaw
Pentland Hills
West Kilbride
East Kilbride
Chatelherault
Carluke
Dolphinton
hre 1
Beith
RSHIRE
Dalry
Stewarton
Larkhall
Carnwath
rossan
Kilwinning
Strathaven
Lanark
New Lanark
Biggar
SCOTTISH
altcoats
Cunninghame
esmahagow
BORDERS
Irvine
Kilmarnock
Galston
Douglas
Upper Tweeddale
lyde
Troon
Tarbolton
Mauchline
Muirkirk
Abington
Tweed
Prestwick
Auchinleck
Crawfordjohn
830m Broad Law
Ayr
Coylton
Cumnock
SOUTH LANARKSHIRE
Alloway
EAST AYRSHIRE
Nith
822m
Kyle
Doon
Sanquhar
Moffat
ulzean Castle & Country Park
Dalmellington
unure
rberrySOUTH AYRSHIRE
C
D

The Great Glen The area surrounding this coast-to-coast fault line that splits the Highlands takes in Scotland's highest mountains and greatest lochs. With the exception of the gentler landscape around Nairn on the inner Moray Firth, and the greenness of the far end of Kintyre, reminiscent of pastoral Ayrshire, most of this terrain is rugged. Though the central Cairngorms have been almost tamed in recent years by ski lifts, which spill visitors all year round on the fragile arctic plateau, the western Cairngorms remain the province only of the hardy hill-walker. West of the Great Glen, the big glens of Cannich and Affric carry hydroelectric dams, but emptiness still lies beyond. Loch Morar, deepest of all in the far west, still leads in to the trackless reaches of the Rough Bounds of Knoydart. Even some of the shores of Loch Linnhe are roadless.

As for the Great Glen itself, its hills just fail to reach truly magnificent proportions: it is large without being impressive. Yet it remains firmly on the touring route of those determined to "do" the Highlands in a day or two and especially of those who hope to find the essence of the Highlands in the busy town of Inverness. Excursions off this main through route are rewarding, to places such as Glen Roy with its curious Parallel Roads, or to the far reaches of Loch Arkaig and the mysteries of hidden Jacobite treasure.

Speyside This region, among the old pinewoods, is subtly different. The blue shadows on the Cairngorm backdrop change as the sun goes round, first highlighting then casting shadows deep into the Larig Ghru, the ancient mountain pass that links Speyside with Deeside. Adding to the enticements of birch and Scots pine, lochs with ospreys and other unusual birds, long hill passes and high level excursions, are the commercial developments which range from steam railroads to Highland estate safaris.

The Western Highlands The Argyll area, taking in Loch Linnhe, is different again. Here is the picture postcard interplay of sea loch and wooded hillslope. The mountains diminish in height the farther south you travel, yet the landscape still retains a ruggedness, among the drowned valleys of Knapdale, for example. It is only toward the far end of Kintyre that a sense of the Highlands is lost almost entirely.

Most of the main population centers in the area have been involved with catering to the needs of generations of tourists. Inverness is a large commercial center serving all of the Northern Highlands. Aviemore was a custom-built 1960s development. Re-development seems always just around the corner: it is looking seedy and is a definite culture shock for those expecting quaint little cottages on the road north. Fort William is an all but unavoidable natural route center in the West Highlands. It has no pretensions toward the picturesque but is practical in

The Great Glen
The wrenching and sliding of the earth's crust formed this coast-to-coast fault line from the sea roads of Loch Linnhe to the inner Moray Firth. Granite from Foyers above Loch Ness on its eastern side matches granite around Strontian, nearly 60 miles away to the west, in the hills of Ardgour.

Western Highland contrasts
One example of the inter-play between loch and high ground that typifies the Western Highlands is the summit of Ben Nevis. Though it is the highest point anywhere in the U.K., it is only 5 miles from the salt waters of Loch Linnhe.

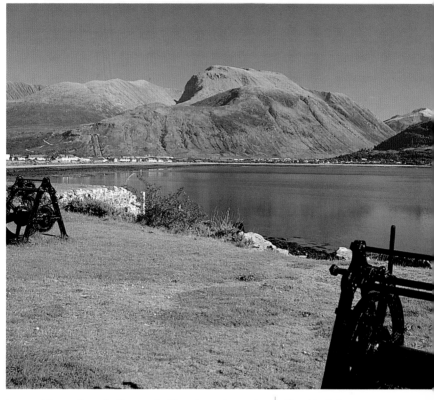

Ben Nevis from
Corpach

terms of its services. Farther south, Oban is a gateway to the Hebrides and an old established resort. The often overlooked Campbeltown at the south end of Kintyre is a self-contained working community.

Away from the main towns, there are plenty of smaller places but the essence of this area is definitely rural and rugged, with extensive forestry plantings and a sense of mossy green lushness. When the cloud is down on the hills and the prevailing southwesterlies are dumping their moist contents on campsites and luxury hotels alike, consider it only to be an interlude in the ever-changing pattern of western weather (though it has to be admitted that some of the wettest parts of Scotland lie around the Great Glen). When the sun returns, the colors of hill and loch shine out in with breathtaking clarity and the West Highlands can be for-given for everything (except perhaps the midges). This is picture postcard Scotland, if you time it right.

Highland calf

Controversial name
The area around the River Spey is sometimes known as Speyside and sometimes Strathspey. The local tourist board's introduction of "Spey Valley" to its name provoked fierce correspondence in Scotland's serious press from numerous partisan Scots decrying the "anglicizing" of Scotland's place-names. Even road signs, at one stage, had the new name unofficially blanked out.

▶▶▶ **(Aviemore) and Strathspey** 185D4

The transformation of Aviemore▶ from sleepy Highland railroad junction to upscale St. Moritz-type ski resort never quite worked. Concrete shoe boxes among birches failed to appeal to the desired clientele who, unaccountably, still preferred the Alps. Skiing is very popular here, however, although a combination of gale-force winds and the icy upper slopes of the Cairngorm might deter those who just want to pose in fashionable skiwear. Aviemore bustles all year round with tourists and skiers, but is fortunately a very small blot on a very large and impressive landscape. Strathspey▶▶▶ itself is magnificent. Use Aviemore as a good *après-ski* base or at other times of the year for its shops and variety of leisure facilities: ice rink, theater, movie theater, restaurants, discos, amusements, snooker, and so on, all within the Aviemore Centre itself, plus a range of activities and places to visit within easy reach.

The innovative Landmark Visitor Centre▶▶▶ at Carrbridge was the first of its kind and portrays many aspects of Scotland, from history to wildlife, by means of audiovisuals and displays. There is also a range of outdoor attractions: mazes, nature trails, and adventure playgrounds (*open*: all year).

Rothiemurchus Estate▶▶ This working Highland estate, only minutes southeast from Aviemore, offers estate and farm tours by tractor and trailer, Land Rover safari-type excursions, guided walks, a trout farm, fishing lochs, and other activities. Its visitor center opens all year.

Highland Wildlife Park Not just today's wildlife, but fauna such as wolves (now extinct in Scotland) can be seen safely fenced off at the Highland Wildlife Park at Kincraig (*open*: daily all year).

Loch an Eilean▶▶▶. There is a good walk right around this inspiring loch close to Aviemore amid ancient pinewood, a low-level option well within the capabilities of most visitors. Crested tits and crossbills are a specialty. Watch your head on the door lintel of the visitor center beside the loch (*open*: daily).

Inshriach Nursery▶▶ This wonderful specialist nursery on B970, 1.2 miles (as the crow flies) west of Loch an Eilean,

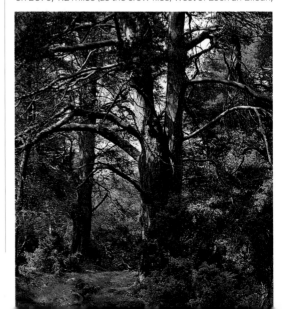

The Great Wood of Caledon—natural pine forest on Speyside

is popular with rock garden enthusiasts. It has a good range of arctic alpine species—and if it grows at Inshriach, it will probably survive in your garden. Its setting makes it a pleasant diversion from a trip to Loch an Eilean. *Open*: Monday to Saturday.

►► Boat of Garten   185D4

Though singling out just one little community from the many in Speyside seems arbitrary, Boat of Garten is typical. It makes a peaceful base for exploring the area, being at a little distance from Aviemore. It has an excellent golf course and a choice of walks through sheltered pinewoods. It is also a steam railroad base.

Offering the best view (the Cairngorms) of any preserved steam railroad line in Britain, the **Strathspey Railway**►►► is pure nostalgia, especially at the original Boat of Garten Station, hard by the Boat Hotel. There is a small museum here as well. The line runs to Aviemore. Check the opening hours in advance, but it operates most of the season.

Bird life
Speyside is home to a number of rare bird species, not only the osprey, but the increasingly rare capercaillie. This is like a cross between a large grouse and a very aggressive turkey. It is still found in the old Scots pinewoods, but its habit of failing to spot high deer fences when it is in flight does little for the species' well-being.

Loch Garten►►► Another gem lies within easy reach. This is where you can spy upon the domestic arrangements of Scotland's most famous pair of ospreys. They get on with the serious business of first catching fish and then feeding it to their voracious offspring, all before the relentless gaze of closed-circuit television cameras, large telescopes, and terribly earnest wardens. Ospreys are again becoming almost common in quite a few lochs and rivers hereabouts, though they were extinct in Scotland by the early years of this century, persecuted by gamekeepers guarding fish stocks, and returned only in 1959. Look for large, hovering, broad-winged birds, a little like giant lapwings at first glance. The visitor blind is open daily (ospreys permitting) in the breeding season (May to August), the reserve opens daily all year.

Steam on Speyside

Cairngorm chairlift

A Cairngorm ghost
Few Scottish ghosts are rugged enough for life on top of the Cairngorms plateau, except for one: the Gray Man of Ben Macdhui. He first terrified the life out of a respectable professor who was walking on the plateau in mist when he became aware of something that followed him, taking one step for every three of his. In 1943, another walker, who happened to be armed, fired his revolver at a "thing" that loomed at him out of the mist. Other tales are told by climbers and local stalkers around the fireside—especially after a dram or two.

Skiing in the Cairn-gorms—big business for Aviemore

▶▶ **Cairngorms** *185D4*

The Cairngorms contain four of the five highest mountains in Britain, some of the finest hill passes and arguably the best ice, snow, and rock climbing. They represent the country's largest continuous stretch of high ground—an arctic tundra plateau. They are flanked by foothills whose slopes carry Britain's largest surviving fragments of natural pine forest. There are endless opportunities for ski touring, walking, climbing, and other activities that respect the fragile environment. The area is under threat from intrusive skiing and tourism developments (see page 188), excessive deer numbers, the proliferation of bulldozed tracks, and commercial afforestation, but still remains magnificent.

▶ **Caledonian Canal** *185C4*

The Caledonian Canal, linking east and west coasts, was started in 1803 under the engineer Thomas Telford. It took 19 years to complete and is about 65 miles long. Approximately 45 miles is along the natural passage formed by three lochs: Lochy, Oich, and Ness, which lie in the Great Glen fault line. The canal has 29 locks, the most famous being the series of eight near Banavie (2 miles north of Fort William), known as Neptune's Staircase. The project received priority as it was considered to have strategic importance for Britain's navy, but was never wide enough to accommodate large naval craft. Today its chief use is recreational. One good place for watching canal activity is at Fort Augustus, with its series of locks through the center of the village.

▶▶▶ **Cawdor Castle** *185D5*

Some castles in private hands impress with their opulence, others display stuffy collections while the owner lives elsewhere. Cawdor Castle, the romantic family home of the earls of Cawdor, does neither of these things, but instead combines the appearance of a fortified stronghold with an air of friendliness.

Though it has a legendary association with Shakespeare's *Macbeth*, it postdates the historical events around which Shakespeare wrote the well-known tragedy. Most of Cawdor is 16th- or 17th-century, though the central tower dates from around 1370, with 15th-century fortifications. Unoccupied for about 100 years after the last Jacobite uprising in 1745, the castle owes much of its charm to its unaltered appearance since those days.

Generations of the family have accumulated a variety of artifacts: portraits, Flemish tapestries, Venetian bed hangings, and so on, as well as historical material, including the iron gate or yett from Lochindorb Castle (see page 195) which the sixth Thane of Cawdor was ordered to destroy. But Cawdor is much more about the overall effect than individual display items.

Best of all are the room notes. Far from breathlessly tiptoeing past objects, visitors can be heard laughing out loud at the witty captions—a scenario unique in a Scottish castle which makes it well worth visiting for that reason alone. There are also attractive gardens. *Open*: daily, except in winter.

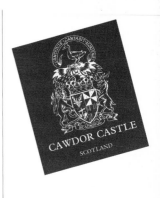

► **Cowal and the Kyles of Bute** *184B2*

Cowal reaches down toward the island of Bute and is bounded by the long fjord-like sea lochs of Loch Long and Loch Fyne. It is sometimes overlooked in the headlong dash for the west coast but is a most attractive part of Argyll. It is also easy to reach from the south via the Gourock to Dunoon ferry crossing. The Arrochar Alps guard its northern approaches and it has a number of scenically spectacular roads, of which the Rest and Be Thankful, the A83 west of Arrochar, is the best known.

Much of this area is contained within the **Argyll Forest Park**, with its diversity of walking and pony trekking routes. There are more exotic trees to see in the **Younger Botanic Garden** at Benmore. This outstation of Edinburgh's Royal Botanic Garden features some of the largest trees anywhere in Scotland and a world-famous rhododendron collection. It is closed in winter.

Cowal's outstretched fingers on either side of Bute form the **Kyles of Bute** (from the Gaelic *caolas*, a strait) These peerless stretches of coastal scenery can be enjoyed from A886, en route to or from the Bute ferry at Colintraive.

Brodie Castle
After Cawdor, castle enthusiasts can travel eastward, just into Moray, to enjoy Brodie Castle (see page 177). The long and unbroken line of Brodies (they were here by 1160) has allowed a unique continuity in its acquisitions. Cawdor and Brodie could be fitted into a morning and afternoon, with lunch at Brodie Country Fayre en route.

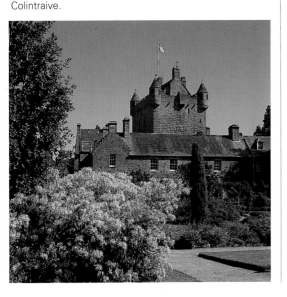

Cawdor Castle

▶▶▶ Crarae Garden   *184B2*

If there is time for only one Argyll garden, then Crarae should be chosen. All the natural advantages of topography and climate have been used to create this woodland garden on a hillside with a tumbling brook. Snow does not linger, rainfall is copious, and these soft conditions are appreciated by many tender shrubs, acer and eucryphia, and a range of Himalayan species. Particularly arresting are the large-leaved rhododendrons, including *R. macabeanum*. There is good color here in spring and autumn, too. Be prepared to walk a little way uphill to take it all in—that way you will see why Crarae has been described as being like a wild corner of some Himalayan gorge. *Open*: all year.

▶▶ Crinan Canal   *184B2*

Designed so that ships could avoid the long haul around the Mull of Kintyre, the 9-mile Crinan Canal was begun in 1794. After many construction problems and the help of

On top of the mountain
A weather observatory operated from 1883 to 1904 on Ben Nevis, surviving the fierce winds and driving snows that so often beset the dangerous summit plateau. There was also a hotel till 1915.

Empty threat
Do not be unnerved by the stacked powder barrels in the Grand Magazine at Fort George. They are empty replicas. Besides, the building was designed to withstand a direct hit.

Crarae Garden

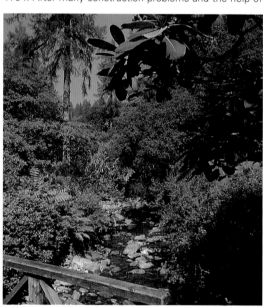

troubleshooting engineer Thomas Telford, it was pronounced satisfactory in 1817. Once used by the Loch Fyne herring fleet seeking new grounds, the canal is mainly used now by yachts, picturesque concentrations of which can be found at the Crinan end, where there is a good hotel and a coffee shop.

▶▶▶ Fort George   *185D5*

Fort George is one of the most vivid experiences of Scotland's history available today. It is also Europe's finest surviving piece of 18th-century military architecture—a huge Georgian fort filling a headland, jutting out into the Moray Firth like a vast battleship forever anchored to the land.

It was built as a response to the Jacobite rebellion of 1745, to ensure that the Highlands never rose again in rebellion. It has never fired a shot in anger. Weapon development soon made it redundant. Yet, oddly, it still has a military presence. (It is slightly unnerving to ask a heavily armed but unerringly polite young soldier for directions to the visitor center.) You can stroll along the great walls with their sentry boxes and embrasures, noting that the

Crinan Canal, west end, at Crinan

whole design is in the form of a pentagon with a bastion at each angle. This is the place to learn a whole new military language: ravelin, casemate, counterscarp, firing step, and so on. There is a visitor center, period rooms of soldiers' quarters, and the regimental museum of the Queen's Own Highlanders. *Open*: all year.

► ▉▉▉ **Fort William** *184B4*

The fort that was founded here in 1690 was named after William, Prince of Orange. It was finally demolished in the 1880s to make way for the railroad. Fort William is a natural route center in Lochaber, all but unavoidable for touring traffic heading for the Great Glen. Like Inverness at the northern end, Fort William is far from picturesque but has an excellent selection of services and shops for books, outdoor wear, tartans, tweeds, woolens, and so on.

The toughest of all mountain races, the Ben Nevis Race

The West Highland Museum►► has an exhibition on tartan and touches upon the area's Jacobite connections; there is a fascinating hidden portrait of Prince Charles Edward Stuart (Bonnie Prince Charlie), painted on a cylinder and viewed with a mirror. *Open*: Monday to Saturday, May to October.

Fort William is famed for its proximity to **Ben Nevis**, though Britain's highest mountain, at 4,407 feet, hides its best profile from the town itself. There are good views from both the Mallaig road and B8004 on the west bank of the Caledonian Canal. A trip into Glen Nevis is also worthwhile for its spectacular hill scenery. Look for the signpost from the roundabout (traffic circle) at the north end of the town.

Parallel Roads of Glen Roy►► These curious parallel lines etched on the sides of the glen are the shorelines of an Ice Age loch, dammed by a glacier at the mouth of the glen, which melted in stages, hence the parallel shorelines, the highest being the oldest.

The Glen Coe Massacre
There have been several larger massacres in the bloody history of clan warfare. However, none convulsed Scotland as much as the killing of around 38 members of the MacIan MacDonalds of Glen Coe on February 13, 1692 by a force of Campbell militia (that is, government troops). The official line was that the clan chief had been late in taking an oath of allegiance to King William (of Orange) and his clan were taught a lesson. Nevertheless, the troops had been billeted with their MacDonald hosts, observing an old Highland custom that no one was ever refused food and shelter, even bitter enemies. It was the breaking of this code and the resulting "murder under trust" that shocked Scotland. The king had blood on his hands—and, besides, the job was botched.

194

The Glenfinnan Monument

►►► Glen Affric   185C5

Glen Affric has a reputation as one of the most beautiful glens in all of Scotland—and this even with a hydro-electric dam.

As a way of getting into the excellent hill and (in some places) natural pinewood scenery, there is a choice of Forestry Commission walks. The best known is around the **Dog Falls**, themselves close to the twisty road up the glen. This trip could also take in the **Aigas Dam Fish Lift►**, on scenic A831 through Strathglass to the north-west, a facility for viewing migrating salmon. *Open*: daily, 10AM and 3PM, June to October.

►► Glen Coe   185C3

Glen Coe is probably the most famous glen in Scotland, partly because it carries a main road which allows some of the finest hill scenery in the central Highlands to be viewed with no effort whatsoever. This includes the impressive view of Buchaille Etive Mor guarding the eastern approaches to the glen, and the "Three Sisters," the three long spurs running off Bidean nam Bian, the highest peak in Argyll. Matching these south-side features is the long wall of the Aonach Eagach ridge enclosing Glen Coe to the north. This is the most spectacular ridge walk on the Scottish mainland—but definitely not for the fainthearted, the unfit, or the novice.

The National Trust for Scotland is in charge of much of the glen, hence the obtrusive visitor center (closed in winter), though even without their presence the sheer grandeur would draw tourists anyway. These hills are awesome and high—but certainly not lonely. Also worth exploring in the vicinity is Glen Etive, a road down to the head of a sea loch with a fine, wild flavor.

At Ballachulish, a former slate-quarrying village west of Glen Coe, **Highland Mystery World** explores the myths and spirits believed in by the Highlanders of old (*open*: all year).

►► Glenfinnan   184B4

The view down Glenfinnan is an image used on everything from postcards to place mats to capture the typical landscape of the Western Highlands. The rash adventurer, Bonnie Prince Charlie, hardly chose this location for scenery alone when he raised the flag of rebellion in August 1745. However, the subsequent Glenfinnan Monument, recalling the escapade, adds interest to the foreground in the view from the main Mallaig road. There is a National Trust for Scotland visitor center here, which tells the story of the prince's campaign (*open*: daily, from April to October).

Equally photogenic is the nearby **Glenfinnan Viaduct▶▶▶** on the "Mallaig Extension" of the West Highland Railway of 1901. The engineer Robert MacAlpine ("Concrete Bob") pioneered the use of mass concrete for such large works while building

the line. Unlike Bonnie Prince Charlie's excursion here, this brought only benefit to the Western Highlands.

Glenfinnan Station and Museum

▶　　　**Grantown-on-Spey**　　　*185D5*

James Grant of Castle Grant planned his new town in 1766, intending to get some return on the poor moorland site. Using the local silver granite, handsome buildings soon sprang up. As well as having local trades such as weaving, the town became popular with tourists. Today, it is still a handsome place and well worth strolling around, especially for a complete contrast to Aviemore. It has interesting shops, if quality souvenirs and gifts are on your list, and a good café or two.

The Speyside Heather Garden Centre▶▶ Within easy reach of Grantown, this center sells a huge variety of heather species, but will also inform you by way of a Heather Heritage Centre on the many different and remarkable uses of heather in the Highland economy of old, from folk remedies to rope-making. *Open*: daily, closed January and Sundays between November and February.

Another excursion north of Grantown-on-Spey leads across endless moors to lonely Lochindorb Castle, a shattered remnant on an island, once the lair of the Wolf of Badenoch (see page 175).

The railroad viaduct
Concrete Bob's railroad viaduct at Glenfinnan has 21 spans and is 1,280 feet long. It receives much attention from photographers when it is carrying one of the steam locomotives running a regular summer service between Fort William and Mallaig.

The "Lone Rowan"
On the way to Glen Coe from the south, on the left-hand side beyond Loch Tulla, look for the "Lone Rowan" on the approaches to the empty stretches of Rannoch Moor. This single tree grows from a crack on a large boulder. For years it has survived the nibbling of sheep and deer and as such has become a kind of symbol among conservationists seeking to restore Scotland's natural tree cover.

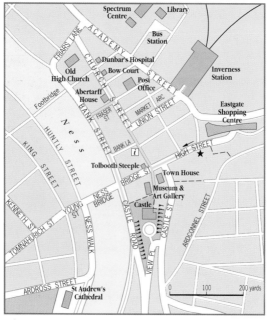

Walk **Around Inverness**

Ancient Inverness was regularly burned by marauding clansmen and little remains. Today, downtown Inverness is a noisy and bustling gateway town serving the north of Scotland. Allow one hour for this walk.

West along High Street, the **Tolbooth Steeple**'s spire dates from 1791, and was damaged and repaired after an earth tremor in 1816. Opposite is Inverness **Town House**, where Prime Minister Lloyd George held the first-ever Cabinet meeting outside London in 1921.

Walk up Castle Wynd to **Inverness Castle**. Though its site is ancient, the present building only dates from 1834–47 and is the Sheriff Court. Note the nearby statue of Flora MacDonald, helpmate of Bonnie Prince Charlie.

Go down steps and follow the River Ness north to Fraser Street. **Abertarff House**, one of the oldest houses in the town, is on Church Street. Farther down Church Street is the much restored **Dunbar's Hospital**. The plaque on the side of the nearby **Bow Court** dates from the 17th century.

Turning south, the best shopping is on Church Street, and in the fine Market Arcade, to the east of Church Street. Return to High Street.

Inverness Castle and the River Ness

■ **Culloden was the last major battle on British soil, fought two and a half centuries ago in order to decide a civil war between the ruling House of Hanover and the Jacobites, who wished to return the exiled House of Stuart—in the guise of Bonnie Prince Charlie—to power. The battle, just to the east of Inverness, accelerated the final demise of a way of life already beginning to disintegrate in the Highlands: the Scottish clan system was something of an anachronism in an increasingly mercantile age ...■**

Anti-Jacobites Only 5–6,000 of the estimated 30,000 fighting men in the Highlands rose in support of the young Stuart prince Charles Edward, known as Bonnie Prince Charlie or the Young Pretender. Anti-Jacobite sentiment prevailed in many parts of Scotland. On his way north from his expedition into England, the prince had no help from Dumfries; and Glasgow was reluctant to supply him with the provisions he demanded. Edinburgh gave the Freedom of the City to the Duke of Cumberland as he took government troops north to confront the Jacobite forces.

197

The battle On a sleety day in April 1746, about 5,000 Jacobites, exhausted after marching for an aborted surprise attack on the Hanoverians, faced 9,000 regular soldiers, including 15 infantry regiments. Through a tactical blunder by the prince's Irish adviser, the Highlanders were lined up at perfect shooting range for the superior government artillery.

Butcher Cumberland
Butcher Cumberland acquired his unsavory nickname due to the conduct of his army after Culloden. Because the rebels were judged to be beyond the law and also because London was a long way off, no mercy was shown, a state of affairs made easier by the fact that the victims were perceived as being racially different in dress and language. This may explain the slaughter which took place on the road to Inverness where bystanders, including women, who had come to watch, were sabered. Wounded rebels were dispatched wherever they were found. Military looting was legalized throughout the Highlands, irrespective of the sympathies of the victims.

The Jacobites were blown away in less than an hour. The Highland charge, when it finally came, was ragged and ineffective. The government troops then went on to commit, with their commander's blessing, the worst series of atrocities ever carried out by the British Army.

Today, the episode is graphically described in an excellent audiovisual in the **Culloden Visitor Centre**. This does much to counter the myth that this was a simple Scottish–English conflict. (Some say there were more Scots on the government side than with the rebels.) Whatever the truth, Culloden Moor is a strange and poignant place, the scene of much waste and little glory.

Drive A loop to the isles

You could use part of this drive to reach Skye via the Mallaig to Armadale ferry link, or to make an excursion to the Small Isles from Arisaig—but, if the weather is good, the stupendous island views from Moidart alone make the trip

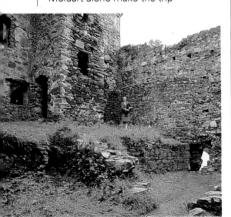

Castle Tioram

enormously worthwhile. Without the Ardnamurchan option (an extra 41-

mile round trip) the drive is 115 miles: it can be driven in three or so hours, using the Corran ferry, but it is best to allow a whole day.

If approaching from the south, note the Corran Ferry off A82, useful for your return. Go through Fort William to take A830 along the shores of Loch Eil. You climb away from the seaweedy levels of Loch Eil to reach the **Glenfinnan Monument** by Loch Shiel. Though the hills on either side of the loch are not especially high, their steeply tilting slopes receding down the loch into a blue haze make them the very distillation of Scottish scenery. The National Trust for Scotland Center outlines the story of (Bonnie) Prince Charles Edward Stuart's rebellious escapade here.

Rail buffs will doubtless admire the **Glenfinnan viaduct** (see page 195). Take care, the train enthusiasts traveling by car are occasionally inclined to chase the locomotive—and it's quite possible that you may be passed several times along this stretch.

Continue to Lochailort, then keep right on A830 for Mallaig. Do not expect to have the dazzling **Sands of Morar** all to yourself in high season. You could also drive down for a close-up view of **Loch Morar,** though its supposed monster, Morag, has been extremely quiet in recent years. Back on the main road, the approach to the town of **Mallaig** is picturesque, with plenty of interest. Actually being

hands on it after the 1715 Jacobite rebellion. It has a grand setting, and a pleasingly unkempt and forgotten air, on a bracken-covered islet barely attached to the mainland by a sandy beach.

Continue through Acharacle and Salen to Loch Sunart to decide on the Ardnamurchan option. If taking B8007 across the peninsula to the most westerly point on mainland Scotland at

there, at the end of the road (and railroad), is, however, something of an anticlimax. The **Mallaig Marine World** has fishing displays on the local fleet, a marine aquarium, and exhibition. *Open*: daily, closed late January to early February.

Return to take the A861 loop at Lochailort. Here are the classic Scottish views of islands set in ultramarine—over the Sound of Arisaig to Eigg, Muck, and Rum—unless it is raining, which is statistically and regrettably very probable. Beyond Kinlochmoidart, **Castle Tioram** is a worthwhile diversion. It was the home of the chief of the MacDonalds of Clan Ranald, who burned it in order to prevent the Campbells getting their

Mallaig harbor

the lighthouse, then allow plenty of time as the road is single lane and winding. Otherwise, continue east to **Strontian**, the community that gave its name to the element strontium, formerly mined nearby. If you go up the road which led to the mining area, you will see a variety of craft businesses on the way.

Continue on A861 through **Glen Sanda**, joining the faster double lane section and, unless returning to Fort William, exit via the Corran Ferry. Alternatively, note the two roads going south into Morven. Both are attractive ways to reach Mull, via the backdoor short ferry crossing at Lochaline.

Inveraray Jail with live jailer

Bridges
Some 18th-century town planning is seen at its best at Inveraray. The stylishness even extends to its bridges, a notable feature on its northern approaches by A83. One of the best examples is the Garron Bridge of 1747–9, reminiscent of those seen on willow pattern plates.

Kilmartin grave slabs

▶▶▶ **Inveraray**   *184B2*

Inveraray is one of the most handsome of Scottish towns and owes its appearance to the mighty chiefs of the Clan Campbell. One of them, Archibald, third Duke of Argyll, planned his grand new town in 1743 at a little distance from his castle. Churches and courthouse, bell tower, and handsome Georgian façades all stand together in harmony. Sadly, Inveraray is one of the wettest places in the Highlands. However, it has some indoor attractions. These include **Inveraray Castle**, the stately pile of the present duke (*Open*: daily during summer; closed Friday, April to June and September to October); there are fine interiors and valuable portraits to admire.

Inveraray Jail▶▶▶ This is a re-creation of a 19th-century county prison, complete with courtroom and cells with live prisoner and jailer. (It is more enticing than it sounds and opens daily throughout the year.) Beware, the prisoner can be extremely talkative—do not mistake him for a wax figure!

Auchindrain Old Highland Township▶▶▶ This fascinating survivor from an earlier age and authentic glimpse of Highland rural life of the past is the last communal tenancy farm township to have survived on its original site in something like its original form. Many of the buildings have been restored and there is an on-site museum. *Open*: daily in summer.

▶▶ **Kilmartin and Dunadd**   *184B2*

Argyll has plenty of early sites and there is a profusion around Kilmartin, a small village on the main Oban–Lochgilphead road. The youngest are the medieval grave slabs in the churchyard at Kilmartin, the work of craftsmen from the so-called Loch Awe school of carving. The prehistoric monuments of the valley to the south of Kilmartin are also curious: 3,000-year-old cairns at **Nether Largie**, one with ax head and cup and ring decoration on the slabs of the cist (burial place) within. Among other early sites, the **Templewood Stone Circles** are close by, and the **Ri Cruin Cairn** farther south is in a group of five cairns in a straight line.

Dating from around AD 500, on a rocky hillock dominating the mossy flatland all around, **Dunadd Fort▶▶** was a stronghold or capital of the first kingdom of the Scots after they arrived from Ireland. This kingdom was known as Dalriada. Some early walling survives, but the chief point of interest of this hill fort is the carvings: a boar, an outline of a footprint, and a hollowed-out basin can be

Shopping in Inveraray

Ogham script
Ogham writing as seen at Dunadd and in other early sites is thought to have originated in Ireland. It consists of groups of strokes scored at various angles to a baseline. At Dunadd, natural cracks and fissures make up this line.

201

seen, as well as several lines of inscription in the ancient ogham system of writing (see panel). These features have been linked to the early kingship rituals of the embryonic Scotland. Altogether, it is a mysterious place, with superb views across the levels towards the Crinan Canal. Access at all times.

▶ ▶ ▶ **Kingussie**   *185D4*

Kingussie (pronounced "kin-yoo-see," from the Gaelic for the head of the pinewood) is a typical Speyside tourism community which benefits from the visitor trade, summer and winter. Nearby **Ruthven Barracks▶**, destroyed by retreating Jacobites after Culloden, still dominate the valley floor near Kingussie. They can be visited en route to the Royal Society for the Protection of Birds' **Insh Marshes▶▶▶**, Scotland's largest inland marsh. Goosander and red-breasted merganser breed here, spotted crake and water rail are often heard; and there are wood and common sandpipers in summer, with hen harriers and buzzards all year. In winter, 10 per cent of the United Kingdom's population of whooper swans is found here, along with greylag geese and goldeneyes.

Highland Folk Museum▶▶▶ Not just a passive show of half-forgotten artifacts, this museum in Kingussie tries to recapture the past with a program of events and activities: you are likely to smell bannocks (oatmeal cakes) toasting or hear a horse being shod if you choose the right day. Costumes, musical instruments and everyday bits and pieces can be seen, as can authentically reconstructed buildings such as a "black house" from Lewis. *Open*: all year, closed weekends in winter.

HIGHLAND WILDLIFE PARK
KINCRAIG

▶▶ **Kintyre** 184B1

This is the longest peninsula in Scotland, with the Mull of Kintyre at its tip. Kintyre's gateway is Tarbert on the isthmus, where there is a heritage center. Some visitors get no farther, which is a pity, as Kintyre offers splendid sea views from both its east- and west-facing coasts, as well as an unexpectedly Lowland air in places. (The Campbell Dukes of Argyll once settled the area with Lowland farmers.) The raised beaches backed by ancient sea cliffs, typical west side landscapes, are bright pasture lands, echoing Ayrshire over on the "mainland."

Near Southend on the Mull of Kintyre

202

Columba's Footsteps
This is the name given to two footprint-shaped impressions on a flat-topped rock near an ancient chapel site. Traditionally, this is where Columba first stepped ashore on Scottish soil. As he could still see Ireland, his home, he took to the sea again before fetching up on the island of Iona.

With the impressive outlines of Islay, Jura, and Gigha parading along the horizon, the main road leads down to Campbeltown, a substantial town, busy with whisky, creameries, and fishing. It seems a lot farther than 12 miles down the narrow roads to the Mull of Kintyre itself. Facing west from this spot is very romantic at sunset. The best views are from the moorland before the road drops to the lighthouse, which is built well down the steep slope. This trip can also be combined with the loop which goes past **Columba's Footsteps**, on top of a flat-topped rock at Keil, moments from the road. Return north from Campbeltown by B842 (on the east side of the peninsula), which is narrow but scenically rewarding.

▶▶ **Knapdale** 184B2

Knapdale is an area defined by the Crinan Canal to the north and West Loch Tarbert to the south. Without high mountains or overwhelming scenery, Knapdale nevertheless has a special charm. The woods which drop to the salty tide-lines of the sea lochs clothe rugged hills. There are primroses in spring and, later, twining honeysuckle. As well as extensive plantings supplementing the natural oakwoods, there is some farming and the area was once noted for its beef cattle. There are no large towns; instead the small villages have often grown up around natural anchorages.

The stone walls of **Castle Sween**▶ overlook the loch of the same name. Possibly dating from the mid-12th century, the ancient fortress is one of the oldest in Scotland, and can be viewed at any time. There are also finely carved medieval grave slabs and crosses of the Knapdale School to be viewed at Kilmory and farther south at Kilberry, with the further advantage of a good pub near the latter. Knapdale is a spot for an unhurried visit. Choose a fine day for the sea views.

►► Loch Awe 184B3

Loch Awe is Scotland's longest loch. Once it drained southward, until with the last Ice Age a breach was made in a fault line. The loch now empties by the Pass of Brander westward to Loch Etive. Loch Awe is most often seen from A85, the main Perth to Oban road, where its length is not appreciated. However, there are numerous points of interest along this stretch.

At the **Cruachan Dam Visitor Center►►►** there are displays about the impressive hydroelectric project which generates 400MW of electricity by running water from a dam high on Ben Cruachan down into Loch Awe (and pumping it back at off-peak times). Minibuses take visitors half a mile into the mountain to see the turbine hall. *Open*: daily, April to mid-November.

The former 15th-century Campbell stronghold of **Kilchurn Castle►►►** is just a short walk across the flats by the loch. Interpretive boards help identify features in the extensive panorama. The castle itself is open at all reasonable times.

Duncan Ban McIntyre Monument►►► Take the road behind Dalmally for one of the very finest vistas in the Western Highlands—an even better view than from Kilchurn. Also worth a look are **Ardanaiseig Gardens►** (*open*: daily in season) and, farther west by Loch Etive, the **Bonawe Iron Furnace►** (*open*: daily in summer), Here Historic Scotland looks after the well-preserved remains of a charcoal furnace for iron-smelting founded in 1753, a reminder that industry even reached these peaceful Highland shores 250 years ago.

203

Kilchurn Castle by Loch Awe

An unsuccessful speed attempt
Between Invermoriston and Drumnadrochit on A82, a cairn recalls the world water speed record attempt by John Cobb. He was killed here in 1952 when his jet-boat hit a mysterious patch of ripples at high speed. Inevitably, this tragedy is linked to the monster phenomenon, as the loch was otherwise calm.

▶   **Loch Ness**   *185C5*

Loch Ness has a larger volume of water than any other Scottish loch. It is around 825 feet deep in places, and the water in this great glacier-gouged trench is said never to freeze. Because of its mysterious reputation, it is very popular with tourists. Take time to explore the area away from the main loch itself, particularly the big glens to the west around Strathglass and also peaceful Stratherrick eastward. Though Loch Ness ends up on most people's touring list, like Inverness, Loch Lomond, and the Trossachs, the loch itself can be a faint anticlimax—a big sheet of water, certainly, yet lacking in real grandeur.

The west-bank road, the busy main A82, goes through Drumnadrochit with its "Official Loch Ness Monster Exhibition" and "Original Loch Ness Monster Visitor Centre," among other enticements. With souvenir shops and cafés as well, it is all-year monster marketing here. Nearby **Urquhart Castle** was once one of the largest castles in Scotland but was blown up in 1692 lest it fall into Jacobite hands. The castle viewpoint is popular with fast-moving tour buses "doing" Scotland in a day. It is a relief to escape to the gentler and more subtle attractions of the east-side road. These include **Loch Tarff**, north of Fort Augustus on B862, and the superb viewpoint beyond (toward Inverness) with its panorama of the Monadhliath and waves of northern Highland hills. The route here follows the old military road, completed by General Wade's men in 1726. The road runs to Whitebridge, with a handsome preserved Wade bridge, then on to Foyers, where the **Falls of Foyers**▶▶ are worth a visit. (Park beside the post office, but take care with young children on the slippery paths). Inverfarigaig is lower down. Starting from the Forest Centre, a forest walk leads up to a fine view of the loch.

Castle Urquhart,
Loch Ness

The Loch Ness Monster

■ Scottish folklore has plenty of references to water spirits, which lurk in and around lochs and burns (brooks), often with evil intent. The water kelpie is blended with Gaelic *each-uisge*, the water horse, and other beasts in a fantastic menagerie of the Celtic imagination ...■

The start of the story One quiet week on the *Inverness Courier* in May 1933, there was space for a report that had come from a local correspondent and water bailiff. He had heard of a couple who had seen a strange animal disporting itself in the dark waters of the loch. The couple were thought to be running one of the hotels in Drumnadrochit.

Soon other sightings flooded in. National papers took up the story and "monster mania" hit the headlines. A pre-war patrolman from a motorists organization reported that he could create pandemonium among the lines of cars parked by the loch merely by pointing over the water. Meanwhile, Inverness Town Council voted to reduce its publicity expenditure substantially for 1934.

The story has refused to go away. It has spawned books, supported a variety of tourism-related businesses both by the loch and in Inverness, and attracted both dedicated amateurs and hoaxers. It has generated dubious movie sequences and still photographs, echo soundings, and sincere testimony from dozens of eyewitnesses who have seen something.

There is undoubtedly a strange phenomenon to be witnessed here, whose manifestation is of great importance to the local economy. Its appearance is in inverse proportion to the number of cameras trained on the loch at any given moment. Loch Ness is a very large body of water, prone to mirages in still, calm conditions—ideal visitor and monster-spotting weather.

In the Scottish legal system there is a verdict "not proven." Without enough evidence for a conviction, Nessie has to remain a modern myth—the water kelpie with an excellent publicity machine.

Sunday observance
A Free Church minister in Fort Augustus wrote of the 1930s monster craze: "the word 'monster' is really not applicable to the Loch Ness animal, but is truly applicable to those who deliberately sin against the light of law and revelation." He was objecting to visitors going monster-spotting on a Sunday.

Some explanations
Swimming red deer, diving otters, floating logs or vegetation, cormorants, boats' wakes, seals, and many more everyday things have been suggested as explanations.

Not the real thing at Drumnadrochit

Road-building expectations
One explanation often given for the sudden flurry of sightings in the 1930s was the new road which gave better views of the loch. Some even said the beast or beasts had been disturbed by the blasting. Yet General Wade and his men built a military road down the east side of the loch to supersede the first high level road of 1726. They also blasted out rock above Inverfarigaig and must therefore have created quite a disturbance. Perhaps Wade's forces were too busy keeping a sharp look-out for Jacobites to notice long-necked creatures.

At Oban harbor

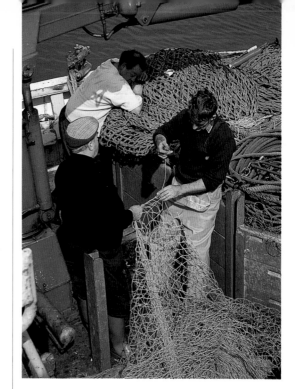

Two cultures
It was once the boast of the Stuart monarchs that they had a town in their realm that was so large that the inhabitants spoke different languages at either end. This was a reference to Nairn, where the Lowland fishers at the sea end of town used the Scots tongue (still heard eastward along the Moray Firth today). At the landward end of the town, the farmers spoke Gaelic. Thus Nairn has for long been on the dividing line between Highland and Lowland cultures.

The Atlantic Bridge
The Clachan Bridge is a single arched bridge of 1792 linking the island of Seil with the mainland. Seil is one of the so-called slate islands, recalling an industry that lasted for 200 years until a violent storm in 1881 flooded the quarry workings and closed down the industry overnight. The Clachan Bridge is often called the Atlantic Bridge, because it spans an arm of that ocean. Other bridges on the western seaboard do likewise, but only the Clachan Bridge is so labeled.

►► **Nairn**   *185D5*

More Lowland than Highland, Nairn, with its resort air and famous golf course, always seems to have had a split personality. The former fisher town by the harbor is separated by the main road from the main shopping streets of a center once dependent on agricultural activities. Both lie apart from the mansions and hotels of the seaside resort development that benefited from the arrival of the Highland Railway in the mid-19th century. The resort atmosphere is doubtless helped by the low rainfall—a mere 22 inches annually.

Nairn Fishertown Museum►► This pleasingly informal local museum, staffed by helpful enthusiasts, tells the story of how the harbor was built by Thomas Telford in the 1820s and how, about a hundred years later, the herring fishery business declined. The harbor is now mainly used by pleasure craft. *Open*: afternoons except Sunday, in the main season.

The **Nairn Literary Institute Museum** is a classic, slightly old-fashioned museum which includes relics from Culloden. *Open*: Monday to Saturday, afternoons only June to September. Then there are a golf course and miles of beach backed by dunes, stretching east to the Culbin Forest. Fort George, and Cawdor and Brodie Castles are also within easy reach.

► **Newtonmore**   *185D4*

Newtonmore is a Speyside community made more peaceful by the A9 bypass. The old Celtic game of shinty (like a boisterous form of field hockey) has quite a hold here and at nearby Kingussie. The village also has the **Clan Macpherson Museum**► (*open*: daily in summer) with its display of clan artifacts, some relating to the '45 rebellion. Within easy reach of Newtonmore, along A86, west of Laggan, a track leads on to the **Corrieyairack Pass►**, completed by General Wade's men in 1732. This high-level military route from Speyside to the Great Glen that zigzags up to approximately 2,500 feet, soon fell into disuse because of the severe Scottish winters. Now this piece of Scotland's story is disintegrating due to the attentions of four-wheel-drive enthusiasts.

►► Oban   184B3

When the railroad arrived in 1880, Oban was described as the new "Charing Cross of the Highlands"—a reference to London's busiest train station. The rail company initiated trips to the islands and the sea lochs around. Today, the railroad is still here, though most of Oban's visitors now come by road.

On the way from the east, A82 passes the **Falls of Lora** at Connel Bridge. This curious turbulence at the mouth of Loch Etive can be seen below the bridge when the tide runs strongly. Even nearer to Oban is the 13th-century **Dunstaffnage Castle** (*open*: in summer), an old MacDougall stronghold which once controlled the sea roads of Argyll. There are spectacular views back to Ben Cruachan.

Oban is built around a sheltered bay. Unashamedly visitor-centered, many of the well-built solid houses have "B & B" signs outside, and there is a wide choice of hotels. Oban is both a transit point for the ferry connections and a resort. Within the town is a good choice of commercial attractions with long main season opening hours, including scale-model rooms, a distillery, audiovisual shows, plus other summer entertainments.

McCaig's Tower► is prominent above the harbor. Sometimes called McCaig's Folly, it recalls a local banker who had it built as a family memorial to ease local unemployment. It is open at all times. Both the tower and **Pulpit Hill►** make excellent viewpoints over this quite handsome town. There are numerous excursions by boat—on spectacular Loch Etive, for example.

Sea Life Centre►►► This is at Barcaldine, 10 miles north of Oban, and makes a popular and rewarding excursion. Britain's marine life is revealed to be every bit as flourishing and exotic as anything in the tropics. *Open*: mid-February to November.

A world in miniature—½-scale exhibition, in Oban

Feeding seals at the Sea Life Centre, Barcaldine

THE NORTHERN HIGHLANDS

The Northern Highlands From a southern viewpoint, it is easy to assume that Scotland shrinks as you go north. But take care when route planning in this area, as there is still a lot of ground to cover. Inverness to Thurso, for example, is farther than Carlisle to Glasgow, and the divided highway sections of A9 come to an end not very far over the Kessock Bridge beyond the Highland capital.

However, this is an area that has seen many road improvements in recent years. Ullapool is no longer a single-lane crawl made hazardous by southbound fish trucks. Instead, it is an easy hour from Inverness. Scourie and Laxford Bridge, far north on the western seaboard, are another two places that can be reached without resorting to single-lane driving.

All of this means there is more time to look at the scenery, the chief attraction of the north. The eastern side continues to resemble a Lowland farming strip most of the time. Look for the use of lines of Caithness flagstones set on edge as field boundaries, highly characteristic of the sparse wind-honed pastures of the north. Yet the moors with their attendant sense of wildness reach down to the eastern seaboard in places—around Helmsdale, for example. There are also spectacular sea cliffs.

Traveling westward, away from the coastal cultivation,

Destitution Road and the shoulders of An Teallach, near Ullapool

Weatherbeaten hills
Some mountains are disappearing fast. The popular Stac Polly in Coigach has lost a few pinnacles in recent years and its red sandstone is powdering and strewing great screes down its flanks. Meanwhile, it is said that on Foinaven, a northern peak just below the magic Munro mark, you can hear erosion—the gentle tinkle of chips of Cambrian quartzite intermittently falling from its fast-weathering gray rock summits. So visit soon—before it is too late.

you soon reach uplands—the boggy flows of Caithness, for instance, with their long open vistas ending in blue hills beyond the blocks of alien and controversial conifers. In the far north, the transition westward into uncultivated landscape is gradual. In the old county of Ross-shire it can be more abrupt. One point that typifies this transition is on the main A832 west of Contin, near the Falls of Rogie (see page 223). Quite suddenly, the last of the Lowland barley, woods, and pasture drops back eastward and its vivid greenness is replaced, at a single bend, by enveloping Highland pinewoods, gray hills, and a choppy loch.

Empty spaces Beyond, you enter the empty quarter. Settlement in the north is mainly, though not exclusively, coastal. The interior conforms to the pattern of much of Highland Scotland. Generally, it is a network of substantial privately owned estates, with vast areas given over to deer stalking, often bought as an investment by absentee landlords. It is the owners of these exclusive sanctuaries, determined to make their land pay by offering shooting rights, who feel threatened by the increasing numbers of other countryside users, notably hill walkers intent on "bagging" not a stag, but another Munro.

Fortunately, some of the very best chunks of landscape, such as the Torridons, Kintail, and parts of Coigach, are owned or managed by conservation agencies determined to compromise with all parties.

Beyond the backbone of Scotland in Wester Ross and particularly in Sutherland, the old sandstone peaks sit on their plinth of ancient glacier-scoured rock. It is this spare and empty landscape of a thousand lochans (tiny lakes) scratched out of the Lewisian gneiss (granite-like rock), overlooked by cliffs, rock terraces, and shattered hills that is the essence of the far north.

Summer daylight hours lengthen noticeably hereabouts—it is perfectly possible to read outdoors at 11PM around midsummer (if the midges will let you) and it never seems to get dark. However, the climate does not alter in a uniform way. The far north sometimes has periods of a curious flat calm, especially away from the hills and out on the headlands. Golfers can be enjoying a round at Gairloch in good conditions while climbers in the Torridons are taking compass bearings and extracting rain jackets from rucksacks. Even at low level, for example, walking by Loch Clair, admiring the profile of Liathach in Glen Torridon, you may well experience four seasons within an hour.

It is all too easy to be hopelessly beguiled by the northwest landscapes, especially in the Torridon hills or, farther north, around Inverpolly. Certainly, the Northern Highlands have attracted lots of permanent newcomers from other parts of the United Kingdom throughout the 1980s, with a noticeable improvement in eating-out options, compared with 20 years ago. Though many visitors want to make their way north and west, do not forget the gentler attractions of Easter Ross and Caithness with their old communities such as Cromarty and Dornoch, just two of the handsome little places on the eastern seaboard.

In this northern region, all roads seem to lead to the "Capital of the Highlands." Inverness is now bypassed but is still a natural route center, with roads to the north and west leading out like the spokes of a wheel. And though caution is advised when planning touring routes—it may be farther than you think—it is also true that no matter how great the sense of emptiness, of remoteness and spare beauty in these lands of ancient rock, if it all becomes a little too intimidating, then you can always rush back in a few hours to Inverness with its supermarkets, traffic lights, and other comforting signs of civilization...

Durness schoolchildren's wallhanging of the Highland Clearances

An overview of the North
From the summit of Ben More Assynt, one of Sutherland's Munros (see page 149), on a clear day it is possible to see not only a great sweep of the Northern Highlands but simultaneously Orkney and the Western Isles.

Duncansby Stacks, near John o Groats, Caithness

Remembering Queen Victoria's Diamond Jubilee, Dingwall

212

High-level grouse
There are few places in Scotland where you can see ptarmigan from the car, but this sometimes absurdly tame high-altitude grouse makes its home among the frost-shattered boulders on the exposed plateau at the top of the Bealach-na-Ba (Gaelic, meaning the pass of the cattle). This is the spectacular way to Applecross, reaching 2,050 feet with magnificent views to Skye.

Fossil fish
Cromarty-born Hugh Miller (1802–56) was a pioneering self-taught geologist, who started work as a stone-mason. He developed an interest in the fossils he found in the local sandstone quarries, and eventually achieved an international reputation for his discoveries and classi-fication of primitive fishes. His birthplace cottage is in the care of the National Trust for Scotland and may be visited in Cromarty.

The road to Applecross, toward the Bealach-na-Ba

▶ **Achiltibuie and the Summer Isles** *208B3*
A side road through Coigach beyond Ullapool offers spectacular views of the impossible crenellations of Stac Polly on the skyline. The single track road eventually runs through the 3-mile straggle of homesteads that is Achiltibuie—a place certainly far removed from urban pressures. The Summer Isles make up part of the peer-less sea views. This bleak group off the mainland of Wester Ross hold a strange fascination for some. Cruises go from Ullapool (inquire at the tourist information center) and from Achiltibuie (ask at the post office).

▶▶ **Applecross** *208A1*
Access to Applecross used to be easiest by sea, especially when the high-level Bealach-na-Ba was closed by snow. Since the 1970s, the settlement has had a low-level road built from Shieldaig. Applecross is associated with St. Maelrubha, who established a monastery here in AD 673. Only a few fragments of early crosses survive from its ancient religious past, but the place still has the air of a remote sanctuary.

▶▶▶ **Cromarty** *209C2*
Well worth the Black Isle diversion, this is one of the most satisfying of Scottish towns: full of character, a place that has seen its fortunes rise and fall, with herring and coastal trading, and rise again with oil.
Cromarty Courthouse▶▶▶ is perhaps the best place to start a tour of the town. Now a visitor center, it portrays the development of Cromarty into a prosperous 18th-century trading burgh (town). If time permits, take the "personal tape tour" of the town's fine buildings. It is closed January.

▶ **Dingwall** *209C2*
The former county town of Easter Ross is pleasingly workaday with a good range of shops. It has long been an administrative center—its name, from the Norse *thing-vollr*, place of assembly, is a reminder that it was an important settlement in 11th-century Viking times. Within easy reach is the little-known **Black Rock Gorge**▶▶ above Evanton. The River Glass runs through a gorge, about 100 feet deep in parts, yet hemmed in by black and mossy rocks only 13 feet apart at their narrowest. The spot has a decidedly sinister atmosphere.

The Brahan Seer

■ **Brahan is an estate near Dingwall whose name is now strongly associated with the most famous of Highland prophets, the Brahan Seer. Various stories and legends have become attached to him, and fact and fiction are blended. The Brahan Seer is thought to have been a certain Coinneach Odhar (the Gaelic for "Brown Kenneth," pronounced "co-in-yach oar") who came to work on the estate in the late 17th century ...■**

His prophecies The seer predicted the railroads: "long lines of carriages without horses will run between Inverness and Dingwall and Skye." The rise of Strathpeffer as a spa was likewise noted. Of the well he said: "Uninviting and disagreeable as it now is...the day will come when it shall be under lock and key." Some prophesies are eerie, especially one curious prediction concerning the terrible disaster which would befall the world when the River Ness in Inverness was spanned by five bridges. A fifth bridge was opened on the river a few days before the outbreak of World War II.

The most unsettling of his prophesies has already partly come to pass. In it he saw the 19th-century coming of the sheep and the emptying of the glens of people. Complete fulfillment of the ending has yet to happen: "the deer and other wild animals in the huge wilderness will be exterminated and browned by horrid black rains. The people will then return and take undisturbed possession of the lands of their ancestors." This meaning is still discussed in the Highlands, with oil pollution and nuclear fallout as two unpleasant alternatives.

An unforeseen end Brown Kenneth came to an unfortunate end when, at an aristocratic gathering to which he had been invited, perhaps as a novelty act, he reported what the husband of Lady Seaforth was doing at the time (being unfaithful while on a visit to Paris). For such an insult in front of her assembled guests, the furious Lady Seaforth had him burned in a tar barrel—or at least that's how the story goes.

Burned in a Brahan tub
On the orders of Lady Seaforth, the Brahan Seer was rolled down a hill in a burning tar barrel at Chanonry Point near Fortrose in the Black Isle. A memorial can be seen there to this day. However, this may not have happened to the 17th-century seer but to another Brown Kenneth accused of witchcraft a century earlier. It seems unlikely that someone with a gift for foretelling the future could not have foreseen the consequences of insulting his hostess.

Inverness; the fifth bridge over the Ness at Inverness turned out to be "a bridge too far"

Drive — Dunnet Head to Durness, along the north coast

By traveling in an east–west direction on this north coast drive, you can see the open, flagstone-bordered fields of the edge of Caithness gradually giving way to the moors and mountains of wild Sutherland. This route (in all 82 miles long) could be driven in two hours or so, but to get the best from it you might wish to arrange an overnight stay in either the Durness or Tongue area.

Crossing the Kyle of Durness, for the Cape Wrath minibus

Dunnet Head is the most northerly point in Scotland and makes a worthwhile short excursion from **Thurso.**

Heading west from the town, you will see the unmistakable profile of **Dounreay**, which became the world's first fast reactor to produce commercial electricity, on a site about as far from the Houses of Parliament as it could possibly be. It is now being decommissioned.

At **Melvich**, the landscapes start to become more rugged. If time permits, divert to lighthouse-tipped **Strathy Point,** with the dunes and coastal grasslands en route harboring some rare plants, notably the tiny Scots primrose in May and June. (The more conspicuous blue among the grass is spring squill.) Back on the main road, **Bettyhill** is a post-clearance settlement. The name refers to Elizabeth, Countess of Sutherland, whose husband ordered the removal of 1,200 people from their dwellings to the coast during the shameful Highland Clearances (see page 38), as the **Strathnaver Museum** relates. More cheerfully, little coastal loops lead down to empty and beautiful, if windswept, pale sand beaches.

A836/838 leads on to the **Kyle of Tongue**, with its breathtaking view of spiky Ben Loyal from the causeway which shortens the route around the sea loch. Across the empty moors,

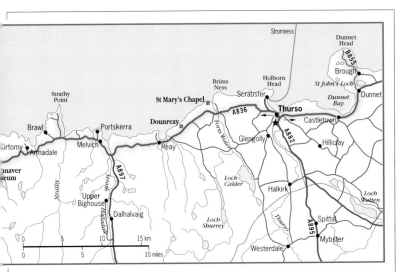

with vast and remote seascapes around Whiten Head to the north, lies the next great sea inlet. **Loch Eriboll** was a former wartime convoy assembly point, known to mariners as Loch 'orrible. There is a well-preserved prehistoric wheelhouse, among other barely acknowledged sites in the vicinity, just a walk across the moorlands—but you should take a map.

Smoo Cave by Durness is a popular spot, a series of caverns by the shore, cut into the limestone by water action. The other Durness attraction is the excursion to **Cape Wrath**, the northwesternmost tip of mainland Scotland. Note that you cannot take your car. A small ferry crosses the Kyle of Durness and then a minibus does the lighthouse run. The tallest mainland cliffs are nearby as well, with the whole area carrying a faintly sinister air, thanks partly to the military range that lies between the Kyle and the Cape. A calmer option is puffin-watching at Faraid Head, a very pleasant walk from Durness: leave the car near the beach at Balnakeil.

Smoo Cave, Durness

THE NORTHERN HIGHLANDS

The Destitution Road

The roads from Gairloch to Poolewe and northward were built in a poverty relief program following the famine after the failure of the 1840s potato crops. Government boards put up half the cash on the understanding that local landowners would match the funds. The lairds benefited from the improved communications, their estates increasing in value. Instead of wages, the half-starved locals were paid in meal, as both government and land-owners wished to avoid a "dependency culture" developing. Part of A832 is still known as the Destitution Road.

▶▶▶ Dornoch   209C2

Were it not for its northerly location, Dornoch would be better known: a mellow sandstone burgh (town) with a handsome cathedral on its skyline and a picturesque setting by a great sweep of beach and a famous golf course. The opening of the Dornoch road bridge on A9 has, however, been of benefit. It is one of the most pleasingly attractive of Scottish towns, also known as the "St. Andrews of the North" because of its reputation for great golf. Though much rebuilt and altered, **Dornoch Cathedral▶**, open daily, dates from the 13th century. The town was the seat of the Bishops of Caithness. As well as just strolling around, admiring how the yellow sandstone sets off the roses in the little gardens, things to do in Dornoch include visiting the town jail, now a craft and exhibition center (closed weekends in winter). Another of the peaceful little town's delights are the golden beaches to the north and south. Ripple-patterned and unpolluted, the long shoals and banks at the mouth of Dornoch Firth are exposed at low tide.

Between Dornoch and Golspie stands **Beinn a Bhragaidh**, a hill west of A9 whose top is crowned by a statue of a size usually associated with Eastern Bloc dictators. This colossus by Sir Francis Chantney is in memory of the first Duke of Sutherland (d. 1833), a prime mover in the Highland clearances which resulted in mass emigration. (See Dunrobin, immediately below.)

▶   Dunrobin Castle   209C2

The largest house in the Northern Highlands, Dunrobin started as a 13th-century sandstone keep on a raised

Gairloch

beach overlooking the Dornoch Firth. The original keep was progressively enveloped by newer work, the last and most spectacular being 1835–50 extensions. These were by Sir Charles Barry, architect of the Houses of Parliament in London. He gave the structure its present French-style look with spires and elaborate stonework.

For centuries this has been the seat of the dukes and earls of Sutherland. The third duke (d. 1892) was Western Europe's largest landowner—his holdings included most of the county of Sutherland. However, Dunrobin has also been an auxiliary naval hospital and a boys' school in the present century. Stuffed with the goods acquired by one of the wealthiest families in the land, it has a makeshift air, a series of rooms laid out to impress with displays of uniforms, trophies, medals, endless portraits, tapestries, and such eccentricities as the duke's own steam-powered fire engine. The old summer house is a museum containing hunting trophies, from which you gain the impression that the Sutherlands must have kept a squad of taxidermists in work over the years. The attractive gardens laid out below the castle were inspired by Versailles. *Open*: daily except Sunday mornings, Easter to October.

Fortrose 209C2

With its neighbors, Avoch and Rosemarkie, on either side, Fortrose is an attractive village by the shores of the Moray Firth. The community originally grew around the cathedral, completed in 1485 but now a red sandstone roofless ruin. Avoch (which is pronounced <u>aa</u>ch with a long Scots frontal "a" or "ao" and a Scots "ch"), with its fishing heritage, is like the Lowland towns on the south side of the Firth. North of the three villages is Eathie beach, where Hugh Miller (see panel, page 212) made important discoveries about the origin of the local sandstones.

►► Gairloch 208A2

Gairloch overlooks the safe anchorage of the Gair Loch. Largest of the settlements along this fine stretch of Wester Ross seaboard, Gairloch combines some sea fishing (and processing) activity with tourism, an industry which established itself here in mid-Victorian times. It is a small resort which relies on its own scenic charm. The local sandy beach helps attract families, as does the golf course. Also in the vicinity are **Inverewe Garden** (see page 221) and the beauties of **Loch Maree** (see page 218), as well as **Gairloch Heritage Museum►►** (*open*: daily except Sunday in summer).

Dunrobin Castle 217

In Fortrose

■ **The mountains of Torridon are exactly to the taste of modern leisure travelers eager to escape from urban pressures. Austere and uncompromising, notched and carved into terraces and ridges, they have a beauty that has made an impact for as long as tourists have made their patient way over the long reaches of Strath Bran to Achnasheen, then the high pass over Glen Docherty ...■**

A trail with views
From a clearly marked parking area by the shore of Loch Maree, a hill path ascends the steep slopes leading on to the flanks of Beinn Eighe. This Scottish National Heritage nature trail is for the well-shod walker, but gives excellent views over Slioch and Loch Maree as height is quickly gained and the ancient pinewoods peter out.

Far from being a long way off across the backbone of Scotland, now that the roads have been improved across the empty middle the western seaboard and the Torridons are all too accessible—an easy excursion from Inverness will give a taste of the region, though the mountains deserve much more time.

The Main Mountains Glen Torridon runs from the sea toward the southern end of **Loch Maree**. A single-lane road runs through the glen, becoming double-lane by the shores of **Loch Torridon**. It is from the southern side of Loch Torridon, on the way to or from Shieldaig, that the best views of **Beinn Alligin** can be obtained. This is the most westerly of Torridon's peaks, a half-horseshoe ridge of red sandstone with a spectacular gash on its southern cliffs, casting a sinister shadow by late afternoon. Its equally lofty companion, **Liathach**, lies east of it. Rising precipitously from sea level, its quartzite-topped sandstone terraces and summit pinnacles are best appreciated from the east, by Loch Clair. Next is **Beinn Eighe**—several miles of summits on a quartzite ridge with gray-white rocks, cascading down its flanks in long scree slopes. These three mountains are the main performers in the Torridon spectacular.

The National Trust for Scotland owns much of the land by the glen and above Loch Torridon—about 10,700 acres. The visitor center by the Diabaig road junction is the starting point for ranger-led walks, as well as giving an introduction to the unique geology and wildlife of the area. The east end of the glen and much of the west side of Loch Maree was Britain's first National Nature Reserve, now under Scottish Natural Heritage, which operates a visitor center by the loch (on A832).

Take your time—but do not hold up the locals!

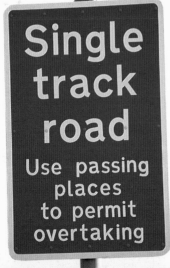

Single track road Use passing places to permit overtaking

Walks in the area Though much can be seen from the roadside, the Torridons are best explored on foot. All the rules of Scottish mountain walking obviously apply: and even at lower level, the terrain is rough enough to make proper hiking boots a necessity. One popular but demanding low-level walk is the "circumnavigation" of the Liathach massif. This demands either two cars, extreme fitness, or a confident approach to hitchhiking. Start either at the waterfall parking lot beyond Torridon House on the Diabaig road or at the lot halfway along Glen Torridon. The off-road section of the walk is 7 miles. The views take in the northern slopes and corries (deep basins) of Liathach and, notably, the less well-known **Beinn Dearg** with its spectacular rock terraces.

Another popular excursion is to view the mighty triple buttresses of **Coire Mhic Fhearchair** (pronounced corrie-vich<u>err</u>icher). This diverges from the "round Liathach" path to circle into one of the most magnificent corries in the Scottish hills. Alternatively, take advantage of the nature trails on the Loch Maree side, though the mountain trail goes steeply up through the old pines and demands careful footwork. There are breathtaking views over the loch to Slioch, the peak on its eastern shore.

Fit hill walkers have many possible excursions. The pinnacles of Liathach are not for the vertigo-prone, though there is a path around them. The **Horns of Alligin**, on Beinn Alligin's eastern end, demand a little bit of handwork and need great respect. Meanwhile, the long ridge of Beinn Eighe should not be underestimated. If in doubt, stay at low level, explore the shore path by Diabaig, or the route to the headland near Shieldaig, or stroll by Loch Clair, admiring one of Scotland's finest views, with Liathach filling the skyline like an upturned boat.

Norse place-names
Diabaig is derived from the Norse *deop-vik*—deep bay, while Shieldaig is *sild-vik,* herring bay. Both little villages are in attractive locations and both offer some accommodations, though Kinlochewe at the east end of the glen is a slightly larger center.

219

Beinn Eighe from Glen Torridon

Caithness craftsman

Spaniard's Peak
Eilean Donan's destruction by naval gunfire in 1719 came about because of its involvement in the Jacobite rebellion of that year. A force of 300 Spanish soldiers landed nearby to link up with local Jacobites, mainly Mackenzies and Camerons (plus Rob Roy and a few Macgregors). They joined battle in Glen Shiel with government forces, whose superior firepower made retreat or surrender inevitable. The Glen Shiel place-name Sgurr na Spainteach (Spaniards' Peak) recalls the incident.

Kintail sunset

▶ **John O' Groats** 209D4

An anticlimax at the end of the road, though some of the craft goods on sale here are attractive, John O' Groats cannot even claim to be the most northerly point of mainland Scotland—that distinction belongs to **Dunnet Head▶▶** to the west. The seascapes here are, however, spectacular, notably around **Duncansby Head▶▶▶** with its rock stacks. There is a passenger-only summer service from John O' Groats to Orkney.

▶▶▶ **Kintail** 208A1

Just how much landscape perceptions have changed is indicated by Dr. Johnson's remark, when traveling hereabouts. He described the main mountains west of the Great Glen as "...matter incapable of form or usefulness, dismissed by nature from her care and disinherited of her favours." Kintail today is highly prized for the same elemental qualities that so appalled the urban doctor. The National Trust for Scotland cares for much of the area, which includes the famously picturesque **Five Sisters of Kintail▶▶▶** as its centerpiece. These five peaks are all Munros (see page 149), as indeed are many others farther east up Glen Shiel. Also within the National Trust for Scotland sphere are the spectacular **Falls of Glomach▶▶**, tumbling 370 feet in remote Glen Elchaig, accessible only by a 5-mile path over rough country—treat it as a hill walk and dress accordingly.

The best-known (and most photographed) low-level landmark is **Eilean Donan Castle▶** on its islet on Loch Duich. This was wrecked in 1719 (see panel) and rebuilt between 1913 and 1932 (*open*: daily in summer). It includes a memorial to the Clan Macrae, whose seat it was.

A dead-end minor road heads off from the end of Glen Shiel to GlenElg. This route is worth exploring, to view not only Skye and Knoydart but also the best preserved brochs (circular defensive structures) on the Scottish mainland. **Dun Telve** stands over 30 feet high. Also nearby are the ruins of the **Bernera Barracks**, originally built around 1722 to control Jacobite activities (see pages 34–5).

Inverewe

■ **Inverewe Garden is on the same latitude as Labrador, but it has a cool and temperate climate because it is favored by the lapping waters of the North Atlantic Drift. The western seas blunt the keen edge of the winter frosts and extensive shelter belts create the microclimate beloved of rhododendrons, mahonia, and other lovers of dappled shade and moisture. Plants from cool temperate zones all over the the world can be found here ...■**

History Until 1862, the garden site was a windy, bare headland with only the island of Lewis between it and northern Canada. But Osgood Mackenzie, whose father and grandfather had been lairds of Gairloch, started his lifetime's work to create a garden in this unpromising landscape. Some of the first trees were planted, not by digging a hole in soil (since often there was none), but by carving out solid rock.

Osgood Mackenzie died in 1922, with the now maturing garden appreciated by temperate eucalyptus trees from Tasmania, species rhododendrons from the Himalayas, and pernettyas, olearias, nothofagus, and other Southern Hemisphere plants that found this Highland home compatible with the Patagonian plains or the high forests of the Andes. By 1952, the garden was in the care of the National Trust for Scotland.

The garden today Inverewe is a late garden, which can mean that you might add a month to six weeks onto flowering times quoted in the gardening manuals—particularly in the early months. This cautious start also means that there is a running together of late spring and early summer flowering plants into a more continuous display than in many southern gardens. Its most attractive feature is the sense of different "rooms" within the overall structure—turn a corner to reinvigorated plantings and geographically linked species, a deliberate management policy in which the team of gardeners are given comparatively free rein within their own patches.

Earth moving
Osgood Mackenzie's labors in creating Inverewe did not only involve excavating holes in solid rock for trees. Soil by the basket load had to be moved in as even the thin blanket of peat that had originally thinly overlaid the rock had been stripped off for fuel by previous crofting tenants.

221

Inverewe Gardens

Guillemots, razorbills, and kittiwakes on Handa's cliffs

An unsightly scar
When a proposal was made to put a deep-water oil rig platform site near Drumbuie, close to the rail-head at Kyle of Lochalsh, the National Trust for Scotland, which owns land nearby, fought hard for an alternative site. The yard was eventually built near Kishorn, arguably a more conspicuous spot, with its breathtaking mountain backdrop. In the boom years it had a workforce of 4,000 and was the birthplace of the largest mobile structure ever built, the Ninian Central rig. After a period of dormancy, plans were announced in 1994 to construct giant oil storage tanks on the site.

Ardvreck castle
On the main road to Lochinver, look for the ruins of Ardvreck Castle by Loch Assynt, a ruined MacLeod stronghold, noted as the place where the Marquis of Montrose was captured after his army's defeat in 1650.

► **Lochcarron** 208A1

Glen Carron seems mostly empty: its soaring hills are clothed with forestry. The blueness of Loch Carron, on the western seaboard, is almost a relief after the unpeopled wildness. The village of Lochcarron is a long ribbon of dwellings, shops, guest houses, hotels, and so on, without a real focal point (it even boasts a golf course). Across the loch, beyond the road and the railroad with its avalanche shelter, is one of Scotland's larger virtually uninhabited areas. With the Applecross Hills and the Torridons to the north, Lochcarron is ideal for exploring wild country. A896 northward passes through Kishorn and then opens up breathtaking views of the series of cor-ries on the Applecross hills. Also nearby is the **Rassal Ash Wood►** nature reserve (administered by Scottish Natural Heritage), where fenced grazing "exclosures" show a rich woodland fauna, contrasting with the overgrazed moors around.

►► **Lochinver** 208B3

Lochinver is the largest center in Assynt, and a busy little fishing port. Seen from across the sea loch, the blunt bows of Suilven (2,398 feet) rise end on in the rough lands behind the village, as a reminder of the eye-catching Assynt landscapes. Though far north on the map, Lochinver has double-lane road all the way, and also offers magnificent touring options on (single-lane) loops both to north and south. B869 goes around via Stoer and Drumbeg, giving fine views of **Quinag**. From this road at Stoer, there are unclassified roads leading out to the Stoer peninsula with its scattered crofts (small tenant farms). Park near the lighthouse for a cliff-top walk to see the rock stack, the **Old Man of Stoer►►**. (It is farther than you think.)

For equally spectacular coastal scenery, a longer excursion (by car) goes via the Kylesku Bridge and on beyond Scourie to Tarbet, where a boatman will take you over to **Handa►►►**. This RSPB (Royal Society for the Protection of Birds) reserve has impressive seabird colonies—including puffins—on awesome cliffs, as well as skuas in the interior which alarmingly dive-bomb intruders near their nests. Southward, there is more wildlife interest to be found by taking the unclassified road leading toward the **Inverpolly National Nature Reserve►►** (look for wildcats and golden eagles). There is a reserve information center at Knockan Cliff, by A835.

►► Plockton 208A1

Too impossibly neat to be true, Plockton was a fishing settlement but now has a number of vacation properties. Complete with rambling roses and hardy palm trees, the trimly painted coastal village makes the most of its sheltered east-facing position—unusual in Wester Ross—and turns its back on the prevailing westerly winds. Other points of interest in the Lochalsh peninsula include the **Lochalsh Woodland Garden►**, a National Trust for Scotland woodland garden with pleasant sheltered walks by the lochside (open throughout the year). Many of the trees are over 100 years old, but the garden is still being developed.

►► Strathpeffer 208B2

The mineral springs in this spa town were described in print by 1772. The first pump room was built in 1819. The local lairds gave the town their blessing and further development took place, assisted by the arrival of the railroad

which conveyed a regular clientele to take the sulfurous waters. The spa attracted royalty and even George Bernard Shaw. The great Victorian heyday lives on in the town's confident and solid architecture. The waters can still be sampled. Though the railroad has gone, the station is now an attractively converted craft, gift, and coffee complex with a small **Highland Museum of Childhood►** (*open*: daily, mid-March to October, and evenings in July and August).

Nearby are a number of points of interest, including the vitrified walling of the fortified hilltop of **Knock Farril** (as yet unexcavated), which can be reached on foot from Strathpeffer. **Strathconon** is also worth exploring as this long glen often offers good views of red deer. The **Falls of Rogie** are signed from the main road west of Contin and also make a worthwhile short stroll.

The Battle of Strome Pier
Sabbatarianism is still quite strong in certain parts of the Highlands, and in May 1883 it resulted in a bizarre incident. East coast fishermen started landing herring at Strome Pier for rail shipment seven days a week. The west coast fishermen opposed the Sunday activity. Along with the locals, they seized the pier, thus preventing the loading of fish onto the trains bound for the London market. The protestors fought off six local constables and the loading crews. Matters escalated. The War Office in London was informed. Only a large police presence and a troop train on standby the following Sunday ensured that religious beliefs did not stand in the way of commerce.

Plockton, arguably Wester Ross's prettiest village

Inspiration by Loch Carron

Wick harbor

An unsafe sanctuary
Tain may have been a
shrine and sanctuary of St.
Duthac, but that did not
stop it from being violated.
In 1306, the wife and
daughter of King Robert I
(the Bruce) fled the tight-
ening English siege of
Kildrummy (see page 182)
to find sanctuary at Tain.
This proved no obstacle to
the local Earl of Ross (who
supported Balliol, not
Bruce). He snatched them
from the sanctuary and
made them prisoners. In
the next century, a
MacNeil warrior pursued
his foes to the chapel and
set fire to it.

*Whaligoe Steps near
Ulbster—not for the
vertigo-prone*

► **Tain** *209C2*

Some say Malcolm Canmore granted Tain's first charter
in the 11th century. The little town has a fine tolbooth (jail)
and steeple. The ruins of nearby **St. Duthac's Chapel**
(built 1065–1256) mark the site of the birthplace of St.
Duthac, an early missionary to the Picts. Tain was a place
of pilgrimage for centuries, the chapel a sanctuary and
shrine. **St. Duthus Church►** was built in 1360 and also
served the many pilgrims. **Tain and District Museum**
and a center for Clan Ross now stand in the grounds.
(open: daily except winter mornings).

►► **Timespan Heritage Center** *209C3*

Timespan, in Helmsdale, is the work of a local group of
enthusiasts who wanted to preserve the area's heritage,
and knew how to acquire funding. The center portrays
many aspects of life in the Highlands of old, from
Neolithic and Pictish times right up to the Clearances,
with a mixture of tableaus, artifacts, and audiovisuals. It
also has a fascinating account of the "gold rush" of 1869,
which took place in the nearby Strath of Kildonan. What
makes Timespan different is the thought-provoking way
the exhibits tell the story. There is only one jarring note:
the center also has a bizarre shrine to the romantic
novelist Barbara Cartland, who has property nearby—in
fact, there is a minor Cartland cult within Helmsdale. The
center is closed in winter.

Farther up the Strath is the site of the gold rush town. At
Baile an Or "gold town," 8 miles to the northwest, it is
still possible to pan for gold, using equipment rented from
a craft shop in Helmsdale. Do not expect to be able to
subsidize your trip this way!

►► **Ullapool** *208B2*

In contrast to many ancient settlements with obscure
origins, Ullapool can be dated precisely. The abundant
herring in Loch Broom inspired the founding of a fishing
station and village there soon after the formation of the

British Fisheries Society in 1786. This society paid for the infrastructure of curing sheds, storehouses, a pier, inn, and even a school and some of the dwelling houses. All was laid out to a regular grid plan and mostly completed by 1792. However, it soon became clear that the herring were not a reliable harvest. Ullapool's fortunes rose and fell, and many turned to the land for a living. Overall, however, Ullapool has maintained a strong fishing connection, rising into prominence with the arrival of the Eastern Bloc "klondykers"—vessels buying fish direct for onboard processing—in the 1980s.

Two small museums in the town, plus a number of shops and a pottery factory, provide diversion for the strolling tourists, as this is one of the largest centers on this stretch of seaboard. Ullapool also has an important ferry link with Stornoway in the Outer Hebrides.

Corrieshalloch Gorge►►► On A835 south of Ullapool, this is just one of the area's many scenic attractions. Meltwater from a glacier at the end of the last Ice Age cut a 200-foot-deep gorge, into which the **Falls of Measach** now plunge, half hidden by trees and lush greenery. It is viewed from a spindly, vertigo-inducing suspension bridge.

►   **Wick**   *209D3*

The workaday, east-wind-flavored town of Wick made a big contribution to the development of fishing. **Wick Heritage Centre►►**, with its wide-ranging displays of fishing artifacts, recalls the time when herring brought great prosperity to the town in spite of a dangerous and inadequate harbor. *Open:* daily except Sundays, June and September.

North of the town, a pleasant walk along the coastal grazings from the signposted parking lot soon leads to **Castles Girnigoe** and **Sinclair**, perched on the cliffs above Sinclair's Bay. These adjacent gloomily ruined strongholds were the works of the Sinclair Earls of Caithness and can be visited any time—but take care, their situation is exposed.

Cheap food
Before slavery was abolished, Wick herring, salted in barrels and exported, was used as a source of cheap food for plantation slaves.

Along A9
Diversions off A9 near Wick include: trips to Whaligoe Steps where a vertigo-inducing set of steps leads down the cliff to a former fishing station; and, inland from Whaligoe, to the Grey Cairns of Camster, Neolithic burial cairns of the area's first farmers. Nearby is the Hill of Many Stanes: 200 stones arranged in 22 rows, dating from the early Bronze Age. Their purpose is a mystery.

225

On the Stornoway to Ullapool ferry

THE ISLANDS

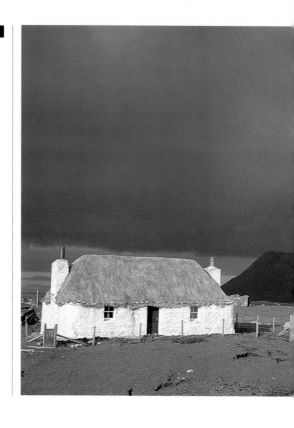

*Changeable weather,
Cladach Chairinis,
North Uist, with
Eaval beyond*

*The CalMac ferry
making the Ardrossan–
Brodick (Arran) run*

The Islands Scotland's western seaboard is about 260 miles in a straight line but, counting all the indentations and island shores is around 2,000 miles long. On such a complicated and rocky coast, even counting islands can be difficult—it all depends on the definition, but it is usually said that Scotland has 790, of which 130 are inhabited.

Apart from the outliers like North Rona or St. Kilda, the island clusters fall into natural groupings: the islands of the Clyde which lie within the estuary between the mainland and the Kintyre peninsula; the Inner Hebrides, comprising the main islands of the western seaboard between Kintyre and Skye; the Outer Hebrides, now usually called, somewhat confusingly, the Western Isles, and stretching in a long line from the Butt of Lewis to Barra and beyond; and finally Orkney and Shetland, utterly different in culture and outlook from anything western.

The Clyde islands Access has much to do with character. The Clyde islands were for generations an easy-to-reach vacation playground for the workforce of metropolitan Glasgow and, no matter how much the local authorities try to change this image, just a little of earlier days still hangs around. A 1950s air clings on in the occasional café in Arran or Bute—that is part of their charm. **Arran** is sometimes labeled "Scotland in miniature" because of its scenic attractions. The granites of the Goatfell ridges (the principal hill complex) have enticed generations of outdoor enthusiasts.

Bute, meanwhile, still echoes the old days of traditional

THE ISLANDS

228

Fair Isle
Sometimes the P & O ferry between Lerwick and Aberdeen sails close to Fair Isle to give passengers a glimpse of this isolated island midway between Orkney and Shetland. It is called the remotest inhabited island in the U.K., and has outstanding coastal scenery, bird colonies, and a bird observatory, as well as the George Waterston Memorial Centre, displaying the island's folklore and history. A ferry runs from Grutness, Sumburgh.

Mendelssohn and the Hebrides
The basalt columns carved by the sea into caves on the island of Staffa, west of Mull, inspired the composer Mendelssohn to write his overture, *The Hebrides*, or *Fingal's Cave*. This little island has recorded a series of famous literary visitors: Scott, Tennyson, Keats, and Wordsworth, as well as the artist Turner, all came to admire the soaring cathedral-like symmetry. It can be visited from Iona or from Mull.

Orkney tractor

vacations, with its seafront mansions built by wealthy industrialists in Victorian times. It is now a very peaceful place, with an attractive rural hinterland, to which the spectacular Victorian Gothic Mount Stuart House provides an unusual contrast.

The Inner Hebrides Islay and Jura are often grouped together because of their proximity and ferry connections (the Jura ferry leaves from Islay). Yet they are completely different in character. Because of its farming and whisky, Islay, at least in part, still has a sense of a community held together without recourse to too many cute craftware ventures earnestly worked by urban refugees—the characteristic feature of all too many parts of the west.

Jura is simply empty. Not literally devoid of people, perhaps, but there are few other places where depopulation has been so spectacular. The island has been divided up into a few sporting estates. Some come to the island because of its connection with George Orwell's *Nineteen Eighty–four*, which was written at Barnhill, a remote house well up the east coast. Neither this spot nor the famous but seldom seen Whirlpool of Corrievreckan, a tidal conflict at the tip of Jura, is accessible by ordinary car.

Mull boasts the only other island Munro apart from Skye: Ben More. There is also some highly attractive coastline. Like Skye, Mull has proved a magnet for a new breed of resident, eager to escape the pressure of life in the south of the U.K.

As for the smaller Hebridean islands, **Colonsay** is the very distillation of Hebridean charm. With only 14 miles of roads it is hardly worth bringing a car. Colonsay is popular both as the ultimate in relaxing Scottish hideaways and as a good place for bird watchers, with its variety of habitats. These include sand, cliff, machair (see page 283), moor, and garden, and its own (stunted) woodland. Note that **Oronsay**, its companion to the south, with an interesting ruined priory, is only really a separate island at high tide—take your rubber boots for the walk. **Coll** and **Tiree** are also interesting Hebridean destinations, with machair and long beaches. The so-called Small Isles—**Rum**, **Eigg**, **Muck**, and **Canna**—also offer a true island experience, very definitely away from it all, with Rum the best for scenery.

Skye and the Western Isles Skye—strictly part of the Inner Hebrides—is the most scenically spectacular island of the western seaboard, with glorious mountain landscapes. It is therefore very popular. However, the main ridge of the Cuillins is not a place for the inexperienced climber (with the possible exception of Bruach na Frithe). The ascent of many of the Cuillins peaks demand rock climbing skills or, at the very least, a good head for heights.

One way in which the **Outer Hebrides (Western Isles)** differs from most of the mainland is in the

Scottish brochs
These are circular defensive structures, dry-stone walled and double skinned, of which the Broch of Mousa is the best preserved. There are about 400 of them scattered in Shetland, Orkney, Caithness, and Sutherland and farther down the western seaboard. Brochs are presumed to have been built for defensive purposes around the 1st century BC to 3rd century AD, probably against seaborne raiders in the turbulent Celtic world of the time.

Orkney Farm and Folk Museum, Kirbister, Orkney

deeply felt Sabbatarianism. Once widespread in the west, the setting aside of Sunday for almost exclusively religious pursuits has retreated to a stronghold here. All too easy for outsiders to dismiss as curiously joyless, the staunch faith must be a source of strength for those who choose to live among the bleak landscapes of the north end of the island. Visitors should respect it.

The lower end of the island chain is Catholic, with a more relaxed community to be found there. Beaches receding to infinity, corncrake-haunted hayfields, and outhouses tied down to escape the wind, are just a few of the far Hebridean images—as is the very real sense of a rhythm of life attached to tide and ferry times.

Orkney and Shetland Orkney and Shetland look to their Scandinavian heritage. **Orkney** also looks further back, to a time when the climate was warmer and the ancient peoples who farmed here left more prehistoric monuments than anywhere else in Britain. These include Skara Brae, an ancient settlement where, amid the Stone Age furniture, an idea of the life of these shadowy ancestors can be gained.

Most northerly of all, from a British citizen's viewpoint, **Shetland** is almost like a foreign destination—yet still within Britain. Shetland's specialties include awesome seascapes—Esha Ness on Mainland, for example—and brochs (see panel).

Do not let the sea be any kind of barrier to visiting any of these islands. Access by the main ferry gateways—Oban, Mallaig, Ullapool, Scrabster, Aberdeen, and others—is straightforward. All of Scotland's main islands are viable communities, with reliable car-ferry links and, in the case of the Outer Hebrides, Islay, Orkney, and Shetland, with good air services as well. And if you want the island experience but do not like ferry travel, then the new bridge to Skye is the answer.

Trimming hooves, Shetland

Hutton's Unconformity

A rough 10-minute walk over the sheep-cropped raised beach beyond the north shore of Loch Ranza takes you to Hutton's Unconformity. In 1787, the geologist James Hutton noticed a change in the angle of the rocks, where 600-million-year-old gray-green Cambrian schist dips and is overlain by the sprightly young red Devonian sandstone, a good 200 million years its junior. This observation helped Hutton work out his theories about the age of the earth.

The Arran tapestry, Brodick

Islands of the Clyde

▶▶ **Arran** 230A1

Arran has for long enjoyed a reputation as an island for outdoor-lovers and walkers. The Highland Boundary Fault runs through the island: Arran's southern end is accordingly less hilly. Its largest township is Brodick, with a frontage spaciously set back from promenade and beach.

Brodick Castle and Country Park▶▶ is Arran's most famous attraction. On the north side of Brodick Bay and in the care of the National Trust for Scotland, the former seat of the dukes of Hamilton displays furniture, paintings, silver, and sporting trophies, but the real attractions are the rhododendrons, particularly in late spring and early summer. There is also a walled garden, and many other shrubs among the great-trunked trees. The castle is open daily in summer, the garden and country park open daily all year.

Much of the settlement on Arran is clustered around the coast: pottery and crafts at **Corrie**, with its mountain backdrop; even better views at **Mid Sannox** with its bay of ground-down granite; **Lochranza**, where Loch Ranza spills in shallows up the flat-bottomed glacial glen, is yet another focus of crafts activity. Here, too, is **Lochranza Castle** where Robert the Bruce is said to have first landed in 1307 at the start of the independence campaign. Look for the "**Twelve Apostles**" at Catacol—a row of former fishermen's houses, identical except for differing window shapes, in order to be identified from offshore.

On the west side, the standing stones of **Machrie Moor** are very atmospheric. There are a number of early sites around Machrie: chambered cairns, hut circles, and standing stones. Back on the east shore, **Lamlash** has a cheerful air and views to Holy Island (now a religious settlement), and a sobering boulder memorial to the Highland Clearances (see pages 38–9).

▶ **Bute** *230B3*

The old traditional waterfront resort of **Rothesay** contrasts with the pasture, peace, and brackeny woodland on the rest of this little island. The resort was popular in the heyday of the steamer network on the Clyde, a story told at the **Bute Museum** in Rothesay (*open*: all year except most Sundays; closed Mondays in winter).

Rothesay Castle▶▶ This fortress in the town center is built around a circular courtyard. The Norse assailed it in 1230, breaching the wall. *Open*: all year, except for Thursday morning and Friday in winter.

Just outside Rothesay is **Mount Stuart House**▶▶▶, ancestral home of the marquesses of Bute. A splendid Victorian Gothic palace, there is plenty to admire inside, from the Marble Hall, with galleries, stained glass, and astronomical painted vault, to outstanding furniture, paintings, and tapestries (*open*: in summer, closed Tuesdays and Thursdays).

Bute has beaches and interesting walks up the west coast overlooking the Kyles of Bute. There are also ancient hill forts and faint echoes of neolithic folk, but the most peaceful place is **St. Blane's Chapel**, a 6th-century religious foundation with a 12th-century ruined chapel, set amid the hushed trees and sheltering mossy rocks.

Evening calm on Bute

Medical supplies
The soft and mossy woods of Bute once provided an unusual harvest. During World War I, cotton became scarce and sphagnum moss, with its antiseptic and absorbent properties, was used instead for dressing wounds. It was gathered from the Balnakeilly Woods, dried, sorted, and packed for hospitals and field units.

The Cumbraes
Often overlooked, these are the smallest of the main Clyde islands. Like Arran they are fondly regarded by many visitors, who come for the beaches, sailing, biking, gentle walks, and traditional entertainment. Great Cumbrae and its even smaller neighbor are only a few minutes off Largs on the Ayrshire coast, to which they are linked by ferry.

Cart decoration, Arran & Argyll Transport Museum, Brodick

Choughs

These very rare crows (pronounced "chuffs") are a Colonsay (and Islay) specialty. From a distance, they look black, in common with most of their cousins. If you observe choughs closely as they poke about for insects in old cowpats, you may glimpse their bright red beaks and feet. In flight they look like square and ragged-winged jet-black jackdaws. Their survival, research shows, seems to be dependent on the overwintering of cattle outside. Hence the cowpats.

Spectacular coastline, Colonsay

Jura

Jura has one road, one distillery, one hotel, six sporting estates, and 5,000 red deer—outnumbering the people by at least 20 to one. Jura's human population was cleared to make the island into a deer forest and sheep pasture. It is a haunting kind of place, with a few traces of the vanished villages—the faint shapes of the "lazy-beds" (cultivated strips) still show through the heather. Otherwise, especially near the road end, the bracken and yellow flag-irises, mossy woods, and strands of sea-weed crisping on the salty grass form idyllic pictures of summer on the Hebrides.

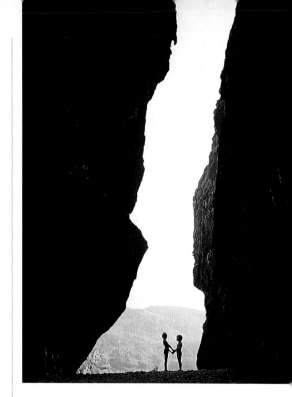

The Inner Hebrides

►   Coll and Tiree   *233A4/A3*

Coll and Tiree duck low on the Hebridean horizon to let the Atlantic weather systems pass over, thus boasting good sunshine records. Tiree looks friendlier in cream and green, while Coll is rockier, with more acid moorland. Tiree has long been famed for its fertile, sandy soil, and the crofting way of life is still followed, more so than in Coll with its cattle rearing. Both islands were cleared, at least in part, with Ayrshire dairy farmers the new tenants in Coll in the 1850s. In Tiree the clearances were less severe: even today its population, around 750, is five times that of Coll.

Long beaches with crashing Atlantic surf are popular with surfers. Tiree has reliable conditions almost all year. Visit these islands if wide skies, open seas, wildflowers on windy dunes, and a pace of life governed by the tide and the ferry is your idea of Hebridean bliss.

►►   Colonsay   *233B2*

Two hours from Oban lies 8-mile-long Colonsay, its gray rock rubbing through threadbare moorland. If you only have time for one Hebridean island, this is the one to choose. Colonsay's farms raise sheep and cattle, the rabbit-cropped coastal strip is shadowed by hunting buzzards, while wild goats browse around the edges of protected patches of unusual Hebridean natural wood-lands of oak, hazel, and willow. Bird habitats include gleam-ing sandy beaches and extensive tidal sand flats as well as impressive sea cliffs and a loch. Colonsay's most famous (and scarcest) bird is the chough (see panel, page 232).

Lord Strathcona's family owns Colonsay, residing at Colonsay House. The grounds of this rambling pink mansion, **Kiloran Gardens**, with their tender rhododendrons, thickets of rampant escallonia, and many much rarer species, are open to the public all year.

►► Gigha
233C1

Tucked out of the weather off Kintyre, 5-mile-long Gigha has a mild climate. Its main attraction is **Achamore House Gardens**. These 325-acre gardens were originally created by Sir James Horlick in 1944, who saw the place as ideal for exotic shrubs. Within the wooded windbreaks he created one of Scotland's finest woodland gardens. There are thickets of camellias, azaleas hoary with lichen, heather banks, and damp places as well as a superb viewpoint revealing Jura's spectacular profile. The gardens are open all year and it is possible to visit the garden by ferry from the mainland in a long morning or afternoon.

Oronsay

Oronsay is separated from Colonsay at low tide by 1.2 miles of sandflats, a splashy cockle-strewn haunt of plover. Bring waterproof boots to visit Oronsay Priory, an abandoned 14th-century Augustinian foundation with impressive grave slabs and a magnificent early 16th-century cross. Keep an eye on the tide to avoid being cut off.

Around Islay

Islay has a quite different feel from the rest of the Hebrides. In the western half in particular, it is a place of large farms, rather than crofts, and a number of distilleries provide work for the local community. For both the 56-mile round trip from Bowmore and the southern excursion via Mull of Oa (52 miles), make sure you allow plenty of time for short walks and sea views.

Bowmore is a tidy little town which gives its name to the whisky made in the distillery (founded 1779) by the shore. The dominating parish church of 1767 was built to an unusual circular design so that the devil could not find a corner to hide in.

Take A846 north out of Bowmore to Bridgend, then A847 to skirt the sandflats at the head of Loch Indaal, following its shores to

Portnahaven, Islay

Bruichladdich, a village with a distillery and another malt whisky name. Continuing south for a few minutes you reach Port Charlotte. On the right of the road, in a converted church, is the **Museum of Islay Life**, a pleasantly haphazard but informative display of times past.

Return north to turn onto B8018, then take a minor road which ends close to **Machir Bay** with its superb sandy beach. The nearby derelict church of **Kilchoman** has some interesting grave slabs and two late medieval crosses. Circle **Loch Gorm**, pausing to enjoy the fine seascapes at Saligo Bay beyond the former wartime camp.

Return east, turning right onto B8018, then left on B8017. Take a left for **Kilnave**, where the chapel is associated with the massacre of Maclean clansman after a skirmish with the Macdonalds in 1598. In the graveyard is a weathered 8th-century carved cross.

The Royal Society for the Protection of Birds has several farms here, including **Aoradh Farm**, a visitor center with full information on its nature reserve. The low-lying lands are still farmed, the extensive acreage providing a wintering ground for geese around the splendidly wild dunes and endless beaches of **Loch Gruinart**. Drive up its east shore and park before a gate, where the road deteriorates. Walk as far as the headland—Killinallan Point—on this

peerless and lonely coast before returning to Bowmore.

To the south of the island is the southern peninsula of **The Oa**, a region of caves, cliffs, and smuggling tales. At the tip, the **Mull of Oa**, a monument recalls 650 men who lost their lives when the troopships *Tuscania* and *Otranto* went down nearby in 1918. Farther east near Ardmore Point is the highly wrought 8th-century **Kildalton Cross**, carved from a single slab of epidiorite rock.

En route for the Jura ferry take in the **Islay Woollen Mill** and, a little farther, **Loch Finlaggan**, former power base of the Macdonalds, the Lords of the Isles. Their story is told in a small visitor center overlooking the loch with its little island on which their headquarters stood.

The magnificent Kildalton Cross

Torosay Castle, Mull

Sunken treasure
After England's defeat of the Spanish Armada, several vessels were driven into northern waters. The *San Juan de Sicilia* put into Tobermory for supplies. Rumors spread that it was carrying £300,000 in gold. Donald Maclean of Duart sneaked on board and fired the ship's magazine, though why this would have helped him acquire a fortune is unclear. The ship blew up and sank in 11 fathoms, just offshore, with the loss of over 300 lives. Since then, every so often, salvage attempts have been made but with little success.

►► **Mull** *233B3*

Eilean Moula, Isle of Mull, is an island of great beauty and emptiness. It has a history of emigration and eviction. Today, it is sometimes called "The Officers' Mess," from its popularity with retired military men.

You can take the ferry from Oban to Craignure, though it is more interesting to use the short (summer-only) ferry crossing from Lochaline to Fishnish. Both ferries are within easy reach of Torosay and Duart Castles.

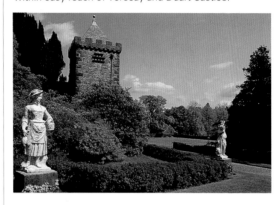

Torosay Castle►►► Scottish baronial-style Torosay (closed in winter) is a lot of fun: full of interest and humor by way of its idiosyncratic information boards and informal family albums. The energetic can walk along the shore from Torosay to **Duart Castle**►, otherwise reached off the A849. This ancient Maclean seat was restored by Sir Fitzroy Maclean in 1911 (also closed in winter).

Tobermory is the largest settlement, and, like Ullapool (see pages 224–5), was founded as a fishing station. Its gradual decline was hastened by the arrival of the railhead at Oban, which took away fish traffic. However, the brightly painted crescent of mainly 18th-century buildings give Tobermory a faintly Mediterranean air. A museum and a distillery stand on the waterfront, both opening weekdays all season.

Mull's attractions tend to the ruggedly scenic. Near the tip of the dramatic cliff ramparts of Ardmeanach is **The Burg**►, with its fossil tree, a National Trust for Scotland property reached by a rough walk. There is more coastal spectacle at Carsaig, where a very rough path leads west, below lava cliffs, to the impressive **Carsaig Arches**►►.

Even from the road, there is plenty of dramatic scenery, notably on the west coast loops. North of Loch Scridain, B8035 breaches stepped cliffs and drops to the shore with fine views of the island of Ulva. This stretch has a very remote flavor, with unnervingly fresh-looking rock splinters strewn on it in places.

In Torosay Castle Gardens, Mull

Isle of Mull Weavers

■ **Although St. Ninian, the first named missionary to Scotland, is said to have built a church at Whithorn in Galloway around** AD **397 (see pages 120–1), it is the tiny island of Iona that is called the cradle of Scottish Christianity, because of its association with St. Columba ...■**

Foundation of the monastery The fiery and argumentative Irish monk Columba chose Iona for the setting up of a monastery in AD 563 because it was the first place he reached from which Ireland could not be seen—or so the tale is told. The word of St. Columba's church was spread widely among the northern Picts, these early missionaries being regarded as some kind of superior "medicine men." Such was the importance of this religious community that it eventually became the burial place of the kings of Scotland.

It also suffered dreadful atrocities during repeated Norse sackings which finally caused the evacuation of the community to Kells in Ireland. Even after this it was not abandoned entirely and many monks were martyred here. It became a Benedictine foundation around 1203, finally falling into ruin by the Reformation. Restoration work began at the turn of the present century, the Iona Community was founded in 1938, and today the restored buildings are a spiritual center under the jurisdiction of the Church of Scotland.

Iona today Today the ambience within the complex is a curious mix of the ancient and the earnest, but beyond the restored cloisters the most mystifying aspect of all is the little island's ability to mop up its visitors and still feel peaceful. Most people only make the short walk from the ferry pier via the nunnery to the abbey. They miss the beautiful white shell beaches and the machair with its undisturbed rich insect and bird life beyond the bare rocks and the thin pasture of the interior. The best place to see the shape of the island is from the top of the low (and oddly named) hill Dun I (see panel).

A literary location
From Dun I (a low hill), look for Erraid island, lying close inshore to the south, and difficult to see separately from Mull. Robert Louis Stevenson came from a famous lighthouse engineering family and knew the area well, as there was a shore base and quarry on Erraid in 1867 for the building of the Dhu Heartach lighthouse, on an outlying tooth of rock 11 miles southwest. In *Kidnapped*, Stevenson set the wreck of the brig *Covenant* on the reefs offshore, the treacherous Torran Rocks.

237

The 15th-century MacLean's Cross, Iona

Kitchener's memorial
The huge bird colonies of Marwick Head are below the cliff-top memorial to Lord Kitchener. He was on his way to Russia in 1916 aboard HMS *Hampshire* when it hit a mine and sank, with the loss of the warlord and most of the ship's crew.

Stromness garage

Orkney

▶▶   **Mainland**   238A2

Orkney is an ancient archipelago of gently contoured islands, with place-names identifiable from the rich Norse heritage of the Viking sagas. It has the greatest concentration of prehistoric sites anywhere in Western Europe. With the exception of Hoy, the prevailing color on these whaleback islands is green—the emerald of pasture, the yellow-green of cut hayfields, and the golden tinge of ripening oats and barley.

Mainland is the largest island and quite a lot of short-stay visitors never venture beyond it. **Kirkwall** is the largest town and island capital, built by a natural harbor. It was an early Christian settlement, taking its name from the Old Norse *kirkjuvagr*, "church bay," and has several attractions.

Earl Patrick's Palace and the **Bishop's Palace**▶▶ The Bishop's Palace dates originally from the mid-12th century as accommodations, close to the then new cathedral. Earl Patrick's Palace was built in 1600 for the cruel Patrick Stuart, ruler of the islands, executed for treason soon after. This is the finest example of French Renaissance architecture in Scotland. Both buildings close in winter.

St. Magnus Cathedral▶▶▶ This magnificent church's harmonious proportions belie its smallness. Founded in 1137 by Earl Rognvald Kolsson and dedicated to his uncle St. Magnus, the red sandstone structure took three centuries to complete. Visit any day to admire its Romanesque, Transitional, and Gothic styles.

Tankerness House▶▶ This 16th-century merchant-laird's mansion is now a museum of Orkney life from prehistoric times to the present. *Open*: Monday to Saturday all year, and Sunday afternoons in the main season.

Maes Howe▶▶▶ Off A965 8 miles from Kirkwall, this

ORKNEY

Taking the air in Kirkwall

huge burial chamber dates from around 2500 BC and has workmanship unsurpassed in Western Europe. It was already almost 3,500 years old when Vikings broke in and scratched graffiti on the walls. It is closed on Wednesdays and Thursday mornings in winter.

Marwick Head Nature Reserve▶▶ Orkney has a wealth of wildlife, notably seabird colonies. These easily reached great red cliffs are stacked with 35,000 guillemots, among other species.

The Ring of Brogar▶▶▶ This is Orkney's best-known stone circle, with 36 stones surviving from around 60, and other mounds and standing stones all adding to the fathomless mystery of these monoliths. The **Stenness Standing Stones** are also in the vicinity in this extraordinarily rich area. *Open*: daily.

Skara Brae▶▶▶ At this unforgettable prehistoric site, 5,000-year-old stone dressers, beds, and cupboards have survived as furnishings to the snug circular dwellings built before the pyramids. *Open*: daily.

Stromness is the main ferry port for mainland Scotland connections. The little town became important in the 18th century as a watering place for shipping. Whalers, Hudson's Bay traders, and round-the-world explorers all stopped off here. Today, with its own fishing fleet and boatyards, its narrow lanes and old traders' houses, it has a decidedly pleasant period feel. Visit the **Pier Arts Center** (*open*: Tuesdays to Saturdays) for exhibitions and a permanent 20th-century collection.

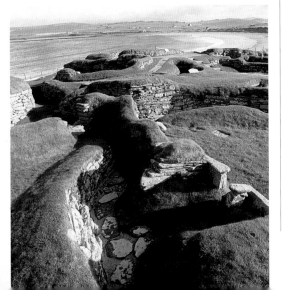

A famous mariner
Captain Bligh (of later *Bounty* fame) was one of many well-known mariners who called at Stromness. This was in 1780 when he was with the *Discovery* and *Resolution*, returning home from the South Seas after Captain Cook's death. He dined at the Whitehouse of 1680, which can still be seen today.

Viking inscriptions
The party of Vikings who came into the Maes Howe tomb in the winter of 1153 not only contributed to one of the largest surviving collections of runic inscriptions, but also executed some fine animal drawings on a buttress. These include the Maes Howe Dragon (though some say it looks like a lion) which has inspired artists and jewelry designers ever since its rediscovery in 1861.

Skara Brae on Mainland Orkney is perhaps the most spectacular of the island's prehistoric sights. This extraordinary slice of Stone Age life lay buried beneath the sands until a storm revealed it in 1850

►► Hoy *238A1*

Hoy, the second-largest island in the group, is the exception to Orkney's prevailing low-lying greenness, its north and west being high and craggy. Here the red sandstone has weathered into almost Highland scenery, with a west coast of spectacular natural beauty, glimpsed from the ferry en route to Stromness. With the most northerly natural woodland in Britain, glacial features such as small corries (hollows) at comparatively low levels, and U-shaped valleys, plus an arctic-alpine flora (and mountain hares), Hoy has a very distinct character.

A scuttled fleet
It was off the islands of Cava and Flotta that the interned German High Seas Fleet scuttled itself on midsummer day of 1919. In doing so, they not only created a massive amount of scrap metal which was salvaged for years after, but they also became what is now rated as Britain's best amateur diving site, as not all of the German ships were cut up.

St. Margaret's Hope, South Ronaldsay

A walk on Hoy
Naturalists who want to explore the rugged Hoy hinterland can reach Rackwick on foot by a well-marked track which goes around the north side of Ward Hill, the highest point on Orkney at 1,571 feet. Look for great skuas bathing at the Sandy Loch on the way.

The eerily deserted **Lyness Naval Base** on the east coast was the shore base that served the key anchorage for the Royal Navy in two world wars. The former Pump House is an interpretation center. Here, too, is the cemetery as an inevitable epilogue to warfare, with sailors' graves from many famous ships, including HMS *Hampshire*, mined and sunk in 1916, HMS *Vanguard*, accidentally blown up off Flotta in 1916, and HMS *Royal Oak*, torpedoed at anchor here in 1939. Also nearby are the **Martello Towers**, on either side of Longhope Bay, first built in 1813–15 as protection for Baltic-bound British convoys against American privateers.

A road leads west to **Rackwick**, a crofting township gradually coming back to life after a period of decline. This is one of the most attractive parts of all of Orkney, amid the heathery hills with steep shoreward cliffs nearby. From here a footpath leads to the **Old Man of Hoy**, a spectacular sea stack.

North Hoy Nature Reserve►►► This area takes in the Old Man of Hoy and is noted not only for its seabird colonies, but also species such as the piratical great skua, of which 1,500 pairs breed on the island. It is administered by the Royal Society for the Protection of Birds.

Dwarfie Stane► Yet another curiosity, reached on foot from the Rackwick Road, is the so-called Dwarfie Stane, the only rock-cut tomb in Britain. Quite why its 3rd millennium BC excavators should have bothered to chip away at this natural block of red sandstone in its windy valley is a mystery. The tomb has been empty since recorded time.

SEBAY FARM

► **South Ronaldsay**

Though strictly speaking a separate island, this can be easily visited from Mainland by the road link over the Churchill Causeway, formed by lines of tipped concrete blocks. Sir Winston Churchill ordered its construction during World War II in order to close off the eastern arm of the Scapa Flow anchorage after a German U-boat slipped in and torpedoed HMS *Royal Oak* with great loss of life. Rusty shipwrecks, previously scuttled as part of the navy defenses, still line part of the route, adding a surreal quality to the scene.

Italian Chapel►► Starting with a Nissen hut, Italian POWs in 1943 built this extraordinary trompe l'oeil building (even the windows are painted on), creating an intricate embellishment with only scrap metal, cement, and other scrounged bits and pieces. It is on Lamb Holm, halfway along the Churchill Causeway, and open at all times.

The road continues to **St. Margaret's Hope**, gray houses tucked next to a seaweedy harbor and, on its way to Burwick on the southern tip, passes by the **Orkney Wireless Museum** (*open*: daily in summer). Crammed together are numerous examples of wartime communications equipment, including some tiny radio sets, used by spies, as well as gramophones and other wireless memorabilia.

Other Orkney islands Among the farther-flung Orkney islands are **Papa Westray**, where two 5,000-year-old dwellings (believed to be the oldest houses in Europe) at Knap of Howar can be seen; **Sanday**, where a tomb of the Maes Howe type—and many other remains—suggest that this was a burial place of great importance in the 2nd millennium BC; and **Westray**, with its ancient church and **Noltland Castle**, a very impressive 16th-century Z-plan edifice, guarding the natural harbor at Pierowall. These and almost all of the other northern outliers of Orkney are well served by the interisland airplane and ferry network from Kirkwall.

241

The Old Man of Hoy

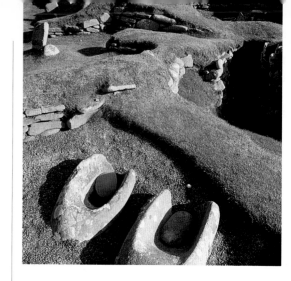

*Many-layered
Jarlshof, Shetland*

Sumburgh Head
With its cluster of attractions, South Mainland
alone needs a couple of
trips from Lerwick, particularly if you are interested
in the bird life. Though
there are plenty of other
places to see puffins, the
Sumburgh Head colony is
particularly convenient.
Park before the wall that
marks the lighthouse area,
go through the gap in the
wall, and walk up the road
to the first hairpin bend.
Look over the cliff to the
right for the puffins.

Shetland

With its ever-changing seascapes, its Norse heritage, and
the sheer challenge of its ocean-girt northerly setting,
Shetland confounds any stereotypes of tartans and glint-
ing lochs. Nowhere is more than 5 miles from the sea,
thanks to the voes and (smaller) geos, the long fingers of
sea that find their way far inland. The ocean is a glittering
or grim backdrop to every view, and has historically made
Shetland into a surprisingly cosmopolitan place.

The islands themselves are subtly different, with a
prevailing inland landscape of crofts and small fields or
eroded peatland vegetation, and virtually no trees. The
biggest island, Mainland, has the island "capital" Lerwick,
the only town of any size, and also some excellent
seascapes and nature interest as well as historic sites.

▶▶▶ Mainland   243A2

Esha Ness▶▶▶ Here the sea has hammered away at the
cliffs and quarried out awesome rock features: the Holes
of Scraada, the Heads of Grocken, and the Grind of the
Navir. South of B9078, **The Drongs**, sea stacks in the bay,
resemble a Norse galley under sail. North of Ronas Voe,
the scoured hump of Ronas Hill can be seen. Though only
1,476 feet high, its northerly and exposed situation has
created a low-altitude arctic environment, with a variety of
interesting arctic and alpine plants on its boulder fields.

*A fairly quiet day at
Esha Ness*

At Jarlshof

Minutes from Sumburgh Airport, the important archeological site of **Jarlshof▶▶** (in the care of Historic Scotland) represents waves of settlement from the Bronze Age right through to medieval times. Among the earliest huts was a bronze smiddy (blacksmith's). The buildings were then covered by an Iron Age broch (see panel, page 229) whose walls still stand about 6 feet high. This in turn became a wheelhouse, and there are examples of others on site. Then there are traces of possible Pictish occupation, probably between the 6th and 8th centuries AD, before the Viking farm was built over them. A series of medieval homesteads and finally a late 16th-century house of the Earls Patrick and Robert Stuart were built. The latter's ruins dominate the site today. *Open*: daily in summer, closed in winter.

Nearby look for puffins and otters on **Sumburgh Head** and bonxies (great skuas) loafing around the Loch of Spiggie before their next spot of air piracy. Also within easy reach is **St. Ninian's Isle**, where a treasure was discovered in 1951 at an ancient chapel site. **St. Ninian's Isle** is a tomboloan—an island joined to Mainland by a spit of dazzling cream sand.

The **Shetland Croft House Museum▶▶▶** is a 19th-century thatched building once typical of the style of croft house found throughout the islands. The museum provides an excellent way of understanding rural life in Shetland, especially if you ask the helpful attendant any questions. Walk down to the fascinating "click mill"—a miniaturized horizontal water mill powered by a tiny burn (stream). *Open*: daily in summer.

► **Lerwick** *243B1*

This is by far the largest town in Shetland. No settlement existed here before the 17th century, as the area was not considered very fertile. The Norsemen named the area *leir vik*—mud bay—but muddy or not, the sheltered stretch of water between modern Lerwick and the island of Bressay was a safe anchorage for enterprising Dutch fishermen. Lerwick started as a fishing season trading post, then in the Anglo-Dutch wars of the mid-17th century, it became a permanent town, built around Fort Charlotte, whose walls still survive. Now it has around 8,000 people, one third of the total Shetland population.

Today, "downtown" Lerwick is full of character, especially the waterfront, with the older buildings hard against the sea still retaining their "lodberries" built out over the water. These were shops/houses/storage areas with their own private loading and unloading areas. The main commercial street is at least partly for pedestrians only, with as good a range of shops as you will find anywhere else in Scotland. There are also fine and sturdy Victorian buildings as well as the housing boom on the

A Norse legend
The Orkneyinga Saga tells how Mousa Broch, or Moseyjarborg, already a thousand years old, was used as a refuge in 1153 by a wayward Orkney earl who had abducted the woman of his dreams (a rival earl's mother, hence the complications).

Lerwick harbor

edge of town prompted by the oil developments. The **Shetland Museum** (*open*: all year, closed Sundays) covers the principal Shetland themes of folk life, shipping, art, and archeology.

Once solitary on the edge of a boggy loch, now with lots of new housing nearby, **Clickhimin Broch**►► has the complication of being a broch built within an Iron Age fort. Open any time, it makes a good preamble to an excursion to Mousa Broch.

Exclusive knitwear labels, Lerwick Museum

Mousa Broch►►► is the most complete example of a broch anywhere in Scotland, with 40-foot walls. As it is on the island of Mousa, the visit involves taking a boat, which runs daily in summer—check with the tourist information center in Lerwick. Mousa Broch is impressive because it is eerily complete. Boats can be rented on summer afternoons, also weekend mornings and some evenings.

Made in VOE, Shetland Isles
expressly for
THE LONDON SHOP
100% PURE SHETLAND

100% SHETLAND WOOL
HAND FRAME KNITTED
IN THE
SHETLAND ISLES of SCOTLAND
EXPRESSLY FOR
Macy Associates
IMPORTED BY R.H.MACY & CO.,INC.

The Shetland Bus
This was the name given to the small craft which maintained the highly dangerous sea connection from Shetland to Norway during World War II. It was used by the Norwegian Resistance for taking in saboteurs and taking out refugees.

Scalloway Castle

Another very worthwhile Lerwick excursion is across the neighboring island of Bressay to visit the nature reserve of **Noss►►►**, a much smaller island looked after by Scottish Natural Heritage. Though its vertiginous seabird colonies are not for the fainthearted, the puffins and rapier-beaked gannets offer spectacle on a grand scale. Take the regular Lerwick-Bressay ferry, then walk, cycle, drive, or take a taxi 3 miles across Bressay for a small boat crossing to Noss, and walk all around the island.

By the Town House, Lerwick

Scalloway►► The second-biggest settlement on Mainland (and in all of Shetland) is older than Lerwick. It lies in a more fertile area on the west coast and was the original main town. Dominating the roofs of the town are the ruins of **Scalloway Castle**. After the demise of Norse power, Shetland gradually came under the sway of a particularly predatory breed of Scottish baron, of which Earl Patrick Stuart was a typical specimen. As the displays within the castle tell, he used forced labor from the surrounding area to build his fortress in 1600. He was executed in Edinburgh in 1615, the castle thereafter gradually falling into ruin. The key-keeper lives nearby and access is at any reasonable time.

Also nearby (*open:* in summer, closed Sunday, Monday and Friday), is the locally run **Scalloway Museum** which, among other maritime matters, tells the story of the Shetland Bus (see panel) which used Scalloway as a base. (The museum can be visited at other times by telephoning one of the numbers displayed outside). Access to the lesser islands of Trondra and East and West Burra is by B9074, also near Scalloway. All are linked to Mainland by bridges and the road eventually ends at Papil. At the road end, walk through a little gate to find another fine beach, with views to distant Foula framed by rocky headlands.

THE ISLANDS

Curious enclosures

First-time visitors to "the bonnie isle" of Whalsay are often puzzled by the small circular stone-built enclosures which dot the landscape. The locals will inform you that they are "planticruives" (variously spelled). They were used to grow winter fodder of the brassica variety. The round wall kept the sheep out and provided shelter. The structure was usually covered with net to keep out birds.

Foula

Foula (from a Norse word for bird island) offers spectacular coastal scenery even by Shetland standards. The Kame on the west coast is a sheer 1,197-foot cliff, the second highest in Britain. (Only the cliff by Conachair on St. Kilda is higher at 1,411 feet.) Foula is 27 miles west of Scalloway.

A variation on the theme of a boathouse at Gutcher, Yell

►► Unst 243B3

Thanks to cheap prebookable interisland ferries, getting up to Unst is not a problem. It is worth going, if only to see the United Kingdom's most northerly just about everything from post office to lighthouse.

Muness Castle► Scotland's most northerly stone castle was built on low ground by the sea for yet another tyrannous Shetland laird, Lawrence Bruce, half brother to Scalloway Castle's Earl Patrick Stuart. Muness shares approximately the same building date as Scalloway (1598) and the same architect, Adam Crawford. He created a handsome yet functional oblong fortress flanked by two towers on the diagonal, though the third floor and roof are now missing. His client's invocation in verse carved above the main entrance "To help and not to hurt his work always" did not impress the French privateers who burned the building within 30 years of its completion. Access is at all reasonable times, via a key-keeper, and the building can also be seen from the road.

Hermaness National Nature Reserve►►► At the other end of Unst from Muness, this is the very end of the United Kingdom. However, the RAF community at Baltasound and the conspicuous radar station on top of Saxa Ford, one of the twin headlands on top of Unst, give the area a slightly sinister ambience. To make the most of the headland, climb the 660-foot-high Hermaness Hill. Strong shoes are advised on the rough moorland path. There is a good hilltop view of Muckle Flugga with its lighthouse. Take care if investigating the puffin-hollowed cliffs and gannet-plastered stacks on the west side as the grassy edges slope away treacherously. Keep an eye out, too, for dive-bombing great and arctic skuas breeding on the moor and keep on the path.

Other features of Unst to note are the most northerly post office at **Haroldswick**, as well as a number of broch sites and other prehistoric places; also, for the botanist, the **Keen of Hamar**, a low, domed hill near Baltasound with plant species from the arctic tundra (Scottish National Heritage permits access only—though the general terrain can be seen from the road).

Whalsay   243B2

The Hanseatic League, the trading confederation of European cities which flourished until the 17th century, was important for Shetland. The most vivid reminder of those sea-trading days can be seen at Symbister on the island of Whalsay. The **Bremen Böd** (booth) is a curious little building by the harborside, a restored Hanseatic storage and trading booth, possibly dating from the 17th century. The key-keeper is nearby, so visiting is possible at reasonable times. Otherwise, Whalsay is an island for bird lovers, with several rarities recorded on migration here. It is also a wealthy island, as it is the home of many of the successful local skippers.

▶   Yell   243B2

Yell is a dark brown stepping stone between Mainland and Unst. It has more peat than any other part of Shetland, and this is widely cut for fuel. The **Old Haa of Burravoe** is a 17th-century house (or hall) built by the local laird on the best spot to keep an eye on shipping entering Burra Voe. It has been restored as a local museum with extras such as genealogy, crafts, and a good cup of tea (*open*: in summer, closed Monday and Friday).

Up at the north end of Yell, it's worth tracking down the **Gloup Fishermen's Memorial** in a field behind one of the crofts. Gloup Voe is long and narrow, and at one time had a large fishing community, which was devastated in July 1881 by the loss of 58 men from 10 "sixerenes," the native six-oared craft.

Clickhimin Broch, Lerwick

Viking quarries
Among the variety of rock types in Shetland is steatite or soapstone, a soft, easily worked rock extensively used by the Vikings for making a variety of vessels including lamps. One source was near Clibberswick, east of Haroldswick on Unst, where traces of quarrying can still be seen. Sometimes the vessels were formed while still attached to the main rock body. They were chiseled into shape, upside down, then removed and hollowed out.

The White Wife
On the way up Yell by B9081, look toward the sea edge for the White Wife near Otterswick and Queyon. She was the figurehead of the German sail training ship *Bohus* and now looks over the waters in which her ship was wrecked. The Old Haa at Burravoe has a copy of her, as well as details of the drama.

Skye and the Western Isles

►   **Barra**   *251A1*

The seagoing Macneil clan owned Barra for centuries, and often practiced piracy. One chief sold the island to pay debts in 1838, and part of it was bought back in 1937 by the 45th chief, an American architect, who restored **Kisimul (also known as Kiessimul) Castle►** in Castlebay (limited opening, in summer). Castlebay itself was once a thriving fishing port.

As well as the open shell-sand beaches, one of which achieved fame as the island's landing strip, and the rough inland walking, other points of interest on Barra include **Kilbarr Church**, a ruinous medieval church dedicated to the saint who gave his name to the island. The last thatched croft house on the island is at **Craigston**, northwest of Castlebay. It is now a little museum, but with limited hours—check with the tourist information center at Castlebay.

Caledonian MacBrayne
Hebridean and Clyde Ferries

BOARDING CARD
ULLAPOOL 0082740

This card is only valid for boarding
purposes on the sailing for which it is issued.
Passengers also require valid travel tickets.

248

         Benbecula   *251A2*

Benbecula, joined to the Uists by causeways, is patterned and interlaced with inland waters. It presents great sweeps of sand to the Atlantic, with flowery machair beyond and attendant crofts. To the west, a missile range points into the ocean. To the east there is much rough bogland. The highest point, Rueval, is barely 393 feet above sea level and overlooks endless peaty lochans (small lochs), beloved of fishermen.

►►   **Harris**   *251B3*

Harris has austere rocky landscapes, except for some western machair and the highest hill in the Outer Hebrides, **Clisham**, at almost 2,598 feet. The "border"

Leverburgh
One odd chapter in Harris's story is encountered at Leverburgh, near Rodel, which recalls the efforts of one of Britain's most successful industrialists, the soap magnate Lord Leverhume, to spend some of his riches turning a tiny fishing village into a major fish processing port. He owned most of Lewis and Harris at the time.

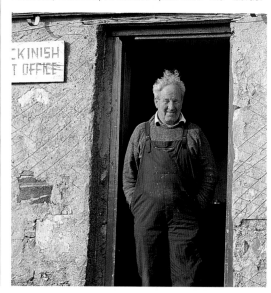

Stockinish post office and postmaster, on Harris

between Lewis and Harris runs east from Kinlochresort. Traditionally, the Macleods of Lewis held the island of their name, while Harris was under the sway of the Macleods of Dunvegan in Skye.

Hiking, fishing, bird-watching, and visiting beaches are the main activities. **St. Clement's Church▶▶** at Rodel, on the southern tip, is a cruciform church built around 1500 by the eighth chief of the Macleods, sometimes

Kisimul (Kiessimul) Castle and Castlebay, Barra

Above East Loch Tarbert, Harris

Eriskay
This island between Barra and South Uist was the place where Bonnie Prince Charlie first landed on Scottish soil. Its other claim to fame is that the SS *Politician* was wrecked there in 1941 while carrying 20,000 cases of whisky. The subsequent events inspired Compton Mackenzie's *Whisky Galore.*

known as Alasdair Crotach, who died 20 years after the construction of his magnificent tomb within the church. Visit it at any reasonable time.

If visiting Rodel from Tarbert, take in the endless empty sands of **Traigh Luskentyre▶▶▶**, and loop back toward Tarbert from Rodel by the east coast road, enjoying the wild and remote boulder country before a mountain is removed and a new sea loch is created. A superquarry is planned here. Another very twisty drive along B887, northwest of Tarbert toward uninhabited Scarp passes the former whaling station at **Bunavoneadar** (abandoned in 1930—look for the chimney stack by the road), and **Amhuinnsuidhe Castle** with its "no stopping" notices. This grand structure was built by the then owners of Harris, the earls of Dunmore, in the 1860s.

Unsightly benefits
Benbecula's missile range has been there since 1957. More than half its 520 civil staff are from the Uists, 38 per cent of them living in croft houses. It supports a further 300 local "spin-off" jobs in the area, generating £10 million for the local economy. Like superquarries, missile ranges may not be picturesque, but provide employment in a geographically disadvantaged area.

THE ISLANDS

*Callanish Standing
Stones*

*An abandoned croft
at Barvas, Lewis*

▶ **Lewis** 251B4

Most of Lewis's townships are close to the coast,
forming a narrow green strip between the ocean and the
inland brown sea of endless lochan-dotted peatlands.
This initially unpromising landscape has a long history of
settlement dating from neolithic and Norse times.

Callanish Standing Stones▶▶▶ This is the most
famous of the prehistoric sites, possibly dating from
3000 BC, sometimes described as Scotland's Stonehenge.
This is a cruciform setting of stones: 19 monoliths form
an avenue running north–south from a circle of 13 other
stones, with outliers adding to the inexplicable design.
View any time.

Dun Carloway Broch▶ A fairly well-preserved
structure visible from the main A858. The walling stands
in part over 30 feet high. View any time.

Black House at Arnol▶▶▶ This once typical local
dwelling is in the care of Historic Scotland. The byre (cow
barn) is under the same roof. *Open*: Monday to Saturday,
closed Friday in winter.

Callanish, Carloway, and Arnol are all on the west coast.
It is worth continuing northeast on the main road, A857,
all the way to Port of Ness to see the **Butt of Lewis** and
its lighthouse. Though the cliffs are not spectacularly
high, the ambience is wild and windswept. There are
streams of gannets, other seabirds, skuas, and sometimes dolphins or whales can be seen.

Lewis also offers good seascapes on the way to Great
Bernera, an island joined to the "mainland" by a causeway: there are plenty of diving gannets and terns off the little beach at the road end at **Bosta**. Arguably the finest
beach on Lewis is on the east coast: **Tràigh Mhór** (literally
in Gaelic "big beach") can be seen toward the end of the
Tolsta road.

Stornoway is the main administrative center for the
Western Isles. It is not overtly picturesque and is very
hushed on Sundays but has a fine asset in the **An Lanntair
Gallery** with its changing exhibition program.

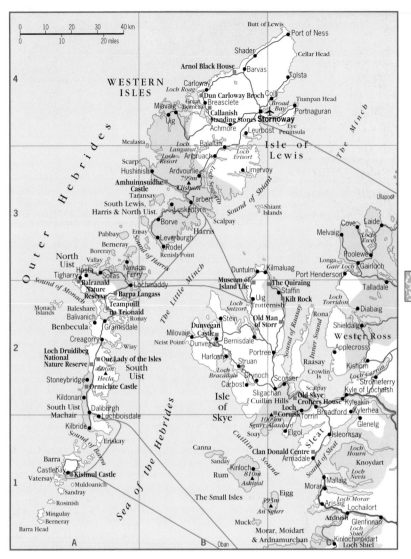

▶ **North and South Uist** 251A2

These are classic Hebridean islands of shell-sand and peaty lochans, golden beaches with crashing Atlantic surf and a rocky, wild, and forbidding easterly coast. All of this provides a varied habitat for wildlife, hence the importance of the RSPB's **Balranald Reserve** on North Uist. There is a reception cottage (for information on what to see on the reserve), which is open all summer.

On South Uist **Loch Druidibeg** is another wildlife area under the care of Scottish Natural Heritage and noted for its breeding greylag geese, among many other species. Check with the warden's office for visiting details. There is access to machair land at several points on the Uists, where the full glory of wildflowers and bird life can be seen in late spring and early summer.

The tallest monolith
The Callanish stones may be tall, but tallest of all on the islands is the Clach an Trushal, a solitary monolith standing by the township of Ballantrushal (between Barvas and Shader) on A857 (north of the junction with A858). This gray, grizzled, lichen-covered tooth reaches a height of around 20 feet.

*Pony trekking at
Sligachan, Skye*

*Roadside shrine,
South Uist*

Skye road sign

▶▶▶ Skye   251B2

Superlatives and Skye scenery go together. The big hill masses catch southwesterly weather systems, so it does rain a lot here, but when it is clear, the hills make the heart ache. Skye is unforgettable.

Though there is a Mallaig–Armadale link, most people arrive via the new Skye Bridge near Kyle of Lochalsh, which replaced the ferry to Kyleakin. Among attractions on the way to Portree is the **Luib Folk Museum▶**, north of Broadford. (*Open*: daily in summer.) This thatched, traditional period piece shows the kind of dwelling that the crofters of Skye once lived in.

En route for Portree, the **Cuillins** first show themselves around Sligachan and are still distantly in view from the "capital" of Skye itself. Fairly picturesque (depending on the angle of view) **Portree** has quite a good range of shops and services.

The **Skye Heritage Centre▶▶▶** is a good starting point for understanding the island, particularly the struggles of the crofters. It tells Skye's story from the viewpoint of the ordinary folk who lived there in the fairly bad old days, rather than dwelling upon heroic tales of clans and chieftains. The center uses headphones to pick up and relay information, depending on which part of the exhibition you are in. It is open throughout the year (even Sundays), though opening is variable in winter.

The most interesting of Skye's scenic road loops is the **Trotternish** peninsula. Beyond the curious rock form of the **Old Man of Storr▶▶**, a popular stop is **Kilt Rock▶▶** at Elishader. Seen from a reassuringly safe viewing platform, the cliff edge has alternate bandings of sedimentary rock with dolerite, giving the strong impression of kilt pleats. Much of the coastline around here is scenically spectacular, including the 300-foot seaward vertical fall of the **Mealt Falls**.

Beyond the impressive **Quiraing►►►** with its rock towers and pinnacles, and around the top of the peninsula, the Skye **Museum of Island Life►►** by the main road at Kilmuir portrays crofting life as it was lived in a self-contained township. The staff are helpful and eager to tell you more. Flora Macdonald's grave is nearby. *Open:* daily except Sundays in the main season.

Though there are other places with Jacobite associations to track down on your way around Trotternish, **Dunvegan Castle►** is the big attraction in the northern half of Skye.

For 700 years the chiefs of the Clan Macleod have inhabited this rock above the sea lake, and between the 19th-century front entrance and the 14th-century keep there is plenty of historic lumber to enjoy. Among the relics is the Fairy Flag. All true Macleods believe this ancient cloth has the power to save the clan one more time if waved in battle. *Open:* daily in the main season.

Clan Donald Center► The Sleat peninsula is sometimes overlooked by visitors heading for Trotternish and the Cuillins, unless they are traveling from the ferry port at Armadale. The area's principal attraction is this center in a restored portion of Armadale Castle. It tells the story of the MacDonalds when they held sway over the western seaboard and beyond as the Lords of the Isles. Around the castle are gardens and nature trails. *Open:* daily in summer.

The Small Isles►► This is the collective name for Muck, Eigg, Rum, and Canna. Accommodations are very limited (though not impossible) on all of them, so these little green chunks are usually visited on a day trip from either Arisaig or Mallaig. Rum is the most spectacular and entirely in the care of Scottish Natural Heritage. Red deer are studied here and there are also large numbers of breeding burrow-nesting shearwaters.

A view of the Cuillins
B8083 runs to Elgol and offers a close view of the Cuillins. Hardy walkers can get into the interior via a rough track, which leads to Camasunary. This starts some 4 miles from Elgol itself. There is also a coastal path from Elgol.

...and another Cuillins viewpoint
Follow the minor road, off B8009 near Drynoch, into Glen Brittle. An obvious road, starting from the large parking lot right at the end of the road by Loch Brittle, rises onto rough moorland for a closer view of the Cuillin ridges. Strong footwear is advised, otherwise enjoy the roadside views, especially from where the road descends into Glen Brittle.

Dunvegan Castle

Skye's landscapes

■ **Skye's 50-mile length is the distilled essence of Scottish scenery. In geological terms it has a greater area of basaltic plateau than anywhere else in the United Kingdom. It also has what some writers claim to be the finest view: the view of the Cuillin Hills from Elgol. Sir Walter Scott was inspired by it, so was the painter Turner, who was one of many artists who journeyed here ...■**

Skye marble

Among the many geological complexities of Skye, the island even has its own marble. This gray-, green-, and white-striped rock is not only found in lamp bases and paperweights in souvenir shops, but is also exported for decorative, building, and agricultural purposes from the Torrin Quarry on Loch Slapin (visible from the Elgol road). The marble has come about by "thermal metamorphis" millions of years ago—limestone in contact with neighboring igneous rocks in their molten state has been converted and hardened into the attractive stone found here today.

*Sgurr nan Gillean
from the Old Bridge
at Sligachan*

South of the island Skye starts off gently enough, from a tourist's point of view, with the **Sleat** peninsula. Even the bulky granite flanks of the **Red Hills** (sometimes known as the Red Cuillin) give no hint of the spectacle just around the corner. Then the pinkish granite gives way to dark toothed gabbro, and the **Cuillins** reveal themselves at Sligachan with the spire of Sgurr nan Gillean, well over the 3,000-foot contour. More than 20 of its high companions also reach this magic mark, the highest being Sgurr Alasdair at 3,310 feet, on a spiky arête which eventually tumbles into **Loch Scavaig** in the west. Complicated volcanic geology has been further notched and splintered by more recent glaciation.

The Trotternish peninsula Yet even with the Cuillins Skye has not finished with scenic spectacle. Most of the north of the island is basalt plateau, the ancient lavas suddenly ending in a long line of slipping cliffs, again the most spectacular of their kind in Britain. The **Old Man of Storr** on the horizon is a 161-foot pinnacle adrift from its parent cliff. It stands insecurely on a jumbled complication of clays and limestones unable to support the weight of the lava plateau above. The infinitesimally slow rotational slippage of great slabs of lava cliff has also created the extraordinary rock forms of the **Quiraing**, into whose confines only surefooted walkers should venture. Skye is unbeatable—when the sun shines.

Communications map

Legend:
- M90 — Motorway
- A9 — Main Road
- A390 — Other Road
- Railway
- Vehicle Ferry
- Canal
- ✈ Airport

256

**Places and labels on map:**

Cape Wrath, Durness, A836, Tongue, Kinbrace, Butt of Lewis, Port of Ness, A857, Scourie, A838, Isle of Lewis, Stornoway, Knockan, Lairg, A835, A836, Dornoch, A859, The Minch, Ullapool, A832, A835, Garve, Dingwall, Tarbert, Gairloch, Harris, Achnasheen, Inverness, Lochmaddy, The Little Minch, Uig, A890, A9, North Uist, A856, Portree, Kyle of Lochalsh, A82, Loch Ness, Aviemore, Benbecula, Isle of Skye, A850, A87, Fort Augustus, Caledonian Canal, South Uist, A865, Armadale, Kingussie, Lochboisdale, Mallaig, Lochailort, A830, Barra, Castlebay, Inner Hebrides, A861, Fort William, A828, A82, Coll, A884, Connel, Pitlochry, Arinagour, Tobermory, A848, Lochaline, Bridge of Orchy, Scarinish, Craignure, A82, Tiree, Isle of Mull, Oban, A85, Crianlarich, A84, Crieff, Fionnphort, A849, Firth of Lorne, Inveraray, A816, A83, Tarbet, Loch Lomond, Stirling, ATLANTIC OCEAN, Colonsay, Scalasaig, Lochgilphead, Jura, A82, A811, M90, A816, Greenock, A8, Dumbarton, GLASGOW, Port Askaig, Islay, Kennacraig, Rothesay, Paisley, A78, A77, M74, Hamilton, A71, Port Ellen, A83, Arran, Brodick, Ardrossan, Irvine, Kilmarnock, Campbeltown, Ayr, A76, Firth of Clyde, Girvan, A77, Sanquhar, IRL, North Channel, Larne, Belfast, Newton Stewart, Castle Douglas, NORTHERN IRELAND, Stranraer, A75, Solway

Shetland
Islands

same
scale

Orkney
Islands

Lerwick

Kirkwall

Burwick

John
O'Groats

Wick

sdale

gin

Buckie

Macduff

Fraserburgh

Peterhead

Huntly

Ellon

Inverurie

NORTH

SEA

Ballater

Aberdeen

Braemar

Stonehaven

Laurencekirk

Forfar

Montrose

Blairgowrie

Arbroath

Dundee

St Andrews

Perth

Kinross

Dunfermline

Firth of Forth

Dunbar

EDINBURGH

Eyemouth

Peebles

Galashiels

bington

Jedburgh

Hawick

Moffat

Langholm

Dumfries

Annan

ENGLAND

In all, Scotland has
about 800 offshore
islands, most of which
are uninhabited. Ferry
routes between larger
islands, and between
them and the main-
land, are shown on
this map, as are other
communication routes

258

By air
You can fly direct from London to **Edinburgh**, **Glasgow**, **Aberdeen**, and **Inverness**. There are also Scottish connections from other English airports. Main operators within Scotland are British Airways, British Midland (New York office call 203/661-8980, fax 203/661-9221) and Air UK. British Airways flies many routes within Scotland as well as cross-border routes. Some carriers offer fly-drive deals; check with your travel agent for information.

There are direct services by many major carriers from a number of European cities into Scotland's larger airports, principally Edinburgh, Glasgow, or Aberdeen. All transatlantic scheduled services fly into Glasgow, though this option is under increasing pressure, particularly from London Heathrow, and there has been a reduction in the number of North American carriers serving Glasgow. Transatlantic visitors can also fly to Frankfurt or Amsterdam, and connect with a wide choice of flights to Scotland.

There is a departure tax of £5 for flights within the European Union, and £10 for flights elsewhere.

By sea
From Europe There are frequent ferry services from the Continent to the north of England within easy reach of the Scottish border. There is a variety of Scandinavian connections from **Newcastle**, within 90 minutes of the border, and Hull, three–four hours away, has ferries to Rotterdam and Zeebrugge.
From Northern Ireland There are frequent regular sailings from **Larne** to **Stranraer** and to **Cairnryan**. Complete details are available from Sealink or from P & O appointed travel agents. There is also a SeaCat service from **Belfast to Stranraer**.

By train
InterCity rail services connect the main cities of Scotland with the south, though with privatization of the rail network, matters are in a state of flux. Fast electrified routes run from **London Kings Cross** to **Edinburgh**

Waverley and between **London Euston** and **Glasgow Central**. Some Kings Cross services also run to Glasgow Central. In addition, there are some (nonelectrified) direct services from London to Aberdeen and Inverness. The travel time between Edinburgh and London is just under four hours (the fastest timing) with many services taking around four hours 30 minutes including stops. The fastest direct service between London Euston and Glasgow Central takes around five hours, with services linking Glasgow and Kings Cross taking about the same time.

InterCity also connects main English cities and towns with Scottish destinations: for example, Birmingham, Carlisle, Crewe, Manchester, Newcastle, Penzance, Peterborough, Preston, Plymouth, York, and many others. For overnight travel, sleeping cars are available.

By bus
There are a number of companies in the United Kingdom that operate express service to Scotland. They offer direct service (often daily throughout the year) to a variety of destinations. Overnight travel is available on most major routes.

Many companies offer facilities such as steward or hostess service with hot and cold drinks and light refreshments, rest rooms, air-conditioning, and seating in smoking or no smoking areas. Further details on all services and ticket prices can be obtained from appointed travel agents or main city bus stations.

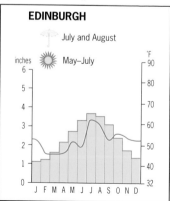

EDINBURGH

July and August

inches
May–July

°F

By car

Many travelers from the south use the M6 expressway, which becomes M74 and A74 north of the border. Using this route to Glasgow, and then taking M80 north, it is possible to reach Aberdeen by expressway or divided highway all the way from London or even Bristol in the south-west of England.

Alternatively, M1, A1(M), and A1 is the main route in the eastern half of the country, though it is not possible as yet to reach Edinburgh, the capital, without encountering some undivided stretches of A1 north of the border. Allow around seven or eight hours to reach Edinburgh comfortably from London, including stops and keeping reasonable average speeds.

WICK

October–January

inches April–June

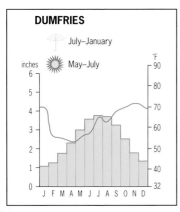

DUMFRIES

July–January

inches May–July

Customs

There are no border checkpoints between England and Scotland. Transatlantic visitors flying direct to Glasgow will find the standard U.K. regulations apply with regard to quantities of duty-free cigarettes, alcohol, perfume, and so on. There are higher allowances for duty-paid goods bought in the E.U.

When to go

In terms of the weather, there is no reliable time to go, though most Scots would say that May and June are the best months. Peak vacation months are July and August, and accommodations may be scarce in some of

the smaller, western places during this period. Festival time in Edinburgh (late August to early September) is very busy.

Most visitor attractions belonging to the National Trust for Scotland (see address page 269) are closed by the beginning of November and open again at Easter. However, the grounds of many of these properties stay open throughout the year. Many Historic Scotland properties are open throughout the year, though some opening times are quirky, with Thursday afternoon and all day Friday closing between October and March. Many castles that are still in private hands also close between November and March.

Scotland does not close down entirely in winter. Most municipal museums and art galleries stay open, as do some nature reserve visitor centers, plus a surprising number of other types of attractions. For example, Cromarty Court House and Scotland's Lighthouse Museum are just two places of interest in the north that are open all year (but remember winter days are short).

Temperature and rainfall, Edinburgh

Average daily maximum temperatures and average rainfall in inches (1951–1980)

	Jan.	Feb.	Mar.	Apr.	May.	Jun.	Jul.	Aug.	Sep.	Oct.	Nov.	Dec.
°F	43	44	47	52	58	63	64	65	61	56	48	45
inches	1.8	1.5	1.5	1.5	1.9	1.8	2.7	2.9	2.2	2.2	2.3	2.2

Climate

The Scots say that Scotland does not have a climate: it only has weather. Scotland's position on the edge of Europe, surrounded by sea on three sides, means that the weather is very varied—though plenty of east-coast places have less rain than Rome.

The east coast of Scotland tends to be cool and dry, the west coast milder and wetter. Remember also that only a short distance can make a great deal of difference. The occasional outbreak of haar (summer sea mist) along the east coast is usually a sign of brilliant sunshine only a little way inland. Most important, if you do meet rain, with Scotland's ever-changing weather patterns, the chances are that it will not last for long. See also **When to go** on page 259.

Public holidays

In Scotland, "bank holidays" apply only to banks and some other financial and commercial offices, although in England and Wales they are general public holidays. **Christmas Day**, **Boxing Day (December 26)**, and **New Year's Day** (and **January 2**) are usually taken by everyone.

In place of the general holidays in England, Scottish towns and cities normally have a spring and an autumn holiday. These holidays vary from place to place, but they are almost invariably on a Monday. In general, all visitor-oriented places, including restaurants and so on, remain open, but a holiday in a small town means that local businesses and many stores will be closed for the whole day.

Time differences

Scotland observes the same time as the rest of the United Kingdom. Between the end of October and the end of March, Greenwich Mean Time operates: thus at 12 noon in Edinburgh it is 8–10PM in Australia, 4–8:30AM in Canada, 12 noon in Eire, midnight in New Zealand, and 4–7AM in the U.S.A. From the end of March to the end of October, British Summer Time operates (one hour ahead). There are longer summer daylight hours in the north of Scotland.

Visas and vaccinations

Scotland's visa requirements are identical to those of the rest of the United Kingdom. U.S. citizens need a valid passport, though visas are not required for a stay of less than six months. No special vaccinations are required. Scotland's indigenous biting insect, the midge, is no more than an irritation and does not pose any serious threat.

Money and banking

English currency is accepted in Scotland and a sign to this effect can be seen decorating the till of many a Highland shop.

There are five major banks with branches throughout Scotland: Bank of Scotland, Royal Bank of Scotland, Clydesdale Bank, TSB Scotland, and Girobank, three of which issue their own bank notes.

The hours of Scottish banks are approximately 9:15AM–4:45PM, with some closing later on Thursdays. Very few banks are open on Saturday mornings.

All Scottish bank notes are legal tender in the rest of Britain, and Bank of England and Northern Ireland bank notes are legal tender in Scotland. Note also that, unlike England, Scottish banks still issue £1 notes, rather than coins.

In Scotland generally, banks give the best exchange rates for foreign currency. All banks offer this service. It is also possible to change money in airports, larger train stations, travel agents, and some of the larger hotels (if you are a guest). Traveler's checks can be used in some shops, and can be cashed in banks.

Several major English banks have branches in Edinburgh, Glasgow, and Aberdeen. There are also several foreign banks in Edinburgh and Glasgow. For details of these see the *Yellow Pages*, the *Phone Book*, or ask at local tourist information centers.

Credit Cards Most larger shops, stores, hotels, and restaurants in Scotland will accept the majority of international credit cards, such as American Express, Diners Club, MasterCard, and Visa. Despite this widespread acceptance of credit cards, it is advisable to carry some cash in case of difficulty. Many smaller establishments offering accommodations such as bed-and-breakfasts are unlikely to accept any form of credit card. American Express has offices in Glasgow, Edinburgh, and Aberdeen.

Near Aberfeldy in Tayside…

Car rental

Scotland has a large selection of car rental companies. Both national and local companies offer competitive rates. Major operators can often arrange in advance for a car to be available at your destination. Alternatively, several hotels in Scotland offer this service. It is advisable to contact more than one company and compare the rates offered. Away from the main cities and in the north of Scotland, you may be restricted to a few local operators. There are car rental companies at the major airports in Scotland.

Skye ferry from Kyle of Lochalsh, now replaced by a new bridge

Aberdeen Airport

Avis Rent-a-Car Ltd.
tel: 01224-722282
Europcar
tel: 01224-770770
Hertz
tel: 01224-722373

Edinburgh Airport

Alamo
tel: 0131-344 3250
Avis Rent-a-Car Ltd.
tel: 0131-333 1866
Eurodollar
tel: 0131-333 1922
Europcar
tel: 0131-344 3114
Hertz
tel: 0131-344 3260

Glasgow Airport

Avis Rent-a-Car Ltd.
tel: 0141-887 2261
Eurodollar
tel: 0141-887 7915
Europcar
tel: 0141-887 0414
Hertz
tel: 0141-887 2451

Inverness Airport

Avis Rent-a-Car Ltd.
tel: 01667-62787
Hertz
tel: 01667-462652

At the smaller airports in Scotland, local car rental companies will often deliver and collect cars from the airport by prior arrangement.

Car rental at a British Rail station

You can arrange to collect a Hertz car at any station on the rail network. Hertz has offices at many principal stations. When traveling to such stations during normal office hours, make your reservation just before starting your train journey and your car will be waiting on your arrival.

Hertz reservation centers

Aberdeen
tel: 01224-210748
Edinburgh
tel: 0131-557 5272
Glasgow
tel: 0141-248 7736

Car rental companies can, in many instances, arrange for your rental car to be available at a ferry terminal.

Driving in Scotland

Driving in Scotland, like the rest of the United Kingdom, is on the left side of the road.

Scotland's roads include an efficient motorway (expressway) network in central Scotland, with good roads to key places farther north such as Aberdeen—a divided highway, now A90(M)—and Inverness (partly divided highway via A9). In some parts of the north and west there are still some single-lane roads with passing places.

Radio Scotland (FM 92.4–94.7MHz/

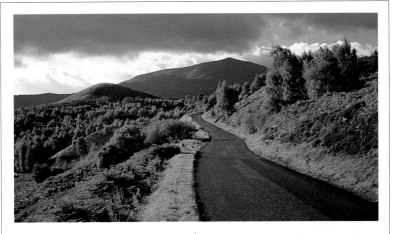

Rush hour in the Highlands

MW 810kHz) broadcasts details of road conditions throughout the day, as do the many local stations.

Insurance Visitors bringing their own cars from overseas will require "green-card insurance" and should also have in their possession the registration documents of their car.

Driver's License Any holder of an overseas driver's license may for a period of up to one year drive a motor vehicle in Britain, but only for a class of vehicle that the original license authorizes.

Speed Limits On expressways and divided highways 70mph/112kmh; on undivided highways 60mph/ 96kmh; in built-up areas 30mph/ 48kmh unless otherwise signposted.

Drinking and Driving The police in Scotland strongly advise against drinking alcohol and driving afterwards. This advice applies to citizens of Britain and overseas visitors alike. Anyone caught driving with more than the legal limit of alcohol in their bloodstream by the police is subject to prosecution.

Breakdowns If you break down on the expressway there is a "hard shoulder" where you can stop your car. Emergency telephones are positioned at regular intervals on the hard shoulder. This shoulder is for emergency use only. You must never stop to rest on it.

Single-Lane Roads In some of the more remote areas of Scotland there are still some single-lane roads. When two cars are approaching from opposite directions, the car that first reaches a passing place should pull in or stop opposite to allow safe passage. It is an offense not to allow a vehicle that's following you to pass, and you shouldn't think of passing places as places to park.

Parking Parking is difficult in Scotland's cities, and you are advised not to take chances. Traffic wardens are vigilant, fines for parking offenses are high, and you could even have your car impounded.
  There are usually coin-operated meters for individual parking spaces or else ticket-issuing machines. There are also parking lots run by the local authority or National Car Parks (NCP).

An unusual cast-iron milepost in Fife

	MILES		MILES
LAWHEAD	½	BREWESTER WELLS	½
PEAT INN	1	NORTH BANK	1
FALFIELD	2½	LATHOCKAR	2
NEW GILSTON	4	KINALDY	3
TEASSES	6	BRIGHTON	3
MONTRAVE	7½	STRAVITHIE	4
CROSSGATES	1½	BONNYTOWN	5
WILKIESTON	2½	BOARHILLS	7
DRUMCARRO	4	CAMERON	1½

By train

Scotland has a reasonable internal network, with fast connections to the four main Scottish cities and points between. In addition, there are 161 miles of track north of Inverness and west coast railheads such as Mallaig and Kyle of Lochalsh, with the attraction of superb scenery on the way. Privatization of the service means changes to the current structure of tickets and, possibly, Rover or flexible ticket arrangements. Check with your travel agent, main train station, or the nearest tourist information center in Scotland.

Glasgow Underground

By bus

A network of operators covers the smaller towns and rural areas of Scotland. Local tourist information centers have complete details and timetables. Alternatively, for further information on getting around, contact the following:

Aberdeen and Grampian Tourist Board
102 Migvie House
North Silver Street
Aberdeen AB1 1RJ
tel: 01224-632727
fax. 01224-848805

Angus and City of Dundee Tourist Board
Market Place
Arbroath
Angus DD11 1HR
tel: 01241-877883
fax. 01241-878550

The Borders Council
Public Transport Unit
Newtown St. Boswells

Melrose TD6 0SA
tel: 01835-823301, ext. 523

Dumfries & Galloway Council
Public Transport Unit
Council Offices
English Street
Dumfries DG1 2DD
tel: 0345-090510

Edinburgh and Scotland Information Centre
3 Princes Street
Edinburgh EH2 2QP
tel: 0131-557 1700
fax. 0131-557 5118

Fife Council
Public Transport Unit
Fife House, North Street
Glenrothes
Fife KY7 5LT
tel: 01592-754411

Highland Council
Public Transport Unit
Glenurquhart Road
Inverness IV3 5NX
tel: 01463-234121

Orkney Tourist Board
6 Broad Street
Kirkwall
Orkney KW15 1DH
tel: 01856-872856

Shetland Islands Tourism
Market Cross
Lerwick
Shetland ZE1 0LU
tel: 01595-693434

Stirling Council
Public Transport Unit
Viewforth
Stirling FK8 2ET
tel: 01786-442707

Strathclyde Passenger Transport Authority
Travel Centre
St. Enoch Square
Glasgow
tel: 0141-226 4826

Tourist Information Centre
Granada A1 Service Area
Oldcraighall
Musselburgh

East Lothian EH21 8RE
tel: 0131-653 6172

Western Isles Council
Public Transport Unit
Sandwick Road
Stornoway
Lewis, Western Isles
tel: 01851-703773, ext. 319

Postbus Many remote areas are served by Postbuses, small minibuses that deliver mail and also have seats for fare-paying passengers. Space is limited, so do not plan an entire or a tight itinerary around the Postbus network, especially if you have a lot of luggage. There are over 130 rural routes throughout Scotland: time-tables are available from:

Royal Mail
7 Strothers Lane
Inverness, IV1 1AA
tel: 01463-256200

By ferry
Ferries are a major means of trans-portationt on the western seaboard and around Orkney and Shetland.

MacBrayne Ltd. The Ferry Terminal, Gourock PA19 1QP
Renfrewshire, tel: 01475-650100, fax 01475-637607
Car ferry reservations: tel: 01475-650000, fax. 01475-637607
  P & O Scottish Ferries sails regularly to Orkney and Shetland from Aberdeen and Scrabster (near Thurso). The main Orkney crossing is from Scrabster to Stromness. There are sailings between Orkney and Shetland, although these are not as frequent as the ferries to and from the Scottish mainland. Make sure that you book in advance for cars on all sailings and also for passengers from Aberdeen to Lerwick.
Information is available from:
P & O Scottish Ferries, P. O. Box 5, Jamieson's Quay, Aberdeen AB9 8DL tel: 01224-572615, fax 01224-574411
  Western Ferries operates between the mainland towns of Gourock and Dunoon and between the islands of Islay and Jura. Information is available from:
Western Ferries (Clyde) Ltd., Head Office, 16 Woodside Crescent,

Kirkwall harbor

Caledonian MacBrayne Ltd. (CalMac) operates the majority of ferry services on the River Clyde and west coast of Scotland, sailing to 23 islands. Most ferries carry vehicles, although some (to the Small Isles, for instance) only convey passengers. On many services, it is advisable to make advance vehicle reservations, especially during the summer and at other peak times. Caledonian MacBrayne offers flexible tickets that make island touring easier. Contact: Caledonian

Glasgow G3 7UT, tel: 0141-332 9766
  Orkney Islands Shipping Co. Ltd. has service between the various Orkney islands. Information is available from:
Orkney Ferries Shipping Co. Ltd., Head Office, Shore Street, Kirkwall KW15 1LG, tel: 01856-872044, fax 01856-872921
  The **Shetland Isles Council** operates ferries within Shetland. Information is available from:
Shetland Isles Tourism, Market Cross, Lerwick, ZE1 0LU, tel: 01595-693434, fax 01595-695807.

The Media There is a reasonably widespread circulation and availability of quality and tabloid newspapers printed in England, partly serving the many English people living in Scotland. Scotland also has its own indigenous media, again at both the quality and tabloid ends of the market. *The Scotsman*, based in Edinburgh, aspires to the crown as Scotland's national newspaper, though challenged by its Glasgow-based competitor, *The Herald*. Both are exceeded in circulation by the unashamedly regional, if not parochial, Aberdeen-based *Press and Journal*. (It is said that the *P & J* headlined the Titanic's sinking with "North-East Man Drowns at Sea.") All of these papers have their evening equivalents. Scotland's other popular daily is the tabloid *Daily Record*.

The Sunday Post is a top-selling

'ALL OF SCOTLAND'

networks north of the border include Border Television, the influential STV (Scottish Television), based in Glasgow, and Grampian Television from Aberdeen. One anomaly of the 1990s is the availability of funding for the making of Gaelic programs, which both the BBC and independent TV networks beam out not just to the Gaels but to chunks of Scotland where the

THE SCOTSMAN

The Scotsman, *voice of Edinburgh*

Scottish institution peddling its own unique brand of homespun, conservative, family-oriented journalism, while *Scotland on Sunday*, from the same stable as *The Scotsman*, is a heavyweight production that sees off *The Sunday Times* north of the border. Scotland also has many local weekly newspapers that list entertainment opportunities. *The List* is excellent for Glasgow and Edinburgh options.

Scotland's television consists of what is broadcast from south of the border, with home-based material slotted in as appropriate. Both BBC1 and BBC2 have Scottish opt-ins, including, on BBC1, substantial Scottish news coverage (and the all-important weather forecasts).

The commercial television

language has not been spoken since the 13th century (such as the Northeast), or even Orkney and Shetland, where it has never been spoken.

BBC Radio Scotland has a loyal following. Though also on FM, its medium-wave transmissions can easily be found by locating Radio 4 on long-wave (sometimes referred to as "Radio England" north of the border) and pressing the medium-wave button (not guaranteed to work on all radios!). Radio Scotland is very useful for *Scottish* (rather than English) weather forecasts. Otherwise, the station broadcasts a broadly based mix of news, discussion, travel, magazine format, and music programs.

There are also various local commercial radio stations, some good, with just one or two of startlingly amateurish quality.

Post offices

Post offices in reasonably sized Scottish towns were formerly instantly recognizable and housed in distinguished, often handsome, buildings. However, recently they have become heavily disguised as pharmacies or grocers, for example,

Some old-style red phone kiosks survive in Scotland

and are much harder to identify. Look for the sign "Post Office," in yellow lettering on red. Beware of the tendency for small post offices to close on half days and local holidays,

which means a trip to the nearest large town if postal services are required urgently. Otherwise, all post offices open for "conventional" shopping hours, approximately 9AM to 5PM and also on Saturday mornings. Most smaller post offices close for an hour at lunch.

Telephones

Telephones are standard throughout the United Kingdom. Modern payphone equipment usually means that the amount of money inserted is shown on a display that "counts down" throughout the conversation. Fax machines are often available at hotels, as well as at printing and photocopying shops in larger towns.

Language guide

English-speakers will be able to understand just about anyone north of the border unless people are being deliberately obtuse and using a dense form of Scots. Scots speakers often "modulate" almost unconsciously into some form of "standard English" when dealing with non-Scots. As for the Gaels, all speak English anyway, so there should be absolutely no problem. See also page 283 for a select glossary of Scots terms and phrases.

Scottish post offices come in all shapes and sizes

In general, Scotland is an extremely safe destination, though the police would certainly advise using common sense. Thefts from cars (and of cars) do occur, especially in major cities and at popular sights (you may want to be careful in the crowded parking lot at the Cairngorm chairlift, for example). It is not a good idea to keep valuable material of any sort in an unattended vehicle. If you must, then keep things out of sight.

As for personal safety, again, use common sense. You are probably perfectly safe late at night in any Scottish city center, but from time to time, incidents—muggings and worse—do occur, often alcohol-related.

One Scottish activity that all too often requires emergency action by the authorities is hiking. It must be strongly emphasized that Scotland's hills are rugged and should be treated with respect. Snow can occur above 3,000 feet in any month, and hill conditions can change *very* rapidly. Proper water- and windproof clothing and equipment and—most important—properly soled hiking boots (definitely not with a cut-away heel) should be worn. **Always** take a map and compass, and know how to use them. The police also advise leaving word, for example, with your hotel, on your proposed route and estimated time of return. Though there are some obvious security implications, it is also advisable to leave a similar note displayed on or in your car.

Embassies and consulates
As Scotland is part of the United Kingdom, the chief foreign embassies are in London. However, a number of representatives for other nations have consular offices within Scotland and these can be found in the *Yellow Pages*. These include:

The Australian Consulate,
25 Bernard Street,
Leith
Edinburgh, EH6 6SH
tel: 0131-555 4500

The U.S.A. Consulate General,
3 Regent Terrace,

Edinburgh,
tel: 0131-556 8315.

Emergency telephone numbers
As in the rest of the United Kingdom, dial 999 to summon police, fire, and ambulance services, as well as coast guard and mountain rescue. These calls are free from all phones, including public pay phones.

Lost and found
The police operate an efficient lost and found service, as do the railways and major bus operators. Broadly speaking, the Scots are fairly honest people, and if an item is lost in a restaurant or other establishment it is always well worth making inquiries.

Health
Medical Insurance If you fall ill in Scotland, unless you are a U.K. or E.U. (European Union) citizen, you are eligible only for free emergency treatment at National Health Service Accident and Emergency departments of hospitals. If you are hospitalized, even from an Accident and Emergency department, or referred to an out-patient clinic, you will be asked to pay. Therefore you are strongly advised to take out adequate insurance coverage before traveling to Scotland. Your travel agent can advise you.

Pharmacies Except in remote areas, where some doctors do their own prescribing, you must take a doctor's prescription to a pharmacy. These part-prescribing, part-retail businesses have normal shopping hours plus a system whereby one pharmacy in a given area stays open to cover half-day closings and other holidays. In cities, there is usually a pharmacy that stays open at other times to deal with urgent prescriptions. In all cases, a notice—usually prominently displayed on the shop door—will tell you where you can get the prescribed medication. In addition—in an emergency—police can contact a pharmacist and request his or her assistance.

Camping and caravanning

There are over 400 licensed and recognized camping and caravan (trailer) parks in Scotland, many greatly upgraded in recent years. All area tourist boards carry listings of parks within their own area, and the Scottish Tourist Board produces an annual guide *Scotland: Caravan and Camping* with a comprehensive listing of parks in Scotland. This is available both direct from the STB (address on page 272) and from bookshops.

Caravanning is popular in Scotland. Any roads that are unsuitable for towed caravans are clearly marked. Towing a caravan on single-lane roads demands extra vigilance, and you should be careful not to hold up traffic behind you. Please note that most local authorities do not permit overnight parking of caravans in pull-offs and other parking lots, and in several places barriers of a suitable height prevent the entry of caravans.

So-called "wild camping" is still fairly popular in Scotland. In fact, Scotland is recognized as one of the last areas of the United Kingdom where camping away from recognized parks is still possible. It is always polite and in your own interests to seek permission from the landowner before camping in the countryside.

House rentals

The main source for house-rental listings is the Scottish Tourist Board's *Scotland: Self-Catering* guide, published annually and available direct from the STB (address on page 272) or from bookstores. There are also a number of agencies that specialize in short-term property rental.

Visitors with disabilities

Disability Scotland has a comprehensive vacation database with information on hotels, camping and caravanning, sports and leisure facilities, guest houses, and so on. A vacation directory is also published, covering all of Scotland. Information is available from: Disability Scotland, Princes House, 5 Shandwick Place, Edinburgh EH2 4RG, tel: 0131-229 8632.

A wide range of information for visitors with disabilities can also be found in the Scottish Tourist Board's *Practical Information for Visitors with Disabilities to Scotland,* available directly from them or from tourist information centers.

Opening times

Times are given within the text for all main attractions and tourist sights. Information on opening times has been provided for guidance only. We have tried to ensure accuracy, but things do change, and we advise you to check locally before planning visits to avoid any possible disappointment.

Scotland's supermarkets and home improvement centers often open on Sundays even in quite small towns, and in the main cities shopping malls may also be open. In popular tourist areas, most shops will open daily. Beware the local half-day, usually a Wednesday or Thursday, on which many little stores in small towns close. Evening hours for shopping are usually confined to Thursdays in the cities, though, certainly in Edinburgh, bookstores tend to stay open late in the evening. In addition, many super-stores remain open most nights till around 8PM.

Conservation bodies

Historic Scotland, Longmore House, Salisbury Place, Edinburgh EH9 1SH (tel: 0131-668 8600). The government agency that is responsible for the preservation of a huge range of monuments, from standing stones to castles and industrial buildings. Many of its properties have standard hours: April–September, Monday–Saturday 9:30–6, Sunday 2–6. October–March, Monday–Saturday 9:30–4, Sunday 2–4.

National Trust for Scotland, 5 Charlotte Square, Edinburgh EH2 4DU (tel: 0131-226 5922). The leading charitable organization that cares for castles and other grand properties, as well as a smaller range of humbler places, and also untouched land of great beauty.

Scottish Natural Heritage, 12 Hope Terrace, Edinburgh EH9 2AS (tel: 0131-447 4784). The main government agency with responsibility for environmental matters and nature conservation, it operates nature reserves in some of Scotland's finest unspoiled places.

Royal Society for the Protection of Birds, 17 Regent Terrace, Edinburgh EH7 5BN (tel: 0131-557 3136). The leading charitable body in the preservation of habitat suitable for bird life, this operates a number of nature reserves of high ornithological interest.

Scottish Wildlife Trust, Cramond House, 16 Cramond Glebe Road, Edinburgh EH4 6NS (tel: 0131-312 7765). Scotland's own charitable conservation agency, concerned with the preservation of habitat for all kinds of wildlife, operates a number of nature reserves.

Places of worship
Scotland recognizes many religions. The most widespread is the (Presbyterian) Church of Scotland. Roman Catholics, Episcopalians, Baptists, and Free Presbyterians are also represented as well as a variety of nondenominational "chapels" and other sects. Because of liberal Sunday drinking laws and shopping

Dunblane Cathedral

hours, Sabbath observance is fairly low-key, with the notable exception of Lewis and Harris and also Skye. The local press usually carries church notices with times of worship, and tourist information centers will also help.

Toilets
Public toilets in Scotland are fairly good but vary in standard between local authorities. Some are free, some attended toilets require a small fee.

Photography
With its spectacular scenery, Scotland is a great place for landscape photography. Because it is also a popular hobby north of the border, even quite small towns often have photography shops where a wide range of film can be obtained. Pharmacists and other stores, particularly in popular tourist areas, also carry stocks of film. Films of larger format than 35mm can sometimes be slightly trickier to find.

Electricity
Voltage is 240V 50Hz AC, as in all the United Kingdom. Almost all accommodations in Scotland have square-pin sockets for 3, 5, and 13amp fused plugs.

Etiquette: dealing with the Scots
Preconceived images of Celtic volatility or dour Calvinism make it easy to see the Scots as being more "different" than they actually are. Certainly, the Scots can be defined as an ethnic minority within the United Kingdom, but they differ from other groups only in subtle ways. However, the Scots have an intense dislike of being labeled English by other English-speaking visitors.

   Also to be noted is the curious double meaning of the word "national," which within the Scottish media can mean either Scottish or U.K.-wide British, depending on the context. Radio Scotland, for instance, announces itself as "The National Network." Many of the subtle distinctions that mark the Scots are actually linguistic, and in everyday speech, there are opportunities for misunderstanding.

It is worth remembering a number of minor points of etiquette that apply to food and drink. If invited to someone's house for coffee or tea, do not be surprised if they insist that you have biscuits or "Home-Bakes"—no matter what the hour of the day. When ordering beer in Scottish pubs listen for the local words "export," "heavy," and "special," rather than the English word "bitter," which is virtually absent north of the border. And finally, if your host offers you a dram (a glass of whisky) and suggests malt whisky rather than an everyday blend, make sure that you only add water, if anything, to it. Ginger ale or lemonade will be at least an irritation, if not an insult.

However, no one will mind if you put sugar instead of salt in your porridge; nobody will arrest you for wearing the "wrong" tartan (there is no such thing); and hardly anyone will even notice if you get the words of "Auld Lang Syne" wrong at the end of the ceilidh. (Most Scots do as well.)

Please note: For reasons quite unknown, the Scots do not like to be "Scotch" and much prefer "Scottish." See also below.

❏ **Scotch** a word for whisky never used by Scots people.

Scotch broth broth made with a meat stock, plenty of vegetables and lots of barley to give it a glutinous texture.

Scotch egg a boiled egg in sausage meat and bread crumbs.

Scotch mist a characteristic western weather condition of relentlessly damp misery, created to test cheap summer raincoats.

Scotch bluebell *Campanula rotundifolia*, called the harebell south of the border, and common on Scottish heaths.

Scotch thistle the national emblem of Scotland, sometimes called the cotton thistle, though not a native plant.

Scotch verdict "not proven," a peculiarity of Scotland's legal system. ❏

CONVERSION CHARTS

FROM	TO	MULTIPLY BY
Inches	Centimeters	2.54
Centimeters	Inches	0.3937
Feet	Meters	0.3048
Meters	Feet	3.2810
Yards	Meters	0.9144
Meters	Yards	1.0940
Miles	Kilometers	1.6090
Kilometers	Miles	0.6214
Acres	Hectares	0.4047
Hectares	Acres	2.4710
Gallons	Liters	4.5460
Liters	Gallons	0.2200
Ounces	Grams	28.35
Grams	Ounces	0.0353
Pounds	Grams	453.6
Grams	Pounds	0.0022
Pounds	Kilograms	0.4536
Kilograms	Pounds	2.205
Tons	Tonnes	1.0160
Tonnes	Tons	0.9842

MEN'S SUITS							
U.K.	36	38	40	42	44	46	48
Rest of Europe	46	48	50	52	54	56	58
U.S.	36	38	40	42	44	46	48

DRESS SIZES						
U.K.	8	10	12	14	16	18
France	36	38	40	42	44	46
Italy	38	40	42	44	46	48
Rest of Europe	34	36	38	40	42	44
U.S.	6	8	10	12	14	16

MEN'S SHIRTS						
U.K.	14	14.5	15	15.5	16	16.5	17
Rest of Europe	36	37	38	39/40	41	42	43
U.S.	14	14.5	15	15.5	16	16.5	17

MEN'S SHOES						
U.K.	7	7.5	8.5	9.5	10.5	11
Rest of Europe	41	42	43	44	45	46
U.S.	8	8.5	9.5	10.5	11.5	12

WOMEN'S SHOES						
U.K.	4.5	5	5.5	6	6.5	7
Rest of Europe	38	38	39	39	40	41
U.S.	6	6.5	7	7.5	8	8.5

Tourism in Scotland is in the overall control of the Scottish Tourist Board (STB), 23 Ravelston Terrace, Edinburgh EH4 3EU, tel: 0131-332 2433. Visitors in Scotland are asked to use the Edinburgh and Scottish Travel Centre (see below). There are two other STB offices for visitors en route to Scotland:

Scottish Tourist Board
19 Cockspur Street
London SW1Y 5BL
tel: 0171-930 8661-2/3

Southwaite Tourist Information Centre (Southwaite Service Area M6, south of Carlisle) tel: 01697-473445

Within Scotland, there are a variety of area tourist boards. As well as comprehensive information services, they offer on-the-spot accommodations reservations both locally and into other areas (Book-A-Bed-Ahead). Some of the 170 tourist information centers are open all year. The main year-round "TICs" are given below.

Edinburgh and Scotland Information Centre
Waverley Market
3 Princes Street
Edinburgh EH2 2QP
tel: 0131-557 1700
fax. 0131-557 5118

Greater Glasgow and Clyde Valley Tourist Board
39 St. Vincent Place
Glasgow G1 2ER
tel: 0141-204 4400
fax. 0141-204 4772

The South
Burns House
Burns Statue Square
Ayr KA7 1UP

tel: 01292-262555
fax. 01292-269555

Whitesands, Dumfries
tel: 01387-253862

Murrays Green
Jedburgh TD8 6BE
tel: 01835-863435
fax: 01835-864099

Horsemarket
Ladyacre Road
Lanark ML11 7LQ
tel: 01555-661661

Granada Service Area
Oldcraighall
Musselburgh
East Lothian
tel: 0131-653 6172

Burgh Halls
The Cross, Linlithgow
tel: 01506-844600

Central Scotland
41 Dumbarton Road
Stirling FK8 2QQ
tel: 01786-475019

45 High Street
Perth PH1 5TJ
tel: 01738-638353

70 Market Street
St. Andrews KY16 9NU
tel: 01334-472021

4 City Square
Dundee DD1 3BA
tel: 01382-434664

The Northeast
St. Nicholas House
Broad Street
Aberdeen AB9 1DE
tel: 01224-632727

17 High Street
Elgin IV30 1EG
Moray
tel: 01343-542666

The Great Glen and the Western Highlands
Castle Wynd
Inverness IV2 3BJ

tel: 01463-234353
Grampian Road
Aviemore
Inverness-shire
tel: 01479-810363

Cameron Square
Fort William
Inverness-shire
tel: 01397-703781

7 Alexandra Parade
Dunoon PA23 9AB
Argyll
tel: 01369-703785

Boswell House
Argyll Square
Oban Argyll
tel: 01631-563122

The Northern Highlands
Whitechapel Road
Wick
Caithness KW1 4EA
tel: 01955-602596
fax: 01955-604940

Auchtercairn
Gairloch
Wester Ross
tel: 01445-712130

The Square
Dornoch
Sutherland IV25 3SD
tel: 01862-810400
fax: 01862-810644

The Islands
4 South Beach Street
Stornoway
Lewis PA87 2DD
tel 01851-703088

Market Cross
Lerwick
Shetland ZE1 0LU
tel: 01595-693434

6 Broad Street
Kirkwall, Orkney
tel: 01856-872856

Meall House
Portree
Skye IV51 9BZ
tel: 01478-612137

HOTELS
AND RESTAURANTS

HOTELS AND RESTAURANTS

ACCOMMODATIONS

Finding good accommodations is not a problem. (Use the Scottish Tourist Board's grading and classifications if in doubt. Go for any place that is at least "commended" or higher, irrespective of the facilities.) Off-season rates vary, and may be negotiable.

As a rough guide in this listing $$$ is over £60 ($90) per person for dinner, bed, and breakfast; $$ is between £20 ($30) and £60 ($90); and $ is under £20 ($30) for bed and breakfast only.

EDINBURGH

Ashdene House ($) 23 Fountainhall Road, Edinburgh EH9 2LN (tel: 0131-667 6026). Five-room Victorian town house in quiet conservation area, close to bus to center.

Balmoral Hotel ($$$) Princes Street, Edinburgh EH2 2EQ (tel: 0131-556 2414). $23 million bought a total refurbishment of Edinburgh's landmark hotel in the early 1990s. High standards in 189 rooms.

Caledonian Hotel ($$$) Princes Street, Edinburgh EH1 2AB (tel: 0131-459 9988). Another old-established top-flight hotel: Like the Balmoral, a former railroad hotel: 236 rooms.

Channings ($$) 12–16 South Learmonth Gardens, Edinburgh EH4 1EZ (tel: 0131-315 2226). A superbly stylish conversion of five Edwardian terraced town houses. A place for comfort and indulgence. 48 rooms.

Edinburgh Grand Sheraton ($$$) 1 Festival Square, Edinburgh EH3 9SR (tel: 0131-229 9131). This opulent and stylish hotel, adds a subtly Scottish stamp to Sheraton quality without resorting to clichés.

Ellesmere Guest House ($) 11 Glengyle Terrace, Edinburgh EH3 9LN (tel: 0131-229 4823). A six-room house in a side street, near the green space of the Meadows, with easy access to the city center.

Galloway Guest House ($) 22 Dean Park Crescent, Edinburgh EH4 1PH (tel: 0131-332 3672). Friendly family-run house with 10 rooms. Good choice for a base near the center.

George Hotel Inter-Continental ($$$) George Street, Edinburgh EH2 2PB (tel: 0131-225 1251). Supremely convenient, luxury standard in elegant surroundings. 195 rooms.

Howard Hotel ($$$) Great King Street, Edinburgh EH3 6QH (tel: 0131-557 3500). Ideal central location amid New Town refinement. Very comfortable. 16 rooms.

King James Thistle Hotel ($$) 107 Leith Street, Edinburgh EH1 3SW (tel: 0131-556 0111). Conveniently situated modern hotel, slightly anonymous in feel, with helpful staff. 147 rooms.

Roselea House ($$) 11 Mayfield Road, Edinburgh EH9 2NG (tel: 0131-667 6115). A seven-room guest house close to Commonwealth Pool and minutes by bus from center.

Silverburn Steading ($) Silverburn, Penicuik, Midlothian EH26 9LJ (tel: 01968-678420). A pleasant farm conversion overlooking Pentland Hills within easy reach of Edinburgh. Two rooms—ask for the one away from main road.

Stuart House ($$) 12 East Claremont Street, Edinburgh EH7 4JP (tel: 0131-557 9030). Comfortable Victorian house in convenient New Town location. No smoking. Seven rooms.

Turret Guest House ($) 8 Kilmaurs Terrace, Edinburgh EH16 5DR (tel: 0131-667 6704). Refurbished Victorian house in quiet area.

GLASGOW

The Devonshire ($$$) 5 Devonshire Gardens, Glasgow G12 0UX (tel: 0141-339 7878). Note the correct address of this simply sumptuous town house. Superb throughout. 16 rooms.

Glasgow Hilton ($$$) 1 William Street, Glasgow G3 8HT (tel: 0141-204 5555).

Hilton style hit Glasgow in 1992 with themed eating and drinking, wide-ranging leisure facilities, and 319 rooms.

Hunter, Elsie ($) Easter Glentore Farm, Greengairs, Airdrie, Lanarkshire ML6 7TJ (tel: 01236-830243). A friendly out-of-town option within easy reach of Glasgow.

Kelvin Park Lorne Hotel ($$) 923 Sauchiehall Street, Glasgow G12 9LG (tel: 0141-314 9955). Fairly large hotel, friendly staff, making excellent base for Kelvingrove and Hunterian or Transport Museums. 99 rooms.

Kirklee Hotel ($$) 11 Kensington Gate, Glasgow G12 9LG (tel: 0141-334 5555). A nine-roomed Victorian house in a quiet residential area, near the Botanics. Breakfast served in your room.

Moat House International Hotel ($$$) Congress Road, Glasgow G3 8QT (tel: 0141-306 9988). In what seems rather like an endless parking lot by the river, a stylish modern hotel with 282 rooms.

Morton, Jean and Andrew ($) Lochend Farm, Carronbridge, Denny, Stirlingshire FK6 5JJ (tel: 01324-822778). Get the best of both worlds here: farmhouse accommodations in two rooms of the highest standards, situated in a tranquil setting within easy reach of the city.

One Devonshire Gardens ($$$) 1 Devonshire Gardens, Glasgow G12 0UX (tel: 0141-339 2001). Adjoining elegantly furnished town houses. Very high reputation in all departments. 27 rooms.

The Terrace House Hotel ($$) 14 Belhaven Terrace, Glasgow G12 0TG (tel: 0141-337 3377) A 19th-century town house; a good standard of comfort and service in the West End. 15 rooms.

The Town House ($$) 4 Hughenden Terrace, Glasgow G12 9XR (tel: 0141-357 0862). Elegantly refurbished Victorian property in the West End. In quiet conservation area. 10 rooms.

THE SOUTH
Abbotsford
Woodlands House Hotel ($$) Windyknowe Road, Galashiels TD1 1RG (tel: 01896-754722). Gothic Revival-style hotel with stunning views over Tweeddale.

Ayr
Langley Bank Guest House ($) 39 Carrick Road, Ayr KA7 2RD (tel: 01292-264246). Sympathetically modernized Victorian house. Good touring base. Six rooms.

Piersland House Hotel ($$$) Craigend Road, Troon, Ayrshire KA10 6HD (tel: 01292-314747). Fine Edwardian mansion with 23 rooms, originally built for whisky firm owner.

Castle Douglas
Balcary Bay Hotel ($$) Auchencairn, by Castle Douglas, Kirkcudbrightshire DG7 1QZ (tel: 01556-640217). Shoreline-set, family-run, country-house-style hotel with bay views.

Castle Kennedy Gardens
North West Castle Hotel ($$–$$$) Stranraer, Wigtown-shire DG9 8EH (tel: 01776-704413). Excellent range of leisure facilities at this former home of Arctic explorer. 71 rooms.

Châtelherault
Strathaven Hotel ($$–$$$) Hamilton Road, Strathaven, Lanarkshire ML10 6SZ (tel: 01357-521778). Adam fireplace and stairway feature in this refurbished house, making ideal base for Glasgow. 10 rooms.

Culzean Castle
Ladyburn ($$$) by Maybole, Ayrshire KA19 7SG (tel: 01655-740585). Impressively rambling, elegant, and tranquil house in rural valley. Good base for Burns fans. Five rooms.

Dalbeattie
Auchenskeoch Lodge ($$) by Dalbeattie, Kirkcudbrightshire DG5 4PG (tel: 01387-780277).

Victorian shooting lodge, peaceful, rural hideaway setting, with friendly, thoughtful owners. Well worth traveling for.

Dirleton (Castle)
Open Arms Hotel ($$–$$$) Dirleton, East Lothian EH39 5EG (tel: 01620-850241). Old established, much-loved, comfortable hotel in attractive village, easy access to Edinburgh. Seven rooms.

Galloway Forest Park
Glendrissaig Guest House ($) Glendrissaig, Newton Stuart Road, by Girvan, Ayrshire KA26 0HJ (tel: 01465-714631). Modern house with fine views over Mull of Kintyre. Three rooms.

Gatehouse-of-Fleet
Cally Palace Hotel ($$) Gatehouse-of-Fleet, Kirkcudbrightshire DG7 2DL (tel: 01557-814341). Georgian mansion in large forested estate. Extensive leisure facilities. 56 rooms.

Haddington
Steven, Mrs. N. ($) Under Bolton Farmhouse, Haddington, East Lothian EH41 4HL (tel: 01620-810318). Elegantly furnished farmhouse in the lush East Lothian countryside. Ideal for golf or city. Two rooms.

Jedburgh
Larkhall Burn ($$) Larkhall Burn, Jedburgh, Roxburghshire TD8 6AX (tel: 01835-862040). High-quality modern terraced cottages overlooking town, self-catering or meals delivered.

Spinney Guest House ($) Langlee, Jedburgh, TD8 6PB (tel: 01835-863525). Converted, modernized farm cottages offering B & B at astonishingly good prices for its high standards. Three rooms.

Sunlaws House Hotel ($$$) Heiton, Kelso, Roxburgh-shire TD5 8JZ (tel: 01573-450331). Luxurious country house of the highest standards, owned by the Duke of Roxburghe. 22 rooms.

Willow Guest House ($)
Willow Court, The Friars, Jedburgh, Roxburghshire TD8 6BN (tel: 01835-863702). On spacious grounds overlooking town; family-run, home cooking. Four rooms.

Logan Botanic Garden
Fernhill Hotel ($$) Heugh Road, Portpatrick DG9 8TD (tel: 01776-810220). The same owners for 30 years; coastal site, excellent service. 20 rooms.

The Machars
Corsemalzie House Hotel ($$) Port William, by Newton Stuart, Wigtownshire DG8 9RL (tel: 01988-860254). Welcoming country house in total seclusion.

Melrose
Burts Hotel ($$) Market Square, Melrose, Roxburghshire TD6 9PN (tel: 01896-822285). Friendly, family-run hotel of the kind that generates a loyal local clientele. Ideally placed for Borders touring.
Dunfermline House ($–$$) Buccleuch Street, Melrose, Roxburghshire TD6 9LB (tel: 01896-822148). Comfortable home overlooking Melrose Abbey. No smoking. Five rooms.

Moffat
Moffat House Hotel ($$) High Street, Moffat, Dumfriesshire DG10 9HL (tel: 01683-220039). Elegant Adam house, near town center, strategically placed for north-bound travelers and Borders explorers. 20 rooms.

North Berwick
Greywalls ($$$) Muirfield, Gullane, East Lothian EH31 2EG (tel: 01620-842144). Architecturally exciting house by Edward Lutyens adjacent to some of Scotland's best golf. A hotel of much finesse.

Peebles
Cringletie Hotel ($$$) nr Peebles, Peebles-shire EH45 8PL (tel: 01721-730233) Plenty of personal and

275

professional attention in rural, family-run, 13-room baronial mansion.

Traquair Arms ($$) Traquair Road, Innerleithen EH44 6PD (tel: 01896-830229). Family-run traditional inn with simple, unfussy rooms.

CENTRAL SCOTLAND
Aberfeldy
Farleyer House Hotel ($$$) by Aberfeldy, Perthshire PH15 2JE (tel: 01887-820332). Historic former seat of the Clan Mackenzie. Excellent cuisine and high standard of comfort. 11 rooms.

Guinach House ($$) by The Birks, Aberfeldy, Perthshire PH15 2ET (tel: 01887-820251). Small country house emphasizing great cuisine in peaceful, rural surroundings.

Weem Hotel ($$) by Aberfeldy, Perthshire PH15 2LD (tel: 01887-820381). Refurbished 17th-century inn with plenty of country pursuits close at hand in Perthshire countryside.

Arbroath
Redroofs ($) Mrs. Milne, Redroofs, Balgavies by Forfar DD8 2TN (tel: 01307-830268). A peaceful, secluded and friendly house, formerly a World War I nursing home. Three rooms.

Sandhutton Guest House ($) 16 Addison Place, Arbroath, Angus DD11 2AX (tel: 01241-872007). Comfortable Victorian villa with modern facilities. No smoking. Three rooms.

Blairgowrie
Drumnacree House Hotel ($$–$$$) St. Ninians Road, Alyth, Perthshire PH11 8AP (tel: 01828-632194). A family-run country-house hotel well worth considering as a base for exploring rural Angus. Seasonal garden produces in well-thought-out menus.

Kinloch House Hotel ($$$) by Blairgowrie, Perthshire PH10 6SG (tel: 01250-884237). Mid-19th century oak-paneled country house with 21 rooms, fine antiques (and 130+ malt whiskies).

Callander
Dundarroch Country House ($$) Brig o Turk, by Callander, Perthshire FK17 8HT (tel: 01877-376200). Dedicated professionalism and high quality in three-room Victorian house.

Roman Camp Hotel ($$$) Callander, Perthshire FK17 8BG (tel: 01877-330003). Beautiful riverside site for this charming 17th-century house, like a small château. 14 rooms.

Dumbarton
Cameron House Hotel ($$$) Loch Lomond, by Alexandria, Dunbartonshire G83 8QZ (tel: 01389-755565). Luxury resort hotel by loch shore. Very wide range of leisure facilities. 68 rooms.

Dundee
Old Mansion House Hotel ($$$) Auchterhouse, by Dundee, Angus DD3 0QN (tel: 01382-320366). 16th-century baronial house with original plasterwork and other features, on spacious grounds. 6 rooms.

East Neuk Villages
The Spindrift ($$) Pittenweem Road, Anstruther, Fife KY10 3DT (tel: 01333-310573). Victorian house with original features. No smoking.

Perth
Auchterarder House ($$$) Auchterarder, Perthshire PH3 1DZ (tel: 01764-663646). A sumptuously furnished country house with notable conservatory. The "house guest in private home" approach makes for an interesting alternative to neighboring Gleneagles. 15 rooms.

Gleneagles Hotel ($$$) Auchterarder, Perthshire PH3 1NF (tel: 01764-662231). Arguably Scotland's best-known hotel, with the ambience of an oceangoing liner. 236 rooms and every need catered for—you will never need to step outside the grounds.

Green Hotel ($$) 2 The Muirs, Kinross, Perthshire KY13 7AS (tel: 01577-863467). An independent hotel, recently refurbished with excellent range of leisure facilities. 47 rooms.

Pitlochry
Knockendarroch House ($$) Higher Oakfield, Pitlochry, Perthshire PH16 5HT (tel: 01796-473473). Victorian mansion, 12 rooms, of considerable charm and style.

St. Andrews
Aslar Guest House ($$) 120 North Street, St. Andrews, Fife KY16 9AF (tel: 01334-473460). Family-run terraced house in central location. Five rooms.

Rufflets Country House ($$$) Strathkinness Low Road, St. Andrews, Fife KY16 9TX (tel: 01334-472594). Country house in its own grounds; garden provides fresh produce for restaurant. 26 rooms.

St. Andrews Golf Hotel ($$$) 40 The Scores, St. Andrews KY16 9AS (tel: 01334-472611). Close to the Old Course, large Victorian building with high standards throughout. 23 rooms.

Stirling
Castlecroft ($) Ballengeich Road, Stirling FK8 1TN (tel: 01786-474933). Very comfortable six-room modern house offering excellent value for money—a good base for Stirling excursions.

Stirling Highland Hotel ($$$) Spittal Street, Stirling FK8 1DU (tel: 01786-475444). Fascinating conversion of former high school, full of character and very comfortable. 76 rooms.

THE NORTHEAST
Aberdeen
Atholl Hotel ($$) 54 King's Gate, Aberdeen AB9 2YN (tel: 01224-323505). Handsome building in residential area, close to city center. Personally run establishment, friendly staff.

Craighaar Hotel ($$) Waterton Road, Bucksburn, Aberdeen AB2 9HS (tel: 01224-712275). Behind a plain exterior there is plenty of design flair and a high level of comfort.

Mannofield Hotel ($$) 447 Great Western Road, Aberdeen AB1 6NL (tel: 01224-315888). Ideally placed for exploring Deeside, this family-run hotel offers superb value for money.

Marcliffe at Pitfodels ($$$) North Deeside Road, Pitfodels, Aberdeen AB1 9PN (tel: 01224-861000). Luxury hotel run by proprietors who have plenty of experience. 42 rooms.

Thainstone House Hotel and Country Club ($$$) Thainstone Estate, Inverurie Road (N), Inverurie, Aberdeenshire (tel: 01467-621431). Upscale Georgian mansion on large grounds. 48 rooms.

Ballater

Darroch Learg ($$) Braemar Road, Ballater AB35 5UX (tel: 013397-55443). Country-house-in-town hotel, with Deeside views.

Stakis Balmoral Hotel ($$$) Braemar Road, Ballater, Aberdeenshire AB35 5XA (tel: 013397-55858). This is the place to go for if you have the budget and a family that needs all-weather entertaining. Superb leisure facilities. 44 rooms plus lodges available for rent.

Craigellachie

Craigellachie Hotel ($$) Craigellachie, Banffshire AB38 9SR (tel: 01340-881204). Imposing fishing and shooting hotel with excellent food and well-appointed rooms.

Elgin

Mansion House Hotel ($$$) The Haugh, Elgin, Moray IV30 1AW (tel: 01343-548811). Peacefully situated baronial mansion with excellent leisure facilities.

Fochabers

Chalmers, Mrs. E. ($) Broom Farm, Sandend, Banffshire AB45 2UD (tel: 01542-840401). Accommodations in self-contained wing of working farmhouse. Very high standard of furnishings and decoration.

Leith, Mrs. S. ($) Academy House, School Road, Fordyce, Banffshire AB45 2SJ (tel: 01261-842743). Very well appointed family home in conservation village. Three rooms.

Fyvie Castle

Eden House ($$) by Banff AB45 3NT (tel: 01261-821282). Handsome Georgian house in impressive setting overlooking river; friendly atmosphere. Golf and fishing.

Huntly

Kildrummy Castle Hotel ($$$) Kildrummy, by Alford, Aberdeenshire AB33 8RA (tel: 019755-71288). Imposing mansion house close to ancient castle in rural setting. Very high standard of accommodations and cuisine. 16 rooms.

Old Manse of Marnoch ($$) Bridge of Marnoch, by Huntly, Banffshire AB54 5RS (tel: 01466-780873). 19th-century country house in secluded gardens. Fine food and high standards throughout. Five rooms.

Tomintoul

Minmore House ($$) Glenlivet, Banffshire AB37 9DB (tel: 01807–590378). Stylish country house offering excellent ambience and cuisine. 10 rooms.

Village Guest House ($) 83 High Street, Banchory, Kincardineshire AB31 3TJ (tel: 01330-823307). Pleasingly substantial Victorian house in village center. Four rooms.

THE GREAT GLEN AND WESTERN HIGHLANDS
Aviemore

Corrour House Hotel ($$) Inverdruie, Aviemore PH22 1QH (tel: 01479-810220). A secluded country house with lots of character and Cairngorm views.

Cowal

Ardfillayne Hotel ($$) Bullwood Road, Dunoon, Argyll PA23 7QJ (tel: 01369-702267). Victorian mansion on large grounds. Seven rooms.

Crinan

Crinan Hotel ($$$) Crinan, by Lochgilphead, Argyll PA31 8SR (tel: 01546-830261). Substantial hotel, much frequented by yachting types and seafood enthusiasts. 22 rooms.

Fort William

Corriegour Lodge Hotel ($$) Loch Lochy, by Spean Bridge, Inverness-shire PH34 4EB (tel: 01397-712685). Former shooting lodge, on imposing site overlooking the loch. Nine rooms.

Crolinnhe Guest House ($) Grange Road, Fort William, Argyll PH33 6JF (tel: 01397-702709). Elegant Victorian house overlooking Loch Linnhe. Five rooms.

Inverlochy Castle Hotel ($$$) Torlundy, by Fort William, Inverness-shire PH33 6SN (tel: 01397-702177). The byword for luxury country-house-style accommodations in Scotland. 17 rooms.

Kilcamb Lodge Hotel ($$$) Strontian, Argyll PH36 4HY. (tel: 01967-402257). Sturdy Georgian house with private shoreline on Loch Sunart. 11 rooms.

Moorings Hotel ($$) Banavie, Fort William, Inverness-shire PH33 7LY (tel: 01397-772797). Canal-side location with panoramic mountain views. Ideal touring base. 24 rooms.

Old Pines ($) Gairlochy Road, Spean Bridge, Inverness-shire PH34 4EG (tel: 01397-712324). Scandinavian log cabin-style accommodations with relaxing and informal atmosphere. Nine rooms.

Glen Coe

Ballachulish Hotel ($$) Ballachulish, Argyll PA39 4JY (tel: 01855-811606). Imposing old baronial hotel with 54 rooms, overlooking main road and Loch Linnhe.

Holly Tree ($$) Kentallen, by Appin, Argyll PA38 4BY (tel: 01631-740292). A comfortably converted Edwardian station, on superb loch-side location.

HOTELS AND RESTAURANTS

Grantown-on-Spey
Ardconnel House ($$)
Woodlands Terrace,
Grantown-on-Spey, Moray
PH26 3JU (tel: 01479-
872104). Victorian villa with
deluxe, non-smoking
accommodations and Taste
of Scotland menu.
Ravenscourt House Hotel
($$) Seafield Avenue,
Grantown-on-Spey PH26
3JG (tel: 01479-872286).
Award-winning small hotel
with very high standards
throughout. Seven rooms.

Inverness
Ballifeary House Hotel ($$)
10 Ballifeary Road, Inverness
IV3 5PJ (tel: 01463-235572).
Charming small hotel with
very high standards and
home cooking; quiet
residential area. Eight rooms.
Braemore Guest House
($–$$) 1 Victoria Drive,
Inverness IV2 3QB (tel:
01463-243318). Attractive
Victorian house with fine
antiques. Quiet location
easy distance from town
center. Three rooms.
Clach Mhuilinn ($) 7 Harris
Road, Inverness IV2 3LS (tel:
01463-237059). No smoking
modern house; 20-minute
stroll from town center.
Three rooms.
Culduthel Lodge ($$) 14
Culduthel Road, Inverness
IV2 4AG (tel: 01463-240089).
Georgian house in large
gardens; quiet and relaxing,
elegantly furnished. 12
rooms.
Dunain Park Hotel ($$)
Inverness IV3 6JN (tel: 01463-
230512). Georgian country
house in secluded grounds,
six bedrooms, eight suites,
pool, and sauna.

Loch Ness
Knockie Lodge Hotel ($$$)
Whitebridge, Inverness-
shire IV1 2UP (tel: 01456-
486276). A 10-room hotel
with simple high quality.

Oban
Ardanaiseig Hotel ($$$)
Kilchrennan, by Taynuilt,
Argyll PA35 1HE (tel: 01866-
833333). Superb, country
house in a romantic setting
with an outstanding attractive garden.

**Invercreran Country House
Hotel ($$)** Glen Creran,
Appin, Argyll PA38 4BJ (tel:
01631-730414). Secluded
luxury in sylvan setting.
High standards in all
respects.
Isle of Eriska ($$$) Ledaig,
by Oban, Argyll, PA37 1SD
(tel: 01631-720371). Family-
owned baronial mansion
offering the highest
standards of comfort and
emphasizing fresh local
cuisine. 16 rooms.
Knipoch Hotel ($$$) Kilniver
by Oban, Argyll PA34 4QT
(tel: 01852-316251). Family-
run hotel with sea-loch
setting. 15 rooms.

THE NORTHERN HIGHLANDS
Dornoch
Altnaharra Hotel ($$)
Altnaharra, by Lairg
Sutherland IV27 4UE (tel:
01549-41122). Rural peace
on a grand scale in this old
established Highland hotel:
Ardgay House ($) Ardgay,
Sutherland IV24 3DH (tel:
01863-766345). Close to the
main A9; family-run guest-
house with fine views across
Dornoch Firth. Six rooms.
Dornoch Castle Hotel ($$)
Castle Street, Dornoch,
Sutherland IV25 3SD (tel:
01862-810216). Originally
the local bishop's palace; a
hotel with plenty of
ambience in the center of
this pleasant town.

Gairloch
Little Lodge ($$) North
Erradale, Gairloch, Wester
Ross IV21 2DS (tel: 01445-
771237). Isolated crofthouse
7 miles from Gairloch. Three
rooms.
Mellondale Guest House
($$) 47 Mellon Charles,
Aultbea, Wester Ross IV22
2JL (tel: 01445-731326).
Modern house overlooking
Loch Ewe. Inverewe Gardens
within easy reach. Five
rooms.

Lochinver
Inver Lodge ($$$) Lochinver,
Sutherland IV27 4LU (tel:
01571-844496.) Modern
hotel with wide coastal
views; 20 rooms with good
facilities.

Kinlochbervie Hotel ($$$)
Kinlochbervie, Sutherland
IV27 4RP (tel: 01971-
521275). Family-run hotel
overlooking sea loch and
fishing harbor. 14 rooms.
Newton Lodge ($$) Newton,
Kylesku, Sutherland IV27
4HW (tel: 01971-502070).
Large, modern-design guest
house overlooking wild
northern panorama, seven
rooms.

Torridons
Loch Torridon Hotel ($$$)
Torridon, by Achnasheen,
Wester Ross IV27 2EY (tel:
01445-791242). Extensively
refurbished hotel, now of
very high standard and
earning excellent reputation.
21 bedrooms.
Tigh an Eilean Hotel ($$$)
Shieldaig, by Strathcarron,
Wester Ross IV54 8XN (tel:
01520-755251). Recently
refurbished, personally run
hotel offering good seafood.
11 rooms.

Ullapool
Ardvreck Guest House ($)
Morefield Brae, Ullapool,
Wester Ross IV26 2TH (tel:
01854-612028 or 612561). 10
rooms on secluded site out-
side Ullapool, overlooking
Loch Broom.
Dundonnell Hotel ($$)
Dundonnell, by Garve,
Wester Ross IV23 2QR (tel:
01854-633204). Family-run
for over 30 years; popular
haven in wild country.
Quality accommodations.
30 rooms.

Wick
Shieling Guest House ($$)
Melvich, Sutherland KW14
7YJ (tel: 01641-531256).
Spectacular bay views and
home-cooked meals. Three
rooms.

THE ISLANDS
Arran
Apple Lodge ($$) Lochranza,
Arran KA27 8HJ (tel: 01770-
830229). Detached house
on its own grounds. Easy
access to ferry terminal for
Kintyre.
**Auchrannie Country House
Hotel ($$$)** Brodick, Arran
KA27 8BZ (tel: 01770-
302234). Previously home to

a dowager duchess; 28 bedroom hotel with luxurious add-on leisure facilities.

Colonsay
Isle of Colonsay Hotel ($$–$$$) Colonsay, Argyll PA61 7YP (tel: 01951-200316). A superb location and a very well-equipped hideaway. (Try the fresh oysters.) 11 rooms.

Harris
Allan Cottage Guest House ($) Tarbert, Harris, Western Isles PA85 3DJ (tel: 01859-502146). Very comfortable conversion of former island telephone exchange. Good food. Three rooms.

Ardvourlie Castle ($$) Aird a Mhulaidh, Harris PA85 3AB (tel: 01859-502307). Impressive-looking castle on loch shore amid wild scenery. Excellent home cooking and personal attention. Four rooms.

Scarista House ($$$) Scarista Isle of Harris HS3 3HX (tel: 01859-550238). Elegance and comfort in Georgian house overlooking endless shell sand beach. High reputation for its cuisine. Five rooms.

Two Waters Guest House ($$) Lickisto, Harris, Western Isles PA85 3EL (tel: 01859-530246). Home cooking; own smokehouse set amid wild hill and loch setting. Four rooms.

Lewis
Caberfeidh Hotel ($$$) or ($$) Manor Park, Stornoway, Lewis HS1 2EU (tel: 01851-702604). 46-room modern hotel thought to be Lewis's finest. Good local seafood.

Galston Farm Guest House ($$) South Galston, Lewis, Western Isles HS2 0SH (tel: 01851-850492). 18th-century restored working croft by the shore with Butt of Lewis views. Three rooms.

Mull
Strongarbh House ($$) Tobermory, Mull, Argyll PA75 6PR (tel: 01688-302328). Comfortable Victorian House, superb seafood in the restaurant. Four rooms.

Shetland (Mainland)
Busta House ($$$) Busta, Brae, Shetland ZE2 9QN (tel: 01806-522506). Scotland's most northerly top-flight, country-house-style establishment; considerable charm and elegance. 20 rooms.

Kveldsro House Hotel ($$) Lerwick, Shetland ZE1 (tel: 01595-692195). Comfortable accommodations close to the town center. Fresh seafood assured.

Shetland Hotel ($$) Holmsgarth Road, Lerwick ZE1 0RB (tel: 01595-695515). Modern 66-room hotel convenient for ferry.

Unst (Shetland)
Bremner's Guest House ($) Barns, Newgord, Westing, Uyeasound, Unst, Shetland (tel: 01957-755249). Modern, practical house, ideal for exploring northernmost island in Britain. Two rooms.

RESTAURANTS

It is possible to eat very well in Scotland, though sometimes the locals would argue that the very best of produce—the seafood, the prime beef, and so on, is sent south to market. This is not entirely true. As well as Scottish cuisine, often influenced by the French, Scotland's cities are notably cosmopolitan in their offerings, which range from Turkish to Thai.

As a rough guide in this listing, $$$ is over £25 ($37) per person for a three-course meal excluding drinks, $$ is between £25 ($37) and £15 ($22), and $ is under £15 ($22).

EDINBURGH
Atrium ($$$) 10 Cambridge Street, Edinburgh EH1 2ED (tel: 0131-228 8882). Fresh Scottish produce, notably meat and fish, with a strongly theatrical element. Very popular with locals.

Cramond Gallery Bistro ($$) 4 Riverside, Cramond, Edinburgh EH4 6NY (tel:

0131-312 6555). Quayside bistro in "village within the city." Take your own wine.

Henderson's Salad Table ($) 94 Hanover Street, Edinburgh EH12 1DR (tel: 0131-225 2131). A downtown self-service healthy refueling stop for hungry shoppers in the daytime, with an entertaining ambience by night.

Jackson's Restaurant ($) or ($$) 209–213 High Street, 2 Jackson Close, Edinburgh EH1 1PL (tel: 0131-225 1793). On a main tourist thoroughfare and achieving authentic Scottish tastes without resorting to "whisky sauce with everything."

Kalpna ($) 2–3 St. Patricks Square, Edinburgh EH8 9EZ (tel: 0131-667 9890). How do they manage these flavors at this price? One of the most distinctive places in town. You'll not even notice it's vegetarian.

Kelly's Restaurant ($$) 46 West Richmond Street, Edinburgh EH6 9DZ (tel: 0131-668 3847). Confident, thoughtful cooking in a friendly little restaurant, favored by the locals.

La Lanterna ($$) 83 Hanover Street, Edinburgh EH2 1DJ (tel: 0131-226 3090). Authentic Italian food at a (near) budget price. Cheerful, popular, and often busy. Convenient central location.

Laigh Kitchen ($) 117a Hanover Street, Edinburgh EH2 1DJ (tel: 0131-225 1552). Subterranean eating in a curious café—homebakes, salads, and so on—with devoted regulars who make it nearly a club.

Martin's ($$$) 70 Rose Street North Lane, Edinburgh EH2 3DX (tel: 0131-225 3106). Tucked well away in a downtown service lane but of top quality. Simply one of the very best anywhere in Scotland.

Pompadour ($$$) Caledonian Hotel, Princes Street, Edinburgh EH1 2AB (tel: 0131-459 9988). Dignified and gracious, old established, offering supremely high standards with a Scottish flavor.

HOTELS AND RESTAURANTS

Scottish National Gallery of Modern Art Café ($) Belford Road, Edinburgh EH4 3DR (tel: 0131-332 8600). The art is fine, but the downstairs self-service food is equally appealing. Just smell that coffee and scones…

Vintner's Room ($$$) The Vaults, 87 Giles Street, Leith EH6 6BZ (tel: 0131-554 6767). An eating place of high repute, housed in a 17th-century historic building in Edinburgh's port.

GLASGOW

Babbity Bowster ($$) 16–18 Blackfriars Street, Glasgow G1 1PE (tel: 0141-552 5055). Merchant City spot with reputation for good Scottish food, more elaborate in the upstairs restaurant.

The Brasserie ($$) 176 West Regent Street, Glasgow G2 4RL (tel: 0141-248 3801). Clublike ambience and an air of quality.

The Buttery ($$$) 652 Argyle Street, Glasgow G3 8UF (tel: 0141-221 8188). Behind an uninspiring tenement façade is a transformation: an old established restaurant with famously polite and unobtrusive service—great food as well.

Café Gandolfi ($$) 64 Albion Street, Glasgow G10 1PE (tel: 0141-552 6813). An (almost) budget restaurant with identity and style. A Merchant City trendsetter.

Café October ($) or ($$) Princes Square, 46 Buchanan Street, Glasgow (tel: 0141-221 0303). Persevere—go to the roof of the modern shopping mall to find this 1930s-style café in black-and-white, serving exciting but simple food, faintly U.S.-style.

Camerons Restaurant ($$$) Glasgow Hilton, 1 William Street, Glasgow G3 8HT (tel: 0141-204 5555). Highland hunting lodge theme, but plenty of style and panache with Scottish produce.

Drum and Monkey ($) 93–95 St. Vincent Street, Glasgow (tel: 0141-221 6636). Atmospheric pub with appetizing snacks, moving up a gear in backroom bistro—more expensive but still with friendly ambience.

Malmasion Café Bar and Brasserie ($) 278 West George Street, Glasgow (tel: 0141-221 6401). British favorites mix with classic French dishes in this booth-lined restaurant.

One Devonshire Gardens ($$$) 1 Devonshire Gardens, Glasgow G12 0UX (tel: 0141-339 2001). Stylish cuisine in the most luxurious surroundings.

Rogano Restaurant and Café Rogano ($$$) 11 Exchange Place, Glasgow G1 3AN (tel: 0141-248 4055). Remodeled in art deco style in 1935, the Rogano is older than most locals, yet has retained its reputation as a top-class restaurant.

Ubiquitous Chip ($$) or ($$$) 12 Ashton Lane, Glasgow G12 8SJ (tel: 0141-334 5007). A sophisticated interpretation of Scotland's larder is guaranteed at "the Chip"—the discriminating Glaswegian's favorite restaurant.

Victoria and Albert ($) 159 Buchanan Street, Glasgow G1 2JX (tel: 0141-248 6329). Yet another spot—an upscale bar-restaurant—straddling the categories, depending on chosen menu. Popular with businessfolk.

THE SOUTH
Ayr

Dunure Anchorage ($) Harbour View, Dunure, by Ayr KA7 4LN (tel: 01292-500295). Overlooking the harbor, this cozy place offers food with a distinctly Scottish flavor.

Fouters Bistro Restaurant ($$) 2A Academy Street, Ayr KA7 1HS (tel: 01292-261391). A highly regarded establishment taking full advantage of Ayrshire's own produce. Exciting food, interesting ambience—old bank vaults.

Stables Restaurant and Coffee House ($) Queen's Court, Sandgate, Ayr KA7 1BD (tel: 01292-283704). A wee place in a Georgian courtyard. Try the clootie dumpling.

Dunbar

Courtyard Hotel and Restaurant ($) Woodbush Brae, Dunbar, East Lothian EH42 1HB (tel: 01368-864169). Sympathetic conversion of shore-side fishermen's cottages; good value, interesting food.

East Neuk Villages

Cellar Restaurant ($$$) 24 East Green, Anstruther, Fife KY10 3AA (tel: 01333-310378). Probably one of the best seafood restaurants in Scotland. Don't miss it if visiting Fife.

Haddington

Browns Hotel ($$) 1 West Road, Haddington EH41 3RD (tel: 01620-822254). Reliable, short but enterprising menus in a Georgian house. Cooking with panache.

Logan Botanic Garden

Knockinaam Lodge ($$$) Portpatrick DG9 9AD, Galloway (tel: 01776-810471). A place of pilgrimage for food lovers in the far west, basically modern French and highly inventive.

New Lanark

Grape Vine Bar Restaurant and Café Bar ($) 27 Main Street, Bothwell, Lanarkshire G71 8RW (tel: 01698-852014). Take a break from M74 driving (East Kilbride turnoff). Fresh local produce.

North Berwick

La Potinière ($$$) Main Street, Gullane EH31 2AA (tel: 01620-843214). Near-legendary, sophisticated restaurant in golf resort.

Open Arms Hotel ($$) Dirleton, East Lothian EH39 5EG (tel: 01620-850241). Food with panache from very experienced hoteliers.

Station Cottage Restaurant ($$) 2 Station Road, North Berwick EH39 4AU (tel: 01620-894737). Relaxed and informal in this seaside resort, offering reliable food at good prices.

CENTRAL SCOTLAND
Arbroath

Byre Farm Restaurant ($) Redford, Carmyllie, Arbroath DD11 2QZ (tel: 01241-860245). Home-bakes and good home cooking without pretension. Try the Arbroath smokie pie.

Gordon's Restaurant ($$) Homewood House, Main Street, Inverkeilor, by Arbroath, Angus DD11 5RN (tel: 01241-830364). Cozy village restaurant, decorated in cottage style.

Blairgowrie

Peel Farm Coffee and Crafts ($) Lintrathen, Angus (tel: 01575-560205). Attractive coffee shop in the peaceful Angus Glens, near Reekie Linn Waterfall.

Trumperton Forge ($) Letham, by Forfar, Angus (tel: 01307-862516). Attractive wee tearoom offering light lunches and teas, while the children ogle the farm animals.

Callander

Roman Camp Hotel ($$$) Callander, Perthshire FK17 8BG (tel: 01877-330003). Cooking with Scottish flair at the restaurant of this old country house situated by the river.

Dumbarton

Grill Room ($$$) Cameron House Hotel, by Alexandria, Dunbartonshire G83 8QZ (tel: 01389-755565). Very sophisticated cuisine of the highest standards at this country club hotel over-looking Loch Lomond.

Dundee

South Kingennie House Restaurant ($$) Kellas, by Broughty Ferry, Dundee DD5 3PA (tel: 01382-350562). Farmhouse conversion, now pleasing restaurant with sophisticated Scottish cooking.

Perth

Auchterarder House ($$$) Auchterarder, Perthshire PH3 1DZ (tel: 01764-663646). The style and flair of this opulent Victorian country house is reflected in the imaginative menus.

Deil's Cauldron Lounge Bar and Restaurant ($) 27 Dundas Street, Comrie, Perthshire PH6 2LN (tel: 01764-670352). Atmospheric ambience in 200-year-old

protected building. Food freshly produced daily.

Smugglers Restaurant ($) Glenturret Distillery, The Hosh, Crieff, Perthshire PH7 4HA (tel: 01764-656565). Daytime only, both self-service and waitress. Venison, trout, salmon, and many other Scottish touches.

Tullybannocher Farm Food Bar ($) Comrie, Perthshire PH6 2JY (tel: 01764-670827). Straightforward self-service restaurant nodding toward healthy eating. A popular stop on A85.

St. Andrews

Ostlers Close ($$) Bonnygate, Cupar, Fife KY15 4BU (tel: 01334-655574). Hidden up a "close" or alley-way is outstanding cuisine, consistent over the years.

Trossachs

Byre Restaurant ($$) Brig o Turk, Perthshire FK17 8HT (tel: 01877-376292). On the Trossachs road, this professionally run, welcoming establishment offers both bar and restaurant meals of high quality.

THE NORTHEAST

Aberdeen

Faraday's Restaurant ($$) 2 Kirk Brae, Cults AB1 9SQ (tel: 01224-869666). This converted electric pumping station now serves traditional Scottish food, with a pronounced French flavor.

Gerard's Brasserie ($$) 50 Chapel Street, Aberdeen AB1 1SN (tel: 01224-639500). Long-established, with "garden room" decor and excellent use of Scottish produce.

The Marcliffe at Pitfodels ($$$) North Deeside Road, Pitfodels, Aberdeen AB1 9PN (tel: 01224-861000). A team of chefs emphasize local produce here: among them are lobster, halibut, Aberdeen Angus beef, venison, and so on.

Poldino's ($) 7 Little Belmont Street, Aberdeen AB1 1JG (tel: 01224-647777). Italian flair with relaxed service. Pleasantly uncrowded.

Ballater

The Green Inn, 9 Victoria Road, Ballater, Aberdeenshire AB35 5QQ (tel: 013397-55701). Fresh cooked, health-conscious, local dishes (and specialty Scottish cheeses).

The Oaks at Stakis Balmoral ($$$) Braemar Road, Ballater AB35 5XA (tel: 013397-55858). Arguably the best restaurant for miles around; very sophisticated and imaginative cuisine, without being "over the top."

Craigellachie

Ben Aigan Restaurant, Craigellachie Hotel, ($$$) Craigellachie, Banffshire AB38 9SR (tel: 01340-881204). Thoroughly Scottish in ambience, with professional hotel cooking of the highest standard.

A Taste of Speyside ($) or ($$) 10 Balvenie Street, Dufftown, Banffshire AB55 4AB (tel: 01340-820860). Good home cooking with extra touches (plus a huge malt whisky selection).

Crathes Castle

Crathes Castle Horse Mill Restaurant ($) Crathes Castle, Kincardineshire AB31 3QJ (tel: 01330-844634). Tea and scones, traditional soups and Scottish dishes.

Elgin

Old Monastery ($$$) or ($$) Drybridge, by Buckie, Banffshire AB5 2JB (tel: 01542-832660). The best for miles around in a culinary desert. Sophisticated, honest cooking without pretension.

Forres

Brodie Country Fare ($) Brodie, by Forres, Morayshire IV36 0TD (tel: 01309-641555). Popular self-service restaurant attached to a large and tempting gift-ware complex.

Kildrummy Castle

Clatt Village Hall ($) Clatt, Aberdeenshire. People come from all around to this rural spot where the locals serve home-bakes for afternoon tea. An institution—summer weekends only.

HOTELS AND RESTAURANTS

THE GREAT GLEN AND WESTERN HIGHLANDS

Boat of Garten
Ecclefechan Bistro ($) Main Street, Carrbridge, Inverness-shire PH23 3AA (tel: 01479-841374). Attractive, family-run bistro serving straightforward Scottish food.

Cowal
Beverley's Restaurant ($$) Ardfillayne Hotel, Bullwood Road, Dunoon, Argyll PA23 7QJ (tel: 01369-702267). Classical French meets Scottish traditional amid high Victoriana.

Crinan
Lock 16 ($$$) Crinan Hotel, Crinan, by Lochgilphead, Argyll PA31 8SR (tel: 01546-830261). Fishing boats land only 50 paces from here. Freshness is assured and discriminating diners come from all around.

Fort William
Arisaig House ($$$) Beasdale, by Arisaig, Inverness-shire PH39 4NR (tel: 01687-450622). Special country house in impressive location with food to match.
Crannog Seafood Restaurant ($$) Town Pier, Fort William, Inverness-shire PH33 7NG (tel: 01397-705589). Here the catch is unloaded directly into the kitchen, so fresh is the seafood. Good value.
Old Library Lodge and Restaurant ($$) High Street, Arisaig, Inverness-shire PH39 4NH (tel: 01687-450651). Seafront restaurant with creative cuisine and growing reputation.

Inveraray
Loch Fyne Oyster Bar ($) or **($$)** Cairndow, Argyll PA26 8BH (tel: 01499-600236). Lots more shellfish as well as oysters on the road to Inveraray. Adjacent smokehouse—learn a little about smoked fish.

Inverness
Dunain Park Hotel ($$$) Inverness IV3 6JN (tel: 01463-230512). Top-quality Scottish game and seafood, with

home-grown vegetables and home-baking, are merged in Scottish-French cuisine.

Kingussie
The Cross ($$$) Tweed Mill Brae, Ardbroilach Road, Kingussie, Inverness-shire PH21 1TC (tel: 01540-661166). A mill conversion full of character, but do not be distracted from the high-quality food.

Oban
The Gathering Scottish Restaurant & Ceilidh Bar ($$) Breadalbane Street, Oban, Argyll PA34 5NZ (tel: 01631-565421). Seafood and steaks in generous proportions in historic restaurant.
Shoreline Restaurant ($) Sea Life Center, Barcaldine, Oban, Argyll PA37 1SE (tel: 01631-720386). Self-service restaurant with a good choice of all-day meals. A good off-season place to eat.

THE NORTHERN HIGHLANDS

Cromarty
Thistles ($$) 20 Church Street, Cromarty, Easter Ross IV11 8XA (tel: 01381-600471). Cromarty is worth the trip just for this restaurant alone, with simple, clever cooking.

Gairloch
Aultbea Hotel and Restaurant ($$) Aultbea, Wester Ross IV22 2HX (tel: 01445-731201). Two-stream dining in all-day Waterside Bistro or the more formal Zetland Restaurant. A culinary haven in far northwest.

Lochinver
Lochinver Larder's Riverside Bistro ($$) Main Street, Lochinver, Sutherland IV27 4JY (tel: 01571-844356). Panoramic bay views, with steaks and seafood prominent on the menu.

Timespan (Helmsdale)
La Mirage ($) 7–9 Dunrobin Street, Helmsdale, Sutheland (tel: 01431-821615). Less a restaurant, more an institution on A9; claims to be "north's premier restaurant."

Ullapool
Altnaharrie Inn ($$$) Ullapool IV26 2SS (tel: 01854-633230). Guests talk in hushed and reverent tones about food here. It can only be reached by boat—so you will want to stay.
Ceilidh Place ($) West Argyle Street, Ullapool, Wester Ross (tel: 01854-612103). Healthy eating in the far northwest.
Summer Isles Hotel ($$$) Achiltibuie, Wester Ross IV26 2YG (tel: 01854-622282). Impressive cooking by a bleak shore. A haven for gourmets.

THE ISLANDS

Islay
Kilchoman House Restaurant ($$) by Bruachladdich, Islay PA49 7UY (tel: 01496-850382). Historic Georgian building with relaxed atmosphere. The emphasis is on local scallops, lobster, venison, and steaks.

Mull
Old Byre Heritage Center ($) by Dervaig, Mull PA75 6QR (tel: 01688-400229). Unpretentious wholesome cooking in this tearoom, especially delicious warming soups.

Orkney
Creel Restaurant ($$) Front Road, St. Margaret's Hope, South Ronaldsay, Orkney KW17 2SL (tel: 01856-831311). Award-winning, very popular restaurant working wonders with seafoods, as well as Orkney beef and lamb.
Foveran Hotel ($$) nr Kirkwall, St. Ola, Orkney KW15 1SF (tel: 01856-872389). Some well-chosen dishes to represent the best of Orkney's foods, served in an airy, bright modern hotel dining room.

Skye
Three Chimneys Restaurant ($$$) Colbost, nr Dunvegan, Skye IV55 8ZT (tel: 01470-511258). Cuisine of the highest order at the most westerly point of Skye in a converted crofter's cottage.

Glossary

Entries with asterisks indicate words of Gaelic origin

bastel a characteristically Scottish fortified house (*cf* French *bastille*)

ben* a mountain, hill (usually used as a prefix)

bonnie bonny, pretty, fine, handsome

brae* slope, road with steep gradient, hillside

broch a late-prehistoric round tower

burgess a citizen of a burgh (see below)

burgh Scottish town with special privileges granted by (royal) charter

burn a stream

byre a cowshed

cairn* a pile of stones, often now marking hilltops or landmarks, or a memorial

ceilidh* originally an informal gathering or visit to neighbors at which stories and songs were performed, now a concert or entertainment in hall or hotel

clachan* a small Highland village

clan* a Highland family group or tribe, owing allegiance to a chief

claymore* a large double-edged sword, often a basket-hilted, single-edged sword

Clearances the economic reorganization of Highland estates, mainly taking place 1800–50, which resulted in the suppression or discouragement of arable farming and the clearing and resettlement of tenants, either on less productive coastal ground or by forced emigration

corrie* a deep hollow on the face of a mountain, scooped out by glacial action

Covenanter a supporter of the National Covenant (1638), a manifesto drawn up in protest against King Charles I's religious reforms

craig* a crag, cliff

croft a small holding

dram a single drink (or "nip") of whisky, to drink whisky

factor a Scottish estate manager

firth a wide sea inlet or major river estuary

Gael* a Gaelic-speaking Highlander

Gaeltacht* the Gaelic-speaking community.

geo in Orkney, Shetland, and Caithness, a narrow gully-like sea inlet

glen* a Highland valley, often U-shape in profile

haar coastal mist, often occurring in summer on the east coast

howe a hollow or low-lying piece of ground

Jacobite a (Catholic) supporter of the exiled King James VII (of Scotland), his son, and grandson (Bonnie Prince Charlie)

kirk church

kirk elder an ordained member of the Presbyterian Church, elected to hold office

kyle* either an inlet or strait between the mainland and an offshore island

laird the owner (or the landlord) of an estate

linn* a cataract or the pool below a cataract or waterfall

loch* a lake

lochan* a small lake

machair* grassland lying immediately behind a sandy beach

manse the house of the kirk minister

mercat cross a market cross, symbol of the trading rights of a Scottish burgh

Munro a Scottish peak over 3,000 ft (914m) in height (named after Sir Hugh Munro, the first compiler of such mountains)

neuk corner, as in East Neuk, the eastern corner of Fife

ogham,ogam an ancient Celtic alphabet with 20 characters

policies the enclosed grounds or parkland of a large house

quaich* a shallow, two-handled drinking bowl, now usually ornamental

sassenach* a non-Gaelic speaking Lowlander—Scots or English —often now used simply to indicate a non-Scot

strath* a broad open valley

tolbooth the former administrative center of a Scottish burgh

tombolo a narrow sand strip joining an island to the mainland

voe a bay or creek in Orkney and Shetland

Index

INDEX

288

Picture credits

The Automobile Association would like to thank the following photographers, libraries, and associations for their assistance in the preparation of this book.
ABERDEEN UNIVERSITY LIBRARY 42–3 Embarking at Broomielaw, Glasgow   MARY EVANS PICTURE LIBRARY 25 19th-century shipbuilding, 28 Bannockburn, 30–1 execution warrant, 30b Mary Queen of Scots, 34–5 Battle of Prestonpans, 104–5 Robert Burns, 197a Culloden   D HARDLEY 110 Culzean Castle, 120 Logan Gardens, 202 Mull of Kintyre, 231a Rothesay Harbor, 232 Colonsay, 234 Islay, 235b Kildaton Cross   HULTON DEUTSCH COLLECTION LTD 205a Loch Ness Monster   NATIONAL GALLERY OF SCOTLAND 33 Earl of Seafield   ROYAL GEOGRAPHICAL SOCIETY 37a map   SCONE PALACE 150 Scone Palace   SPECTRUM COLOUR LIBRARY 39 Dunrobin Castle   THE MANSELL COLLECTION LTD 26a seal and coins of Alexander III, 28–9 Bannockburn Battle, 30a Mary Queen of Scots, 36b Adam Smith, 41 Andrew Carnegie, 42 Building of Queen Mary, 123a Lanark, 123c Robert Owen
The remaining photographs are held in the Automobile Association's own library (AA PHOTO LIBRARY) and were taken by the following photographers: M. ADLEMAN 38, M. ALEXANDER 6–7, 18–9, 23b, 40b, 76, 77, 78a, 81a, 81b, 82a, 82b, 83b, 83c, 86a, 86b, 87a, 90, 91, 94, 97, 98, 99, 100a, 100b, 101, 102, 106a, 106b, 107, 112a, 112b, 113a, 114a, 115, 118a, 124, 125a, 125b, 127a, 127b, A BAKER 17a, 131, 147a, 154, 155a, 155c, 172–3, 190a, 190b,J. BEAZLEY 5c, 35a, 108b, 109a, 109b, 114b, 116a, 117, 118b, 121a, 121b, 122a, 122b, 128b, 192, 193a, 196, 200b, 213b, 216, 221a, 221b, P. & G. BOWATER 169b, J. CARNIE 2, 9a, 10a, 10b, 14, 15, 20b, 31, 34, 130, 138b, 151c, 184, 189, 191, 199, 200a, 204, 205b, 212a, 213a, 226, 230, 231b, D. CORRANCE 9b, 20a, 23a, 48a, 50, 51a, 51b, 55, 59a, 64, 67, 111, 119, 129a, 129b, S. L. DAY 11a, 13b, 18, 19, 21b, 22a, 22b, 24a, 29a, 29b, 35b, 128a, 132, 133a, 133b, 135a, 135b, 135c, 136, 137, 138a, 139, 140, 141a, 141b, 142b, 143a, 143b, 144a, 144b, 145a, 145b, 147b, 148–9, 148, 149, 151a, 151b, 152, 153a, 153b, 156, 157, 158, 159a, 159b, 160–1, 160, 161, 167b, 186, 187a, 187b, 188a, 193b, 194, 195a, 195b, 198, 203, 206, 207a, 207b, 260, 261b, 263a, 263b, 266a, 270, E. ELLINGTON 5a, 7, 16–7, 26b, 163, 164, 165a, 166, 167a, 168, 170b, 174, 175a, 176a, 176b, 177a, 177b, 179, 182a, 210, 211a, 212b, 214, 215, 217a, 217b, 218–9, 218, 220a, 223a, 223b, 224b, 228, 229a, 229b, 238, 239a, 239b, 240a, 240b, 242a, 242b, 243, 244a, 244b, 245, 245b, 246, 247a, 247b, 262, 265, 267a. R. G. ELLIOTT 49, 64–5, 68, 69, 70b, 95b, 96, 220b, 225, 226–7, 236a, 236b, 237a, 237b, 248, 249a, 249b, 250a, 252b, 252c, 254a, 254b, 255, 267b, 273, S. GIBSON PHOTOGRAPHY 43, 79b, 80, 83a, 85a, 88a, 88b, 89a, 92, 93a, 93b, 95a, 108a, 264, D. HARDLEY 27, 146, 219, A. J. HOPKINS 188b, 222, R. JOHNSON 241, S. & O. MATHEWS 126, K. PATERSON 3, 11b, 12a, 12b, 13a, 16, 17b, 21a, 32a, 32b, 36a, 37b, 44, 46, 47, 48b, 52a, 52b, 53, 54a, 54b, 56a, 56b, 57, 58, 59b, 60a, 61a, 61b, 62, 63a, 63b, 65, 66, 70a, 71, 72a, 72b, 73, 74a, 74b, 75a, 261a, 266b, D. ROBERTSON 5b, P. SHARPE 84, 103a, 103b, 105, 170a, 201, M. TAYLOR 171a, 171b, 171c, 178, 180, 211b, 224a, R. WEIR 4, 24, 134, 165b, 169a, 172, 173, 175b, 182b, 197b, 252a, 283.

Contributors

Revision copy editor/Americanizer: Donna Dailey   **Original designer:** Design FX
Revision verifier: Gilbert Summers   **Indexer:** Marie Lorimer